Another Anthology by

WALTER DE LA MARE

Come Hither

A COLLECTION OF RHYMES AND POEMS

FOR THE YOUNG OF ALL AGES

EMBELLISHED BY ALEC BUCKELS

xxxix + 823 pages   1923, revised edition 1928

"This is indeed a marvellous collection, quite different from any other that has ever been printed. What makes it unique is the happy genius which has given an atmosphere of unity to the whole book. It is not merely an anthology of beautiful poems; it is a creation — warm, colored, living — poems, notes, and introduction being all somehow blended together." — *Westminster Gazette*

Published by ALFRED A. KNOPF

Behold, this Dreamer!

BEHOLD, THIS DREAMER!

Of Reverie, Night, Sleep, Dream, Love-Dreams, Nightmare, Death, the Unconscious, the Imagination, Divination, the Artist, and Kindred Subjects

WALTER DE LA MARE

NEW YORK: ALFRED·A·KNOPF

mcmxxxix

TO

LASCELLES ABERCROMBIE

Contents

[vii]

★ *Contents* ★

PART ONE

Dream and Imagination

L'homme est né si médiocre qu'il n'est bon que quand il rêve. . . .
*Our life is no dream, but it should and will perhaps become
one. . . .*
That which is unreal, never was: that which is real, never was not.

Dream and Imagination

The Collection of poems and passages in prose that follows may be opened at random, browsed in, and then laid aside, until (as I hope) it is returned to again. It is a hope which may be expressed without presumption since its editor is responsible only for the choice of its contents and for their arrangement; and that arrangement, although it has been given thought and care, and although it has a definite object in view, can be ignored. One reader may prefer the glancing flight of the kingfisher, even over waters as profound and mysterious as these so frequently are; another the patience of the heron intent on the slow-moving current of his stream or the placid fringes of his pond. And both of them, needless to say, are very welcome.

An *anthology* may be restricted to any kind or period or province of literature; to any subject, interest or pursuit — birds, flowers, kisses, eating and drinking, moths, trees, fairies, mysticism, infancy, infamy, old age, weather, wisdom or witchcraft. And not one of these, I fancy, is completely ignored in the pages that follow. But this volume is rather a Survey — a panorama — of a wide theme, endlessly inviting, in much obscure, viewed from many different angles, by many diverse minds, and in differing states of the mind. It ranges fitfully over an immense area of human experience; and of speculation concerned with it. Still its area is limited. All that relates in life to broad daylight, to what we all call actuality, to the wholly wide-awake, and to complete consciousness is outside its aim, although even " If seven maids with seven mops had Swept it for half a year," they would have failed to keep out every trace of that.

The word " experience " usually implies that of which we are fully aware; the direct traffic in life between the within and the without, between mind and matter. This conscious mind may often deserve the epithets " prim, smug, self-satisfied, owlishly wise," but *its* is the life which (with notes of exclamation) Longfellow described as real, and which he accepted as earnest. This is the life which we can, to some extent, lead as well as follow; control, order, and arrange; although we may appear, on reflection, to be little more than passive if well-meaning pawns on the chequered board, and dubious of the true players, of the rules, the stakes and the motive of the game.

It is the kind of life that occupies some two-thirds of our stay on earth. One aggregate year out of three is spent otherwise — on the borderland of consciousness, or on its further outskirts, or beyond them, and in a state and region which may still merit the compliment of being called life and experience, however widely and oddly either of them differs from that of the waking day. Nor need broad daylight debar us from this borderland. When the sun is high in the heavens we may find — and lose — ourselves only just this side of it. The degree of our trespass into it is then measured by the degree of attention we give to it, and it is complicated by the problem of time.

Whether time is considered as " one side of a four-dimensioned continuum that is perfectly isotropic," or as but an imposture of consciousness, or as the despair alike of the poet and the metaphysician, or as a lifelong enemy only to be disposed of by death; it remains an elusive enigma in which the humblest mind can delightfully entangle itself. We plead, Hasten! Time stands still. We cry, Stay! It flies like a swallow. We attend to it; it tarries. We forget it; it (usually) forgets us. The more we have of it at our free disposal, the less likely, perhaps, we are to make good use of it. A little may go a long way. Certain drugs—hashish, for example—play ducks and drakes with it; and time gone, like the tides of the sea, leaves only flotsam for the records of its ebb. Time to come appears to be oceanic in extent; but may become eternity in the twinkling of an eye. It is a strange medium or solution for anything so solid-seeming, so insistent and inevitable as human experience. Time is childhood's leaden wings; it is age's rushing, soundless river. It is common coin — copper or golden — to be spent, saved, or wasted, of which instant by instant we each of us, according to Big Ben, have precisely the same amount. It is the bars of our cage or aviary which vanish away the moment we begin to sing, or to listen to a fellow-captive engaged in the same inexplicable pursuit. But borderland time, and time beyond it, is the strangest kind, not to mention that of the " serial " order discovered by Mr. J. W. Dunne.

THE BORDERLAND

Time in our waking state, whatever inward yardstick we may apply to it, is supervised by the world at large, and kept in order by a clock that obeys the sun. When consciousness, in whatever degree, either in quantity or quality, withdraws from that clock's, that heavenly sun's exacting sway, other conditions no less mysterious and more private immediately supervene.

It is with these conditions that the following pages are concerned. With sleep, and its associations; with dream, and the state of dreaming; with the Unconscious, and its fringes; with fantasy and the imagination; with the art and genius that reveal their value and significance; and with Death, either as incredible end or as inscrutable beginning — these are this book's chief landmarks and divisions.

Each of them has been an agelong problem; for even the term, the Unconscious, used for the first time in this sense so recently as 1909, was only thereby made specific. Centuries of human meditation have achieved no final solution of any one of them. The awake may scrutinize the sleeper for hours together, and, as we shall see, discover certain curious facts about him; but of sleep itself, no more than of life itself, can any vestige be laid in any balances; and where shall we find the ethereal swansdown to weigh against it in the scales? Every dream, too, is and must always remain the secret possession solely of the dreamer. Waking recollection of it is the only proof he has that it has come and gone; and even this is difficult to translate into those obstinate and artificial symbols, words. From the earliest times there may have been agreement in the classification of dreams. Further than that, concord is far to seek. Yet in their variety, habits, and characteristics, they appear throughout Man's centuries to have changed no more than have his bones. A palaeolithic troglodyte asleep under his stalactites was hardly more of an insoluble riddle to his fellows than we in the same relation are nowadays to one another.

Evidence again for the *Unconscious Mind,* a phrase that borders on self-contradiction (and the necessity for which is not universally accepted even by authority), is attainable only when it has ceased to be wholly unconscious. And our own sensuous, shallow and noisy side of Death, even when the quietude of contemplation stills a restless mind, is a poor vantage ground wherefrom to attempt to divine what Death itself portends. That we ourselves must die indeed, remains only an overwhelming inference based solely on external evidence, even if it be ratified by intuition and the heart. We deduce its event only from its effect upon others. Even if we could discover the link between self and mind and body, how much nearer should we be to realising the sequel to its fracture?

THE CONTENTS

This is no more than a brief summary of the contents of this book — for those who care for its currency, riches indeed. Its arrangement is of infinitely less value and importance than what has been arranged. In its course and sequence, it wanders and wavers, shallows and deepens; and this with no more, perhaps, but I hope with no less, excuse than has the Thames for its meanderings from its source to the sea. Much has been omitted that would have been equally appropriate, but nothing is here which failed to interest or to delight its editor. And that ensures as safe a hope as any of delighting his reader. Many omissions have been deliberate; many more have been due either to lack of insight or good fortune or, worse, of industry. Very few translations find a place in it. What influence and effect, then, the race or climate or language of the dreamer has on the kind and quality of his dreams, and on similar operations of the mind, is a seductive question that has been left unanswered. Certain things much desired have been denied. Book-makers are restricted even more than is the spirit of man by a horrid necessity called Space; there is a vineyard called copyright; and that reminds one of sour grapes. But apart from these deficiencies, a collection of so wide a scope as this, over harvest fields so various and so abundant, could only glean rather than garner.

Poetry has been its main incentive; its prose being chiefly intended as comment and explanation — to indicate, like a fingerpost, what for the most part it so inadequately exemplifies. The two may make rather uneasy company at times; and there are good reasons not only against making poems serve their subject matter, since that is always subsidiary in the value of any work of art, but also against glossing, as it were, what is self-contained and self-sufficing with material of a different nature and intention. A poem *is* a work of art. It is personal and individual. It is not usually, though it may be, concerned with Fact, or even with Truth, except that of the imagination. Poetry itself, indeed, in A. E. Housman's words, springs from and appeals to " something in man which is obscure and latent," " in some region deeper than the mind." Proof, then, even of its presence is impracticable. Psychology, on the contrary, deals with the ascertaining of certain facts, and these can be checked and confirmed.

Yet there need be no enmity between them; since poetry is a remote province of Psychology and may enshrine a profound knowledge of Psyche — the mind and the soul. Still, when prose concerned with science is neighboured by poetry, it is the poetry which, in the reader's mind, is likelier for the time being to make the greater sacrifice. Two poems, again, equal in technical merit and in a similar vein, may either become telling foils one to the other, or each may thus lose something of its virtue. If their merit is unequal, one may suffer vital loss, the other ensure to itself an equivalent gain. Nevertheless, the planet Venus is no less lovely and is certainly no less serene when Sirius is sharing with her the same quarter of the heavens; and precious stones, if they are deftly arranged, may win colour and lustre from others in the same setting.

The material, then, in this volume is miscellaneous. It may be charged (according to taste) either with providing an unconscionable deal of sack or too little bread.

> But " IS " and " IS-NOT " though with Rule and Line
> And " UP-AND-DOWN " by Logic I define,
>   Of all that one should care to fathom, I
> Was never deep in anything but — Wine! —

the wine named *poetry*. To praise what is here in such abundance would be impertinent; much of the loveliest poetry in English is concerned with my theme. And, with no foolish intention of suggesting that scientific knowledge and poetry need be inimical, I have been frugal with the bread. Certainly not because I cannot enjoy and delight in it, and, I hope, be nourished by it. But the quartern loaves of Psychology, amply provided with an inviting provocative crust, are difficult to cut into adequate and truly representative slices. Science, too, is fare for the day-mind, rather than for that of the night. It can richly and acutely theorise on dreams, it cannot finally impale a specimen upon a pin. The extracts included here, however, even if some of them were not so intended, may be of invaluable help to the novice and entice any reader to the fountainhead.

Bread or sack, " Hollo, my fancy! " has been one will-o'-the-wisp for guidance; but certain supremely good poems have been omitted because they are very familiar, while others no less familiar have been included either for their own irresist-ible sake alone, or because the context here given to them might lend a slightly novel or a less evident tinge than usual to their meaning.[1] To quote fragments of poems — a few petals rather than the complete flower — may need excuse; and a better excuse, perhaps, than that of sheltering behind Robert Bridges. But that he did not condemn the practice, and himself followed it, is very far from being in its disfavour. A fine poem is of course a complete unity; but so also may be one of its stanzas, even one of its lines. Less fine poems, *pace* the poet, like Apollo's laurel, may be improved by judicious pruning — especially in respect to their conclusions. Also, one may cut, and come again.

The sources of this book, then, are very numerous and diverse; it is intended to suggest rather than to demonstrate; to present ideas and sentiments either in accord or in conflict, rather than to prove. Many books have been searched; few even of the most delightful and instructive have been ran-sacked. When one picks a bunch of flowers, either for their rarity, or their beauty, or their fragrance, or their associations, one cannot but — when the meadows of the Hesperides are one's happy hunting ground — leave many behind. And al-though in these tranquil meadows, never more welcome and covetable than now, one cannot " trespass," one may yet at times grow weary. Moreover, the dense savours and flavours of our everyday existence can be at least temporarily destruc-tive of all that in life or in books we associate with the word " dream."

Even the most partial survey of the literature on the sub-ject of sleep alone is out of the question here. In one volume devoted to it in general, upwards of 550 several treatises are

---

[1] As to spelling: consistency, of course, has a great advantage. Nevertheless, while much archaic spelling is apt to become tedious, in moderation it may be welcome, and it at least reveals what is lost, and gained, by modernisation.

listed. And dreams — a glance at an extract in Part II will hint at what lies in wait for the conscientious enquirer intent on mastering this engrossing but elusive theme; and that summary is by no means exhaustive, since it excludes poetry, autobiography and fiction, and the moderns. Many books on dreams have little value. No other common and universal human experience has been more densely obscured with superstition, is so beset with absurdities, may prove so tedious to the wayfaring man, and has been so silly a byword to the rational. Even the expert who, like most of us, is apt to accept his theories as statements of fact, may only succeed in estranging as well as astonishing the amateur, although in positive first-hand evidence he may himself be even less well endowed. Indeed, in his efforts to remove the comfits and gilt, he may only succeed in making the gingerbread uneatable or at any rate indigestible; and a mere pretension to the "scientific" is worse than valueless. As a consequence of this, perhaps, we many of us nowadays keep secret our little squirrel-hoard of nocturnal experiences, especially those which are touched with the *outré* and egregious. You never know what horrid revelations may not be divined in the lingo so frequently scrawled in sleep on the blackboard of the Sub- or the Un-conscious. Why dredge beneath the shimmering surface of its priceless and healing waters? Although, then, a dream may to all appearance have no more guilty or unseemly inspiration than a scrap of cheese for supper, a blanket too many, the notes of a nightingale, or an eloquent sprig of geranium under the pillow, and even if neither its origin nor any meaning that can be read into it can lessen the mystery of this metamorphosis, and our joy in it, or the reverse; yet perhaps caution is best. What if an expert happens to be sharing our morning coffee, our substantial bacon and eggs?

We cannot deny, of course, that our dreams are seldom of any value or much interest — even to ourselves. On the other hand, alike on the authority of "Napoleon's Dream Book" and that of many eminent interpreters, we may be

convinced that they may be not only occasionally precognitive, prophetic, but that, in their own abstruse language, they
may reveal our deeper instincts and our hidden wishes (a
belief at least fifteen centuries old), and that they may be
meaningful communings between self and self, revelations of
the spirit within. We may accept Mercutio's, "Dreams are
the children of an idle brain, begot of nothing but vain fantasy"; or may prefer Romeo's,

> "Oh! Speak again, bright angel, for thou art
> As glorious to this night, being o'er my head,
> As is a winged messenger of heaven."

The former is a curious comment on man's vaunted common-
sense, if not upon his sanity. And dreams, alas, resemble far
too frequently a tale told by an idiot, signifying even less than
the literature he may reserve for the noonday.

If, when our drowsy eyelids consign us to sleep's care, we
could always rely on an entertainment even comparable with
the old transformation scenes and harlequinades of our
childhood's pantomimes, an enchanting reward apparently
merely for being alive, well and good. We cannot. Contrariwise, we may at least return thanks that our hours of darkness
so seldom afflict us with their own wilder and more wanton
representation of the cares, anxieties and anguish of waking,
and of its follies and futilities. We may pine in vain for the
fulfilment of our dearest wishes in our dreams (however
extreme the disillusionment of the morning) — the child for
his coveted toy, the lover for the loved one; for the illumination of a devoted taskwork, for a relief from our stupidity, or
a refuge from despair. But an existence resembling a panorama of precisely the same kind of experience, now observed
in waking, now in sleep, would be a poor alternative. Life's
punctual magpie serial is at least more amusing for being the
work of two collaborators so unalike in style, so much at odds
regarding form and matter and method, so various in their
shocking disregard of our tastes and ideals; and so remote

one from the other apparently in motive, value, and moral code, and in their notions of the sane, the significant, the welcome, and the useful.

But sleep, as we shall see, like dreaming, is a state of many degrees. Our matchless blessing is that no tyranny can finally deprive us of the one, or, when we are under its sweeter domination, spy upon the other. That the famous metaphor of the gates of horn and of ivory is due to a Greek pun, and — since ivory is a pleasanter, rarer and more beautiful substance than horn — to a questionable pun, is a minute indication of the state of the subject. Bishop Ken's:

> I, waking, called my dream to mind
> Which to instruct me heaven designed;

Ben Jonson's:

> And Phansie, I tell you, has dreams that have wings,
> And dreams that have honey, and dreams that have stings,
> Dreams of the maker, and dreams of the teller,
> Dreams of the kitchen, and dreams of the cellar;

and Robert Herrick's:

> Here we are all by day; by night w'are hurled
> By dreams, each one into a sev'rall world,

are epitomes of widely differing points of view. And so, in quite another tongue, is:

" Dreams are usually transmutations, translations of bodily, coenesthetic, organic feelings into psychical feelings of which we do not become directly and immediately conscious, but merely as the results or as the kernels of dream-dramas which are improvised from experiences of vital, customary hopes and fears."

Even the discovery that *coenesthesis* is " the undifferentiated complex of organic sensation by which one is aware of the body and bodily condition " left me palely wandering through the mists of this precise statement until — I came out to Ben Jonson again. The one thing clear and certain is that dreams in sleep (and these meandering remarks will return to both subjects) are of an infinite variety in matter, in manner, and also in degree. And some dreams are waking dreams.

DAY-DREAMS

"When ideas," says John Locke, "float in our mind without any reflection or regard of the understanding" (a division of our mental operations which at once sets one speculating again), "it is that which the French call ' revery ' " — a word that for Chaucer signified a state of delight, its English equivalent "day-dream" not being then ready to his pen since it first came into general use nearly three centuries later.

This placid pastime — snare of the idle, scorn of the matter-of-fact — deserves a slender anthology all to itself. It has indeed been recently scrutinised, dissected, and tabulated in more than one treatise slender neither in bulk nor argumentation. Compared with dream, it is what nectar is to honey, tint to colour. It resembles, in its gentle rilling, the circulation of the blood; and *may* be the usual occupation, apart from the needs and dangers of their workaday existence, of bird and beast and fish. A passive looking-glass-life of active reflections — the cow in the meadow, the sheep in the corn. A Painted Lady perched on a flower; a thrush in tranced meditation on her nest; a drowsy cat on her footstool by the fire, are, at least, pictures and emblems of reverie; and a great deal more of our workaday life is spent in this heedless industry than we are likely to realise, or might care to confess. The enjoyment of every tale, of every poem we read, indeed, is largely in the nature of a day-dream, even though it is being built up in an astonishing fashion out of a purely verbal fabric. Every hope, every expectation, every desire and resolve concerning that radiant or dismal region of the life of the mind which we call the Future, and which, in general, might be more precisely designated as the Never-Never-Land, also resembles a day-dream — suspended, like dew-drops, on filaments of fact and truth and fancy, spun out of the silk of memory, and even more flimsy, if no less attractive in design, than a spider's web. " That it was May, thus dremèd me," whispers romance, and Cupid creeps a little closer with his dart.

What indeed is every work of art before it is accomplished but a day-dream with a definite purpose and a particular goal? Ideals, ambitions, sustaining enough for the time being, may prove as illusory. Very few human beings never thus indulge fancy; and not all of those who do, wear rose-coloured spectacles meanwhile. The miser embraces a day-dream from which only a coffin can bring him release. Grief, envy, hapless love, malice and hatred — to each its own colour and livery. With their polite slogan of " service," the vast emporiums and trusts of this Age of Trade, whatever day-mares they may also suggest, are realisations of a certain order of day-dream. Even governments and nations may secrete these bodiless figments — with sovereign advantages to humanity or with appalling catastrophes, possibly, for their outcome. In private life they may be a honey that without cost or trouble sweetens our daily bread. But one cannot live on honey alone.

These musings of the mind, seldom shared even if they are fully shareable, seldom sharply attended to even, or precisely realised, may yet have far more effect on our well-being, on our relations with others, and on our actions than some of the more substantive and evident factors in life. That reverie may cheat us, prove utterly fallacious, be a tragic if pleasant waste of time, is a commonplace. All things in moderation. Sheer habit and subjection to it may convert this particular enticement into a vice. Schoolmasters, moralists, censors — there is never any lack of solemn warning. Men, it seems, are more likely to be the happy visitants and victims of this strain and state of mind than women. A good deal depends on how much of the child they may have retained for solace and companionship; for the day-dream in childhood is notoriously rife.

In his study entitled *Children's Daydreams*, Mr. George H.

Green sorts his specimens into three consecutive types. The first of them, which, he says, manifests itself when the child is about three years of age, is a day-dream of the imaginary companion. When the three-year-old succeeds in becoming ten years old, this imaginary companion is followed by the " team fantasy," showing that the child has somehow or other admitted the necessity of working with his fellow children, and is no longer purely egotistic even in his imaginings — a triumph not always attainable even by the adult! With the approach of puberty, almost needless to say, the day-dream acquires what is called a " sexual tinge " — a phrase that bristles with as many vexatious points of the problematical as a porcupine with quills. Then comes the day-dream of yet another imaginary companion, one who is likely to be a member of the other sex (and may appear in many disguises!), whereas in earlier years sex was a matter of indifference.

One wonders. Day-dreams are chameleonic and exquisitely elusive. Fancy and fantasy of many odd strands may be woven out of our immediate surroundings at any age. I was no more than seven years old when (perhaps not for the first time) I fell in love; and the child of my devotion consisted chiefly, I fear (as in maturer glimpses of the divine and the transitory), of day-dream. Of any imaginary companion at the age of three I haven't any recollection; but this of course does not affect Mr. Green's general statement. A wholly imaginary companion with no less and no more affective sex than an Aunt Sallie, arrived much later. She was a nursery drudge in my young days, dumb, ugly, battered, scorned and reviled. She was called Tatta, played cards with the family, and eventually was joined by " Tatta's brother."

Since a child's vocabulary is scanty and he is apt to scent a trap whenever the adult presents him with a direct question for bait, he cannot be trusted to commit himself to a full exposure of what he holds most personal or most dear. How is he to be sure that his confidences will be received with insight and sympathy? That for imaginative children at any rate reverie or day-dreaming is a state of being brimming over

with solace and delight is beyond question. It trespasses —
what wonder? — into the classroom; and, swift and silent as
the dartings of a hover-fly, will weave its enchanting patterns
beneath the dunce's cap. A child's questions and comments,
one's own memories of childhood, reveal how profound this
day-dreaming may be; and even at times of a poetic or philosophical or mystical cast. Growing older may thin its flow, or
canalise it — for purposes of irrigation, perhaps. All minds,
probably, are shared by a Martha and a Mary.

As a way of escape (in days like ours that sadly need one)
reverie has its dangers. And yet if we could appraise the outcome in achievement, and in practical achievement, due to a
severe rationality and logic and that due to the state of mind
when ideas float in it "without any reflection or regard of the
understanding," reverie would at any rate easily take second
prize! King Alfred let the cakes burn; George Stephenson appeared to be wasting his precious time mooning over a steam-
ing kettle; and no doubt Isaac Newton idly amused himself,
when he sat on the shingle facing the Ocean of Knowledge,
by flinging stones into the sea. Stay a moment, mind and body
completely at rest, in any English solitude — garden, hill-side,
green valley or flowing river, or even at a window looking
down upon the to-and-fro and play of light and sound in a
busy street — and let the whole scene — spring, or fallen
snow, or summer twilight, or autumnal trance — settle, as it
were, in consciousness; then the stealthy outcome will be yet
another day-dream, and none the less lovely or beguiling for
that.

Our English climate, indeed, erratic in everything but its
fascinating variety, our seasons, each one in turn consistent
only in never being perfectly sure to which of the others it
may decide to offer the sincerest form of flattery, the gradual
progress of its every day, from dawn to sunrise, from twilight
on to dark, may be a slender tribute to any system of logic,
human or divine. It may none the less account in some measure for the various richness of the English imagination and
fantasy, unflinchingly matter-of-fact in other aspects of it

though the English genius may be. Its literature is proof of the power and range of that imagination; and even its indolent but deep-seated preference for muddling through is a cloud with a silver lining — a lining, again, that is not called Logic, and yet at inspired moments may suggest Wordsworth's " clouds of glory."

But reverie is of the day; and we are for the dark.

NIGHT

" The sun descending in the West, The evening star does shine." The twilight deepens; the last faint spectral colours in the west vanish away:

> Now the day is over,
> > Night is drawing nigh,
> Shadows of the evening,
> > Steal across the sky.
>
> Now the darkness gathers,
> > Stars begin to peep,
> Birds, and beasts, and flowers
> > Soon will be asleep . . .

With that darkness, those stars and that sleep we are nowadays becoming less and less familiar; even if, by good fortune, we are neither city-bred nor city-pent, but " live in the country." The tolling curfew, if it were still audible, " over some wide-watered shore, swinging slow with sullen roar," would, as heretofore, leave the *world* to darkness. But we ourselves, unless perhaps we are in love or grief or despair or wish to meditate, hasten to switch on our electric bulbs. Paraffin lamps, even the Victorian gas jet (until it dismally hooded itself with a " mantle "), were a less abrupt alternative to the Victorian " gloaming." And to resort to candles even for a few hours is to realise what an aid their gentle light can be to quiet of mind and quiet talk — let alone the beauty thus conferred on quiet face and musing eye. And, summer or winter, candles are even a kind of company.

Darkness itself, nowadays, is steadily narrowing in for most of us to being merely the domain of sleep — which blessedly has a darkness solely its own. We flood not only both living-room and bedroom with a glare rather than with light, but also our cities, towns, highroads, and even our villages and lanes. Until the advent of the motor car, it is true, the magic — fantastic, theatrical or serene — of a country road skirting woodland or arched over with forest trees, and illuminated by this vibrant glare, was undiscovered. But a Guy Fawkes bonfire achieves a similar witchery, and at less expense of spirit to the solitary wayfarer. As for London, one needs to be alone at night in the silent and deserted heart of the city to realise the overwhelming odds nowadays against those who " plan some evil." I can recall no more bizarre solitude than that of the musty fourwheeler in which, to the *clopp* of its horse's shoes, I traversed some years ago in the small hours an exotically illuminated Cheapside; and not another spectre, not so much as a vagrant cat, in sight.

So complete, whatever the advantage may be, is our present slavery to the lamp that, for most of us, it is something of an adventure to go upstairs in the dark, or to enjoy that curious fellowship with ourselves incident to undressing in it. To be naked in the dark is to be naked — myself and no other; but at any rate unashamed. To sit alone in it, and to remain for the time being as far as possible at peace, may bring not only refreshment to the spirit but even be tinged with romance.

Like Thomas Hood's roses and lily-cups, our minds and our moods in differing degree are " made of " light, or of darkness. They respond, then, given the opportunity, to every change of light. A house in the small hours with electricity laid on is a fortress; nimble sentries are instantly ready on its battlements. A wind-ridden or fogbound house of many rooms, with not a tandstickor or stub of tallow to its name, may seem, if there is still any childhood left in us, to be helplessly listening for " the others " — either from without or from within. But how else prove that there are others? A little experience will answer that question quite as well as any " medium."

It was to earthly night — " the dumb hour clothed in black " — that the three sons of Usher's Well returned from the gates of paradise; and Sheridan le Fanu, as every adept of the powers of the air must be, was as familiar with the dark as with his own hands. We dance attendance on daylight by instinct and confirmed habit; we should make an assignation with the night. For years I have intended to enjoy a spell of life which would familiarize me with my complete daily allowance of twenty-four hours — in all their guises — sunrise to sunrise, by merely shifting, say, half-an-hour forward, " my habitual period of repose." Alas, like so many others, this charming project still remains a mere project.

"Our minds," Alice Meynell has said, "our senses, our sensibilities are profoundly affected by the hours of darkness," although (as with the changes of the seasons — spring as opposed to autumn; as with the weather and our physical well-being) we may be only vaguely aware of it. The fancy, the fantasy is then more sharply on the *qui vive*, restless, alert. Our chief and most active spy on actuality, the eye, is now on a precarious footing. The listener within may at any moment be compelled to supersede the sighted. Protracted night-work, moreover, not only, it has been ascertained, affects the poise of the mind, but the action of the heart, and the health. The door of the Unconscious, or of the " Coconscious," edges open, stands less narrowly ajar. And the solemn tide of darkness ebbing and flowing — the dusk of midsummer midnight, the small black hours of winter — is at least as mysterious as the tides of the Seven Seas. By preference or habit, we curtain out the dark; and unless illness compels it, we seldom of set intent watch out its hours, and so taste to the full its solitude, strangeness and emptiness.

How strange at night to wake
　　And watch, while others sleep,
Till sight and hearing ache
　　For objects that may keep
The awful inner sense
　　Unroused, lest it should mark
The life that haunts the emptiness
　　And horror of the dark! . . .

No close acquaintance with it is practicable by means of mere chance glimpses. We must set apart a certain hour and again and again keep quiet watch, from open window, from field or hill or garden, even if over only so brief a period as a lunar month. And of one thing we may be certain, the mistress we are wooing will not cheat us of our tryst.

The world without appears to have been lulled into a tense reverie of attention, or to have withdrawn itself into its own private affairs. We begin to learn what weather means to the shepherd and the sailor. Or heavy rain may be falling — its fragrant sigh overwelling the silence under a dense canopy of cloud. There is a cold sweet freshness in the late summer air, as if the mother of us all were giving suck to her Benjamin, sitting quietly in her chair. Or, the rain over, the leaden minute-drops from leaf to leaf sharpen the quietude, arrest the listener behind the ear. At night, too, the recurrent onset and lulling of the wind is less like a mere formless noise than the accents of a voice roaming through a world countless centuries before the spirit of man stirred its dust.

Night by night, little by little, the stars and the planets creep up towards their zenith. As yet hidden constellations begin to thrust their horns above the horizon line. We realise how delicate are the degrees of dusk and darkness — between the Stygian and even the starlit. And if we stay still, passive and receptive, the stars themselves begin to shake their colours in the sky as if they were endeavouring to transmit us an urgent message in some celestial Morse code of their own. Make friends of them, they will not fail us. Each gigantic

tree wears a gravity and solemnity as of Keats's forest sena-
tors. Every flitting moth becomes a private visitor with an
unspoken message. Every owl-squeak is a half-secret coun-
tersign. And every drift of open grass or road or meadow
becomes at length as familiar as was the forest of Arden to
Titania, to her lovely Indian boy and her elves. At the same
time we find ourselves straying into far less familiar regions
than usual of the mind. An "emanation far within," of the
"fathomless and boundless deep," may awake — and not
always to recall our griefs, our follies, our ruined loves, or our
sins. A tedious restless daybreak does that best.

The imagination bestirs itself in the dark; the serpent
sloughs its daily skin. And perhaps because night actually
attracts less kindly phantom fauna than the day, evil and
disaster are associated with darkness: dark thoughts, a darkened outlook, dark deeds, the night of the soul. The imaginative writers have given the sharpest edge to the word.
What is called realism is usually a record of life at a low pitch
and ebb viewed in the sunless light of day — so often a drab
waste of grey and white, and an east wind blowing. But
imaginative evil, either in thought or act or art is an evil that
is rare and may be almost past endurance — there is an evil
dream in Dostoevski, there are drawings of Goya's — and
this, like the funguses, flourishes in the dark.

By act of grace, we have been given eyelids (silent, untir-
ing twin sisters), which are not only an exquisite means of
expression to those strange, lovely and eloquent, or strange
and equally repellent marvels of life, light, colour and movement that gaze out from beneath them. They are also a priceless refuge and release from the distractions and fatigue of
the world without. Sight, indeed, unlike touch and smell, is
not a local sensibility: it seems to flood one's whole being
with the lustrous scene it bestows. Let there be light; and we
ourselves *are* light. But since safety first, whatever its danger
as a maxim, is a paramount instinct, we cannot at will, alas,
except when the mind is so intent that not even a clap of
thunder may win admittance, refuse to hear. None the less,

how seldom in the waking day do we deliberately close awhile our eyes, and thus regain for the time being the quiet and hospitable vestibule of the mind.

This is because, perhaps, attention tends then to begin to waver; because the signpost in that peculiar small darkness, fenced off, more densely than was Robinson Crusoe's stockade, from actuality, points vaguely out to sleep. We seldom even in reverie, indeed, shut our eyes, since that way again lies night-dream. The precarious authority and power of direction which we have over our faculties slips away, and we presently after become less responsible for what may chance to us — like Hansel and Gretel in the darkening wood. Nor, indeed, in our familiar England is night frequently synonymous with pitch darkness. When cloud is scattered and not dense, the light rained faintly down upon us from the infinitely remote stars resembles a lucent dust in the air. And — surely one of the very happiest of our earthly accidents — there is the moon — "*le* 'lovely moon' *des Anglois.*"

THE MOON

I dreamed many years ago that above a wide stretch of flattish land — hummocks of sea-darkened sand, indented with shoaling-water — no fewer than three moons were in the heavens: one to the east, one to the west, and the third at her zenith. For astronomy, no more than any other science, is slavishly respected in sleep. But, in view of all that she has done for me, even my three dream moons were a poor tribute to the earth's faithful yet fickle satellite. A gifted young poet recently assured me that an image now so trite and so incorrigibly romantic as the moon should henceforth be taboo in English verse. My dream, then, was no more than as old-fashioned a piece of Victorianism as a robin on a Christmas card. Still, the abrupt snapping of her earthly ties and her escape into space (quite apart from any jarring effects on her guardian-planet) would even to the most prosaic of us be an irreparable disaster. In the earth's destiny she was the happiest of afterthoughts, the oddest of grace-notes, the most magical of things " thrown in."

The light and heat of the sun, like air and water, is a human necessity. The moon is in the nature of a luxury. She is sweetheart rather than wife. She is our night-light. The sun excites, challenges, daunts, dazzles, dazes, may even all but stun the mind with radiance. It sucks self outwards; its heat resembles a fourth skin. In its vast shimmering mantle of gold, it pours life into us.

> With open mouth he drank the sun
> As though it had been wine!

" Doth not the glory of the Sun pay tribute to your sight? Is not the vision of the World an amiable thing? " Not so the moon. Like a spy with a bull's-eye, she silently discloses what she shines upon. She pacifies, invites us *in*. Her light gnaws away shadow; and glides, smooth and softly as a serpent, from stone on to stone. Caught, yet unaware of being so, our instincts and our sentiments are instantly affected by her presence. " The Sea! the Sea! " we may shout at sight of an ocean basking in splendour beneath the sun; but what barbarian would go bawling into the night to welcome the moon? We tread softly; look and think with caution; as if to be in keeping with this stealthy and motionless lustre. The preternatural is lurking near, is skulking abroad. And a beauty, or bearing, or character in things, indetectable in daylight, now lies in wait for us. Not only is every flower alone in moonlight, and many refuse to bloom until her hour draws near, not only is the air sweet and heavy with smells and odours, and every rose chilled with dew resembles a rose dreaming of itself; but even so gross and coarse a plant as the vegetable marrow, when its great thorny leaves are dusked over with the moon's silver, becomes not only singularly beautiful, but as individual an organism as a basking alligator.

Unlike her lord and master, a Bluebeard who, in her sluggish rotations, never allows her out of his sight, the moon pre-

sides rather than rules over the earth. Even at her most
brilliant she reflects, we are told, less than half a millionth of
his luminousness, and gives as little heat, I fancy, as would
to the hand a lighted candle some half-a-mile away. Yet, as
human-animals, we can no more evade returning her stare
than Criseyde could escape that of Troilus, or a king his cat's.
Now she will dazzle an eye that can yet face her out; anon,
her gaze is as calm as it is hypnotic. When the heavens are
gracious she may be a marvel of beauty in every one of her
gradual phases — from that slender half-hoop of silvered
ivory in the serene of evening, to her last white parched and
ghostly relic adrift in the blue of noonday. Harvest moon
(which I once mistook for a rounded haystack when she was
capping a hill on the horizon), or Hunter's moon, or May-
day's, or January's, blanching an earth shag and grey with
hoar frost or mantled in driven snow — how choose between
them? She is mistress of so many moods and caprices.

As when, for example, having risen an hour or two before
a faintly veiled and starry summer midnight, she slowly
ascends out of the east, as if she were carrying her own lantern, and *shows*, as it were, the lovely vault of space its beauty;
or as when her full circle is stealthily and funereally devoured
by the monster called Eclipse; or as when, dwindled and all
but evilly bright, she gazes from the heights of winter with the
ferocity of some heraldic lynx. Or yet again, as when, fallen
towards her setting, she casts on the pallid woods and meadows a light as spectral as that of a phosphoric fish in a dark
larder. And hers too is the charming device of enticing into
her service every planet or major star she passes on her way.

She pacifies the peaceful — wood, hill and water; gives
wings and a tumultuous sky to the wildest gale; smiles down
from a pale-blue sky of soapsud clouds as benignly as some
old family Nannie on the children of men — although candour must add that she can be a little dull and commonplace
when gibbous, and rather too sweetly sentimental on the
marine parade. She bestows loveliness and magic even on the
lovely: " How sweet the moonlight sleeps upon this bank! "

She can win back from the darkness their reds and blues into the flowers, its dyes into a Persian carpet; can etherealise the ugly; bestow grace on the commonplace; and will adore her own splintered reflection, as Tchekhov declared, in every unflattering scrap of broken crockery or glass. Her beams, on some old discoloured wall, green bridle-path or dingle in the woods, make stealthy shadows, jet black and soft as velvet, but not shade.

Only the very timid or guilty *fear* her light, and only the furtive would shun it. A bad conscience has an assignation with her; and the earth itself may seem apprehensive of her unflinching gaze. She can intensify darkness; give magic to the bewitched; terror to vacancy; horror to the haunted; an edge to the spectral. Her presence in sky or room deepens solitude; prepares for the ghostly. And no wonder the tide of unreason also obeys her influence. The crazy, the insane, are also described as "lunatics": persons, according to the Law, who manifest lucid intervals, as indeed she does herself. And, although authoritative evidence is conflicting, even one's own experience may suggest that it is not merely an old wives' tale which declares that the mentally afflicted show increasing disquietude and unease at the approach of full moonlight.

Fish, flesh and fowl, it is said, go bad more rapidly then than by day. In early childhood I was warned to shield my sleeping face from her direct rays. And not without reason, apparently. A friend who ventured to challenge the full moon by sleeping on deck in the tropics, his countenance bathed in her reflected beams, paid for it, he tells me, with the most severe and most protracted headache of his lifetime — moonstruck. Even the most popular of fallacies could hardly account for that. But what we are not taught in print is held to be hardly worth the learning. We pay less and less court than our grandfathers to our only satellite, discredit her wiles, and ignore her sweet influences. Of old, the country people, whose books were running brooks, throughout the round of the seasons — killing, culling, felling, sowing, the taking of medicines and the care of the sick — kept a continually heed-

ful eye on her phases. But this was in the darker ages, and before knowledge became Science.

Although, again, the moon is so close a neighbour, only some thirty days' distance in a chaser aeroplane (eighty being fixed on by Jules Verne as an astonishing minimum for a journey round the world), nothing on earth, except its ice-caps and vast deserts, remotely resembles her realm: with its instantaneous extremes of all but absolute cold, of violent heat and wild glaring radiance; with her enormous craters and pro-digious volcanic ramparts; her pocked and arid plains; her unbroken silence, innocent of any twilight, of any odour or fragrance, or even of earth's perpetual falling of fine dust; and, above all, her ink-black skies continually frequented, even at noonday, by a myriad untwinkling stars.

That man should have worshipped the divinity of the Sun or of the Stars is no marvel. What state and circumstance in all its glory could be more divine? Nor is it to be wondered at that he has paid obeisance to, held secret and savage rites un-der, feared, and saddled superstitions on the Moon. It is she indeed, more closely even than the planets and the stars, whom we associate with sleep and with our dreams. Yet what an oddity of a parasite the creature is. That viewlessly teth-ered enormous sterile mass, whether or not torn from the watery hole that is now the Pacific Ocean, refusing to divulge the secret of her hidden side, and reiteratedly revealed to our gaze and telescopic curiosity by the vast bull's-eye of the sun as she skulks on her interminable and circuitous journey through space! [2]

Amateur worshippers, however, at the shrine of Astarte, with her mysteries, must be almost as rare nowadays as they are likely to be lukewarm; and " the implacable Aphrodite " went out of literary fashion with Algernon Charles Swin-

---

[2] According to Hans Hoerbiger, who originated the Cosmic Ice Theory, the moon was once a solar planet, and was gradually seduced from her intermartian orbit until at length — thirteen to fifteen thousand years ago — she became Terra's servile and serviceable satellite. The disaster thus inflicted on the earth's inhabitants would be excelled if in times to come she is gradually attracted nearer and nearer to the earth until she is finally shattered to pieces on its breast.

burne. The astrologer, as in the days of Defoe, it is true, is putting the stars to his own privy use again, and the intelligent pay due attention to his predictions. But our modern tendency to introspection — a far more common, and, perhaps, more perilous hobby — is not much concerned with the subtle influences on our minds and moods of the things of nature. At a chance glimpse through window-glass or spectacles of that slim familiar crescent returned again into the west, we may be a little uneasy (it is a personal confession), and at once hasten out into the open to rattle the money in our pockets, and to bestow on her a series of shamefaced bobs. We then smile inwardly and indulgently at yet another of our little " superstitions." Shallow superstitions they may be — valueless as mere lip service; but even at that, they may spring out of a realisation of wonder and mystery, and from the conviction that our senses are not our only trustworthy witnesses in this world, but that nature itself resembles a veil over some further reality of which the imagination in its visionary moments seems to achieve a more direct evidence. Just as the name for a thing that we love and delight in binds it closer to our minds and hearts — a bird, a wild flower, a butterfly, a fellow creature — so with the ancient belief that chace and stream, rocky sea-coast and unpeopled valley may be haunted by divine presences, whether or not we think of them as dryad, siren, naiad, or are content with a far less evocative phrase, " the spirit of place."

All things stale and lose their virtue, the best and worst, the simple and complicated, the plain and beautiful, impulse as well as artifice, unless we attend to them; give to them as much at least as they can bestow. Not that a forced ardour can restore the tinge of strangeness to the familiar which at least once in life was the secret of its charm. Yet it would never be a loss to ponder an instant on the colours of an apple before we peel it; or on the exquisite green-bronze iridescence of a starling's plumage before we dismiss its owner as a pest. No hunter surely, not even Nimrod himself — unless, like Othello, the pitiable prey of jealousy — could kill any creature at the very moment when he was spell-bound with admiration of its beauty, and therefore of its mystery.

SLEEP

But life goes on, leaks away, melts, attenuates itself — ever more rapidly; and each night, at the habitual or unusual hour, a whispered summons from the nether regions of consciousness, or a glance at the clock, or a yawn, or mere ennui, reminds us that yet another day is done.

> . . . The day gan failen, and the derke night,
> That reveth bestes from hir besinesse,
> Berafte me my book for lakke of light,
> And to my bedde I gan me for to dresse,
> Fulfild of thought and besy heviness;
> For bothe I hadde thing which that I nolde,
> And eek I ne hadde that thing that I wolde.

So wrote Chaucer; and his dilemma is not unknown to most of us. Sharing these lines, we peer straight into the fourteenth century at this solitary and most lovable poet, " retiring to rest," " seeking his couch," " off to Bedfordshire," climbing his dusky staircase, bound for the Land of Nod. The dark-coloured words evoke at least some faint realisation of one of the most usual and profound of life's many enigmas — that of sleep. And yet how seldom do we pay any tribute to it as such, or even to the minute act of resolution involved in committing ourselves to its embraces. We make our usual preparations, undress, don its uniform, and get in between the sheets. It exacts, for the fortunate at any rate, its own solitude, and for its full blessing to solitude we go, or to that of man with his mate. We may read for a while, or think for a while; we may have commended all we love to God and entreated heaven to guard us through the hours of darkness. But if our book is too moving or exciting, or if the mind strays

[28]

into any practical problem, to some care or anxiety or trouble of the heart, then the warning, *No Thoroughfare,* may at once disclose itself on the nebulous road to oblivion. The faintest echo of the word "money," for example, will resound in consciousness like a fiendish cockcrow.

Whether the divinity we no longer adulate be named Somnus, brother of Death and son of Night, or Morpheus, or Hypnos — and the absence of any *goddess* of sleep is curious — as soon as sleep wins within call, then the waking self — and how define it? — now quiet as a swan, as dewfall, as the smile on a gentle face, may slip, like some exquisite shallop at twilight, into the deep waters. And the active, attentive, responsible, eager, talkative creature-of-day-time, the paterfamilias and ratepayer has departed, has become mute, defenceless, presumably irresponsible, is inscrutably " engaged." There are faces which, when they are at rest, continue to wear a faint mask of sleep; some appear to be perpetually haunted by dreams of the day or night beneath the surface of consciousness — as may those of very young children. Others are almost as serene as when sleep has them in its keeping. But whether the contrast be little or extreme, sleep brings to all a like immobility. And an innate reverence, even apprehension perhaps, of this so usual miracle almost forbids one watching too closely any fellow creature in armchair or railway carriage thus lost to the world and actuality.

And whither has the sleeper gone? — without perhaps any conscious volition, merely the prey of a passive surrender? Why all this sleep? — seven, eight, nine, ten hours perhaps — with a living to make, work to be done, thoughts to be thought, obligations to keep, a soul to save, friends to refrain from losing, pleasure to seek, and that prodigious host of activities known as life? Even if so odd a humiliation is Nature's unavoidable device for ensuring the continuance of life, how wasteful a method it appears to be; no less afflicting to the rational victim than the fact that, hardly to our own convenience, we consume in food and drink far more than is actually required by the body. Even if the body must rest —

and but a few moments' day-rest will suffice to restore a runner or oarsman at the point of expiring from his effort — why the mind? And why, indeed, the soul, the spirit?

And again, what description can we give of the brief and blissful journey from the one state to the other? Night after night, the process is repeated. Morning after morning, it is reversed. What happens, then? Despite the fact that we may have submitted ourselves to this experience ten or twenty thousand times, it is extremely difficult to observe it clearly and closely, and to record in memory the content of the few moments immediately preceding the onset of sleep. Here the novice must be his own expert; he can only patiently check any other evidence available. A change in the position of the eye is involved — that is easily noticeable. The body has, as it were, melted out of ken; consciousness is confined in its attic; a narrowing and intensification of the inward darkness may follow, or a curious fluttering of shadows against a neutral background; and very occasionally one is aware of the sensation as of a tiny falling shutter. And then — whether a minute by the clock or several hours have intervened — one is awake again!

I have tried repeatedly to watch and examine the process — the fugitive imagery, the protean " psychic material," that fluttering wavering patterning of retinal luminosity, the abrupt emergence of some mental phantasm having no perceptible relation whatever to its surroundings: and now and then the sound of many voices, or a sudden shout. But it is inordinately difficult to follow it. The mere act of watching indeed may involve an *un*-usual procedure, resembling that of a cat entering a room and suddenly aware that a human occupant has his eyes on her. The positive instant of transition is usually imperceptible. Attention may at once defer it. Or the curtain may descend in the little theatre of the mind as swiftly as the shadow of a cloud over a sunlit town. We were here then; the " now " has evaporated. If the hours that follow leave no dream behind them, the time so occupied seems to have been reduced to a cipher. And the return to the

body may be as instantaneous as was its surrender. Even
after a lengthy period — many days — of what appears to
have been complete unconsciousness, a sentence may be instantly finished which the onset of sleep left broken in half.
On awakening we usually find ourselves seated once more on
the apex of the mount of memory, surveying a world utterly
indifferent to our prolonged absence: and every tiniest wheel
of the great contraption is busily revolving again.

Nor has the man of science, in spite of the knowledge and
instruments he can bring to his enquiry, yet been able to explore and to explain the mystery of sleep. He can do little
more than observe and record its perceptible effects on the
body. " In general," says Mme. Marie de Manacéïne, in her
treatise on Sleep, " we pay no attention to its phenomena, and
do not even include it among the questions deserving of serious study . . . The phenomena of normal sleep in this nineteenth century are still so little studied that we do not yet
know how to modify the conditions of sleep in accordance
with different diseases, or the exhaustion of the various organs, or the changes in daily life."

As we prepare to go to sleep (and " fall asleep " is a singularly clumsy way of putting it), the quiet eyelids, softer than
velvet, than falling snow, descend over the tired eyes, and
these at its stealthy onset converge and turn upward. Contrary, however, to what was for long the common opinion, the
eyeballs do not remain in this position during sleep; and although, as in waking, the pupil dilates or contracts under the
influence of certain emotions, such as fear, it seems now to
be established that in sleep itself the axes of the eyes, while
occasionally divergent, are usually parallel, as if, interesting
fact, they were " directed towards a distant object." The
deeper the sleep, the greater the contraction of the pupils.
And the retrieval of a dream seems to depend in part on an
optical adjustment.

In sleep again, the muscles are relaxed; breathing is retarded, is less deep, is continued without pause, and every
inhalation is more prolonged; the air inhaled being dimin-

ished in quantity by about one-sixth of that in waking life. The gaseous exchange in the body is diminished; the heart beats more slowly and with less energy; the temperature falls and the pulse slackens, but neither of them uniformly; the skin acts more energetically; and the internal organs are by no means inactive. Indeed, with the inconstant exception of the nervous system, their industry and their several orders of consciousness, we are told, never lapse.

Experts, and they are numerous, differ in their views regarding sensibility in sleep: whether it is more intense, or is deadened. But the faintest of whispers in the sleeper's ear; the gleam of a candle; an uncustomary odour; or a mere touch *may* prove that sensibility is not merely present but must have been acute. By day, indeed, when the attention is diverted, interruptions such as these may be unperceived. Nor need the summons during sleep be always from without. I have frequently been awakened by the accents of an inward voice, the words themselves being audible; and no less frequently by a summons clearly of this nature but more furtive and unintelligible. In these cases, the exit from sleep was without haste or apprehension, but immediate. Dreaming, once, that I was sitting with a book by the fireside of the room in which I was sleeping and which was reported to be haunted, I heard approaching footsteps behind me, and was awakened by the murmured summons, "You are wanted, sir." By whom — dream-ghost or earth-ghost — I never knew.

The sentry on the ramparts of the senses, however, usually refuses to pass on any habitual challenge to headquarters. Freight trains passing one another in the small hours not half a mile distant from my bedroom window raise such a din into the darkness as might the warring giants before the Flood; yet I never remember to have been awakened by it, and *have* been awakened by the cessation of the ticking of a clock. And a child I once knew who had been pining his heart out for the first snow of winter, with its magic and beauty and silence and cold, was awakened in the small hours even by the whisper of its falling flakes upon his windowpane. The walker in sleep (who must be distinguished from the sleep-walker, the somnambulist, the noctambulist — hands gently raised, and wide unspeculative gaze) pooh-poohs any such puny feat. Not only may the outwearied postillion, the jaded horseman, the soldier on forced march, the swimmer, the *punkah-wallah* continue in sleep their waking activities; but about four out of five human beings are apt to talk in it, some-times in a rapid gibberish, sometimes in a voice barely recog-nizable as their own. Women asleep are rather apter than men at answering questions, especially questions unlikely to concern them much. And what abject would consent to ask any other kind! But after the age of twenty-five, we are all of us less liable, it seems, to these little defenceless indiscre-tions.

Experiment has also shown — a brass ball dropped into a metal basin, a current from an induction coil — that the " depth " of sleep varies more or less regularly according to its duration. The most profound and therefore the most valu-able sleep is that of the first two or three hours, particularly if these include that immediately preceding midnight — when it is not the " quick " who are most likely to be abroad.

By means of a watch glass inserted in the skull of a living creature, human or animal, it has also been ascertained (al-though here again the experts differ) that the brain pales in sleep, is less abundantly suffused with blood; and that, whereas during life the spinal cord and the nerves sleep never, and the brain itself is never wholly inactive, it is then more truly asleep than are the other organs of the body.

Those drowsy but never dormant watchmen, the senses, on the outskirts of consciousness await only a summons sharp enough from the world without to pass on their challenge. To their commanding officer has been given the rank of an " Intelligism." This intelligism, throughout sleep, is perpetu-ally receiving and recording, as does the aether, a multitude of exquisitely tenuous messages from the microcosm in its subtly intent care. Also, however wide of the mark metaphors may be, it will accept and obey orders given overnight by the waking consciousness — that, for example, it shall arouse the sleeper at a certain hour, or even minute. That auto-suggestions (not always innocent of guile) may induce sleep, as well as banish it, I have myself proved by long practice; albeit with fitful success. To what extent this faculty might be further explored, students of M. Baudouin can attest. The mind, it seems, will do little that we wish until we have "imagined" the wish fulfilled. It has a childlike distaste for compulsion. Persuasion is the sugar that best sweetens its medicine. But, as with the child, the dose may be administered by day or night.

How this intelligism through the dark small hours keeps a record of clock-time is a pretty riddle. It may do so by counting the sleeper's respirations, or the low insistent drumming of his heart, or by registering "more subtle organic processes," or, possibly, inorganic. But the waking mind moves in no less mysterious a fashion, as a minute's scrutiny of, let alone a few hours' companionship with a fixed idea, will reveal. Like those of us who are gifted with double joints; or, like our physical ancestors, can at will move ear or scalp; or are the victims of strange coincidences; or pride themselves on being psychic, or infallible judges of character; anyone who can wake himself at his own pleasure is usually a little vain of the feat. He has no reason to be. Three out of five human beings, it appears, possess the faculty; it is more frequent in men than in women, and in the aged than in the young.

There are several theories as to the causes of sleep. They are conflicting and as yet indecisive. For many years, as has been said, sleep was assumed to be the result of cerebral congestion; and then of cerebral anaemia — the probable cause also of frequent yawning, if not of its infectiousness. That sleep is due to fatigue of the cells (and their occupants) in the body is another theory. That the body produces poisons while we are awake which induce a condition wherein they are

destroyed and expelled is yet another — and a peculiar
paradox.

Man's need for sleep, on the other hand, is beyond dispute
— the need, that is, for the sleep of nature: since narcotics can
ensure none of its really sovereign virtues, except only the
arrest of consciousness. An animal deprived of food for
twenty days, and thus shrunken to half its original weight,
may yet escape death if it is then cautiously fed. But five
days' insomnia is fatal to a puppy. In hunger, the brain is the
last organ to suffer; in sleeplessness it suffers most. Absence
of sleep induces waking hallucinations. The bodily weight
may increase in a prolonged period of wakefulness; the
vision may become more acute; but the memory will begin to
fail, and the attention to wane — and this after only ninety
fully conscious hours. Protract this ordeal, and Death, like
blind Mr. Pew in *Treasure Island,* close on the heels of insanity, is tap-tapping on his way: a fact of which the old
Chinese torturers were well aware.

The weaker the consciousness, the more sleep it needs;
when it is highly developed, less is required. But the well-
known folk-rhyme on the subject is not far wrong. Nor was
King Alfred; who may be transposed into doggerel:

> Eight hours for toil;
> Eight hours for rest;
> And twenty-four
> For Joy is best.

And although many very unusual men — Goethe, Frederick the Great, Napoleon among others — have been frugal
in sleep, this need be no exclusive mark of wisdom. Diver-
sions less inactive but more destructive are common enough;
and few of our days on earth contain no moments worse
spent than when we are thus "away." Moments, indeed!
Sleep is the most modest, the most benign of self-effacements.
In sleep even the wicked may cease from troubling, as also
may the "unco guid." If only one could at any moment

ensure a long draught of it, crystal-clear, how many grievous, dragging hours of suspense, or expectation, or foreboding might be spared us. But no, it is a precarious commodity. Strangely, the sharper the demand for it the less assured is the supply. Indeed, the mere echo of the word in the imagination in the heat and dust of the day resembles an oasis in the wilderness — the music of its wellspring too, rather than its silence; an *active* felicity. And a few nights of shallow or broken or leaden or tormented or artificial sleep — let alone the stark Gomorrah of insomnia — is carking evidence of its usual blessings. That way, instinct whispers, and whispers truly, lies madness. To cease at times to remember rather than to cease to forget — is there any anodyne quite comparable to that? And is there any tribute to a loved one more ingenuous and less earthbound than, " You were with me in my sleep "?

Too much sleep,³ whether of the kind indulged in by Rip van Winkle, or broken and chequered with dream, may have almost as baneful effects as too little. There are maladies, too,

---

³ Example here too is better than precept. Jeremy Taylor maintained " that three hours only out of the twenty-four should be spent in sleep," and he practised what he preached. Richard Baxter " extends the period to four hours, Wesley to six, Lord Coke and Sir William Jones to seven, and Sir John Sinclair to eight. . . . Taking the average of mankind . . . no person who passes only eight hours in bed can be said to waste his time." Since too in sleep the heart beats earthly time away less rapidly than it does by day, and therefore then suffers less wear and tear, a little extra closing of the eyes in slumber *may* a little extend one's span of life! But then again, there is " pernicious sleep " — the too much and the too heavy. " Homer, Virgil and Horace are all represented as early risers." So also were " Paley, Franklin, Priestley and Buffon " — who " ordered his *valet de chambre* to awaken him every morning, before the clock struck six, and then if he evinced any reluctance, to compel him to get up by force." The reward for this horrid duty was a crown a day. " Bishop Jewel and Burnet rose regularly every morning at four o'clock "; Sir Thomas More had set the example; and the denizens of his *Utopia* continue, no doubt, to " attend lectures before sunrise." These are sobering statistics. Not so the assertion that nine hours' exile from the inkpot " will frequently be found not too much for literary men." Even that substantial sage, Samuel Johnson, whom Boswell frequently found still snug between the sheets at noonday, can only slightly tilt the scales in favour of the slug-a-bed — a bed which Kant regarded as " the nest of diseases." Besides, " I fancy," says Boswell, " he must have read and wrote chiefly in the night."

of which sleep is one of the symptoms — Paroxysmal sleep, Narcolepsy, the somnolence of Hysteria, Vigilambulism — " I cannot sleep because I am asleep all the time "; and, even more fantastic evidence of the mystery of life, the sleep that is, as it were, the frontier between two or more several " personalities." We read of an English child, twelve years of age, who, after a severe illness, exhibited " four distinct existences besides the normal "; and of a contented and prosperous father of a family who, all memory of it and of his immediate past deleted, lived and worked at his trade for months unperturbed by any misgiving, miles away from home. Here, however, we are drifting into the pathological, a favoured and enticing province in modern psychology.

But although of course sleep may be misused, and may intensify certain maladies, although sluggards are naughty allies of the thorn and the brier, although the half-awake live semi-dead, and day-dreamers seldom top their form, " sleep," in Dr. Benjamin Ward Richardson's words, " reduces fever, quickens nutrition, increases elimination, soothes pain, and encourages the healing of wounded surfaces. Whoever is first to discover the still secret cause of natural sleep and the mode in which it may be commanded by art, for the service of mankind, will be the greatest healer who has, up to this age, helped to make medicine immortal."

GONE AWAY

All this borrowed and valuable information has been chiefly concerned only with the body. But even with the aid of a minute pane of glass, inserted, after the prizing up of a little circular sawn-out shutter of bone, in the cranium of a fellow creature asleep, the intentest human eye can discern no more what he is *experiencing* than it can divine the thoughts of the " wide-awake absorbed in reflection." The most mobile and tell-tale face by day is stilled and mute in repose. Where, then, shall we seek the human wraith when he has ventured into that region of life and being known as " sleep "? The brain we peep at tells nothing of this; is lapped in a quietude far alien to most machines. Nevertheless, " we must remember that the human body is a complicated machine made out of numerous secondary machines, in themselves composed of a most intricate molecular machinery " — a description that so far transcends any machine contrived by man that the very use of the word in this context seems grotesque. No lens, at any rate, will reveal any trace of a *mind* in the exposed grey matter, whosesoever that mind may be. Unless, that is, mind is no more than a specious synonym for brain — " when the brains were out, the man would die, and there an end." If not, what is the relation between them? It is hardly a novel enquiry; but where is the final answer? The mere user of any machine is immeasurably the superior of that machine. How infinitely more complex, then, must be the mind which controls yet is also restricted by such a nexus of machines as that described above.

Although we are told that the brain itself in some degree, then, " rests " in sleep, how shall we ascertain whether the mind is ever completely in repose, ever wholly withdraws its influence over the body? No method seems to present itself. Nor with any certainty can we discover the self's local habitation — behind the eyes, or in the heart, or in the liver, or in the solar plexus? The last of these seems to be our most sensitive target. It will announce bad news before we realise it was on its way. The body itself only exists for us when consciousness becomes aware of it, or is reminded of it by pain or discomfort. We *think* of hand or foot, of nose or chin, and *there* " we " are; but not until that moment. Sensation travels, but does the mind? These are rudimentary questions; but it is impossible, at any rate, to believe oneself or any fellow creature a fantastic automaton.

But if the mind, in and by itself, is beyond clear conception, and presumably beyond final self-scrutiny, since watcher will have to watch the watcher, and so *ad infinitum,* what of the self, of the soul, of the spirit? The simile of the onion, and of the Chinese nest of boxes at once presents itself, even if definite localization seems absurd. " Indeed," wrote Mary Sibylla Holland to her ardently beloved sister Catharine, " I think I could make my body submit to any discomfort if only that *something* which is neither my mind nor my soul, but which is *me myself,* could be left at peace, to dream and to sleep, and at last to die, nothing attempted and nothing done. Wretched state, and yet true. . . . I dare say you will think all this morbid and depressed, but it is not. It is the result of honest reflection."

That " *me myself* " then — silver cockerel on life's delicious and acrid dunghill — what becomes of, what happens to that, in bodily sleep? Why should its " rest " differ from that of the body?

There is surely an inherent absurdity in the common notion that in a lifetime of thirty or sixty years the self within has spent ten or twenty of them in a reiterated extinction, a fatuous oblivion — *dead* asleep. A sleep wherefrom it has reiteratedly leapt back into its palace of memory, its treasury of the senses, at no more than a tap on a door. To rest, surely, is not to surrender life, but to gain a fuller and fresher life. " Deterioration is to be met in both organic and inorganic worlds, but when we meet with improvement, whether it be that of an army, or an artist, or a vintage of port, we may be pretty sure that it originates in living matter and not in mechanism."

There is an alternative. " The mind during sleep," says Dr. John Bigelow in his *Mystery of Sleep,* " is not in a special mood or state but . . . goes on and develops itself absolutely as in the waking hours." There is, indeed, abundant evidence of many kinds for the latent activities of the mind in sleep, and of the intellect. " ' It is certain,' " and the words are Voltaire's, " ' that in sleep and in dream you may think seven or eight hours consecutively, without having the least desire to think, without even being aware that you think.' " After an untroubled sleep, Dr. Bigelow adds, " do we not awake refreshed, and neither hungry nor thirsty? " The cares that may have haunted us, the anxieties and apprehensions that beset us when we went to rest have been lightened. "We sleep upon our troubles, and with morning the way may be much clearer before us. Mood and temper are usually less obdurate and inflamed; quarrels and arguments have lost in part at least their sting." "A man must be next to a devil who wakes angry."

Our bed may have been a plank, our pillow (like Jacob's in Bethel) a stone; our bodily posture may have remained all but unchanged; yet, in circumstances that in day life would be unendurable, we are conscious of having experienced no physical discomfort. Who, indeed, if only once and again in a lifetime, has not awakened with the conviction that he has issued from a state of happiness as rare and serene as if he had spent the preceding hours with Thomas Traherne in his childhood, or in William Blake's "immortal day"? No direct evidence or proof may be available; nothing of the night-time may have left any clear impression on the mind; and yet, on waking, the recollection of a state of peace and bliss, beyond all gratitude, may be ours for a few fleeting moments.

There is, of course, no novelty or extravagance in this. It is an ancient belief. Throughout the Bible, a book — whether divinely inspired or not — unrivalled in its wisdom and insight, sleep is seldom mentioned except with reference to some of the most vital processes of spiritual growth or degeneration. "What reason," then enquires John Bigelow, "have we for doubting that during our sleep we are in substantially the same society and surrounded by similar, if not the same, influences as we shall be when we enter into 'the sleep that knows no waking'?" Night, at any rate, says an ancient proverb, is "the mother of counsels."

In view, again, of the evidence given in the *Proceedings* of the Society for Psychical Research, and elsewhere, can we dismiss with a shrug of the shoulders the belief, long ago propounded by Paracelsus, that we are possessed of an astral or sidereal body, which is usually coincident with the corporate body, but is of a materiality so subtile as to be invisible to the human eye — a body which in sleep or trance or when freed by certain drugs, may depart into the viewless air on errands of its own? The savage believes that in sleep his mouselike soul creeps out from his thick lips ajar. Nor is it only in sleep apparently that this astral body can thus migrate. Many years ago, being quite alone in the house, I sat reading in the light of a standard lamp, and began, after a while, feeling rather unwell at the time, and wearying of solitude, to "wish for company." The small room which I occupied was surveyable if one drew back the flap of the letter-box, in the front door. Leaving my lamp burning, I at length departed to visit a younger sister. An elder sister, who knew that I was alone in the house, had meanwhile set out to see me; knocked, and knocked in vain. She then looked through the letter-box, saw me sitting in my chair just as I have described, and was so much alarmed at my appearance that she assumed that I had fainted. She at once returned home for help. Arrived at my younger sister's house, I myself remarked in the course of conversation how strange it was that one seems at times to have left a self behind one. "I feel that *now*," I said. "It is precisely as if I were, at this very moment, sitting at home in my chair. I seem to be actually *seeing* myself there." Telepathy [4] may account for this odd occurrence; or, more simply, mere coincidence; namely, that my elder sister and I happened to share illusions at the same time.

However that may be, have we ourselves no assurance that a natural sleep is not only a restorative state of being, but another order of life, and one of an infinite value and efficacy? Certainly if the heart is then at rest, it is at daybreak, at the dayspring, during the first and freshest hour of the morning, that the mind once more confers on us its own and our poor best. Apart from their necessity, again, is one's intuitive dis-

---

[4] In 1883 the Society for Psychical Research circulated the following enquiry: "Since January 1st, 1874, have you ever had a dream of the death of some person known to you, which dream you marked as an exceedingly vivid one, and of which the distressing impression lasted for as long as an hour after you rose in the morning?" "Our conclusion," said Frederic Myers, "was that coincident dreams of death in this country were 24 times as numerous as the law of chance according to the data which the census gave us would allow."

trust of opiate and sedative and the drowsy syrups due solely
to the fear of turning a service into a servitude? No wise doctor commends narcotics except as a *pis aller;* and the skilled
anaesthetist can induce unconsciousness in a progressive
depth and intensity. But although on " coming to " his patient
may sigh his eternal gratitude, an inward monitor may still
whisper its lament. Agonies unperceived by the conscious
mind are not necessarily agonies unrecorded by the self
within — not too happy perhaps in deserting the body in its
acute distress.

I have been told of a child, seven years old, who, some days
after a severe operation, was faced with the ordeal of the
removal from his thigh of a broken hypodermic needle. He
implored his mother to let him face it awake and aware.
Some little time after an almost fatal illness which entailed
three drug-induced departures into the unconscious, I had
shingles. My face happened to be turned away when the
cork was removed from a bottle of lotion containing ether,
which had been prescribed to relieve the irritation. Ignorant
of this, at a mere whiff of the ether I was suddenly seized with
an acute and seemingly causeless terror. Yet my operation,
and certainly the anaesthetist's merciful share in it, had been
faced with no more than a grave misgiving. Some creature
within, in a lair far removed from the waking mind, had contrived this time, yet needlessly, to yelp a warning.

Only twice have I brought back any clear glimpse of the
beyond when under the influence of an anaesthetic: once, of
a bare patch of gravel brilliant with sunshine; and again, of
the shelving sandy banks of a slow-moving river, tranquil,
and strange to me. They may have been mere dream-relics
retrieved from the borderline between one stratum of consciousness and another. But they were unusually vivid; appeared to be fragments (as in waking are many memories)
of an impressive experience otherwise lost; and that of the
river with its shelving banks was suffused with an intense feeling of homesickness. I grieved at having to come away. The
dentist's gas may have accounted for the tragic or sentimental

tears that were on my cheeks — but hardly for the acute regret at finding that I had been brought to, had been called back. And though it may be merely a deceit of the senses, this coming back certainly suggests a definite journey. But whose journey? If the purest and deepest sleep sometimes entails a departure of the spirit from its tenement into a state of happiness very rare in waking life, and then only in fleeting and ecstatic moments seldom without a tinge of sadness and regret; if, too, as an exquisite and unknown Elizabethan poet declares, this sleep is "a reconciling," as well as "a rest that peace begets," it is easy to understand why we may pine for it so ardently, and welcome it without the least apprehension. And this, even if allowance be made for the fact that sleep became a habit when we were as yet in the dark security of the womb.

We are at any rate thus enabled to compare the two conditions of sleeping and waking; and, when the world is too much with us, be tempted to choose sleep. But let Wordsworth's "Solitary" make *his* confession, one that was reproved by Wordsworth himself but must at least have been shared, if only in imagination, by a poet who knew the meaning of rapture, of solitude and of the gravity of human life:

> To me, who find,
> Reviewing my past way, much to condemn,
> Little to praise, and nothing to regret,
> (Save some remembrances of dream-like joys
> That scarcely seem to have belonged to me)
> If I must take my choice between the pair
> That rule alternately the weary hours,
> Night is than day more acceptable; sleep
> Doth, in my estimate of good, appear
> A better state than waking; death than sleep:
> Feelingly sweet is stillness after storm,
> Though under covert of the wormy ground.

THE PAINS OF SLEEP

"We term sleep a death," says Sir Thomas Browne, "and yet it is waking that kills us and destroys those spirits that are the house of life " — the profound and blissful sleep, that is, which the " Solitary " also must have had in mind. There may, however, be as many kinds and conditions of sleep, and ways of spending it, as there are states in our waking life, and ways of spending that. As our physical appetite at times may fail us, so our interest even in life itself — without which it would be scarcely endurable — may wane and flag. The inward wellspring which perpetually vivifies and nourishes the mind lapses into a bare trickle and all but ceases to flow. Even our most tender affections may, for a while, languish, like a flower out of water. The realisation that these vital and inscrutable influences are in peril, and can thus for a while abandon us, resembles the apprehension, which may occur in extreme illness, that we are unable even to breathe without reiterated effort. So, too, sleep may lose its virtue, and fail to revive or even to refresh the mind. It may be fitful and shallow; or so dense and heavy that we emerge from it utterly spiritless and inert.

After even the briefest of afternoon naps, for example, we may awake stupid and morose; or, contrariwise, in a humour so mocking and mischievous that our room at the tea-table is likely to prove far preferable to our company. It is as if an imp within were scoffing at the silly cage into which waking had once more confined him. Sleep, moreover, far from removing, may intensify the dejection and misery from which it is usually our only means of escape; and the woes of the waking day may not only continue into sleep, but be then sharpened and diversified with a skill in torture excelling Torquemada's. Worse yet, the inquisitor may keep as punctual a nightly assignation with us as did the devil with Faustus. To dread the slow onset of the dark that ushers in the hour of sleep; to lie cold with sweat awaiting the approach of an enemy from within who may awake us to an apparent embodiment of himself in the without, and whom we shall be powerless to evade or to resist — it is as if in our infancy we had sickened of our mother's milk, as if the heart had become haunted by the treachery of a friend. "When I say, My bed shall comfort me, my couch shall ease my complaint; then thou scarest me with dreams, and terrifiest me through visions: so that my soul chooseth strangling, and death rather than my life. I loathe it; I would not live alway: let me alone; for my days are vanity." "My fevered eyes I dared not close, But stared aghast at Sleep."

This daylong haunting foreboding of what the night and sleep will bring in their train is more common in childhood than in the later years of life. It falls upon us at an age, that is, when we are least able to describe and to endure the terrors that entangle us, even when the dearest of confidantes is available, or to produce a shred of material evidence for them, apart from our glazed eyes and bloodless faces. The darkness, the play of light and shadow, a door ajar, the folds of a curtain, every familiar object of the daytime are now in connivance with the bodiless persecutor and his devices. How many children — Stevenson, J. A. Symonds, William Hutton, Lafcadio Hearn, Richard Middleton, Mr. Forrest Reid among them — have again and again endured the experience recorded so vividly in Mr. Wilfrid Gibson's poem: —

> Gaunt in the twilight
> The hollow beeches
> Close round the lonely
> Bewildered child,
> Gnarled and writhen
> And caverned with darkness;
> And his young heart flutters
> Fear-shotten and wild
> As sharp through the shadows
> The lych-owl screeches.
>
> Yet happily here through the long day he played
> In the rustling deep gold of the sun-dappled glade.

So lovely the morning
And noon burning bright
The heart hardly heeds
The ebbing of light
Till, a lost child, it shrinks
From the coming of night!

Why the innocent, the good, the wise, and the patient-as-Job should be compelled to endure this malignity is only one question in a lengthy indictment. How it is that the abject, the heartless, even "bloody men Whose deeds tradition saves" may slumber in peace is as mysterious. The virtuous may wish it otherwise; and yet, the more acutely we distrust and detest the face of a fellow creature, the less inclined we may be to fix our eyes too closely on it when its owner is at our mercy, being asleep. Even a pitiless poisoner — awaiting daybreak, the vilest of deaths, and what may follow it — has been known to remain lapped all night in what to the jailer with his lantern resembles the sleep which is assumed to be reserved for the just. The soldier in *The Ballad of Reading Gaol* had murdered the woman he loved. An insensate act of passionate jealousy, not for gain; but he too had to endure the same fate, and he too (if we can trust the poet) was released from all memory of it in sleep.

He lay as one who lies and dreams
In a pleasant meadow-land,
The watchers watched him as he slept,
And could not understand
How one could sleep so sweet a sleep
With a hangman close at hand. . . .

But there is no sleep when men must weep
Who never yet have wept:
So we — the fool, the fraud, the knave —
That endless vigil kept,
And through each brain on hands of pain
Another's terror crept.

[46]

Sleep, however, is in general so usual and so easy a refuge that its strangeness and mystery are apt to be as little heeded as are its incalculable value and its gifts of grace. We rely on it as carelessly as we accept the air we breathe, and that shallow skin of soil which alone ensures us the living company, the verdure and the beauty of the earth. Without sleep, would life be endurable? A dismal night or two of fever will be answer enough to the enquiry; or even the mere misgiving that, by reason of some folly or frailty or stealing incapacity or misuse of the mind, the old faithful habit is deserting us. Is there any ill in life which sleep cannot solace awhile; is there any " remand " comparable to it? From hope deferred, from corroding expectation, from pain, pining, anxiety, grief, anger, and passion, it is our only certain and swift release. What the will and reason are powerless to remove, sleep melts like snow in water. Even an obsession, like the giant in *Mollie Whuppie,* comes to a halt at the edge of that narrow abyss. Byron realised that for lover and loved one " the day returns too soon "; but if we knew that sleep would never again revisit us on earth, with what an agony of recognition should we read again:

> For the sword outwears its sheath,
>   And the soul wears out the breast,
> And the heart must pause to breathe,
>   And love itself have rest.

As for insomnia, insanity alone could depict that particular goddess; and insanity has not the art. Even the Sahara has its oases; and arctic desolation its aurora. But, " Macbeth has murdered Sleep " — the whole universe is instantly dyed with its blood. Death alone would suffice for the consolation of the walking shadow doomed to this disaster. There are, too, degrees even of insomnia. Here, too, is a fringe and a borderline; and by no means the least of sleep's mercies, because it is one frequently bestowed on us, is the way of escape it provides from what we so often outrageously flatter in call-

ing "thought" — the dreary bedraggled kind that takes
Lodgings in a Head
That's to be lett unfurnishèd.

And not only from thought, but also from the scarcely endurable burden of *self*. Like poor Lazarus hoping only for
crumbs from the Magician's table, we may have to endure
what seems a little eternity of this companionship. And in
our beds! The hated presence of an inescapable *ego*, the endless supply of this silly aimless secretion, are as far removed
from the rewards of mere thinking as from the pleasures of
day-dream. Consciousness then resembles a rat-trap whose
bars resound with every frenzied scrape of tooth and claw.

Sleep, however, while she is the shyest of mistresses when
pursued, may be wooed and eventually won; although, alas,
the wooer's wiles are apt to lose their charm with repetition.
Any low recurrence of sound, or sensation, will serve as a lullaby that may entice her — the rocking of a cradle (nowadays declared injurious to its small occupant), a gentle singing voice, the fluttering of flames in the fire, the sigh of wind,
the *pit-pat* of rain at the window, the stroking of the forehead
or of the spine, and merely quiet company at one's bedside,
or a friendly hand. Southey, in *The Doctor*, adds to this list —
but his irony has a tragic edge, since the insomnia due to the
protracted and loving care he gave to his wife in her last long
illness seems to have been part-cause at least of the insanity
that was its sequel.

"I listened to the river and to the ticking of my watch; I
thought of all sleepy sounds and of all soporific things — the
flow of water, the humming of bees, the motion of a boat, the
waving of a field of corn, the nodding of a mandarin's head
on the chimney-piece, a horse in a mill, the opera, Mr. Humdrum's conversations, Mr. Proser's poems, Mr. Laxative's
speeches, Mr. Lengthy's sermons. I tried the device of my
own childhood, and fancied that the bed rushed with me
round and round. At length Morpheus reminded me of Dr.
Torpedo's Divinity Lectures, where the voice, the manner, the

matter, even the very atmosphere and the streaming candle-light, were all alike soporific; when he who, by strong effort, lifted up his head and forced open the reluctant eyes never failed to see all around him asleep. Lettuces, cowslip wine, poppy syrup, mandragora, hop pillows, spider's web pills, and the whole tribe of narcotics, up to bang and the black drop, would have failed — but this was irresistible; and thus, twenty years after date, I found benefit from having attended the course."

But if I may judge from experiences in no wise related to Divinity, not every lecturer has to wait twenty years, or even twenty minutes, for this blissful escape from his glittering eye to exhibit itself in his victims. And apart from Southey's Dr. Torpedo, there are many other simple and effectual aids to " going off." The body must lie at ease; every muscle should be relaxed; the pillow in particular must be nicely disposed. Empty that fermenting receptacle the mind, as far as may be, of its froth and sediment, or repeat what memory can retrieve of its slender stock of poetry. Fix the eyes on any faintly vis-ible or imaginary object, and count five; close them, count five again; and then assure yourself in so many words that sleep is coming, is now on its way: — " I am at peace with myself and with all mankind. Now, now, I am going to sleep, and shall not awake until the morning." Or breathe as if slumber were already yours, and count each exhalation. Or sigh after it, " Another breath gone; another breath gone." If then, alas, sleep still eludes you, heaven itself may yet pro-vide an exit. At least remain as much at peace as possible; for mere tranquillity of the wearied body and of the wearied mind is the next best refuge and anodyne to sleep itself.

Death, however, far from being half-brother to Sleep, is not so much as a near relation. The two rapt countenances bear but a brief and cheating resemblance to one another. Even the relics of life's last smile on the face of the dead mutely hails us only with a surer variant of " Sleep no more." The one tells us, it may be, that the house of the body is vacant, but is quietly awaiting its tenant's return; the other, of an even more inscrutable miracle — that it has been finally forsaken, is empty, and will never in this world be occupied again.

> Do what we will, our hasty minutes fly,
> And while we sleep, what do we else but die?

Not so, surely? — in spite even of Sir Thomas Browne. A motionless sleep may suggest to the onlooker the image of death; but hardly if the sleeper is a young child — the lip and cheek bedewed and softly flushed, the limbs in an exquisite abandon and repose. Then it is as if indeed the occupant of this marvellous small house were absent; the face resembles a flower-like mask of a material as strange as manna.

To Leonardo da Vinci's question, "What is it that is much desired by men, but which they know not while possessing?," we may at times be tempted to reply with him, as do many phantom voices in the pages that follow, not merely "sleep," but, "the last sleep of all." And this particularly if to yet another question of his, "Oh why not let your work be such that after death you become an image of immortality; as in life you become when sleeping like to the hapless dead?," we can no more than desperately echo his own, "Oh why?" Indeed, earthly life itself owes something less unworthy of it than fear even to the assurance that death may ensure a final end to it.

Children, again, enjoy a sleep all balm and roses, but they rarely run to meet it; the aged remind themselves of a completer respite, yet they too make little haste in its direction. But when body and mind are in complete accord, or, less unusual, when we are comparatively at ease with ourselves, or no more than only tired, then may the Mind

> withdraw into its happiness:
> The Mind, that Ocean where each kind
> Does streight its own resemblance find;
> Yet it creates, transcending these,
> Far other Worlds, and other Seas.

Few joys compare with that of pushing the battered dunce's book called Life under one's bolster; or, better yet, that of leaving one's Self, like a flower in a glass of water, to blush and revive unheeded amid the dark hours; hoping, if even against hope, that it may prove sweeter company in the morning.

OTHER WORLDS

But what is this that sleep " creates "; of what texture are these far other Worlds and Seas? If, for the few minutes that precede the lapse of consciousness into sleep, or follow its recovery, one remains quietly attentive and receptive, but refuses to let either random or directed " thought " regain its mastery, one appears to be drowsily floating on the placid surface of a state that is neither limbo nor complete awareness. It is in as close a relation to either as the waxen lily by the wharf of Lethe is to its own unrippled reflection. It is then that some brilliantly vivid and entirely unexpected image out of the nowhere of the mind may, as if in the same moment, be perceived and be gone.

These images — hypnagogic and hypnopompic — are of an endless variety. They are alike only in their intense yet fleeting precision. A Victorian carpeted room strewn with fragments of torn-up paper which vanished as instantly as if they had been devoured by a magical sweeper was one such recent glimpse of my own. A low stretch of sky and cloud, its blue of an unearthly serenity, purity and beauty, immediately afterwards, yet another. Or a voice may suddenly become audible; or a low unintelligible gabble as of many voices. But although the imagery involved in any such moment as this may be of as many kinds — of the ear, of touch, of our neuro-muscular and motor systems and so forth — just as it is in the positive recollection of any swift survey of scene or object in waking life, these wisps, these figments of mind-stuff usually consist of the visual. Are they — like the " faces " one sees in the fire — the handiwork of " fancy " busied with the faint retinal spangling luminosity observable when we close our eyes; are they scraps, mean or precious, from the " rubbish heap" of memory; or are they the relics, wreckage, detritus, or the seeds — doomed to sterility — of dreams? Whatever their composition, we may, if so inclined, read into them a relation to the ideas and thoughts which immediately preceded them. In that case, they resemble the pictures in a book in relation to its text. But in how eccentric a relation.

No effort, at any rate, to discover the origin of these glimpses or to retrieve any part of their context may avail. In waking life, a mislaid word is notoriously difficult to recover. Instead, we are conscious of a mould or hollow where the word should be. As soon as we have ceased to pursue it, it may fill that mould as neatly as a dog that has returned to it fits its kennel. Not so with these bizarre and lively fragments of mind-stuff. They seem to " belong " nowhere. No such mould awaits them. A definite obstacle may often hinder their recovery. If we recall anything, we remain as extraneous an onlooker as an astronomer at his telescope who suspects that he has for an instant glimpsed a race of Selenites in motion in the crater of Linné on the surface of the moon. Indeed, it is as if consciousness had for this instant strayed into some other world, into some other order of experience; or, contrariwise, as if it had come into possession of some random unforeseen image or notion or desire which, during the day, is so unexpected and contrary to the current of our thoughts that it appears to be the outcome of telepathy. We may suspect telepathy, and with good reason; but be unable to make sure. To dismiss these images — common as meteors in the month of November, and often no less wildly vivid and delightful — as valueless is to undermine every workaday impression to which we can call no witness.

THE INWARD EYE

But how, precisely, do we perceive any image, and what faculty is involved? We can usually distinguish between the recalled image of anything we have actually seen and of anything we have imagined. And we refer casually to that inward eye which is not only the bliss of solitude, but which, for every one who possesses it, is in constant service at all times and in any circumstances. But when, like Sir Francis Galton before him, William James invited his fellow professors and the students of Harvard University to give him particulars of what they could see with that eye of the contents of their morning's breakfast table, was he intent on testing a faculty identical with, or only similar to that whereby his brother Henry kept steadily in view the spectre of Peter Quint, through the imagined consciousness of the governess who narrates his story, when he was engaged in writing *The Turn of the Screw;* or that whereby, late in life, he was enabled to recall memories of Paris as he had innocently contemplated it from a carriage window before he was able to talk? Closer to our purpose, is this precisely the same faculty as that which we make use of so freely in our dreams?

Until recently, I had assumed that the visualized image of an object is no less bright than the object itself would be in similar conditions when seen in actuality. There are many poems in this book which will evoke in the mind of the reader many such images, glimpses of actual objects and scenes which appear to be not only radiant, but occasionally even dazzling with light. There are others suffused with the light that never was on sea or land but only visible in dream. And again I had assumed that the latter were equally luminous. But is this so? Experiment suggests otherwise.

Imagine in the light of day — your eyes close-shut and turned towards a lime-washed wall or colourless panel — that you are looking down from a hillside upon a field of wheat, "white to harvest," and bordering a wide smooth-watered river flowing through a valley and reflecting the midday sun; or imagine a flat sea stretching out to its faint horizon-line and flashing with its myriad tiny circular reflections of the round sun itself. Then open your eyes. My impression is that, however vivid these mental images may have been, they will at once be overwhelmed, flooded out, by the light of day.

The inward eye may itself perhaps be dazzled and all but momentarily blinded by the mere visualisation of, say, a chalk cliff, a butterfly, a white muslin frock, or even a white flower held close to the eye in brilliant sunshine. But experiment suggests that both the " dazzled " and the " blinded " are here merely terms of comparison; as when we say that moonlit snow is dazzling, or the minute flame of a match struck in a room until that moment in total darkness.

As moonlight is to sunlight, so may be the light perceived by the inward eye compared with that perceived by the eye itself. To an eye doomed to outer darkness, even the faint flare of a glow-worm would resemble a glimpse of salvation. Similarly, when we examine a picture representing a night-scene of dismal streets and houses, illuminated by an arc lamp which is represented by a minute white spot of paint, we translate in fancy, as it were, the whiteness of the spot into the brilliance of the arc lamp. So also, perhaps, in the recollection of the scene of a dream. Its light may appear to be equal to that which we should perceive in a similar scene perceived in the daytime by the inward eye, yet with our eyes fully open; and we may recall the dreamed-of scene without being aware that in so doing we have turned up the lamp. Leonardo nevertheless enquires, " Why does the eye see a thing more clearly in dreams than the imagination when awake? "

Even those who possess this faculty (and precisely what is substituted for it in those who do not possess it is a riddle to which the habitual visualiser is unlikely to find a satisfactory answer) — even those who possess it may yet be unaware of its unceasing activity, and may value it far less than they value what is directly presented to them by those miraculous mirrors, windows, or slaves of the light — blue, brown, hazel, lilac, green or grey — the eyes themselves. Others can watch alike the remembered [5] or the imagined, and the phantasms of reverie or of the dream-world, with equal facility.

[5] This inward eye appears neither to age nor to weary. My own, at least at present, needs no inward spectacles. It can see its object in detail with the ut-

Again, whatever we look at is in some degree perpetually changing. Even when it is apparently motionless, light is busy with appearances, and so is the mind of the observer. The perfectly static is a rare anomaly. But no less changeable and active may be the scenes and objects which we visualise. And we can ourselves dictate, within certain limits, whatever change we wish. We invoke, for example, the image of a blackboard on its easel. Hardly conscious of having given any definite direction, we can then at will visualise the board painted, first blue, then pink or green; striped, mottled, starred or scribbled over — even if, as is probable, the scribbling upon it remains only partially legible. So with any remembered familiar street or building; we can transform it, in fancy, almost as we please. In the same fashion, we can picture a friend in any attire, shoes to head-dress, that we may care to conjure up. The roué, fiction informs us, thus *un*clothes every female shape he eyes.

But even the most introspective of roués is unlikely to be able to disclose the process. It is one no less obscure than that whereby we order what we intend to say prior to its actually being put into words. A message, a direction of some kind, must obviously precede speech, and usually the words required at once obey the order. But what is the nature of the message and how is it translated? How also, at sight of any object, does memory immediately supply the information needed for its recognition? Occasional errors in this respect only emphasise the general rule. We may be deceived by some minute resemblance in an object into conferring on it qualities entirely alien to it. As when we mistake a withered leaf for a dead butterfly, a midge on the window-pane for a bird in the distance, or when the nocturnal bush becomes a bear. Indeed, the phantasmal, the dream-like image of what we expect to see, frequently if not always precedes the actual seeing of it. To be sure of finding a box of matches at

most clearness; but it cannot, I think, except for a moment or two remain fixed and watch it. At need, it appears to be instantly in focus; and in this resembles attention rather than the external eye itself.

[55]

need, I used to conceal one beneath the hollow base of an old brass candlestick, but sometimes forgot to return the box to its hiding-place; with the consequence that I have again and again lifted the candlestick to discover there only the quite perceptible astral body of the match box! Errors of this kind must occur fairly frequently; we must sometimes fail to detect them.

But however often the heart " with pleasure fills " in presence of the images which throng the inward eye, how seldom in general do we pay any close attention to this priceless faculty. And what is its ultimate range? In talk some years ago with a doctor who was also a psychologist, I ventured to refer to this little problem, and for illustration took the dome of St. Paul's. I suggested how odd was the ease whereby one can at will and at once survey its normal leaden ribs either mantled thick in snow, or parti-coloured green and yellow, or, *absit omen,* in partial ruin, its ball and cross toppled into Cannon Street. Such little mental transmogrifications, that is, as are common in waking life, in reverie, on the fringes of sleep, and in dream. Yet, as I suggested, when its image recurs to memory, the dome will have recovered its familiar and beloved London grey and blue. He listened with patience, and replied that until then he had been unaware of this process. A similar reply was given to me by a distinguished oculist. None the less, Everyman, in due degree, can no more dispense with this sovran facility than can the tale-teller, the poet, the artist, the mathematician (perhaps), the actor, or even the acrobat and the juggler, who must first visualise (and much else) the feat which he prescribes for his hoops and balls before they will consent to make the attempt. And at length, to our joy, he may seem to have hypnotised them into obedience to his every whim. By this means we recognise what we are seeking; sensuously and vividly recall innumerable moments of the past; animate our morrows; transmute, astonishing feat, the print of a tale or poem into phantoms of the mind whose misfortunes may devastate the heart; and enjoy the inward society of our friends. This is indeed the

richest substitute for their bodily presence, even if it be how
poor a second best.

> Take, O take those lips away,
>   That so sweetly were forsworn,
> And those eyes, the break of day,
>   Lights that do mislead the morn;
> But my kisses bring again,
> Seals of love, but sealed in vain. . . .

What vivid, lovely and tragic images are here, enshrined in
verbal music. To realise the mind's exquisite ingenuity, for
which we are no more personally responsible than for the
shape of our craniums, we have only to recognise and welcome them as they appear. But we must look intently if we
are to seize not merely each image in turn, but its Shakespear-
ian uniqueness. If we go on to a second stanza, beginning,
"Hide, O hide those hills of snow " — which often accompa-
nies this song from *Measure for Measure,* but was written by
John Fletcher — we shall detect the difference between visualised images of the first rank, quality, virtue and value, and
those still unusual, but not of this rank.

Nor is this faculty confined either to mere reproduction or
to invention. It may not only be controlled, it may also take
control. In this it resembles the wizardry of Prospero. It is
the means of discovering that a mysterious life has been conferred on our imagery, an active freedom and a curious reality.
As "a poet in the description of a beautiful garden or a
meadow, will please our imagination, more than the place itself can please our sight "; so for him the blue air will then
begin to stir, the budding flower to open, clouds to appear,
and birds to sing. The garden will come alive — and, again,
as if in a dream. Indeed, unless a poet's or novelist's phantasmata, from a snail to Mr. Snodgrass, from Cinderella to Caliban, from Moth to Donne's Angels, possess themselves of
this life, this creative freedom, this intense reality, then his
genius has failed him; his Ariel, without whose aid his magic
is inert, has deserted him. We can no more solve the secret

of life in the world which has consciousness in its gift, than that of sleep. And, again, our anonymous Elizabethan: —

> Come, Sleep, and with thy sweet deceiving
> Lock me in delight awhile!
> Let some pleasing dreams beguile
> All my fancies; that from thence
> I may feel an influence,
> All my powers of care bereaving! . . .

Usually the sweet deceiving lasts out only the dream. We awake from it and recognise as illusion what we shall none the less retain as experience, and even valuable experience perhaps; whereas in all work of the imagination the artist creates — or discovers, and records what comes to him in similar guise, but in so doing he gives it form, and graces it with a design and coherence denied to the hotch-potch of casual events and the response to them of which our daily life is made up.

The vivid visual imagery, then, that suddenly distracts the inward eye on that nebulous border between waking and sleeping, appears to differ from our workaday visualisations only in the fact that it comes unbidden and unsought, and may have no perceptible relation to any context — although this may sometimes apply to the latter also. If in this state of partially suspended consciousness we keep watch on what we see, we may be astonished not only at its rapidity and unexpectedness, but at its beauty and variety.

The transition from wake to sleep, and vice versa, is usually abrupt, but may be gradual. As we voluntarily drowse into sleep, so we may undrowse into waking. It is a state called " sentience." Thus, not long ago, I caught in a fraction of a moment a glimpse, between " thoughts," of one of the most lovely and serene landscapes I have ever seen. A day or two afterwards, in the same state, I saw the right-hand edge of the canvas of a picture of a delicate hazy blue, evidently the work of an old master. The edges were roughly folded over, and there was no frame. The stranger who was showing me the picture remarked on this. I then began to speculate whether pictures in this state are not truer to their intention than when they are hung in cumbrous and ornate gilded frames; and in *that* instant I glimpsed Piero della Francesca's Crucifixion, which I saw in the Italian Exhibition a few years ago, so displayed. Multitudes of similar experiences must pass unheeded. The pretty birds await the fowler.

In a brief time, waking consciousness may be for an instant thus repeatedly submerged, and may repeatedly retrieve isolated peephole glimpses of an imagery at least as vivid as anything bestowed by fancy on the eye of day — glimpses, too, which occasionally have an aptness and a hint of profound significance usually denied to or unnoticed in the actual of the waking day.

They occasionally take the form of outrageous spectres; faces malignantly intent; and with the appalling verisimilitude, as Frederick Greenwood declares, of William Blake's " Ghost of a Flea "; or of " caverns measureless to man "; or of " some fair and stately palace "; or of " Babylon-like walls." In this lethargic No-man's-land, I have myself lain in terrified contemplation of a dome, not of many-coloured glass, but formed of a close mosaic of a myriad pebble-shaped faces, every one of which in scorn and rancorous animosity was intent on the minute and quaking intruder beneath them. How find rhyme and reason for this trickery, if mere trickery it is? Many years ago, I made the discovery also that if, on the brink of sleep, I fixed my eyes at a certain angle, I appeared to be surveying, as if from an aeroplane, a vast expanse of *approaching* scenery — desert, sandy foothill, frowning mountain-peak. But the effort involved was so fatiguing that I made only one or two further experiments. Not long afterwards, I read a letter in the *Saturday Westminster Gazette* (now, alas, no more), precisely describing a similar experience.

It is these outskirts of sleep which are, of course, the frontiers of dream itself. And what is called a dream, we must continue to remind ourselves, is a product of sleep of which we become aware only in our waking moments, and in waking terms. It consists of recollections, garbled simulacra, "condensed," "displaced," "dramatised," rationalised, perhaps. It must be seized as it flies and recorded at once in minutest detail if we are to make anything like sure of it.

A dream adept, I gather, may even at length succeed in watching himself dream. And with practice a recurrent nightmare may be evaded by its victim's decision to awake at threat of its reappearance. Attention, moreover, to one's dreams on waking appears not only to whet one's skill as an angler in the secret waters of sleep,

> that dark tarn of Auber,
> In the misty mid-region of Weir,

but also to multiply the fish. During the last few months, I have dreamed seemingly for this reason more often and more richly than ever; in spite of the sad assertion that at the ripe age of sixty and beyond, we tend to dream less and less. Odd and lovely spoil one may find in one's creel at morning-prime. But there must be at least as good fish in that tarn as ever came out of it, or peeped at dawn above its surface; for dreams, yet again, are as evanescent as the blue of a dewdrop shaken in the sun, or the wash of coral red that will reward anyone who keeps tryst with the Dog Star.

HALLUCINATION?

The experiences of dreaming and waking, moreover, may, as it were, occasionally coalesce or overlap; and the half-awakened one may be deluded into accepting the remnants of a dream as real. I treasure a scanty sheaf of this less common species — dreams, that is, which persisted for a while as hallucinations. So, conversely, the mind-stuff of waking life not only persists in dream but by the denizens of dreamland may be likewise dismissed as hallucination. The "second Me" in dreams at any rate appears to keep approximately true to kind.

Many years ago, I dreamed, for example, that Spring —
Flora of *Primavera* herself, was at that moment passing beneath my bedroom window — a commonplace window
enough. I awoke, this vision and conviction vividly clear in
memory, and at once sprang out of bed in order to verify it.
Thrusting back the slats of the Venetian blind over my left
shoulder I gazed through the glass of the window-pane into
the world without. It was early morning and the scene beyond had that rapt yet absent look which is usually the garb
of natural objects before the business of the day begins. The
street was ineffably quiet; no human wayfarer was in sight;
nor can I recall any sound, even if any were then audible.
And there, beneath me, in the dusty roadway, and precisely
as in my dream, I saw Spring herself advancing slowly up
my way. She sat, uplifted, ethereally lovely, surrounded by
her attendant nymphs and *amorini,* and crowned and
wreathed with flowers. It was with ropes of flowers, also, that
her nymphs were drawing slowly on her low flat Car on its
wide clumsy wooden wheels, like gigantic cotton-reels. And
so I stood, feasting my eyes on a waking vision — easily dissected, if need be, of course into Botticelli, a child's toy-cart
and a circus parade. But many lively and lovely " phenomena " (a frog or a humming-bird, for example) are unim-
proved by dissection; and even a chemical compound is not
merely the sum of its parts. The scene was tranquil and solemn; the very houses seemed asleep; and yet — faces and
garlands, the merry naked pagan children — it was also a
spectacle of a divine gaiety, and of a singular, yet not unearthly, beauty. I retired to bed again, and remember no
more.

To see any such picture as this with one's inward eyes while
the outward are in full view of an unattended-to sunlit objective world is so common and normal an experience that one
gives it no second thought. On that far-off morning, however,
both the dreamed-of and the actual appeared to be not only
equally visible but equally actual. The Car with its celestial
burden shut out the dusty flat macadamized road beneath it.

And it was no less *memorable* an experience than that of surveying in my boyhood from the granite parapet of the Embankment near the old and lamented Waterloo Bridge, the drowned body of some poor outcast which had been tethered to a police-boat and was now swaying idly in the tide of the Thames. Both spectacles, that of this radiant Spring, and of the dead woman, and each in its own fashion, were a kind of touchstone. And this is in the gift of sleep as well as of waking.

A completely ludicrous dream of this odd order, which entertained both my Me's some years later, was concerned with the lost upper section of a glass jar containing "mixed pickles." I hadn't the faintest recollection of its origin or ownership, of why it had been treated like this, by whom, or where, or when; and what the "Censor" may conceal in such symbols as onions, peppercorns, gherkins, cauliflower, I dare not guess. I awoke (early day lit the room) with this peculiar dreamed-of object, the upper half of the jar (resinous cork, vinegar and contents complete), clearly in my mind's eye. Its image remains as lively and isolated in memory as anything I have ever seen.

I at once got out of bed and began a busy and anxious search for it. Thus intently engaged, I pushed a book off a chest of drawers that stood near by. It fell heavily on my bare foot. Perched on the other, I nursed it for a few moments to relieve the pain. My wife, now exceedingly wide awake, enquired what I was about, and on my patiently explaining the situation to her, entreated me to return to bed. She cajoled, she pleaded, she argued with me. "You are only dreaming," she assured me. I angrily repudiated the charge, and casting about for a rational proof that I was not only in my right mind but "all there," I retorted that there were three windows in our bedroom, and that the one nearest to me was a few inches ajar — as indeed it was. This riposte, she afterwards confessed, so much perturbed her that at the first private opportunity she determined to hide my razors.

Hurt and indignant, I continued my futile search until at length the fumes and vapours of sleep, like the mists of an autumnal evening above a marsh, began to rise into, and to dull consciousness. With a mumbled, aggrieved remark that I would postpone the matter until the morning, I returned to bed and instantly fell asleep.

Where now, I wonder, is the nether half of my glass jar? And what in dream symbolism do chillies stand for? That in this world vinegar refuses to remain within the confines of a vessel when its bottom is missing is no reflection on dream-life. Ideas of objects are there infinitely tractable.

A similar dream-*plus*-hallucination once presented me with a visitant *in* my bedroom. On this occasion, however, I recalled no dream at all; merely awoke and found myself steadily scrutinising a dwarfish furtive skulking little man (reminiscent of Mr. Hyde and the renowned Charles Peace) who stood facing me, the panel of a capacious Victorian mahogany wardrobe for his background. There he *was*. I was surprised to see him, but less surprised, presumably, than I should have been if I had been sure that he was real; but I continued to survey him without the least dismay or perturbation. Indeed, to judge from the intentness of the small shabby eyes in the sidelong, clay-coloured face, the dismay appeared rather to be on his side. Presently, quiet as a cat, and with scarcely perceptible movements, he began to back towards the wardrobe, until at length — his outlines very gradually adapting themselves to the pattern of the mahogany panel behind him — he vanished into the wood, and was gone. To what degree was he of the stuff that dreams are made on, a mere illusion, a pure hallucination, or — something otherwise?

Of what, indeed, should we be *aware* if we confronted any being — spirit, seraph, fiend — of whom our senses could give us no recognisable data. Its effects on us might be translated into sensuous terms; otherwise it would remain for us a non-entity. In dream, recognition must be as active as it is in waking life, and may be no less liable to error, especially when its visitants least resemble what the dreamer is most familiar with.

Yet again, when I was once staying at a farmhouse near the sea, I awoke in an almost lightless room fully prepared to confront a fellow being who I was well aware was standing behind me and between my bed and the window of the room. I turned my head, and examined him. On this he too edged back until in a similar fashion he vanished into the folds of the white curtains that concealed the window. I fell asleep, and, first thing in the morning, turned at once towards the window to check this experience, only to discover that a dark-blue Holland blind hung over it and that there were no curtains!

Analogous to these little episodes is that of waking from a dream in which one is " lost." This, a recurrent dream, usually occurs to me in strange surroundings, and when I am far from home. The place dreamed of, whether the mouth of a sea-cave or some dim chamber or gallery of a prodigious building, appears to have cleverly mimicked, in its configurations, that of the room itself in which I am sleeping — with its shadows, drift of light, furniture-contours, its flats and hollows. I awake from the dream, usually terrifying and forlorn if not tragic in kind, and the scene presently thins away into or rather conforms with actuality. May even shut eyes be aware of their surroundings?

Once, yet again, in illness, I awoke with the conviction that I was interned much against my will in a house in Holland. And here, in dreadful fact, was the room itself; and over there, my nurse — now a formidable Dutch woman — who had me in her charge. I refrained from letting her into the secret, although the illusion lasted for some little time. But *that* night I had been given a dose of medinal.

How common and compromising a variant of dreaming any experience of this nature may be, I cannot say. But I remember Edward Thomas telling me many years ago that when one morning he was walking along a deserted country

road, he " came to himself " — still buffeting the empty air —
from a dream in which he was engaged in a lively bout of fisti-
cuffs. On the other hand, I once quietly awoke soon after
dawn as it seemed in a room that I knew was reputed to be
haunted. The house had Roman remains in its cellar. On reflection I was so confident that a veritable ghost now shared
it with me that, arguing that I should probably lie awake for
hours if I lifted my eyelids to make certain of my visitor, I
actually refrained from doing so, and fell asleep again. It was
a graceless reception for so unusual a guest.

Flora herself, my glass jar, my sinister snuff-coloured friend
were, I suppose, no *more* than hallucinations, relics of dream
persisting into waking life. The only difference between my
Mr. Hyde and any character whom I am trying to decoy into
the " making up " of a story is the realisation that the former
was an illusion, and that, as to the latter, I am intent, so far as
words are capable, on persuading him to appear as real and
convincing as I possibly can. The gravity, the earnestness,
the intense preoccupation, the artistic conscientiousness involved in the presentation of the scene, situation, characters
and so forth of a story or a poem, when they are considered
only as so much waking-dream stuff, is indeed little short of
ridiculous — if, again, they are that and nothing more.
Nevertheless, the sage and sober reader may accept them with
equal gravity. *Are* they, however, nothing more? Blake's,
Coleridge's, Vaughan's world of dreams and of the imagination — is all this nothing, or little more? Can we pass the burden of proof to the world of sensuous actuality? Apart from
a certain degree of consent with one's fellow creatures regarding it, that too may, in its own kind, however much, be
also little more. It is we ourselves who are the only thread on
which these beads of experience, bright or dusky, are persistently threaded. For whose trinket box?

Full-fledged dreams, like rabbits at dewfall in a hedgerow,
like shades when the dark is thinning into daybreak, undoubtedly infest the edges, the fringes of sleep; although many a
long night's sleep may come and go, leaving behind it no rev-

ocable trace of dream at all. But expert opinion is still divided on this crucial question — whether, that is, a very profound sleep is vacant of dream, or whether, on the contrary, the sleeping mind is never thus unoccupied. Either view appears to be as incapable of proof as the assertion that Memory resembles a prodigious granary wherein is stored the complete harvest of our past — wheat and tares; every sensation, thought, emotion, word spoken, word heard, every syllable, as they will be recorded in our last account.

Our private quarrel with Memory — strange angel that she is — is likelier, however, to be over her incompetence to give reality *enough* to what we value most in her treasury than to the wish that she should endow us with too much of the far less precious. The gluttony of oblivion is tragic enough; the all that we can recall even of a long friendship is niggardly to the last degree. Still, prodigious supplies of the best-forgotten have long ago gone the way of the much-desired.

But if our complete waking life, as it streams through consciousness (or consciousness streams through it), remains in the keeping of Memory beyond change and decay, so also must our life in dreams. A lost but happy dream may shed its light upon our waking hours, and the whole day may be infected with the gloom of a dreary or sorrowful one; yet of neither may we be able to recover a trace. On the other hand, the moment of awakening may reward us with more than one dream. I have myself frequently retrieved a complete covey of these shy and fugitive creatures securely caged, at least for the time being — three, four, even five; and no single specimen, it would seem, of the same flock or field or coloured feather. Most of us must be contented with what we get, mere pot-luck. The rare few, it is said, can order their dreams in advance. Yet, even for the lover, this might prove a dubious privilege. Certain dreams, too, may be as faithful in winging back to their owner as was Noah's dove to his Ark. Sometimes one may suspect serialisation.

In a dream, for example, of some few months ago I found myself seated at a round rusty iron table in the open air out-

side what appeared to be a low and sinister drinking booth.
A group of four men attired in over-long frock-coats stood in
private confabulation a few paces away. I knew vaguely that
my recent past had been involved with this villainous quar-
tette; and that one of them in consequence was keeping a furtive eye in my direction — a sallow, black-avised figure with
a detestable, rat-like face. After a low guffaw he presently
remarked, raising his voice a little for my benefit, "Ay, but
that was nothing to what we gave Harding (and I realised he
was referring to President Harding) in *his* last twenty minutes." The comment went evilly home; but with this ominous
remark the scene faded.

I next found myself a terrified fugitive in the garden of a
house from which into the darkness and silence streamed out
on sward and bushes a flood of light. I entered the house, fled
up a series of staircases, and found myself at length breath-
lessly perched on a footstool or some other piece of furniture,
and staring down from a narrow window-slit in the side of the
house, which was here topped with a gambrel roof. The light
on the garden beneath me fringed out to an edge of jetty
, blackness; and on the extreme right of the scene presently
emerged a greyhound, the base of its pointed head adorned
with what appeared to be a knot, or possibly Tudor rose, of
vermilion leather.

Eyes fixed, and in dreadful foreboding, I watched the creature intently, realising, as with nose to the turf he followed the
shadow's edge, that he was attempting to pick up my scent —
a notably dream-like piece of invention. Having failed to retrieve it, he turned back, and cunningly snuffing along his
original route, retraced his tracks. What infernal mentor,
then, was responsible for the idiocy that followed? When this
sly animal had reached a spot immediately opposite me and
beneath my slit of window, I deliberately vented a sustained
shrill whistle. He stayed instantly, lifted his head, and still
steadily zigzagging his muzzle upward, as if scenting rather
than seeing his way, quartered, as it were, the whole side of
the house, until at last he paused again, his gaze fixed finally

on me. And so Act iii was over. What had occurred in Act i, and what was the denouement?

A second-class " shocker," it is true (let alone the genius of the author of " Victory "), might have been the origin of that funereal group colloguing on the planks of my dreamed-of drinking booth; but it would hardly have bestowed on them that dismal dream-like *quality*. An evening with the " dogs " — an experience not as yet enjoyed — would produce grey-hounds as elegant and delicately reared, but none with that peculiar intensity of astuteness. And where, except in dream, do we find Tudor roses of so exquisite a vermilion and reeking with a secret symbolism which not even that of the Rosicrucians could excel?

The apparent contempt of the wizard of dream for the restrictions of Time and Space is notorious. Ariel is no fleeter than a tortoise by comparison; and a few moments suffice for a stretch of lively experience and its appreciation which in day-life would occupy a half-holiday, or even weeks. I have dreamed richly between — three nods of a tired head — the calling over of one sum of money to a copyist and that of the next. A friend once told me that in his student days he had dreamed that he had listened to a complete hour's lecture on surgery in the ten seconds that intervened between the two strokes of a bell which his father, for experiment, had sounded at his bedside. The first note of the bell had apparently ushered in an attendant carrying a human arm reserved for dissection, and the second had dismissed him. There is, too, the famous case of the dreamer who, after puffing out his bedside candle, slept, circumnavigated the globe, and awoke to find the wick still smouldering. Numerous dreams of this kind have been recorded; but in respect to the rapidity of dream life, it has been pointed out that the waker, returned to objective clock time, may be deceived in retrospect. He may fail to realise the rapidity with which the imagined flits through consciousness. In less than thirty seconds, one can quietly read over Donne's song, " Go, and catch a falling star." But watch the bodiless and prodigious journeys made in the quietude of the mind during that pregnant half-minute.

A similar characteristic of dreams already referred to, and one as eloquent of life's wanton abundance as an oak beaded with acorns, a sturgeon's roe, or the kisses of Catullus, is their evanescence. Now we have them, now they are flown, irrevocably. But this, alas, is a quality which they share with the vast majority of our waking sensations, perceptions and thoughts.

Most dreams, perhaps (at any rate on waking), appear to have been aimless and disjointed and therefore valueless. In this they resemble much of what we read in the morning's newspaper. Like the newspaper, they may consist of dismal or silly bits of scenes and episodes resembling detached excerpts from a tale told by a clumsy and half-literate tiro whose name appears to be *Self;* and they may signify something less savoury than nothing at all. We are not amused; we may refuse to be humiliated; we may deserve all we get. The challenge, " Tell me your last night's dreams, and I will tell you whether you are a Mormon, a Sadist, an imbecile or a lunatic " is best left unaccepted. But then, who would gladly consent to share, even if he could, and even with his closest confidant, every one of his yesterday's thoughts? Even if it be maintained that our thoughts are wholly under our control, a feat that implies the operation of an active guillotine, my father confessor, I fear, would be a good deal more welcome to my dreams than to the skimble-skamble stuff, and worse referred to by Hamlet and Hippolyta.

DAY-LIFE AND DREAM-LIFE

As for our waking traffic with the world-at-large — and how infinitesimal a fraction of that is solely ours — what a medley this appears to be: loose, chancey, piecemeal, formless. From birthday to death-day we continue to collect and weave together the materials of our minute private universe, as a bird builds its nest, and out of a myriad heterogeneous scraps we give it a certain shape and coherence, wherein to lay our treasured brittle eggs. But how little life itself respects the rational, adapts itself to our convenience, discloses its aim, explains the rules — despite the fact that every thread of it that is ours is weaving itself into a gossamer fabric thinner even than dreamed-of moonshine, which we call the Past; and which, when in recollection we attempt to record and arrange it and to give it something of a pattern, we shall call autobiography. Nature, inscrutable mistress of her vast household, even although man assumes himself to be her fairy godchild, shows him a fickle favouritism, destroys him if he ignores her, and is indulgent only if he obeys to the last iota her every edict, her every whim. She *is;* she perpetuates herself; as if she herself were bemused and in a dream — with her seasons and her weather, her greenery and stars and her multitudes; creating, destroying, never at rest.

And, day and night, aloof, from the high towers
And terraces, the Earth and Ocean seem
To sleep in one another's arms, and dream
Of waves, flowers, clouds, woods, rocks, and all that we
Read in their smiles, and call reality —

the reality conferred by the " human soul of universal earth Dreaming on things to come."

Because " such is life," because we are accustomed to it and have been broken in, because we decline to regard ourselves as mere puppets, because in spite of all argument against it we believe that we *will* it to our own small purposes, and because we may divine in it a celestial design, we accept it more or less as it comes — thankfully or otherwise. And so — why not? — with our dreams.

I pause to listen at the moment of writing, and become aware that a stubborn pen is scratching my paper, that leaves are rustling in the wind beyond my window, that a blind-tassel is faintly thumping on the glass. I hear the clump and clatter of a country horse and cart, the demoniac scream of a motor horn, the rumble of a distant train, the crowing of a

cock, a maid polishing a brass door-handle, the barking of
a distant dog. Of such chance (or pre-ordained) material
" life " is largely composed. That it occupied adjacent moments of time, and my attention, is for me its only linkage.
And so with any other sentient beings who may have shared
their part in it. It concerned me little more than the letter-
press of an old folio concerns the channerin' worm burrowing
through its pages. And so with the play of light and colour
on the familiar objects around me — the faint odours on the
air, the scattered sensations of the body, and so forth. Whatever their cause, these things are purely casual, and as such
have no more rational relation with myself and my own trivial
doings than the diabolic hoot of the motor horn that rent the
air had to Childe Roland, his " slogan," and the Dark Tower.
Has my erratic commerce with them any closer rhyme and
reason, any more coherence and significance than far too
many dreams appear to possess?

If, breaking off, I attend to them, then the hollow tap-tap
of the blind-tassel *may* bring the ominous drumming of Destiny to mind; the motor horn, the dizzy " progress " of civilisation; my scratching pen, Dürer's *Melencolia*. But meditation
itself is at least distantly akin to dreaming. Hypnos also is not
inattentive to the nightly business of the outer world; and
with a mischievous genius he may put to use our faintest sensations of it — the tapping of a beetle in the wall, the rustling
of one's bed-clothes, the squeak of a mouse, the settling and
crawling of a fly on the pillow. Out of hints slender as these
he may concoct his engrossing fantasies — endowing now
and then some romantic favourite such as Robert Louis
Stevenson not merely with a particularly odious hue of brown,
but with a Dr. Jekyll and a Mr. Hyde, with an intensely dramatic theme which he recorded and failed to use, and with
that unique retriever dog which, drowsing in the sun, caught
a fly with its paw, devoured it, and then winked up at the
dreamer. He may also pass off his legerdemain as wholly
our own.

Nor, as day-dream proves, is his gift by any means in abeyance in our waking life. Fitfully, fleetingly, we can detect the hither-thither of imagery flitting into and out of coherent thought and reflection. It insinuates itself even between his spoken words in a talk with a friend. It resembles the flight of a swallow — her exquisite sallies, ascents, pauses, twinklings. Like the swallow's, too, in its mazy vagaries, it follows the viewless prey of which presumably it is in pursuit. But although in waking life, however it may be spent, there is a fragile sense of continuity, and its moments are threaded by the conviction, " This is *real;* and is happening to *me*," at times that conviction wanes. More especially when we are deeply moved, exalted, exhausted, crushed, " beside ourselves." The soul then looks out from its fortress as if upon the illusion of a dream. Few experiences, for example, can have exceeded in intensity and dread that of living through the recent European crisis — one's own small private share in it, I mean — in a world not only gone mad, but, worse, claiming to be sane. Yet even then, on the brink of that abyss, how many of us must have paused, as I did myself for one moment, at the inward enquiry, " Is this a *dream?* "

As has been repeated, the careful dissection of a dream will frequently reveal the memoried scraps of waking experience that went to its making. Whereupon we may disparage the pretty chameleon, " Oh! is *that* all you were! " But then, the dreaming intelligence conferred on these scraps a certain form and sequence. Our day-experience is also largely composed of memoried familiar loosely related scraps; self alone gives them an appearance of form and sequence. We deceive ourselves in assuming that our thoughts or even our actions, any more than our day-dreams, are always consciously purposive. Many are automatic responses to the perpetual bombardment of stimuli from the world without; and others — sigh, laughter, tears; wish, appetite, want; anger, vanity, passionate devotion — we may almost as little purpose and design such reactions as we design the clouds in the sky which at one moment conceal the sun and at the next allow its beams to irradiate the Earth beneath them. " This," says Hippolyta to Theseus of Nic Bottom's play and its characters, " this is the silliest stuff that ever I heard." " The best in this kind," he replies, " are but shadows, and the worst are no worse, if imagination amend them." And she, " It must be your imagination then, and not theirs." And he, " If we imagine no worse of them than they of themselves, they may pass for excellent . . ." — well, dreams, or the things of actuality.

If our remembered dream-life were no less *apparently* consecutive and consistent and devoid of gap and fracture than our waking life, it is hardly its " reality " that we should question. The boot might be on the other leg. But so many dreams leave no more impression than the shadow of a flower on a stone. They lack " the aids of memory," refuse to fit into waking terms; although memory itself may have cheated us in this. Others remain in memory as touchstones and criteria of life and of self even at a pitch of extreme suspense, emotion or danger. To put oneself in this pillory may or may not be good for the soul. A few personal experiences of this kind may at any rate be forgiven, if only on the former account.

I — seemingly myself, yet not my*self* — am standing silent and alert in a stone-flagged lofty room, its opposite wall pierced with three high, stone-mullioned, Gothic windows. In the dusk between night and day I see beyond them, but faintly, the distant horns of a bay and the shores and the breaking waves of an inaudible sea. There is a shut door on my left; and a pace or two in front of me stands a high-backed triangular-topped chair. In this is seated an old lady in black — in clothes of a bygone century; and although I have only a sidelong view of her, she is so tranquil and motionless that I cannot be sure whether she is awake or asleep. What reason I have for wishing her dead, what advantage her death will bring me, I have no notion, even in my dream. But murder is my deliberate intention; and there is no pause for second thoughts between the intention and the act. With extreme caution I approach her soundlessly from behind her chair, and devilishly drive home the dagger clutched in my hand beneath her right shoulder blade. The deed is done.

She utters neither sigh nor groan; remains mute and unmoved.

But now the blood begins to flow. It is trickling noiselessly down on to the flag-stones, and in the thinning dusk forms itself into a dark shallow puddle, which in dream-obedience to the strange law of gravitation, is sluggishly pushing out a blunted tongue towards a crevice between the stones and the door. Once under that, it might be detected by any chance passer-by in the corridor beyond; and I am instantly seized with panic.

Near at hand (dreams leave little to chance) stands a leather bucket; and — though with what, I cannot say — I begin mopping up the blood and wringing it out into the bucket. Heated, and intent on this foul job, I work frenziedly on, my ears on edge meanwhile for the faintest rumour in the house beyond. But it is hard to keep pace with nature; and, suddenly, at sound of an approaching footstep, I twist my head towards the door, and in so doing clumsily overturn the bucket. Its contents spill out of it in a thin wide wash of vivid red over the flag-stones; and simultaneously the walls, the lofty ceiling, the high windows, the sea beyond them and the eastern sky are irradiated with the rose of dawn, flushing with beauty the snow-white foam of the billows breaking on the shore. And I awake to find the colours of actual daybreak at my window, and my room ensanguined with the rising sun.

In this particular dream, as I say, I might have been a character in some old tragedy or romance. I am hardly even a second self. There was no conscience in it; not a trace of motive, or of remorse; only a pitiless purpose, and the mere animal dread of discovery.

Not so, in a dream of many years later. In this dream I find myself quietly talking with a dark-eyed friend whom I have met by chance in a narrow deserted London street just before summer nightfall. Apart from our own low voices, not a sound breaks the hush of the city; the air is cool but stagnant after the heat of the day. The evening sky hangs remotely blue above the shabby clustering roofs of the street. We are isolated in space and time, in our relation to one another, and to the universe. And presently my friend enquires if I have heard that the house, not many streets distant, in which I live alone, has been sold — over my head. Instantly I see the house, known only too well; its grimed lightless windows, its obscure façade, its dingy interior; and also a huddled, black-skirted body dwindled by the ravages of decay and locked up in an empty room on its first floor. It has lain there for at least a year, shut in, unvisited. Appalled at this information, I stare mutely into the face of my guileless informant, conscious that in the darkness the blood in my body is steadily mounting into my face and head, and in a desperate confusion of heart and brain. The news has come too late; discovery of my vile secret, and the sequel, is now inevitable. . . .

And yet, the identity of the victim, the motive for the murder, what preceded its dreadful hour, and what had passed in the intervening months — of all this the dream, as it was remembered, recorded not a trace. Merely this utterly unforeseen casual announcement, and the realisation of what would follow it. And even that dream, alas, by no means concludes the dismal indictment. And, although I have been visited by a host of happy and harmless dreams, I can think of no equivalent in my dream-life (if any such equivalent there can be), no outstanding act of mercy or faith or compassion, or even of mere self-denial, to balance it. There is no plea for my defence. I am yet another infamous nocturnal Hyde. But where is Dr. Jekyll?

In an earlier dream, I am sitting in my usual chair at the window of a familiar room, and again in the peace of evening. Now, however, I am brooding in horror and loathing over the murder, committed only a day or two previously, of one very dear to me. I am conscious solely of this fact; and recall nothing concerning the time, place, or circumstances. Motive and outcome are (again) completely hidden from me. As I fustily ponder the crime and its consequences, my stagnant lethargy of body and mind, my cankering remorse, become almost insupportable; and, suddenly, there flashes into consciousness a hope — the childlike, forlorn hope — that all this may be no

[75]

more than the cheating invention of a dream. Proof lies at
hand. I mount a narrow staircase to my bedroom; this time,
I think, a dreamed-of, not an actual room. It is now — although the blind at the window is drawn up revealing the
sky — nearly dark, and it is cold. Hope is frail; I am abandoned and alone. Stooping on one knee, I open by a few
inches the lowermost drawer of a chest standing against the
wall, and push in a groping hand in search of the clothes
which I remember to have been wearing on the fatal day.
What is *their* evidence? In the gloom and utter silence, my
fingers encounter the thick tweed of a jacket clotted and
sticky with blood.

In real life, would it be possible, I wonder, for so blessed a
surmise to spring up in the heart, only to be thus — re-
doubling the murderer's pangs and anguish of mind — instantly blasted?

Terror, pain, grief, for which the mage of sleep may offer
the slenderest explanation, are common enough in dreams.
Can they be accepted as penalties for dream-misdeeds, or any
others, with which they appear to have no connection? Can
they be even remotely in the nature of an expiation? Two
dreams that might conceivably be accepted as penal continue
to horrify me, even although pain itself, mercifully, is past
acute recall, except as a sort of empty husk or echo.

I find myself alone in a narrow cell or chamber; its polished walls ebony black. In an intense blaze of light, I am
scrutinising an intricate machine consisting of many solid
wheels of specklessly smooth and glittering steel and brass.
They range in size from a monster of some seven feet down to
a midget of a few inches. They are inert, motionless. And yet,
yet — an inward whisper has bidden me watch the largest
of them. *Is* it or is it not, beginning to revolve? In acute
foreboding, I continue to gaze at it. Yes, inchmeal, almost beyond perception, it *is*. Instant by instant, without (I fancy)
the faintest audible sound, the momentum of the wheels is
continually increasing; and — horror of horrors — I am now
myself become, as it were, the machine. And the degree of

its speed is the degree of my own exquisite bodily pangs and mental anguish as its wheels ever more rapidly spin on and on and on. It reaches an appalling crisis and then, instant by instant, its hideous velocity begins to diminish again, until at length every wheel and every nerve in my body is once more at rest. But *is* it? Again, in that pitiless glare, I watch; again the gigantic wheel begins to stir. . . . And yet again. . . . Words can no more than hint at the agony thus endured.

In the other dream, it is pitch black night, and I find myself about to cross a wide shallow stream furiously babbling over its bed of stones and rocky boulders. A faint phosphoric light appears to suffuse the yeasty bubbles of the foam. To my right a street sharply ascends, its dark crowded houses, with high overhanging gables and lattice windows pierced with fiery light from within and thronged with painted faces, topped with outlandish head-dresses. These are either terrifying or in terror. The houses, their jutting angles, every shadow, every stone seem to be stricken with fear. Even the crying tongues of the water clamour only of fear. I realise it is the habitual emotion symbolised in every object around me. I wake; and sit up cold and trembling to ask myself, Is it possible that in some future existence a perpetual horror of mind and heart might be my own miserable human fate? If so, what is the prevailing emotion to which I am subjected in this life? And men, in general?

Once, at least, in a dream, I have made my final exit. I am seated on a narrow bench, back against wall, my wrists bound behind me, my lower-jaw tied up with a bandage. This room is of a primitive kind, longer than it is wide, and whitewashed. Seated immediately opposite me, on a similar bench attached to the wall, are two men in a dark nondescript uniform. They are solid and good-humoured, and are quietly talking to one another, leaning forward as they sit, their guns between their hands and their hands between their knees. A little to my right on their side of the room is a doorway, though I cannot distinguish any door to it, or see more than a few feet beyond it. My one and only chance of life and freedom, I realise, is to leap across the intervening space, and so into the room beyond, and then to risk what may lie in wait for me there. I determine to take the risk, push as hard as I can with my numb and shackled hands against the wall behind me, and in one desperate bound succeed in dodging my guard, and reach the threshold. At that instant, framed in the doorway beyond that, and immediately opposite to me, is entering a man, also in uniform (dark red and blue, I think). He has a calm, resolute and pleasing face. At sight of me, he at once levels his gun. I gaze along the barrel into his grey eye, and, presumably, he fires. All that I am conscious of, however, in this instant is, as it were, a blinding, shattering, soundless explosion of *light*.

Only a night or two divided this experience from that of finding myself sitting on the grass at the wayside — the smokeless cottages of a village (a village in Ireland, I fancy) in view. I am fagged out, but intensely relieved at having accomplished some unrecallable mission, on account of which I have escaped from the upper room of the house in which I had been confined. Safely out of the window — I had edged along a narrow ledge of brickwork thirty feet above the ground — an ordeal which my usual Me could, I fancy, in no circumstances face at all. Exhausted but serene, I watch time silently ebbing away in the tranquil morning light, while I await, I know well, inevitable recapture, and what it will entail.

VALUE AS EXPERIENCE

As Frederick Greenwood suggests, it is difficult to compute the precise value as *experience* of dreams of this order, even if the question of any concealed significance they may have is left out of account. That, in certain respects, they tally with similar events in actuality, and still more closely with those that have been imagined, is obvious. Nothing human — nerves or intellect or heart — seems to have been neg-

lected. And yet there is *a* difference; at times a supreme difference. " I awoke; and lo! it was a dream " *versus* " This,
God help me, is Reality."

It is at any rate easy to condone our dreams, not only the
most tedious and imbecile, but the shocking and shattering;
and not merely because, as with the majority of our waking
experiences, it is so easy to forget them. They may distract,
disappoint, dismay and wound us, but they leave few recognisable scars. It is less easy to forgive life its indelible scars;
since, on this side of the grave at any rate, we can have little
hope, hardly any hope, of forgiving ourselves.

Dreams, wholly rational and coherent, are, it is true, rare.
And these, apart from their peculiar aura, so closely resemble actuality that they suggest relics of a previous life, or
borrowings from that of a fellow creature. But so too may the
reveries, the fleeting imagery, and what we " make up," or
rather what is made up for us in our day-mind. Its fitful
fountain of thought and reflection, yet again, may keep the
shallow basin brimming or at a low ebb; but where is the
tap that turns on the water? We say, We think; but it would
be nearer the truth to say, We are thought into. We may
fondly suppose that these purely inward resources are in
our own control. In our own control, indeed! — when
thought's fickle current is not only severely limited, but so
frequently follows lifelong ruts of prejudice, opinion, convention and ideal; when a logical sequence from *A* to *D* is
something of a feat (otherwise we might grow rich over-
night!); when mere habit and our surroundings supply us
with most of the mind's daily bread; and, at an extreme
pitch, when we are possessed by images and presences
grieved and pined for, loved or feared. As well might a
haunted house sighing in the night wind, and unaided by
bell, book and candle, strive to rid itself of spectre or of
ghost.

All day long the door of the sub-conscious remains just
ajar; we slip through to the other side, and return again, as
easily and secretly as a cat. A dreamlike mood will haunt

the mind as moonlight through a window haunts a room, or the sense of disquietude and foreboding that foretells a storm. Obsessive memories vividly imagined, welcome or unwelcome, will insinuate themselves into our active and open thoughts, and so at length decoy our attention to them. As may the distant singing of a bird which the ear, at first refusing to heed, at length cannot evade; as does the shadow-barred light on the wall in Rembrandt's picture — patiently waiting until St. Jerome peers up from his great open book to welcome its company. Any glimpse of unexpected beauty, that of a lovely face, or of a serene landscape, its hollows receding beyond low hills, or of a tranquil day-break and an eastern sky with its dove-grey low-lying lattice of clouds, the pale blue as of an infinite peace between them — all such things, even an abstracted moment with a pebble, a tea-cup, or a blade of grass, may still the waking mind, and so are reminiscent of the more tranquil and moving of our dreams.

As we cannot be certain that any seemingly casual event in our lives may not prove of the utmost gravity, so we cannot deny that a simple impressive dream may be of a profound intention. Every moment of experience indeed becomes the more complex the more closely we examine it. It is, at the least, whether of dream or wake, the slender bridge that attaches self-past to self-present and to self-to-come. Any meaning we are led to bestow on it, in regard to the source of human life or the goal of human destiny, is at any rate beyond refutation. For it is what in our brooding hearts we think of anything and what we feel about it that matters, rather than the thing itself. Whether we wake or dream, then, how much depends on the quality of the " us."

The only catalogue of this world's goods that really counts is that which we keep in the silence of the mind. And the prices we scribble against them in the margin may be too high or too low; usually, too low; and many are due chiefly to our vanity and self-esteem. At times the price may be both fabulous and precise. Is it conceivable, for instance, that *any* human being (except the one on whom it may have been bestowed) is wholly worthy of the exquisite and divinely generous tribute of an impassioned love? Are *we*? "What *can* she have seen in him?" is the usual question. Well, an Apollo; or Marsyas, at the least. A poor specimen to a cold eye, but still her own, and of an infinite value. Thou lovest what thou dreamest her; I am that very dream. That is the sober truth. And so with every thing else we value and delight in. What we dream into it, divine in it, is what counts most. That gone, wasted, there is nothing left remarkable in it, not even its moonshine.

So, every writer, by the mere mention of any object, and whether he intend it or not, reveals in his context the value he sets on it — the value imposed on it by his own vision and imagination, or the lack of them, of which he cannot be fully aware. In no book in English is this sovereign stamp more apparent than in the best book in English — the Authorised Version of the Bible, a translation that, by a miracle of insight and intuition, enshrines the very genius of our language; and this, with Tyndale for model, the work of a Committee! One word in that context suffices for the revelation of the essential and unique quality of what it signifies — whether that word is lion, island, gold, star, ruby, needlework, horse, love, majesty, flattery or evil.

"He made darkness his pavilions round about him"; "His watchmen are dreaming, talking in their sleep"; "Both chariot and horse are cast into a deep sleep"; "In the twilight, in the evening, in the black and dark night"; "Heaviness may endure for a night, but joy cometh in the morning"; "Who is she that looketh forth as the morning, fair as the moon, clear as the sun, and terrible as an army with banners?"; "One cried, the whole earth is full of His glory." Everything is seen as if in the light of that morning, and with a newly awakened inward eye. Its very daimon looks out of it. For no daybreak, no lingering star or planet, no rising sun

is more serene, more tranquilly effulgent than those perceived by happy chance while the mind is still under the
sway of sleep, and of what sleep bestows on us.

As for the dreams referred to or recorded in the same book,
they may be charged there with falsity and upbraided for
their fleetingness; but they are never scorned. Their vividness is conspicuous even in their context; yet they wear the
livery of sleep; and they share that secret atom of radium
common to all things tinged with genius — Jacob's angel,
Joseph's sheaves, the butler's three-branched vine, the
doomed baker's baskets of bake-meats, his spectral birds of
the air, Pharaoh's ill-favoured kine. They are no less familiar, if at any rate we shared them first in childhood, than
the parables; and they are of as pure a dream *quality* as the
objects mentioned in their company are pure in quality compared with those of waking life.

Indeed, clearly remembered dreams leave an intensely
sharp impress in the wax of the mind. If, then, they were
less fugitive, and the wise could whisper their Sesame into
the sleeper's ear, they would be an excellent means of teaching the young.

INTERPRETATION

But as in the Bible and in the majority of treatises on the
subject, so in the popular dream books — the dream is always
considered to be of less importance than what it signifies. It
is a parable, and its earthly story is secondary to its meaning — heavenly or otherwise. Our day affairs presumably
wear *their* meanings on the sleeve; in these, there is little of
the obscure, the concealed, the cryptogrammic, of Abraca-
dabra! But a dream, it is maintained, like the song of the
sirens, is in a semi-secret language. Its interpretation must
be analysed out of it, or divined. If this language were assured, and could be finally elucidated, well and good. But
where is the linguist on whom we can wholly rely? How

many clearly recalled scraps of dream are likely to prove worthy of translation? Many, it appears. But nowadays our Joseph wears a coat of very curious colours; and even if the novice must modestly attempt to come to terms with his Ego, his super-Ego and his Id (differing only in one letter from another unexplored province commonly known as It), he may, since his dreams are solely his own, prefer to accept them, as he accepts his daily events: at their face value. And that being so, Lavater himself had no more diverse and seductive a field for research.

For Freud, that " daring and original psychologist . . . of a subtle and searching analytic genius," our wizard's main concern is with that source of energy, that incentive and fountain of delight called Sex. Its guardian angels are Love and Lust, whose relation to one another resembles that of vision and nightmare, dew and ice, admiration and avarice, lyric and lampoon. " Male and female created he them " — it is a mystery rampant on every side of us on every fine and jocund morning in Spring. To it we all of us owe our mortal bodies, if not our souls. Freud, defensively, reduces it to almost purely physical terms, but in so doing seems to degrade it; as may, for far other than scientific motives, a music-hall song or a smoking-room story. The right kind of dung may bring the most innocent and winning of blushes to the rose on the bush which it nourishes; then why disparage the dung?

But in most human experience, love between man and woman, surely, precedes conscious physical desire, whatever purpose old mother Nature may have in mind for " the conservation of the species." Views change. The Victorian novel ended with wedding bells, while that of our own day is apt to begin with a decree nisi.

That a Blatant Beast, with virtues of its own nature, is confined in the cellar known as the Unconscious,[6] of which it is

---

[6] This " Unconscious " (so far as it is practicable) is now being actively explored — and the novice should fear to tread. It is a convenient but unanimating term for the reservoir of *elixir vitae* from which, throughout the waking day and

advisable as far as possible to keep the key, is undeniable;
but there is also a caged bird in the attic, and one of a marvellous song. Here, paradoxically, it is the pearl that con-
ceals the oyster. Sexual fruition after all is only one course
in love's banquet, and that the last — though by no means
the least mysterious and valuable. It may satisfy awhile the
body, but never, wholly, the spirit. And what should be said
of a Censor who, it seems, habitually endeavours, by trans-
muting the " latent " into the " manifest " content of a dream,
to mislead the waker and so to conceal from him what in his
dreams might be of sovereign value; and who may convert
the obscure into mere gibberish, even if that gibberish is
sweet to tongue and ear? It would be interesting to over-
hear in some priest's hole of the mind a private colloquy between this Censor and that secret sharer called Conscience.

"The Freudian analysis," says Mr. Neil Montgomery in
The End of Fear, " fails to give satisfaction because of its in-
adequacy. No doubt the dreams fit neatly into a sexual

---

at every moment of dream, is being drawn up into consciousness, even though
it may serve its purpose unperceived, the imagery of recognition, recollection
and re-creation. The submerged portion of an iceberg is the commonest metaphor for it; but that of an archipelago of humanity whose myriad island peaks
are connected under the sea may be nearer the mark. Intuition in part depends
on its resources; and, past calculating, the faculty or poise or, rather, state of
the mind which we call the Imagination. Its influence may be the cause of what
fascinates or repels us in a fellow creature; and for the " mystery," *l'inconnu*,
which Man in his devotion seeks in vain to fathom in Woman. Its precious
metals glint out of the quartz of the confirmed " character "; it inspires the
consummate actor; and more or less controls the born demagogue. It can be the
devil in human affairs. Yet it nourishes the flower of mystical contemplation. It
is the Hesperides of the Muses. As the utterance of verbal sounds with the vocal
organs has its own sensuous aesthetic reactions, and facial expression intensifies
the emotions it represents, so every natural posture of the body is the outcome
and revelation of a state of the mind and of the unconscious mind. Even in the
merest novice mimicry of the attitudes of the Buddha will induce some trace of
the spiritual attitudes which they represent — a kind of empathy; and any true
understanding of a piece of statuary is at least in part dependent on a similar
intuitive process. What — in any original enterprise of mind or spirit — *can* man
achieve, indeed, unaided by the reviving waters of this unplumbable well? A
well lapped in darkness — and every metaphor is only a makeshift — into which
we can peer only with the aid of a feeble taper, introspection.

framework, but there are many other frameworks into which they fit with equal ease." "Much," says Professor J. B. S. Haldane, "of what passes the scientific psychologist seems to me profoundly unscientific." "Who," enquires Mr. Bernard Shaw, "has ever wanted to sleep with the Venus de Milo? Ninety-nine hundredths of the sentiment in the world, including the maddest infatuations, are asexual. The fact is staring the psycho-analysts and the penners of red-blooded thrillers in the face all the time; yet they persist in hunting for what they call *libido* in every manifestation of it."

And again: "In such a poem" — says Mr. Owen Barfield in his *History in English Words* — "as 'I sing of a maiden,' we have once more a kind of cross-section of the growth of European outlook. Between its lines we seem to be able to hear, as in a dream, the monotonous intonings of Egyptian priests, the quiet words of Socrates in the Academy, and the alert speculative hum of the Alexandrian world. It is so graceful that for the moment it seems as though all these things, with all the pillages and massacres and crucifixions and vast imperial achievements of Rome, had been conspiring together merely to load the homely old Teutonic word "loaf-kneader" with new semantic significance, to transform it into that mystery and symbol in the imaginations of men, a *lady*." And yet again: "If there are occasions when a single word seems to throw more light on the workings of men's minds than a whole volume of history or a whole page of contemporary literature, the Middle English *love-longing* is certainly one of them."

As for the multitude of sex-symbols which, it is maintained, embellish so many of our dreams, there is scarcely an object around us that cannot be conceived of as a symbol figurative of anything with which the waking mind is deeply concerned. The four walls of the room in which one is sitting, its opaque ceiling, its window curtains, looking-glass, lamp, fire-place, the key (present or absent) of the door, the flowers, the wine and the bread on the table — what of these when we reflect on them in relation, let us say, to the life beyond the grave? [7]

Unfortunately, as soon as we are concerned with the subject of sex (but not with that of our other appetites), perfectly rational thinking is apt to become even more difficult than is completely free speech. A faint fog steals into the mind. Its cellar door has come an inch open, and there peers out from it a taboo. Instinct as well as custom and convention hinders lucid thought. We cannot detect the tune for the echoes. And although a completely unselfconscious little discourse on " my digestion " or " my nerves " is an only too easy matter, mere ease is less apparent when our theme is other no less vital organs and functions, or " my sex " or " my soul." We realise that we are naked, and resort to an apron. We cannot inhale freely the unemo-

[7] Just as we may think we can " foresee our luck " by any means we care to credit — a new moon, the flight of a bird, the spilling of salt, the fall of a picture, the number on a ticket — so we may invent symbols to suit our mood and purpose. But in day-life as in dream, we may believe that we are actually confronted by the symbolical, although its full interpretation may elude us. A hidden self answers the secret watchword; remote memories are stirred. One cannot, surely, for example, avoid focussing one's imaginative attention a little beyond the surface of the two dreams that follow, recorded for me by the dreamers themselves:

" I saw God (or Don Quixote) seated on a lean brown horse which was standing by a ruined house. He had a short brown beard and looked sad and ill. He was dressed in a long brown robe. In front of Him knelt six monks dressed in brown and cream habits, their hoods covering their heads. Behind them and to my right stood the Blessed Virgin Mary and Christ. The Virgin looked old and was dressed as a nun, but Christ was quite a young boy. He was dressed in a plain white gown reaching to the ankles. Every one was motionless. Then I awoke to find that I could have only closed my eyes for a very few minutes."

" I saw a flat garden of green lawn and flowering beds, with big trees in the background. It was bright sunshine. F. was walking there and a little way in front of her a small child with yellow hair kept running from side to side and stooping down to look at the flowers. After I had seen this very clearly, I noticed that the child's movements were controlled by the gestures of a tall black figure, moving from left to right, and walking close behind F. who never knew she was there. The tall figure was not human: she was entirely black — hair, face, arms, drapery — like a statue made of unpolished black marble. She was majestic and infinitely beautiful; very calm and suave. When I saw what she was doing I was horribly frightened and woke up."

tional aether of pure science. Indeed, this mystery is as difficult to isolate and define as life itself. Shame or humour, common sense or braggadocio may be convenient but are equally poor refuges.

Besides, can any more or less plausible interpretation of a dream be finally refuted? Even the most fragmentary of dreams, other than those to which it is impossible to attach any value at all, may hint at a variety of meanings. A few months ago, I sat reading one afternoon, and drowsed off into a shallow sleep of only a few moments' duration. In these I dreamed that I had opened a dream door at the far end of the room and had looked in on a young woman who appeared to be awaiting me there. I made a quiet remark to her concerning a beautiful child, three or four years of age, of whom she appeared to be in charge. The room in which I found myself was still and tranquil, in a degree unusual in waking experience. When I turned, the child to my astonishment had vanished. On this, I realised that I had meanwhile been vaguely aware of his unreality, but was none the less perturbed at what seemed a strange omen: and then I awoke.

Since almost every morning the ebb of sleep leaves me with vague relics of dreams no less certainly present for being otherwise irrecoverable, this was no more than one minute example of a host of similar dream-experiences. Yet it left a vivid impression. How interpret it?

It might be suggested that the dream insinuates either (a) that I had illicit designs on the young woman; or (b) since there were actual and very lively children in the house, that the child's disappearance was in the nature of a wish-fulfilment; or (c) that, contrariwise, in these days of a falling population, the child's presence there was itself a wish-fulfilment — as it well might be; or (d) that the dream was a warning divulged by my Unconscious regarding an actual child in the house; or (e) that the door was a symbol of Death's wicket; the peace beyond, that of Paradise; the young woman, that of one of its guardian angels; and the

child, an earthly self long ago left behind me but still dis-
coverable even beneath the rags and decay of age. Can
any one of these interpretations (and there may be others)
be refuted?

Similarly, not long ago, a demure flaxen-haired child sidled
up to my table in a crowded restaurant and, head on one
side, smiled at me from under her round white hat with all
the shyness of a three-year-old and the archness and artifice
of a Cleopatra. This little episode, too, might be variously
interpreted; but it was a waking experience. Mere prefer-
ences, of course, are of little value or validity except to their
owner. The fact remains that one may continue to treasure
the memory of both these children for their own sakes only
— to leave the silk, as it were, in the cocoon, Blake's old man
in the thistle, the oyster in its pearl. So, too, one may prefer
to enjoy the rhymes " Old King Cole," " How many miles to
Babylon? " and " The Reverie of Poor Susan " without attempting to explain or to analyse them. In the old folk-tales,
the really beautiful and attractive characters remain so. The
ugly may *conceal* the charming; the beast, the Prince; but it is
very seldom vice versa. Even the asinine Apuleius was at
last rewarded with his bunch of roses. Any moral thus intended may be valuable; but it may be more effective even
for being left implied.

I have seen two interpretations of " Old King Cole," one
metaphysical, and the other — well, ultra-physical. None
the less, left as a mere nursery figure of fun Cole may remain
the wiser monarch. No *meaning* bestowed on it would at
any rate, I think, enrich the experience of being smiled at,
at my time of life, and all for nothing, by a small flaxen-
haired female stranger in a round white hat. May not even
the Censor of dreams be on many occasions less of a meddling tainted Uncle Grundy, intent on his plum-and-apple
jam to sweeten his dubious physic, than a sort of mischievous
laughing angel, or at least a wag whom we may accept as
amusing even when he appears to be serious?

The dissection of a dream, as of a corpse, may of course be as informative as it is destructive, and yet the living dream may be of more value than anything deducible from its remains; just as a child's birthday cake with its lighted candles is no less magical to his own heart and fancy in spite of his ignorance that his elders have first estimated the calories it contains. Good wine also has virtues independent of the quantity of alcohol in it.

The question remains whether the waker is in any degree morally answerable for the open and mortifying antics, or worse, of the dreamer. If we decide merely to delight in our choicest dreams, of any kind, without attempting to derive any " lesson " from them, the risk is ours. It is the *secrets* of all hearts that will be opened on the last day — but should they meanwhile remain secret from ourselves? Moreover, if we waive every responsibility for the Blatant Beast, then the bird of paradise in the attic is also none of ours.

That many men of supreme intelligence and genius have been profoundly and permanently influenced by their dreams is beyond question. What of those who have ignored them? Had his wife's dream occurred to Pilate himself, the whole course of human history might have been changed.

In the autumn of 1664 Blaise Pascal passed through a supreme crisis in his life — his " second conversion." He had recently narrowly escaped death when driving to Neuilly. " But the moment that remained ever sacred in his memory was that of a remarkable vision or ecstasy." On November 23 he commemorated this vision in a few impassioned sentences in an amulet which was discovered, after his death, inscribed both on paper and on parchment, and sewn into his doublet. This amulet, it seems, had been stitched anew into his every change of clothes. Thenceforward, he became an extreme ascetic, utterly self-denying and of a boundless charity. He " wore around his body a girdle of iron, the sharp points of which he would press into his flesh when he felt in danger from worldly temptations and wandering thoughts."

Descartes also was visited by dreams that sharply affected his future life; [8] and the supremely pathetic and tragic state of Cowper's mind in his later years also originated in a dream. "I had," he says, writing on October 16, 1785, "a dream twelve years ago, before the recollection of which all consolation vanishes, and, it seems to me, must always

[8] During the winter months of 1619, Descartes, then a soldier, and quartered at Neuburg on the Danube, first divined the principles of the new Method which he afterwards applied in philosophy. He was then in his twenty-fourth year, and, distrustful of what had hitherto been accepted as "knowledge," he had already abandoned his books in order to form his mind for the reception of truth.

During the night of November 11 in this year he had three dreams. It was the Eve of St. Martin — the Saint of the convivial; but Descartes declared that he went sober to bed, and, indeed, that he had not touched wine during the previous three months. The first of his dreams was one of acute physical distress and terror, a dream of darkness haunted by strange and spectral beings and a tempestuous wind. He awoke in pain, afflicted by the horror that an evil spirit had aspired to seduce him. He prayed God to protect him against any evil consequences of this dream, and that He would preserve him from the ills which might menace him as a punishment for his sins. These, he realised, had been grave enough to draw down the thunderbolts of heaven upon his head: although he had hitherto led a life which, in the eyes of his fellow men, had been irreproachable enough. After prolonged meditation, he fell asleep again.

Terror, caused by the sound as of a clap of thunder, awoke him suddenly from the dream that then followed. On opening his eyes, he perceived a multitude of fiery sparks scattered about the room. This was not a new experience. He had frequently awaked at night with his eyes so filled with sparks of light that in a confused fashion he had been able to discern the objects around him. Now, however, after opening and shutting his eyes, and observing the qualities of what was represented to him, he wished to explain this phenomenon by philosophic reasoning, and he drew from it conclusions favourable to his soul. His fears left him, and he fell asleep again in peace.

There was nothing terrible in the dream which immediately followed this. It was concerned with two books, one a dictionary with which he was delighted; the other, also new to him, an anthology of poems entitled *Corpus Poetarum*. On opening the book to read in it, he chanced on the verse, " Quod vitae sectabor iter? " At this moment in his dream he saw a stranger, who gave him a poem beginning with the words, " Est et non," declaring that it was an excellent poem. Descartes told the stranger that he knew the poem, that it was one of the Idylls of Ausonius. While he was searching for it in the *Corpus*, with which he declared he was familiar, he discovered that the dictionary had vanished. He was explaining this to the stranger when it reappeared at the other end of the table. But it was no longer complete. Unable to find " Est et non " among the poems of Ausonius, he told the stranger of an even lovelier poem by the same poet, " Quod vitae," but failed to find it, discovering instead several little portraits engraved vanish." " It is a long time for a man, whose eyes were once opened, to spend in darkness; long enough to make despair an inveterate habit; and such it is in me." " In one day, in one *minute* . . . she [Nature] became a universal blank to me . . . with an affect as difficult to remove as blindness itself." In 1786 he explained that " the word " he had heard in his dream was uttered by God: " ' *I will promise you any thing:* that is to say much as I hate you, miserable as I design to make you, I will yet bid you be of good cheer and expect the best, at the same time that I will show you no favour . . .' What conclusions can I draw from these premises, but that he who once loved now hates me, and is . . . working distinctly contrary to his promises? " In 1793 Cowper was again haunted with " horrible dreams." " From four this morning," he wrote on February 2 of this year, " till after seven, I lay meditating terrors, such terrors as no language can express." On March 1 he dreamed that he was taking a final leave of his dwelling, on the evening before his execution; and rejected the iron hasp of the garden

---

" *en taille douce.*" Both books and stranger then vanished from his imagination. Still asleep, and doubting whether this experience had been a vision or a dream, Descartes decided that it had been a dream and, still asleep, proceeded to interpret it.

He concluded that the dictionary represented the Sciences, and that the *Corpus* represented Philosophy and Wisdom in union; for even foolish and superficial poets may be full of sentences more serious, more weighty, and better expressed than those in the writings of the philosophers. He attributed this marvel to the divinity of Enthusiasm and to the force of the Imagination, which puts forth the seeds of wisdom that are to be found in the spirit of all men — as sparks of fire may be found in pebbles — much more easily and brilliantly than does the Reason of the Philosophers. He concluded that the poem on the uncertainty as to what kind of life one ought to lead represented the counsel of a wise man or even Moral Theology. He then awoke, continued his interpretation, and was finally convinced that the Spirit of Truth had in this dream intended to open the treasures of all the Sciences to him. As for the little portraits, next day an Italian painter called on him, and Descartes sought no further explanation.

So profound was the impression left on his mind by these three dreams that he vowed in his enthusiasm to make a pilgrimage to the Sanctuary of the Blessed Virgin Mary at Loretto from Venice, and, if his strength admitted this, on foot. But God determined otherwise; and four years were to go by before he set out for Italy.

door which he had thought to carry away with him as a memorial, because he recollected that " the heat of the fire in which I was going to be tormented would fuse the metal." Yet he died so peacefully that no one who witnessed his last moments could tell *the* moment. " The expression with which his countenance had settled was that of calmness and composure, mingled, as it were, with holy surprise."

To the insensitive, any experience of this nature, whether of the day or night, is all but dumb. On the raw nerve it may play far too skilfully. The " criminal tendencies " disclosed in my own dreams *may* have been a reaction from a spiritless respect for the Law in actuality (and a subsequent forgotten dream *may* have produced both rope and gallows); or with equal probability they may have been a sort of rash of " thought forms " incident to a sedentary life. Whether or not, the horror and remorse they caused the dreamer have long outlived their waking day. Every such dream, whether " analysed " or not, sounds its tocsin of warning. Indeed, one may awaken no less poignantly stricken by the fictitious tale which Sleep has told us, by the arrow it has aimed at the heart, than if Nemesis herself had tapped at day's door. Yet again, in spite of its follies and fatuities, its mummery and make-believe, its specious dovetailing and jigsawing, dream-life is self-life — a no less consistent self than the I of waking, if not an " identical twin." There is no proof of any complete rupture between this Box and Cox. The mind's life asleep and awake may be continuous; and there need be no rivalry between them. But if there is any salient difference, the give or take is not on one side only.

The general scene, for example, is usually more confined in dream than in waking, the area of survey more contracted. The company may seem less substantial, the bodily self is more nebulous; the thread, as indeed it may in day-life, keeps on breaking. But we accept every transition, however clumsy. The dream tissue itself appears to be as tenuous as reflections in water; the dreamer is frequently as vagrant and unattached as a ghost. We may be uncertain whether we actually hear our own speech or that of others. One may frequently, none the less, recall spoken words. Every generalisation is dangerous; and the words " always " and " never," when applied to dreams, are extremely insecure.[9]

Certainly the senses share this nightwork even less fairly than that of the waking day. The inward eye is usually the busiest of them, though mind-sight might be a closer word. The sense of form may be admirable; that of colour appears to be debatable; in my own case it is often brilliantly luminous. The sense of space varies and may be the cause of a peculiar horror. That of time is eccentric, to say the least of it. Touch *may* be precise and active; smell and taste are usually less so, though on occasion they may be acute. A friend having assured me one evening that she had never tasted or smelt in her sleep, that very night was presented with a dream-draught as nauseous to her nose as it was to her palate.

Our sensibilities and emotions in dream, although they may be dulled and erratic, may be more delicate, sharper, distressing than in waking life. Fancy dances through dream, light as thistledown; and no one could deny imagination its mastery there. And what of the intellect? It was as if from out of a dream, after years of reflection, that Sir William Hamilton was presented with the answer to the question, What is the square root of -1? And it was during a sleepless night, after many days of neuralgia, that " certain thoughts undesignedly came into Pascal's head concerning the Roulette or Cycloid." These thoughts, we are told, were so numerous that " whether he would or no they discovered even to demonstration everything relating to that piece of machinery, to his great surprise." But he had at that time renounced

[9] Quite recently, for example, as I lay in the serene no-man's-land between wake and sleep, there appeared in the dark field of vision, and against a pearly-grey background, a chalk-white and very beautiful face which, as I watched it intently, began subtly to change in feature until at length it resembled a face familiar to me. Then this too began to change, as if it were formed of wood-smoke. This experience, I think, was a complete novelty. But although we may aver with confidence that we have never had such and such an unusual experience in waking life, to assert this of our dream-life would be far too bold a venture.

these branches of knowledge, and refrained from setting his thoughts down.

In dream itself, reason presides, often fantastically enough. And the intellect may be active. Stubborn problems may then be solved; lost objects may be traced, and by methods denied to the waking mind; the crooked way may be made straight; difficulties that defeated us overnight may vanish with the morning, a morning that, probably with the connivance of dream, may on occasion present us with our happiest " ideas." Experiences of this kind are by no means unusual. Far more frequently, alas, I am myself doomed to spend jaded hours in sorting, say, three papers into their proper order; or in vainly attempting to " undo this button "; or in attempting to placate that old reprobate, Mrs. Grundy. Or even worse: I spend what seem dead lagging hours in company and circumstances — discomfort, depression, humiliation, utter fecklessness — that suggest a " home away from home " reserved for the weak-witted and the deranged. But this is only in the way of nature, and not a syllable of reproach is intended.

Once, indeed, now long ago, I found myself reading the first pages of a dingy and dumpy little book, a visionary book, murkily printed, and bound in what appeared to be shagreen, black shagreen. All that I can recall of its contents is a series of diagrams which appeared on pages 1 and 2. Against the first of these, a blank circle, was printed the word " Reality." Against the next, a blackened circle, was the word " Unconsciousness." The next circle showed a minute segment of white cut out of its black. This was labelled " The Consciousness of an Ant." The next, *minus* a rather larger segment, " The Consciousness of Man." From this I deduced — whether in the dream or on awakening I cannot say — that when, owing to the progress of the Superman, we arrive at Nirvana, *all* the black will have become white; that Reality and Consciousness will be coincident. " I Am That I Am." The Infinite is All in All. This little revelation, as I say, was the subject matter of the first two pages of my dingy dream book. What, I wonder, were its last pages concerned with; and in what celestial library does it now repose? [10]

As Edgar Allan Poe may have been sponsor to my dream of the Valley of Fear, so books read in the daytime may have fathered the duodecimo of my dream. This does not affect the ingenuity of its presentation. Nor does it explain the pretty process (familiar to Dr. Johnson) which enables one to peruse in dream a complete column of print of dream's type-setting, to marvel at its excellent sense, relish its wit, and even accept its authorship. A quite recent dream presented me with a typewritten letter the last but one sentence of which was the winning, " Ever in Your Memory."

Physical feats (*pace* their symbolism) may transcend even these mental gymnastics. That, of course, of flying, for example; or of skimming blissfully on from field to field over intervening hedge and ditch and fence; or of floating fishlike in the viewless air, the body instantly obedient in its move-

---

[10] " After taking the largest quantity of calcium chloride on record," says Professor J. B. S. Haldane, " I dreamt that Edward Lear had written and illustrated a life of Christ. It was a strange book, but not essentially irreverent." The Magician can spin similar fantasies at an invitation even less emphatic than an unprecedented dose of calcum chloride. A normal dose of mescal button sufficed, it seems, for the phantasmagoria — excelling the wildest chapter in the *Arabian Nights* — described by Dr. Weir Mitchell on a later page. Much, of course, depends on the dreamer. The prescription for the broken dream at Nether Stowey, of which the 54 lines of " Kubla Khan " are the unique relics, was not opium *per se*, but opium *plus* Coleridge. Fuseli, it is said, would sup on pork as a bait for dreams that would whet his fancy for his work as an artist. But then he was Fuseli.

Habitual dreamers need seek no bait; it is a gift. Dreams in illness, for example, may tend to either extreme, serenity or horror. It was in illness I dreamed that I held between my fingertips the strangest and most entrancing object I have ever seen. This was a hollow orb some four inches in diameter, interwoven of an exquisite translucent trellis-work resembling crystal, through every vein of which coursed an ethereal fluid continually changing in colour. This, as I watched it in awe and admiration, I recognised as the very citadel of life itself! It was perhaps a phantasmal replica of some humble physical organ — although even the heart itself, to which we impute our sharpest joys and sorrows, is hardly a thing of obvious beauty to the naked eye. Dream would know better. In this same illness, in a wild and solitary valley in winter, I kept an assignation, made I know not when or where, with a white horse — blue-eyed. But this memorable dream has also been related elsewhere.

ments to every whim — now this corner of the ceiling, now that; an aerial tank. And deeds of daring? One sunny morning my elder daughter, then a child, vanished from view in a dream through a crevice between two planks of a marine pier. After perceptibly pausing to listen to the voice of reason assuring me that I should sink like a stone, I jumped over the parapet into the water: certainly not to rescue her but — well, I never knew! Jumping-pole in hand, I once found myself leaping from boulder to boulder down a steep mountain track, the bed of a torrent, in pursuit of a terrified leopard. Whereas in waking life . . .

So, too, in dreams, with our delight in beauty, natural or preternatural; and with our passive acceptance of or revulsion against the hideous, the evil, and the vile. Perhaps the loveliest face I have ever seen, rivalling even the angel's in Leonardo's " Madonna of the Rocks," continued to haunt my waking eyes — poised in the air a few feet above my face as I lay in marvel watching it, many years ago, from my pillow. And as for the music of an enchanting voice, that too *in excelsis* was the gift of dream. And yet again its pure lovely cadences, gliding on from note to note, but in no distinguishable tune or air, not only persisted into waking life; they were overheard also by a niece who was then staying in the same house with me. The voice was hardly of a human quality; it would be a wild guess to assume that it may have been my own — in a cherubic falsetto! Was it then that of the banshee, or Israfel's? " I have dreamed in my life," says Cathie in *Wuthering Heights,* " dreams that have stayed with me ever after, and changed my ideas; they have gone through and through me, like wine through water, and altered the colour of my mind." That, surely, is the very voice of Emily Brontë herself. And with due qualification, this has been my experience also.

The " more-so," or rather the less-so, of humour in dream is another matter. There it inclines to the primitive, as may also one's sense of *politesse* and propriety. Once, idling in dream at the marble counter of a railway refreshment room, I asked a charming barmaid if she thought a glass of *stout* would make me *bitter;* and was so much amused by this little Shakespearianism that I not only woke myself with my own laughter, but continued to laugh in the dark for minutes together. Still, fastidiousness is not yet one of the cardinal virtues. The prig, the prude, and the precious had best keep awake; they must be more at ease in the daytime. Still, if, when they slumber, they dream, they probably enjoy the fare provided, whether coarse, vulgar, shocking, or too delicious. The vigilant Censor himself, too, may be caught napping — as the poets of love-dreams attest; and kisses in dreams, even though feigned by fancy, need not be hopeless. And what if waking re-admits us only to Love's wilderness? Dream will still have shed its manna; and Eros, however small his mercies may be, favours, as do all children, a really thankful heart.

For my own part, I have spent in sleep a far more active and adventurous existence than has been my outward lot in the waking day. What that may foreshadow who can say? The fortunate perhaps may follow the liveliest of careers in both. But the precise relation between the life of the imagination and that in the external world is obscure. My dream-life has assuredly not been roses, roses all the way, although it has had a generous share of myrtle. And, taking the bad with the good, and not merely by reason of a native physical indolence, one may delight in what sleep has to bestow, and set out for it, night after night, as if to keep an assignation with a friend — a second self less easy of access than when earth's sun is in the sky: David and Jonathan.

Far less eagerly and willingly, with what impatience and contempt, must my dreaming self, when the cumbrous and uncouth phlegmatic body in which he is confined begins to stir, welcome my awakening. Would he not much prefer to seal for good the leaden lids? In heaven, we are told, there shall be no giving in marriage; and, in one of the supreme revelations of the riches of the Unconscious, it is said that there shall be no more sea. Yet there might still be sleep. If sleep, then perhaps dream; and this beyond any the mere thought of which set Hamlet temporizing, and appalled Claudio.

CUI BONO

But apart from any pleasure, counsel, warning, or foreknowledge of the future that dreams may bestow, to what purpose may we dream? Is any other advantage to be derived from these scenic self-communings, these fugitive scraps of farce, comedy, tragedy, and melodrama presented night after night, with how few repetitions, in the little playhouse (called the *Globe*) of which the dreamer is, it would *seem*, the sole lessee, playwright, stage manager and audience? Why sleep, and yet thus actively and extravagantly come awake within?

One's first temptation is to make light of dreaming because it is so common. The frequently repeated in life becomes the familiar; and the familiar at length loses for us its strangeness and its mystery. And so with dreams. If there were only one dream on record, and that were vouched for even by Aristotle or by Dr. Johnson, who would give it an absolute credence? Who would not rather dismiss it as a piece of pure hallucination? — as in a fashion indeed dream is. Even Huxley's Centaur, galloping in full career down Piccadilly, would be a less astonishing phenomenon. Every dream, indeed, since it is an emanation solely from sleep, is not only the dreamer's private property, but is also completely beyond positive proof.

Addison quotes a saying which, he says, he was " infinitely pleased with, and which Plutarch ascribed to Heraclitus, ' that all men whilst they are awake are in one common world; but that each of them, when he is asleep, is in a world of his own.' " But again, of what intrinsic use and import is this little private " world of one's own " by comparison with that of the waking day? — itself consisting of hours as richly shot through with the changing colours of vaguely or clearly perceived dream-stuff as is a long-buried scrap of iridescent glass dug up out of the ground. "How I got home," wrote Stopford Brooke in his Diary of 1899, " I do not know, I was East of the Sun, West of the Moon. Or like Gregory, I dreamed of myself in a dream, and told the dream, which was mine, as if it were another person's of whom I dreamed. Indeed, what is life when thinking of the past, but dreaming of a dream dreamt by another who seems sometimes to be oneself?" Without foolishly pitting dream-life against waking-life, we find this one thing in common between them: each is a *kind* of experience.

Expert and amateur alike, we differ widely in our appreciation of both; and especially of the former. Dreams range in interest from zero to the infinite. The over-sharp and the too-clever (it may be hoped) may be the prey of mere fatuities, and even the imaginative may dream very seldom. Nowadays, as in science, so in relation to art, with its surrealism, dreams are regarded with a rather arid solemnity. They are treated as exotics. Yet both in sleep and in the common converse of the usual day, the difficulty is not to decoy the Unconscious into activity, but to regulate it or to keep it out.

Nevertheless, the dreamer has fallen from his high estate. In the ancient religions and civilisations, he was at least held in respect; the prophetic dreamer in veneration. In the courts of the Pharaohs, the art (and craft) of divination was the duty, and at times the dangerous privilege, not of one functionary but of many. They failed to satisfy their lord and master at their own peril. The Hebrews were forbidden to consult the soothsayer, but not the divinely appointed interpreter. Nebuchadnezzar's magicians, astrologers and sorcerers, "the wise men of Babylon," were commanded on pain of being "cut to pieces" not only to interpret the tyrant's dream, but seeing that "the thing" had "gone from him," to retrieve the dream itself. It was a "rare thing" indeed that the King required; yet "was the secret revealed unto Daniel in a night vision." History is almost as rich in dreams as it is in legend and folk tale; and King Nebuchadnezzar is only one

[99]

of many monarchs who, like the saints and heroes, have not merely dreamed dreams, but have accepted if not welcomed them as inspirations, omens and predictions. Alexander the Great, Augustus, Nero, Charlemagne, William Rufus, Abraham Lincoln, St. Paul, St. Jerome, who in a dream was accused of being " not Christian but Ciceronian," St. Francis, Veronica, Joan of Arc — the available record fills many pages of Miss Katherine Craig's study, *The Fabric of Dreams*.

In these days, the diviner would probably combine his office with that of Psychologist to the Crown, rather than, as might be assumed, with that of the Poet Laureate. Even at that, he would risk being dismissed, not as God's, but as the Court Fool. " Here comes this dreamer " is still the ironic jibe of the practical man. Even much of Freud, and of his successors, will remain caviare no less, in one sense, to the gourmet than, in another, to the general. But most of us are as little likely to sacrifice our dreams on the altar of psychology as we are to give up laughing when philosophy has finally disposed of the problem of humour.

> The learn'd is happy nature to explore,
> The fool is happy that he knows no more.

But even if this nightly traffic and merchandise — London's millions of humanity stretched mute on their midnight mattresses and dreaming like one — is of small value in the marketplace, and is laughed to scorn in *Vanity Fair;* even if what thus so swiftly comes and goes be incomparably less important than life's daily duties, thoughts and actions, can it be that so perpetual a deposit is of *no* further use, no service, is nothing more precious than the meteoric dust which feeds the foraminiferous ooze of the oceans?

POETRY

Any reassurance the dreamer here may need will at least be found in abundance not only in all the arts of all the ages, from China to Peru; not only in the works of all men of genius;

but also in the testimony of the mystics. True, in this " those
who speak do not know, those who know do not speak." But,
as Professor Saurat says, " The mystic is the dreamer who
knows that he dreams, and can make the effort, and awaken.
The thinker is the dreamer who does not realise that he is
dreaming, and does not know how to make the effort towards
waking. . . . At some very rare moments in dreams . . . one
knows. And thus, at some very rare moments of his life, the
mystic knows." Moreover, every dream worthy of the name is
itself a creation, an anonymous work of art, and may also be
tinged with the poetic.

Like Mathematics, like Contemplation, like " Nonsense,"
Dream occupies a mental sphere of its own; and the debt
owed to it by poetry, by all imaginative literature, is beyond
computation. A poem may reveal its influence in essence or
in tincture; and even Satire is not invariably free from that
influence. In general, the Elizabethan poets made use of
dream — as they used everything else — when and as they
needed it. The poets of the eighteenth century, submitting
poetry to reason, to invention and to wit, owed far less to
dreaming; the Romantic Revival, perhaps too much.

Fiction, too, no less than poetry differs widely in the degree
in which the elements of dream have affected its conception
and making. In general, little with the French, much with
the Russian. And so with individual novelists, as also with
their outlook on life. An *imagined* " character " makes his
appearance in consciousness no less of his own volition as it
were and no less complete than any similar apparition made
manifest in a dream.

But it was the " authour that hight Macrobes " who, with
his prose commentary on the Dream of Scipio which he had
borrowed from Cicero, set a literary fashion in the fourth
century which has never since ceased to flower — that of
ascribing a story to a dream. From the limpid simplicity and
beauty of *Pearl*; from the workaday directness of *Piers Plow-
man*, by way of *The King's Quair* and *The Golden Targe*, to
Spenser, and on to Byron, Burns and Tennyson, the tale in

verse or allegory or lyric declaring itself to be a dream is so usual a device in English poetry that we question neither its motive nor its justification.

As a literary device, it may be simply what its frame is to a picture; and, as such, is best left intact when the tale is done. But just as a glimpse of what is at least intended to be a poem at once vaguely invokes in our minds all that we associate with poetry, whatever our care for it may be; so when any particular poem has for theme either an actual or a fictitious dream we associate it with all that we think and feel in regard to dreaming. Dream-life becomes its criterion. Anything dream-like may happen in a dream; everything that happens in a dream is dream-like — although the wall between the dream and actuality frequently pares very thin. Any poem of this device, then, appeals at once to the dream-self of its reader, and, that done, *like* dream, it may indulge his credulity in respect to any wonder, marvel, mystery, fantasy or extravagance appropriate to the region of sleep.

The poet, of course, is commonly dismissed as a " mere " dreamer, an owl blinking in life's noonday. Nevertheless, of the English poets conspicuous for their good sense, practical energy, knowledge and conduct of affairs, and for their concern and delight in humanity, Chaucer and William Morris are pre-eminent; and again and again they enshrine in a "dream" these very characteristics — and much else. Wordsworth, whom Blake accused of confusing the facts of Vegetable Nature with the Truths of the Imagination, not only related in verse veridical dreams of a singular precision and gravity, but his Nature herself is of his own reverie-like conception.

> Almost, suspended, we are laid asleep
> In body and become a living soul. . . .

Even " The Leech-Gatherer," " Lucy," and " The Solitary Reaper " are all but as dream-like in *effect*, the creation of " the Mind's internal heaven," as, through " the vapours of Lothbury," was poor Susan's " vision of trees."

George Crabbe, apart from the satirists one of the few habitual " realists " in English poetry, showed in his *World of Dreams* and elsewhere how prolific a dreamer he was. As A E says, " The realists who think they are closer to truth are no less depicting a world created by imagination, though it is begotten by dark desires. The universe itself was nothing but Imagination ceaselessly creative. The Imagination and Will which uphold it are in us also, so that we can make our own world and transfigure it out of the glory still within us." Realism itself, indeed, as in many of Crabbe's landscapes, may be faintly suffused with a dream atmosphere — an atmosphere which, although it is immeasurably deeper and subtler in the one than in the other, is yet as pervasive in the *Divine Comedy* as it is in the *Pilgrim's Progress*. Where else, but in dream, are we likely to stray amid the dismal terrors of the *Inferno* — through the Dark Wood, across the Dark Plain; where else breathe the gloomy and malignant air wherein Paolo and Francesca share their eternal felicity and misery? So too such phrases as " the Wilderness of this World " and " the City of Destruction " invoke in the mind memories not of actuality but of an evilly haunted sleep.

Nor is it the least intellectual of the poets who have paid dreams the highest tribute — Coventry Patmore and Alice Meynell, for instance. As for the visionaries, Vaughan, Traherne, Blake, Gerard Hopkins, their poems veil the very world in which they strayed for the time being with the pure loveliness and the remoteness of a dream. Coleridge owed far more to his dreams than to the " anodyne " that may have clouded as well as coloured them; and where but in the region of dreams is Keats's knight-at-arms palely wandering? When he re-wrote his *Hyperion*, he gave that also the semblance of a dream; and Shelley's poetry lavishes almost equally the enchantments of air and sky and water, and, again, of dream.

Indeed, even if no poem had ever assumed this disguise, if no English poet had ever given thanks to heaven and his language that *dream, beam, gleam, seem* and *stream* make convenient rhymes, poetry would still be no less closely linked

with that condition of the senses and sensibilities in which
sleep may confide into waking our most secret concerns. In
poetry life itself, and everything in nature which the desire
of the mind and the pining of the heart most covet and delight in, are continually being compared with what is after
their own pattern and quality in dream. And how seldom to
dream's disadvantage! If any flattery is intended, then it is
actuality that preens itself in dream's looking-glass, rather
than contrariwise. That all beauty in this world is doomed to
be transient, and so resembles dream, is no intrinsic blame
to either. And what more exquisite tribute could be paid to
an adored mistress, whether as herself or her own phantom,
than Donne's " Therefore thou wakd'st me wisely; yet My
dream thou brok'st not, but continued'st it "?

So also with the wrong side of the patchwork. With the
dreams of the " hot and dry brain," and the " body's mis-
chiefs," which in sleep as in waking may " proceed from the
soul "; the dreams of the melancholy and of the obsessed;
dreams troubleful, ominous, unnatural, violent, terrifying; the
incubus, the appalling figments of fever, of drugs, and delirium. The vilest insult we can attach to any earthly experience is the accusation that it resembled a nightmare.[11] Here
the poets and Everyman are at one.

Sleep, then, triumphs in both extremes: radiance and peace
and loveliness; horror and outer gloom. But some poets, un-

[11] Imagine, for example, a dream in which every detail was precisely similar
to its twin experience in waking life — a dead-alive tea-party, let us say, or a
visit to the dentist, or a fashionable wedding, or a lifeless Play. Could anything
be more alien to the witchery of sleep? The little missing — the Master's twitch
at his puppets' strings, the tinge of excess, the twist of the kaleidoscope, that
queer glaze of the not quite real — and how much away. If, indeed, in our dull
and tedious hours we merely pretend to ourselves, " Why, this, of course, may
be a dream," then a peculiar and reviving transformation will at once follow.
For even Fancy, if she is quick and lively, can with memory's aid supply at least
something of that missing little. And so of Nightmare. The pulsating thud of the
wheels on the rails, the fusty atmosphere, the penned-in impassive human faces
in horizontal row, the flitting sides of that subterranean, claustrophobic, ratlike
gallery in a London Tube — all this may wear for the attentive traveller an uneasy
hint of nightmare. But let that subtle demon, Mara herself, insert a finger into
the pie — what then?

like Everyman, are apt to dwell on the " night-side of Nature "
and of human nature — an insistence that might be consol-
ingly dismissed as morbid if there were no truth in Imlac's
cautious, " Perhaps, if we speak with rigorous exactness, no
human mind is in its right state." And if not in waking,
assuredly not in dream. There are poems in this book, and a
host elsewhere, wherein the mere sound of the words, and
their cold and stagnant atmosphere, darken the mind and cast
a chill on the very spirit within us. As do the old books on
diabolism and witchcraft. They are vignettes of stricken
landscapes glimpsed in an eclipse of life's sun. Nor is Death,
as in his every spectral aspect he is depicted by Holbein, a
stranger to the poetic imagination. There his taper gleams
perpetually in an " outer room." He stands in wait at the
elbow of such poets as John Webster, Tourneur, Beddoes and
some of the old Scottish balladists as if one should have an
anatomy for a man-servant.

> Oh, bonnie, bonnie was her mouth,
>   And cherry were her cheeks;
> And clear, clear was her yellow hair,
>   Whereon the red bluid dreeps.

> Then with his spear he turned her o'er,
>   Oh, gin her face was wan!
> He said — " You are the first that e'er
>   I wished alive again."

" Cover her face: mine eyes dazzle, she died young " — dark
mind in darkest sorrow is here surveying a darkened beauty
that is dead indeed, seeing that sorrow and remorse, that
deadly nightshade which flourishes in the small hours, is powerless to retrieve the faintest whisper of forgiveness from out
of the past. Webster is reputed to have been a sexton by
trade. That, in any case, was the secret occupation of his
mind. Like Poe's, it as nearly neighboured a phantasmal
graveyard as the Yorkshire parsonage so wildly beloved by
Emily Brontë neighboured an actual one.

Referring to one of his cases, in his lectures on *Death and Sudden Death,* Brouardel declares: She was not dead, but like a candle the flame of which has been extinguished, though the wick continues to glow. The tissues of the hand were transparent to the light of the candle I held. No definite sounds of the heart; the eyelids moved in my presence. I kept her unburied until the following day. It is a statement of mere matter-of-fact, but how many pages of matter-of-fantasy it recalls in the old playwrights. These poets as continually frequented this disastrous no-man's-land, this frontier between the known and the only imaginable, as did the merchant adventurers of their era the frontiers of danger and romance. Mangan, Thomson, George Darley, Christina Rossetti, and, in his own peculiar kind, Richard Barham, poring " past midnight over his black-letter folios and his port " — theirs, too, is a limbo of treacherous twilight, or that Egyptian darkness which in nature, but less seldom in their writings, precedes the dawn. Their rhythms echo with " those cadences That breathe in night from the secretive ground " — the secretive ground of the spirit of man.

For moral or conventional reasons, we may regret that every creative work of the imagination had its seed in the " Unconscious," and that its flowers and fruit, like those in Aladdin's magical garden, owed their origin to a graft of the waking mind on the wild and ancient stock of dream. Human dignity would prefer to assume that what we think and do solely by conscious and rational effort, by an act of the will, is of a greater value and merit than anything else we achieve. Indeed, will and effort in this world's affairs — we know it to our cost — are of paramount importance. But that we should owe a debt past all computing to subliminal resources that we cannot even define! Well, our " gifts " are gifts; no faculty of mind or body is self-acquired; the self-made are only the self-adjusted or mal-adjusted; self-interest is not Self-interest; and genius seldom boasts. Nor, again, is it by an act of will or by the exercise of reason that we take pleasure in colour and form and pattern, an acorn, a rainbow, a tree in the wind, a dancer at rest; that we delight in beauty, welcome goodness, recognise truth, acquire ideals, choose our friends, or fall, and stay, in love? Or even, for that matter, see a joke? Can argument, however cogent, finally break us of any innate conviction and belief; that, for instance, in "the vision of the wholeness of life" which inspired T. E. Lawrence?

In a poem, we may demand "meaning": clear evidence of an intellectual aim and purport; and many fine poems have this in abundance. Yet a mere trace, and that perhaps prosaic when it is detached, is all that is needful. "Even," says A. E. Housman, "when poetry has a meaning, as it usually has, it may be inadvisable to draw it out." And so too, again, with dream. The more beautiful the beads or precious stones, the less attention we pay to the thread. Are our wild daisies any the less lovely when only very loosely woven into a chain? A poem's supreme significance, like that of a child or a bird or a loved one or a saint, is purely its own beautiful pregnant self. If music is the most perfect of the arts because it is the least diluted, and if poetry most closely approaches music when it is most poetic, when its sounds, that is, and the utterance of them, and when its rhythms rather than the words themselves, are its real if cryptic language, any other meaning, however valuable it may be, is only a secondary matter.[12]

Since language is acquired and is not innate, the intellect must supervise its use as a medium; but it cannot of itself originate poetry — any more than a craftsman originates the material in which he works. The mind is in the service of the imagination, not vice versa. So too, like Newton voyaging into strange seas of thought alone, the man of a poetic genius discovers his own ocean; he cannot create it. Nor is he wholly responsible for the scrawled chart in his pocket,

---

[12] None the less a piece of music, of equal merit *as* music, can hardly be so rich in the various imagery, thought and emotions it invokes as the briefest of lyrics may be, even if the lyric have only a minute fraction of "meaning." A poem, well spoken, again, is *itself* a most delicate music.

although, if he is to bring his pined-for cargo home, he must be master of his craft. Intent on a stuff as nebulous as that of dream, he must so record this inward vision that his refractory symbols, words, shall lull here, awaken there, any reader enchanted by them into listening. The sounds enshrine a curious and exquisite mimicry of the bodiless phantasmata that were occupying his solitude, that were his joy and his despair. Nor is his incentive a mere John-o'-Dreams lullaby, or a target easily detected or hit. Energy alone can reach that gold, given the archer and the arrows of desire.

"Men," says John Aubrey, "fall into an Ecstasy many ways . . . and Ecstasy is a kind of medium between sleeping and waking as sleep is a kind of middle state between life and death. Things seen in an Ecstasy are more certain than those we behold in dreams: they are much more clear, and far more evident." The effect of a fine poem resembles this ecstasy. The rainbow is on the water; there is a murmur of the deep; the mainland vaguely looms on the horizon; and from out of the green corners of the earth and the blue regions of the day the sirens are singing. If, as I have proved at the suggestion of a friend, Dr. Scott Williamson, if, when at rest we quietly contemplate an object but release our direct attention from it and let that attention stray instead hither-thither over what is to be discovered in motion in the field of vision, not only is the experience likely to be memorable, but, however wide awake the mind may then be, consciousness is apt to stray into a state of delighted abstraction. I recall at this moment a scene so watched — a pool of grey-blue water under an autumn sky and within sound of the sea; reeds, grass, solitude, silence; and a host of martins criss-crossing in their mazy flittings as if they were inscribing some ancient rune on the empty air. This remembrance has all the qualities of a rare dream. So with a poem. Consciousness, as we read, becomes a passive mirror of how wide a field of echo and solitude and beauty; and this also within sound of the Sea. An invocation has transported us, in both senses of the word. The body, as in sleep, is bidden

not to interrupt us, not to attract that attention without
which the workaday world ceases to exist. The poetic experience is an island of rapt realisation. We turn away, as
from the characters in a loved, and yet, at last, elusive face.
If we are interrupted, then the immediate memory of the
poem resembles in its own small fashion the shattered dream
of the Lord God that was the garden of Eden.

All lyrical poetry beats with the heart, tells not of things
coldly and calmly considered, but of things seen and felt in
a sudden clearness of the senses, and with a flame in the
thought. An insatiable delight in life haunts it, and the keen
mortal regret that stalks in life's shadow. It springs from a
height of living, however transitory, a tension of spirit, a
sense of wonder and mystery, a faith in all that is held most
dear, a hope and hunger for an unknown that transcends the
known. This can only be partially expressed in language,
and in glimpses — only in " a net of thoughtless delight,"
perhaps. How, indeed, does the commonplace and the obvious look, when the eye regarding it is haunted with passion or sorrow or despair?

Just, then, as the leopard or the lamb is one species of
living creature, and the hawk or the ox is another, so among
humans stands out this particular temperament. It shares
the life that is common to all men, but it possesses life in this
kind more acutely and abundantly, and it has the faculty of
communicating it. Why this is, and why it is the gift in particular of certain races, who can say? It reveals, past reason,
an unearthly rapture, a desire that will not perish in the
having, the vision of the immortal beyond change.

And in sharp contrast to these graces are weariness and
home-sickness, a vain longing, a craving for sleep and for
death. Yet even to the keenest home-sickness there is an
edge of rapture. Burdened with the complexity of the lives
we lead, fretting over appearances, netted in with anxieties
and apprehensions, half smothered in drifts of tepid thoughts
and tepid feelings, we may refuse what poetry has to give;
but under its influence serenity returns to the troubled mind,

the world crumbles, loveliness shines like flowers after rain, and the further reality is once more charged with mystery.

For this reason every imaginative poem, as we allow it to use us, itself resembles in its onset and in its effect the experience of dreaming. Only listen to a few such onsets: " Fly, envious Time, till thou run out thy race "; " Faire fall all good Tokens "; " Full fathom five thy father lies "; " Hide, Absolon, thy gilte tresses clere "; " Sweet *England's* pride is gone, *welladay! welladay!* "; " Leave me, O Love, which reachest but to dust "; " My Soul, there is a country Far beyond the stars "; " Of all chaste birds the Phoenix doth excel "; " O, what can ail thee, knight-at-arms, Alone and palely loitering? "; " Tyger, tyger, burning bright "; " Wake, all the dead! What ho! what ho! " Is it in *these* terms that our day-life presents itself? What effect on the gravest and sagest conversation, let alone a frivolous, would be the least explosive firework of this order? What kind of self is here self-communing? What order of listener lies in wait for incantations such as these?

A dream-self, surely; as well as a waking self. Just as it was a dream-self that kept the poet company in the conception and in the actual composition of his poem. " I can aver," declares Mr. Herbert Read in his *Collected Essays,* " that all the poetry I have written which I continue to regard as authentic poetry was written immediately, instantaneously, in a condition of trance." In widely differing degree this is true of all poetic experience. But a poem, however ethereal its content may be, has been packed in a material verbal basket, has been distilled into a transparent phial. Yet its symbols carry it as lightly and unobtrusively as a rose carries its dew, or an animal its nature. It therefore has a formal and finished loveliness which few dreams can achieve, but which even dreams may occasionally bestow. It is exquisitely at liberty in a cage of words which it is not only a joy to examine, but which is as necessary to all that it holds for our delight as the skin of a cherry is for the security of its stone.

THE BOURNE

And last, if a poet, greatest to least, is more frequently than are most of us in these remote parts, this night- and day-world of dream and of the visionary, what wonder if he is apt to be concerned with the last good-night on earth of all? Even if, like the moralist or the mystic, he can in this no more than give us pause?

Until his own turn comes, he cannot cross that bourne. And, alas, whether he be Chaucer, Marvell, Donne, Vaughan, Blake or Keats, we cannot conjure him back to bring us news of what lies beyond. The body, whether any reawakening come or not, lapses from decay into dust:

> And dreaming through the twilight
> That doth not rise or set,
> Haply I may remember
> And haply may forget.

That is all. Again and again we may ponder that enigmatic future, admit it to reverie, speculate on it, attempt to divine it. Our love weeps bitterly, emptily, at dread of its reiter-ated, Never more. We may hope; have faith and courage. Death, says Francis Bacon, is no such terrible enemy when a man hath so many attendants about him that can win the combat of him — revenge, honour, grief, pity, satiety, love itself. And yet, we may fear and tremble; and so become like old old children, when, outside the Nursery, waits the Dark. All this — of what must come and what may follow. But we do not *know*. And, as Christina Rossetti intimates, and how many poets have done likewise, we may die into a state of dreaming. However that may be, any such state would surely resemble more closely the state of dreaming than that of the life of our earthly day.

" What place have you been to, O mind? " says Mr. Monk Gibbon in " He Questions his Mind after Sleep," " and from what country are you returned, absent now these seven hours or more, it may be? Tell me all, for it is not right that those who are comrades until sundown should be strangers then. How many times have I questioned you and you say nothing, or put me off with some half-told or foolish tale? Those seven hours have been to me a moment, less than a moment, for even a moment is aware that it has been. . . . Is it fair that you should travel and leave no tidings, that you should journey and bring no news? . . . Tell your secret, Mind, for if I knew where you had been so often, I might know the place to which you one day go."

When this "Mind" arrives at that place, life itself, perhaps, as so many young children have surmised, will prove to have been in the nature of a dream, and death, of an awakening. "How," enquires Calderon, concerning our "ghostly lives,"

> How if our waking life, like that of sleep,
> Be all a dream in that eternal life
> To which we wake not till we sleep in death?

The childish surmise may itself have originated in the vague recollection of a previous life, before the soul came to "this place," let alone began to "understand" it. But if it be the dreaming, the half-hidden one within us that then survives, rather than the waking self — which is continually burdened with a body, however rich its rewards may be; is continually assailed by all that feeds the senses; and busied about so many thoughts, actions, obligations, distractions that are in conflict with deeper and more enduring concerns — what account of his earthly pilgrimage will the *waker* then give? Will it resemble poor Mandrake's in *Death's Jest Book*, who has been falsely persuaded of his own demise? —

"Well, what is, is, and what is not, is not; and I am not what I was — for I am what I was not; I am no more I, for I am no more: I am no matter, being out of all trouble, and nobody at all, but poor Mandrake's pure essence. . . . Marry, I must either have been very sound asleep when I died, or else I died by mistake, for I am sure I never intended it: or else this being dead is a quite insignificant habit when one's used to it: 'tis much easier than being alive. . . ."

Or shall we, in the light and silence of morning, in a
tongue more direct and intimate than any words can be,
find ourselves gaily or gravely relating life's strange engrossing tragi-comedy? And with what verve, amusement, astonishment, vanity and wearisome iteration, perhaps. But to
whom? Instead, what might then chiefly engage ourselves
and our listener might be our dream-self and our dream-life;
now, at long last, made coherent and complete. Alice, like
Heinrich Heine before her, was initiated into this little mystery:

"'Come and look at him!' the brothers cried, and they
each took one of Alice's hands, and led her up to where the
king was sleeping. . . .

"'He's dreaming now,' said Tweedledee: 'and what do
you think he's dreaming about?'

"Alice said, 'Nobody can guess that.'

"'Why, about *you!*' Tweedledee exclaimed, clapping his
hands triumphantly. 'And if he left off dreaming about you,
where do you suppose you'd be?'"

And Mr. Redwood Anderson in his poem entitled "The
World Dream": —

> . . . Without me and my kind
> how could his world have being?
> that multiply his seeing;
> A myriad eyes were blind
> mute were a myriad tongues
> and deaf a myriad ears
> through which he sings and hears
> his choric Zion-songs. . . .
>
> All are his instruments,
> my hieroglyphs of dream:
> Sound echoing to what sense
> where golden eagles scream?
> what crystal simile
> flashes the fish in sea?

and where red lions roar
what burning metaphor?

In the sun's zenithed glory,
stars, and the moon's mild fire,
he writes in me the story
of his unknown desire;
and when my love enraptured
follows the meteor's flame
his thought is almost captured
and christened with man's name.

The Dream goes on for ever
— only the dreamers die —
past reason's last endeavour,
belief's last ecstasy. . . .

Genius — in spite of its insight and energy no more capable of explaining its origin than a flower its own beauty — may so contemplate what we call the Unconscious. And *this* personality? — of what is that in contemplation? But poor man clings passionately to his own individuality, and fears heights and depths beyond his vision's scope. He may dread solitude and strangeness; and has always been easily homesick.

The one dark feature of every love-dream in this book is that only a phantom shared it with the dreamer, albeit it was the phantom of the loved one herself. The tragic feature of the death-dream, as I see it, is that we each one of us have to face that last journey alone. Sad that dawn may be, silent and forbidding the wharf, miscellaneous the company, even if it be solely one's own, and cold the obol clutched in the palm. How welcome then would be the company even of one friend.

PART TWO

Behold, this Dreamer!

Now it is and now it nis,
Thus passeth this world away.

A dream, too, is from Zeus.

Day-Dreaming

My eyes make pictures, when they are shut . . .

Was it a vision, or a waking dream?
Fled is that music: — do I wake or sleep?

Day-Dreaming

IN THE WOODS

And then, as if I sweetly dream'd,
I half-remember'd how it seem'd
When I, too, was a little child
About the wild woods roving wild.
Pure breezes from the far-off height
Melted the blindness from my sight,
Until, with rapture, grief, and awe,
I saw again as then I saw.
As then I saw, I saw again
The harvest-waggon in the lane,
With high-hung tokens of its pride
Left in the elms on either side;
The daisies coming out at dawn
In constellations on the lawn;
The glory of the daffodil;
The three black windmills on the hill,
Whose magic arms, flung wildly by,
Sent magic shadows o'er the rye . . .
And, as to men's retreating eyes,
Beyond high mountains higher rise,
Still farther back there shone to me
The dazzling dusk of infancy.
Thither I look'd, as, sick of night,
The Alpine shepherd looks to the height,

And does not see the day, 'tis true,
But sees the rosy tops that do . . .
Ah, happy hours, 'tis something yet
Not to forget that I forget!

COVENTRY PATMORE

William Blake seems to have been subject to visions all his life. When only four years old, he saw God's face at the window of his room, and screamed with fear. A few years later, he was beaten for saying that he had found the prophet Ezekiel sitting in the fields near his home. On another occasion, he beheld a tree filled with angels, who sang and waved their glittering wings in the branches. And, at fourteen, he refused to be apprenticed to the engraver Ryland, on the ground that the man looked as if he would live to be hanged — as, indeed, some years later, he was. Thinking and reading made the visions more frequent. After the death of his brother Robert, he saw his spirit flying away and " clapping its hands for joy." And it was Robert's spirit also which showed him — this time in a dream — the process by which his books were to be engraved and printed. And once he saw a ghost, a human figure covered with metallic scales, standing at the top of a staircase, and fled terrified from the house. . . ."

P. BERGER, translated by Daniel H. Connor

Most sweet it is with unuplifted eyes
To pace the ground, if path be there or none,
While a fair region round the traveller lies
Which he forbears again to look upon;
Pleased rather with some soft ideal scene,
The work of Fancy, or some happy tone
Of meditation, slipping in between
The beauty coming and the beauty gone. . . .

WILLIAM WORDSWORTH

On a poet's lips I slept
Dreaming like a love-adept
In the sound his breathing kept;
Nor seeks nor finds he mortal blisses,
But feeds on the aëreal kisses
Of shapes that haunt thought's wildernesses.
He will watch from dawn till gloom
The lake-reflected sun illume
The yellow bees in the ivy-bloom,
Nor heed nor see, what things they be;
But from these create he can
Forms more real than living man. . . .

PERCY BYSSHE SHELLEY

MOWING

There was never a sound beside the wood but one,
And that was my long scythe whispering to the ground.
What was it it whispered? I knew not well myself;
Perhaps it was something about the heat of the sun,
Something, perhaps, about the lack of sound —
And that was why it whispered and did not speak.
It was no dream of the gift of idle hours,
Or easy gold at the hand of fay or elf:
Anything more than the truth would have seemed too weak
To the earnest love that laid the swale in rows,
Not without feeble-pointed spikes of flowers
(Pale orchises), and scared a bright green snake.
The fact is the sweetest dream that labor knows.
My long scythe whispered and left the hay to make.

ROBERT FROST

THE NEW HOUSE

Now first, as I shut the door,
  I was alone
In the new house; and the wind
  Began to moan.

Old at once was the house,
  And I was old;
My ears were teased with the dread
  Of what was foretold,

Nights of storm, days of mist, without end;
  Sad days when the sun
Shone in vain: old griefs and griefs
  Not yet begun.

All was foretold me; naught
  Could I foresee;
But I learnt how the wind would sound
  After these things should be.

EDWARD THOMAS

THE PHANTOM HORSEWOMAN

Queer are the ways of a man I know:
  He comes and stands
  In a careworn craze,
  And looks at the sands
  And the seaward haze
  With moveless hands
  And face and gaze,
  Then turns to go . . .
And what does he see when he gazes so?

They say he sees as an instant thing
    More clear than to-day,
    A sweet soft scene
    That once was in play
    By that briny green;
    Yes, notes alway
    Warm, real, and keen,
    What his back years bring —
A phantom of his own figuring.

Of this vision of his they might say more:
    Not only there
    Does he see this sight,
    But everywhere
    In his brain — day, night,
    As if on the air
    It were drawn rose bright —
    Yea, far from that shore
Does he carry this vision of heretofore:

A ghost-girl-rider. And though, toil-tried,
    He withers daily,
    Time touches her not,
    But she still rides gaily
    In his rapt thought
    On that shagged and shaly
    Atlantic spot,
    And as when first eyed
Draws rein and sings to the swing of the tide.

THOMAS HARDY

A DREAM WITHIN A DREAM

    Take this kiss upon the brow!
    And, in parting from you now,
    Thus much let me avow —

You are not wrong, who deem
That my days have been a dream;
Yet if hope has flown away
In a night, or in a day,
In a vision, or in none,
Is it therefore the less *gone?*
All that we see or seem
Is but a dream within a dream.

I stand amid the roar
Of a surf-tormented shore,
And I hold within my hand
Grains of the golden sand —
How few! yet how they creep
Through my fingers to the deep,
While I weep — while I weep!
O God! can I not grasp
Them with a tighter clasp?
O God! can I not save
One from the pitiless wave?
Is *all* that we see or seem
But a dream within a dream?

Edgar Allan Poe

CASTLES IN THE AIR

My thoughts by night are often filled
  With visions false as fair:
For in the Past alone I build
  My castles in the air.

I dwell not now on what may be.
  Night shadows o'er the scene.
But still my fancy wanders free
  Through that which might have been.

Thomas Love Peacock

RESIGNATION

Why, why repine, my pensive friend,
    At pleasures slipt away?
Some the stern Fates will never lend,
    And all refuse to stay.

I see the rainbow in the sky,
    The dew upon the grass,
I see them, and I ask not why
    They glimmer or they pass.

With folded arms I linger not
    To call them back; 'twere vain;
In this, or in some other spot,
    I know they'll shine again.

WALTER SAVAGE LANDOR

FANCIES

Fancies are but streams
    Of vain pleasure;
They who by their dreams
    True joys measure,
Feasting, starve; laughing, weep;
Playing, smart; whilst in sleep
    Fools, with shadows smiling,
      Wake and find
      Hopes like wind,
    Idle hopes, beguiling.
Thoughts fly away; Time hath passed them;
Wake now, awake! see and taste them!

JOHN FORD(?)

It is not much of life that is spent in close attention to any important duty. Many hours of every day are suffered to fly away without any traces left upon the intellects. We suffer phantoms to rise up before us, and amuse ourselves with the dance of airy images, which, after a time, we dismiss for ever, and know not how we have been busied.

Many have no happier moments than those that they pass in solitude, abandoned to their own imagination. . . .

It is easy in these semi-slumbers to collect all the possibilities of happiness, to alter the course of the sun, to bring back the past, and anticipate the future, to unite all the beauties of all seasons, and all the blessings of all climates, to receive and bestow felicity, and forget that misery is the lot of man. All this is a voluntary dream, a temporary recession from the realities of life to airy fictions; an habitual subjection of reason to fancy.

Others are afraid to be alone, and amuse themselves by a perpetual succession of companions: but the difference is not great; in solitude we have our dreams to ourselves, and in company we agree to dream in concert. The end sought in both is forgetfulness of ourselves.

SAMUEL JOHNSON

Talking of constitutional melancholy, Dr. Johnson observed, "A man, so afflicted, Sir, must divert distressing thoughts, and not combat with them." BOSWELL: "May he not think them down, Sir?" JOHNSON: "No, Sir. To attempt to *think them down* is madness. He should have a lamp constantly burning in his bedchamber during the night, and if wakefully disturbed, take a book and read and compose himself to rest. To have the management of the mind is a great art, and it may be attained in a considerable degree by experience and habitual exercise." BOSWELL: "Should not he provide amusement for himself? Would it not, for instance, be right for him to take a course of chemistry?" JOHNSON:

"Let him take a course of chemistry or a course of rope-dancing, or a course of anything to which he is inclined at the time. Let him contrive to have as many retreats for his mind as he can, as many things to which it can fly from itself. . . ."

JAMES BOSWELL

THE WISH

Well then; I now do plainly see
This busy world and I shall ne'er agree.
The very honey of all earthly joy
Does, of all meats, the soonest cloy;
 And they, methinks, deserve my pity
Who for it can endure the stings,
The crowd, and buzz, and murmurings
 Of this great hive, the city.

Ah yet, ere I descend to the grave,
May I a small house and large garden have;
And a few friends, and many books, both true,
Both wise, and both delightful too!
 And since love ne'er will from me flee,
A mistress moderately fair,
And good as guardian angels are,
 Only beloved, and loving me!

O fountains! when in you shall I
Myself eased of unpeaceful thoughts espy?
O fields! O woods! when, when shall I be made
The happy tenant of your shade?
 Here's the spring-head of pleasure's flood;
Here's wealthy Nature's treasury,
Where all the riches lie that she
 Has coined and stamped for good.

Pride and ambition here
Only in far-fetched metaphors appear;
Here nought but winds can hurtful murmurs scatter,
And nought but echo flatter.
    The gods, when they descended, hither
From heaven did always choose their way;
And therefore we may boldly say
    That 'tis the way too thither.

How happy here should I
And one dear She live, and embracing die!
She who is all the world, and can exclude
In deserts solitude.
    I should have then this only fear:
Lest men, when they my pleasures see,
Should hither throng to live like me,
    And so make a city here.

ABRAHAM COWLEY

. . . Men seek out retreats for themselves, cottages in the country, lonely seashores and mountains. Thou too art disposed to hanker greatly after such things: and yet all this is the very commonest stupidity; for it is in thy power, whenever thou wilt, to retire into thyself: and nowhere is there any place whereto a man may retire quieter and more free from politics than his own soul; above all if he have within him thoughts such as he need only regard attentively to be at perfect ease: and that ease is nothing else than a well-ordered mind. Constantly then use this retreat, and renew thyself therein: and be thy principles brief and elementary, which, as soon as ever thou recur to them, will suffice to wash thy soul entirely clean, and send thee back without vexation to whatsoe'er awaiteth thee.

MARCUS AURELIUS, translated by Robert Bridges

Voluntary solitariness is that which is familiar with melancholy, and gently brings on like a syren, a shoeing-horn, or some sphinx to this irrevocable gulf. . . . Most pleasant it is at first, to such as are melancholy given, to lie in bed whole days, and keep their chambers, to walk alone in some solitary grove, betwixt wood and water, by a brook side, to meditate upon some delightsome and pleasant subject, which shall affect them most; *amabilis insania, et mentis gratissimus error:* a most incomparable delight it is so to melancholize, and build castles in the air, to go smiling to themselves, acting an infinite variety of parts, which they suppose and strongly imagine they represent, or that they see acted or done. . . . So delightsome these toys are at first, they could spend whole days and nights without sleep, even whole years alone in such contemplations, and fantastical meditations, which are like unto dreams, and they will hardly be drawn from them, or willingly interrupt, so pleasant their vain conceits are, that they hinder their ordinary tasks and necessary business, they cannot address themselves to them, or almost to any study or employment, these fantastical and bewitching thoughts so covertly, so feelingly, so urgently, so continually set upon, creep in, insinuate, possess, overcome, distract, and detain them, they cannot, I say, go about their more necessary business, stave off or extricate themselves, but are ever musing, melancholizing, and carried along . . . winding and unwinding themselves, as so many clocks, and still pleasing their humours, until at last the scene is turned upon a sudden, by some bad object, and they being now habituated to such vain meditations and solitary places, can endure no company, can ruminate of nothing but harsh and distasteful subjects. Fear, sorrow, suspicion, *subrusticus pudor,* discontent, cares, and weariness of life surprise them in a moment, and they can think of nothing else, continually suspecting, no sooner are their eyes open, but this infernal plague of melancholy seizeth on them, and terrifies their souls. . . .

ROBERT BURTON

The instances of abstraction are so numerous, that a volume might easily be filled with them. The following . . . is a case of one of the most profound and clear-headed philosophical thinkers, and one of the most amiable of men, becoming so completely absorbed in his own reflections, as to lose the perception of external things, and almost that of his own identity and existence. There are few that have paid any attention to the finance of this country, but must have heard of Dr. Robert Hamilton's "Essay on the National Debt," which fell upon the Houses of Parliament like a bombshell, or, rather, which rose and illuminated their darkness like an orient sun. There are other writings of his in which one knows not which most to admire — the profound and accurate science, the beautiful arrangement, or the clear expression. Yet, in public, the man was a shadow; pulled off his hat to his own wife in the streets, and apologised for not having the pleasure of her acquaintance; went to his classes in the college on the dark mornings, with one of her white stockings on the one leg, and one of his own black ones on the other; often spent the whole time of the meeting in moving from the table the hats of the students, which they as constantly returned; sometimes invited them to call on him, and then fined them for coming to insult him. He would run against a cow in the road, turn around, beg her pardon, "Madam," and hope she was not hurt. At other times he would run against posts, and chide them for not getting out of his way; and yet his conversation at the same time, if any body happened to be with him, was perfect logic and perfect music. Were it not that there may be a little poetic license in Aberdeen story-telling, a volume might be filled with anecdotes of this amiable and excellent man, all tending to prove how wide the distinction is between first-rate thought and that merely animal use of the organs of sense which prevents ungifted mortals from walking into wells. . . .

ROBERT MACNISH

MELANCHOLY

Stretched on a mouldered Abbey's broadest wall,
    Where ruining ivies propped the ruins steep —
Her folded arms wrapping her tattered pall,
    Had Melancholy mused herself to sleep.
    The fern was pressed beneath her hair,
    The dark green Adder's Tongue was there;
And still as passed the flagging sea-gale weak,
The long lank leaf bowed fluttering o'er her cheek.
    The pallid cheek was flushed: her eager look
Beamed eloquent in slumber! Inly wrought,
    Imperfect sounds her moving lips forsook,
And her bent forehead worked with troubled thought.
    Strange was the dream. . . .

Samuel Taylor Coleridge

. . . She dwells with Beauty — Beauty that must die;
    And Joy, whose hand is ever at his lips
Bidding adieu; and aching Pleasure nigh,
    Turning to Poison while the bee-mouth sips:
Ay, in the very temple of delight
    Veiled Melancholy has her sovran shrine,
        Though seen of none save him whose strenuous
            tongue
Can burst Joy's grape against his palate fine;
    His soul shall taste the sadness of her might,
    And be among her cloudy trophies hung.

John Keats,
from " Ode on Melancholy "

COWPER AT OLNEY

In this green valley where the Ouse
Is looped in many a silver pool,
Seeking God's mercy and his muse
Went Cowper sorrowful.

Like the pale gleam of wintry sun
His genius lit the obscure place,
Where, battling with despair, lived one
Of melancholy's race.

By quiet waters, by green fields
In winter sweet as summer hay,
By hedgerows where the chaffinch builds
He went his brooding way.

And not a berry or a leaf,
Or stirring bough or fragrant wind,
But, in its moment, soothed the grief
Of his tormented mind.

And since, like the belovèd sheep
Of David's shepherd, he was led
By streams and pastures quiet as sleep —
Was he not comforted?

SYLVIA LYND

THE MOUNTAINS

The days have closed behind my back
Since I came into these hills.
Now memory is a single field
One peasant tills and tills.

So far away, if I should turn
    I know I could not find
That place again. These mountains make
    The backward gaze half-blind,

Yet sharp my sight till it can catch
    The ranges rising clear
Far in futurity's high-walled land;
    But I am rooted here.

And do not know where lies my way,
    Backward or forward. If I could
I'd leap Time's bound or turn and hide
    From Time in my ancestral wood.

Double delusion! Here I'm held
    By the mystery of the rock,
Must watch in a perpetual dream
    The horizon's gates unlock and lock,

See on the harvest fields of Time
    The mountains heaped like sheaves,
And the valleys opening out
    Like a volume's turning leaves,

Dreaming of a peak whose height
    Will show me every hill,
A single mountain on whose side
    Life blooms for ever and is still.

EDWIN MUIR

Hence, all you vain delights,
As short as are the nights
    Wherein you spend your folly!
There's nought in this life sweet,
If man were wise to see't,
    But only melancholy,
    O sweetest melancholy!

Welcome, folded arms, and fixèd eyes,
A sight that piercing mortifies,
A look that's fastened to the ground,
A tongue chained up without a sound!

Fountain-heads, and pathless groves,
Places which pale passion loves;
Moonlight walks, when all the fowls
Are warmly housed, save bats and owls;
   A midnight bell, a parting groan,
   These are the sounds we feed upon;
Then stretch our bones in a still gloomy valley,
Nothing's so dainty sweet as lovely melancholy.

JOHN FLETCHER

Peace, muttering thoughts, and do not grudge to keep
   Within the walls of your own breast:
Who cannot on his own bed sweetly sleep
   Can on another's hardly rest.

Gad not abroad at every quest and call
   Of an unstrainèd hope, or passion:
To court each place and fortune that doth fall,
   Is wantonness in contemplation.

Mark how the fire in flint doth quiet lie,
   Content and warm to itself alone;
But when it would appear to other's eye,
   Without a knock it never shone.

Then, peace, discoursing soul, plough thine own ground;
   Do not thy self or friends importune;
He that, by seeking, once himself hath found,
   Hath ever found a fortune.

OF A CONTENTED MIND

When all is done and said, in the end thus shall you find,
He most of all doth bathe in bliss that hath a quiet mind:
And, clear from worldly cares, to deem can be content
The sweetest time in all his life in thinking to be spent.

The body subject is to fickle fortune's power,
And to a million of mishaps is casual every hour:
And death in time doth change it to a clod of clay;
Whenas the mind, which is divine, runs never to decay.

Companion none is like unto the mind alone;
For many have been harmed by speech; through thinking, few
  or none. . . .

THOMAS, LORD VAUX

TO HIS READER

. . . Wouldst thou divert thyself from Melancholy?
Wouldst thou be pleasant, yet be far from folly?
Wouldst thou read Riddles, and their Explanation?
Or else be drownèd in thy Contemplation?
Dost thou love picking meat? Or wouldst thou see
A man i' the Clouds, and hear him speak to thee?
Wouldst thou be in a Dream, and yet not sleep?
Or wouldst thou in a moment laugh, and weep?
Wouldest thou lose thyself and catch no harm,
And find thyself again without a charm?
Wouldst read thyself, and read thou knowst not what,
And yet know whether thou art blest or not,
By reading the same lines? O then come hither,
And lay my Book, thy Head, and Heart together.

JOHN BUNYAN

. . . Once, only once, never again, never,
  The idle curve my hand traces in air,
  The first flush on the cloud, lost in the morning's height,
  Meeting of the eyes and tremble of delight,
  Before the heart is aware
  Gone! to return, never again, never!

Futurity flows towards me, all things come
Smooth-flowing, and ere this pulse beat they are bound
In fixity that no repenting power can free;
They are with Egypt and with Nineveh,
Cold as a grave in the ground;
And still, undated, all things toward me come.

Why is all strange? Why do I not grow used?
The ripple upon the stream that nothing stays,
The bough above, in glory of warm light waving slow,
Trouble me, enchant me, as with the stream I flow
Lost into the endless days.
Why is all strange? Why do I not grow used?

Eternity! Where heard I that still word?
Like one that, moving through a foreign street,
Has felt upon him bent from far some earnest look,
Yet sees not whence, and feigns that he mistook,
I marvel at my own heart-beat.
Eternity! how learnt I that far word? . . .

> LAURENCE BINYON, from "The Idols"

  . . . One summer evening . . . I found
A little boat tied to a willow tree
Within a rocky cave, its usual home.
Straight I unloosed her chain, and stepping in
Pushed from the shore. It was an act of stealth
And troubled pleasure, nor without the voice
Of mountain-echoes did my boat move on;
Leaving behind her still, on either side,
Small circles glittering idly in the moon,

Until they melted all into one track
Of sparkling light. But now, like one who rows,
Proud of his skill, to reach a chosen point
With an unswerving line, I fixed my view
Upon the summit of a craggy ridge,
The horizon's utmost boundary; far above
Was nothing but the stars and the grey sky.
She was an elfin pinnace; lustily
I dipped my oars into the silent lake,
And, as I rose upon the stroke, my boat
Went heaving through the water like a swan;
When, from behind that craggy steep till then
The horizon's bound, a huge peak, black and huge,
As if with voluntary power instinct
Upreared its head. I struck and struck again,
And growing still in stature the grim shape
Towered up between me and the stars, and still,
For so it seemed, with purpose of its own
And measured motion like a living thing,
Strode after me. With trembling oars I turned,
And through the silent water stole my way
Back to the covert of the willow tree;
There in her mooring-place I left my bark, —
And through the meadows homeward went, in grave
And serious mood; but after I had seen
That spectacle, for many days, my brain
Worked with a dim and undetermined sense
Of unknown modes of being; o'er my thoughts
There hung a darkness, call it solitude
Or blank desertion. No familiar shapes
Remained, no pleasant images of trees,
Of sea or sky, no colours of green fields;
But huge and mighty forms, that do not live,
Like living men, moved slowly through the mind
By day, and were a trouble to my dreams. . . .

WILLIAM WORDSWORTH, from *The Prelude, Book I*

A VISION OF THE MERMAIDS

Rowing, I reached a rock — the sea was low —
Which the tides cover in their overflow,
Marking the spot, when they have gurgled o'er,
With a thin floating veil of water hoar.
A mile astern lay the blue shores away;
And it was at the setting of the day. . . .
The zenith melted to a rose of air;
The waves were rosy-lipped; the crimson glare
Showered the cliffs and every fret and spire
With garnet wreaths and blooms of rosy-budded fire.
   Then, looking on the waters, I was ware
Of something drifting through delighted air,
— An isle of roses, — and another near; —
And more, on each hand, thicken, and appear
   In shoals of bloom; as in unpeopled skies,
   Save by two stars, more crowding lights arise,
   And planets bud where'er we turn our mazèd eyes.
I gaze unhindered: Mermaids six or seven,
Ris'n from the deeps to gaze on sun and heaven,
Clustered in troops and haloed by the light,
These Cyclads made that thickened on my sight. . . .
   Then saw I sudden from the waters break
Far off a Nereid company, and shake
From wings swan-fledged a wheel of watery light
Flickering with sunny spokes, and left and right
Plunge orbed in rainbow arcs, and trample and tread
The satin-purfled smooth to foam, and spread
Slim-pointed sea-gull plumes, and droop behind
One scarlet feather trailing to the wind;
Then, like a flock of sea-fowl mounting higher,
Thro' crimson-golden floods pass swallowed into fire.
   Soon — as when Summer of his sister Spring
Crushes and tears the rare enjewelling,

And boasting, " I have fairer things than these,"
Plashes amidst the billowing apple-trees
His lusty hands, in gusts of scented wind
Swirling out bloom till all the air is blind
With rosy foam and pelting blossom and mists
Of driving vermeil-rain; and, as he lists,
The dainty onyx-coronals deflowers,
A glorious wanton; — all the wrecks in showers
Crowd down upon a stream, and, jostling thick
With bubbles bugle-eyed, struggle and stick
On tangled shoals that bar the brook — a crowd
Of filmy globes and rosy floating cloud:
So those Mermaidens crowded to my rock,
And thickened, like that drifted bloom, the flock
Sun-flushed, until it seemed their father Sea
Had gotten him a wreath of sweet Spring-broidery.
   Careless of me they sported: some would plash
The languent smooth with dimpling drops, and flash
Their filmy tails adown whose length there showed
An azure ridge; or clouds of violet glowed
On prankèd scale; or threads of carmine, shot
Thro' silver, gloomed to a blood-vivid clot.
Some, diving, merrily, downward drove, and gleamed
With arm and fin; the argent bubbles streamed
Airwards, disturbed; and the scarce troubled sea
Gurgled, where they had sunk, melodiously.
Others with fingers white would comb among
The drenchèd hair of slabby weeds that swung
Swimming, and languished green upon the deep
Down that dank rock o'er which their lush long tresses
      weep.
   But most in a half-circle watched the sun;
And a sweet sadness dwelt on everyone;
I knew not why, — but know that sadness dwells
On Mermaids — whether that they ring the knells
Of seamen whelmed in chasms of the mid-main,

As poets sing; or that it is a pain
To know the dusk depths of the ponderous sea,
The miles profound of solid green, and be
With loathed cold fishes, far from man — or what; —
I know the sadness but the cause know not.
Then they, thus ranged, 'gan make full plaintively
A piteous Siren sweetness on the sea,
Withouten instrument, or conch, or bell,
Or stretched cords tunable on turtle's shell;
Only with utterance of sweet breath they sung
An antique chaunt and in an unknown tongue.
Now melting upward through the sloping scale
Swelled the sweet strain to a melodious wail;
Now ringing clarion-clear to whence it rose
Slumbered at last in one sweet, deep, heart-broken close.
   But when the sun had lapsed to Ocean, lo
A stealthy wind crept round seeking to blow,
Lingered, then raised the washing waves, and drenched
The floating blooms and with tide flowing quenched
The rosy isles: so that I stole away
And gained thro' growing dusk the stirless bay;
White loomed my rock, the water gurgling o'er,
   Whence oft I watch but see those Mermaids now no more.

GERARD HOPKINS,
from " A Vision of the Mermaids "

TOM O' BEDLAM

The morn's my constant mistress,
  And the lonely owl my morrow;
    The flaming drake,
    And the night-crow, make
  Me music to my sorrow.

I know more than Apollo;
　For oft, when he lies sleeping,
　　I behold the stars
　　At mortal wars,
　And the wounded welkin weeping.

The moon embraces her shepherd,
　And the Queen of Love her warrior;
　　While the first does horn
　　The stars of the morn,
　And the next the heavenly farrier.

With a host of furious fancies,
　Whereof I am commander:
　　With a burning spear,
　　And a horse of air,
　To the wilderness I wander;

By a Knight of ghosts and shadows,
　I summoned am to Tourney:
　　Ten leagues beyond
　　The wild world's end;
　Methinks it is no journey.

Hear the voice of the Bard!
Who Present, Past, and Future, sees;
Whose ears have heard
The Holy Word
That walked among the ancient trees,

Calling the lapsèd Soul,
And weeping in the evening dew;
That might controll
The starry pole,
And fallen, fallen light renew!

" O Earth, O Earth, return!
Arise from out the dewy grass;
Night is worn,
And the morn
Rises from the slumberous mass.

" Turn away no more;
Why wilt thou turn away?
The starry floor,
The wat'ry shore,
Is giv'n thee till the break of day."

WILLIAM BLAKE

My home
The shimmery-bounded glare,
The gazing fire-hung dome
Of scorching air.

My rest
To wander trembling-weak,
On vague hunger-quest
New hope to seek.

For friend
The dazzling breathing dream,
The strength at last to find
Of Glory Supreme.

ELIZABETH DARYUSH

Evening and Night

The day gan failen, and the derkè night,
That reveth bestes from hir besinesse,
Beraftè me my book for lakke of light. . . .

" Look! the world's comforter, with weary gait,
His day's hot task hath ended in the west;
The owl, night's herald, shrieks, 'tis very late;
The sheep are gone to fold, birds to their nest,
   And coal-black clouds that shadow heaven's light
   Do summon us to part and bid good night. . . ."

Evening and Night

TO DAISIES, NOT TO SHUT SO SOON

Shut not so soon; the dull-eyed night
   Ha's not as yet begunne
To make a seisure on the light,
   Or to seale up the Sun.

No Marigolds yet closed are;
   No shadowes great appeare;
Nor doth the early Shepheard's Starre
   Shine like a spangle here. . . .

ROBERT HERRICK

OF THE GOING DOWN OF THE SUN

What, hast thou run thy Race? Art going down?
Thou seemest angry, why dost on us frown?
Yea wrap thy head with Clouds, and hide thy face,
As threatning to withdraw from us thy Grace?
Oh leave us not! When once thou hid'st thy head,
Our Horizon with darkness will be spread.
Tell's who hath thee offended? Turn again:
Alas! too late Entreaties are in vain!

JOHN BUNYAN

A Saturday afternoon in November was approaching the time of twilight, and the vast tract of unenclosed wild known as Egdon Heath embrowned itself moment by moment. Overhead the hollow stretch of whitish cloud shutting out the sky was as a tent which had the whole heath for its floor. The heaven being spread with this pallid screen and the earth with the darkest vegetation, their meeting-line at the horizon was clearly marked. In such contrast the heath wore the appearance of an instalment of night which had taken up its place before its astronomical hour was come: darkness had to a great extent arrived hereon, while day stood distinct in the sky. Looking upwards, a furze-cutter would have been inclined to continue work; looking down, he would have decided to finish his faggot and go home.

The distant rims of the world and of the firmament seemed to be a division in time no less than a division in matter. The face of the heath by its mere complexion added half an hour to evening; it could in like manner retard the dawn, sadden noon, anticipate the frowning of storms scarcely generated, and intensify the opacity of a moonless midnight to a cause of shaking and dread. . . .

THOMAS HARDY, from *The Return of the Native*

> . . . Look from your windows, lovers, lean
> On bridges in the warm, tired air,
> For now is evening poised between
> Light-hearted day and the dark's snare,
> Like a girl flirting in her glass
> And softly letting down her hair.
> The little moths in seeding grass
> Flutter their life out through the field
> Where starwort gleams, and, as you pass,
> All colours that have loudly made
> A dying declaration, yield
> In whispers to the very shade
> Of lichen, and of sheep that browse
> Dimly below orchard boughs.

Alone among night-scented leaves
Did Sargon's daughter, pining, tend
Her charge, the Babylonian moon;
And singly as the leaning sheaves
That now in darkness seem to blend,
Men love; it is the hour when soon
St. Jerome, putting down his quill,
Unlatches to the secret friend,
Then works, with all Judaea still;
When some will wake at horror's edge,
And women start the pains of birth;
When careful paws creep out to kill
And a bird twitches in the hedge,
While dreams smoke from the quiet Earth.

SHEILA WINGFIELD, from *The Hours*

THE WILD SWANS AT COOLE

The trees are in their autumn beauty,
The woodland paths are dry,
Under the October twilight the water
Mirrors a still sky;
Upon the brimming water among the stones
Are nine-and-fifty swans.

The nineteenth autumn has come upon me
Since I first made my count;
I saw, before I had well finished,
All suddenly mount
And scatter wheeling in great broken rings
Upon their clamorous wings.

I have looked upon those brilliant creatures,
And now my heart is sore.
All's changed since I, hearing at twilight,
The first time on this shore,
The bell-beat of their wings above my head,
Trod with a lighter tread.

Unwearied still, lover by lover,
They paddle in the cold
Companionable streams, or climb the air;
Their hearts have grown old;
Passion or conquest, wander where they will,
Attend upon them still.

But now they drift on the still water,
Mysterious, beautiful.
Among what rushes will they build,
By what lake's edge or pool
Delight men's eyes when I awake some day
To find they have flown away?

W. B. YEATS

The sad wall-flower (*Cheiranthus tristis*) . . . has a sombre and dismal hue, of a dark liver colour, and cannot boast of an ornamental appearance; but it compensates for its deficiency in lustre by the exquisitely delicate fragrance which it diffuses during night.

Night-scented blossoms are rarely beautiful in their tints; but this is of little importance, since they seem rather to belong to the hours of darkness than to the day and sunlight. . . .

In our country night-scented flowers are few; though in the East the moon seems to have as much power as the sun in extracting their perfumes. Several of our native plants, like the lime blossoms, scent the evening air, though until that period of the day their odour is not perceptible. This is the case with one of our wild orchideous plants, the butterfly-orchis. . . . It has large yellowish-coloured flowers, which are at all times fragrant, but during evening more so than at noon. The same may be said of the little moschatel, or glory-less . . . a small green flower, with three lobed leaves on a long leaf-stalk, which, when the dew begins to fall, emits its long-concealed odours, and imbues the air with the scent of

musk. The yellow ladies' bed-straw has, during twilight, a
scent like that of new honey; and the musk-mallow . . .
which during the sunshine has but a faint musky smell, re-
serves the full power of its odours until that period
> " When the lamb bleating doth bid good-night
> Until the closing day."

ANNE PRATT

Now from the fresh, the soft, and tender bed,
Of her still mother gentle night out-flew,
The fleeting balme on hilles and dales shee shed,
With honey drops of pure and precious dew,
And on the verdure of greene forrests spred,
The virgin prime rose, and the violet blew,
And sweet-breathed Zephire on his spreading wings
Sleepe, ease, repose, rest, peace, and quiet brings. . . .

EDWARD FAIRFAX

Sitting in the entrance of their caverns [field-crickets]
chirp all night as well as day from the middle of the month of
May to the middle of July; and in hot weather, when they
are most vigorous, they make the hills echo, and in the stiller
hours of darkness may be heard to a considerable distance.
In the beginning of the season their notes are more faint and
inward; but become louder as the summer advances, and so
die away again by degrees. . . .

This bird [the Nightjar] is most punctual in beginning its
song exactly at the close of day — so exactly that I have
known it strike up more than once or twice just at the report
of the Portsmouth evening gun, which we can hear when the
weather is still. . . . You will credit me, I hope, when I
assure you that as my neighbours were assembled in an her-
mitage on the side of a steep hill where we drink tea, one of
these churn-owls came and settled on the cross of that little
straw edifice and began to chatter, and continued his note for
many minutes: and we were all struck with wonder to find

that the organs of that little animal, when put in motion, gave a sensible vibration to the whole building! . . .

GILBERT WHITE

NIGHT–SKIES

It is at ten o'clock [March 18] that I write this. Stormy weather left the night-sky so clear that Rigel was faintly visible at twenty minutes to seven. Betelgeuse, being better placed, was then much more conspicuous, and Capella and Sirius were dazzling. . . .

At this time the *lumière cendrée* was surpassingly beautiful. The crescent moon was on the edge of the twilight. What a strange glow! Such a tint surely never mortal eyes saw on this many-tinted earth of ours. One feature of it struck me greatly — the augmented brightness of the outer rim, due, probably, to what I may be permitted to call the accumulated " shine " in consequence of the curvature of the lunar surface.

There was something magnetic in the attraction of that *lumière cendrée,* . . . and it was only after a struggle that I was able to tear myself away from contemplating its pale ashen beauty. The sun-glow was then melting into the tender blue of early night. And out of it there faintly twinkled a star close in the wake of the crescented moon. . . .

If the full moon — such as prevails to-night [August 23] — be closely scanned a figure resembling in an extraordinary degree the head of a beautiful woman will be observed. This figure changes its position according as the position of the moon in its orbit varies. For the most part, it will be seen on the extreme right of the moon, with the gaze turned to the left, across the disc, but at times it is in the lower right-hand corner, with the face turned upward. It is a striking apparition, this of the Lady in the Moon, whose beauty captivates the eye at once — especially if the eye be aided with a small opera-glass — as beauty is apt to do. This moon-maiden has found the secret of perpetual youth; she has been young for millions of years. A proud, imperious beauty, with a haughty, almost contemptuous poise of the head. But in the airless moon she remains for ever mute. Though what language could express more than she looks? . . .

JOSEPH H. ELGIE

My room was in my last year the top Tower room, which has a staircase to itself. Of a summer night, when College is asleep, and there is but little traffic in the streets, you hear the rushing of Romney Weir, and, at midnight, the three great clocks: our own, in Lupton's Tower, strikes the quarters and the hour: the big one in the Castle quadrangle has a deep bell for the hour only: the Curfew Tower, where the bells of St. George's are, has more to say. When it has done the hour it sets off upon a psalm tune — that known as St. David's, "How blest the man who ne'er consents By ill advice to walk, Nor stands in sinners' ways nor sits Where men profanely talk." That is followed by a tinkling chime, which is the prettiest part, and thrice is the song repeated. It goes on at three, six and nine o'clock as well as twelve; but unless you are in Windsor Street just beneath it, you can never hear it but at midnight.

I don't know what I thought about when I listened to the Weir and the clocks and the chimes, and smelt the perfume of the lime-blossom in the Long Walk, but if I had been capable of writing poetry, I daresay I should have written it then. A still summer night in one's last half at Eton! I ought to have been filled with great projects for the public good, and wonderings as to what I was going to be and do. But I am sure there was none of that, only a sense of how kind a mother Eton was, and how many people that I was fond of were about me. . . .

MONTAGU JAMES

By the time I had made my arrangements and fed Modestine, the day was already beginning to decline. I buckled myself to the knees into my sack and made a hearty meal;

and as soon as the sun went down, I pulled my cap over my eyes and fell asleep.

Night is a dead monotonous period under a roof, but in the open world it passes lightly, with the stars and dews and perfumes, and the hours are marked by changes in the face of Nature. What seems a kind of temporal death to people choked between walls and curtains, is only a light and living slumber to the man who sleeps afield. All night long he can hear Nature breathing deeply and freely; even as she takes her rest, she turns and smiles; and there is one stirring hour unknown to those who dwell in houses, when a wakeful influence goes abroad over the sleepy hemisphere, and all the outdoor world are on their feet. It is then that the cock first crows, not this time to announce the dawn, but like a cheerful watchman speeding the course of night. Cattle awake in the meadows; sheep break their fast on dewy hillsides, and change to a new lair among the ferns; and houseless men, who have lain down with the fowls, open their dim eyes and behold the beauty of the night.

At what incredible summons, at what gentle touch of Nature, are all these sleepers thus recalled in the same hour to life? Do the stars rain down an influence, or do we share some thrill of mother earth below our resting bodies? Even shepherds and old country-folk, who are the deepest read in these Arcana, have not a guess as to the means or purpose of this nightly resurrection. Towards two in the morning they declare the thing takes place; and neither know nor inquire further. . . .

R. L. STEVENSON

UPON A LANTHORN

The Lanthorn is to keep the Candle Light,
When it is windy, and a darksome night.
Ordained it also was, that men might see
By Night their Day, and so in safety be.

JOHN BUNYAN

Midnight's bell goes ting, ting, ting, ting, ting,
Then dogs do howl, and not a bird does sing
But the nightingale, and she cries twit, twit, twit:
Owls then on every bough do sit;
Ravens croak on chimneys' tops;
The cricket in the chamber hops,
   And the cats cry mew, mew, mew.
The nibbling mouse is not asleep,
But he goes peep, peep, peep, peep, peep,
   And the cats cry mew, mew, mew,
   And still the cats cry mew, mew, mew.

THOMAS MIDDLETON

. . . It was nearly midnight. We traversed a broad trail of white sand, between lines of saplings of pale-barked rubber trees, flooded, saturated, with milky-gray light. Not a star appeared in the cloudless sky, which, in contrast to the great silver moon-plaque, was blue-black. . . .

Suddenly before us rose the jungle, raw-edged, with border zone of bleached, ashamed trunks and lofty branches white as chalk, of dead and dying trees. For no jungle tree, however hardy, can withstand the blasting of violent sun after the veiling of emerald foliage is torn away. As the diver plunges beneath the waves, so, after one glance backward over the silvered landscape, I passed at a single stride into what seemed by contrast inky blackness, relieved by the trail ahead, which showed as does a ray of light through closed eyelids. As the chirruping rails climbed among the roots of the tall cat-tails out yonder, so we now crept far beneath the level of the moonlit foliage. The silvery landscape had been shifted one hundred, two hundred feet above the earth. We had become lords of creation in name alone, threading our way humbly among the fungi and toadstools, able only to look aloft and wonder what it was like. And for a long time no voice answered to tell us whether any creature lived and moved in the tree-tops. . . .

WILLIAM BEEBE

The steamer was on an even keel, with but occasional
spasms of sharp rolling for there was no sea, but only old
ocean breathing deeply and regularly in its sleep, and sometimes making a slight movement. The light of the full moon
was the shining ghost of noon. The steamer was distinct but
immaterial, saliently accentuated, as a phantom. A deep
shadow would have detached the forecastle head but for a
length of luminous bulwark which still held it, and some
quiet voices of men who were within the shadow, yarning.
The line of bulwark and the murmuring voices held us together. The prow as it dipped sank into drifts of lambent
snow. The snow fled by the steamer's sides, melting and
musical. Two engineers off duty leaned on the rail amid-
ships, smoking, looking into the vacancy in which the moonlight laid a floor of troubled silver. As if drawn by its light
a few little clouds were poised near the moon, grouped
round the bright heart of the night. . . .

H. M. Tomlinson

Midnight was come, when everie vitall thing,
With sweet sound sleepe their wearie limbs did rest,
The beasts were still, the little birds that sing,
Now sweetely slept besides their mothers brest,
The old and all were shrowded in their nest,
The waters calme, the cruell seas did cease,
The woods, the fields, and all things held their peace,
The golden starres were whirld amyd theyr race,
And on the earth did laugh with twinckling light,
When each thing nestled in his resting place,
Forgat dayes payne with pleasure of the night,
The hare had not the greedie hounds in sight,
The fearfull Deare of death stood not in doubt,
The Partrich dreamd not of the falchens foot,
The ugly beare now minded not the stake,
Now how the cruell mastiffes doe him teare,
The stagge lay still unrousèd from the brake,

The foamie bore feared not the hunters speare,
All things was still in desart, bush and breere:
With quiet heart now from their travailes rest,
Soundly they slept in midst of all their rest.

THOMAS SACKVILLE, EARL OF DORSET

Look how the pale queen of the silent night
Doth cause the ocean to attend upon her,
And he, as long as she is in his sight,
With his full tide is ready her to honour:
But when the silver wagon of the moon
Is mounted up so high he cannot follow,
The sea calls home his crystal waves to wone,
And with low ebb doth manifest his sorrow.
So you, that are the sovereign of my heart,
Have all my joys attending on your will:
My joys low ebbing when you do depart,
When you return, their tide my heart doth fill.
 So as you come, and as you do depart,
 Joys ebb and flow within my tender heart.

CHARLES BEST

 . . . Dear night! this world's defeat;
The stop to busie fools; care's check and curb;
The day of Spirits; my soul's calm retreat
  Which none disturb!
  Christ's progress, and his prayer time;
  The hours to which high Heaven doth chime.

 God's silent, searching flight:
When my Lord's head is filled with dew, and all
His locks are wet with the clear drops of night;
  His still, soft call;
  His knocking time; The soul's dumb watch,
  When Spirits their fair kindred catch.

Were all my loud, evil days
Calm and unhaunted as is thy dark Tent,
Whose peace but by some *Angel's* wing or voice
        Is seldom rent;
    Then I in Heaven all the long year
    Would keep, and never wander here.

        But living where the Sun
Doth all things wake, and where all mix and tyre
Themselves and others, I consent and run
        To every myre,
    And by this world's ill-guiding light,
    Erre more then I can do by night.

        There is in God (some say)
A deep, but dazzling darkness; As men here
Say it is late and dusky, because they
        See not all clear;
    O for that night! where I in him
    Might live invisible and dim.

                HENRY VAUGHAN, from "The Night"

THE WORLD'S WANDERERS

Tell me, thou Star, whose wings of light
Speed thee in thy fiery flight,
In what cavern of the night
        Will thy pinions close now?

Tell me, Moon, thou pale and gray
Pilgrim of Heaven's homeless way,
In what depth of night or day
        Seekest thou repose now?

Weary Wind, who wanderest
Like the world's rejected guest,
Hast thou still some secret nest
        On the tree or billow?

                    PERCY BYSSHE SHELLEY

[156]

The City is of Night; perchance of Death,
　But certainly of Night; for never there
Can come the lucid morning's fragrant breath
　After the dewy dawning's cold grey air;
The moon and stars may shine with scorn or pity;
The sun has never visited that city,
　For it dissolveth in the daylight fair.

Dissolveth like a dream of night away;
　Though present in distempered gloom of thought
And deadly weariness of heart all day.
　But when a dream night after night is brought
Throughout a week, and such weeks few or many
Recur each year for several years, can any
　Discern that dream from real life in aught?

For life is but a dream whose shapes return,
　Some frequently, some seldom, some by night
And some by day, some night and day: we learn,
　The while all change and many vanish quite,
In their recurrence with recurrent changes
A certain seeming order; where this ranges
　We count things real; such is memory's might.

A river girds the city west and south,
　The main north channel of a broad lagoon,
Regurging with the salt tides from the mouth;
　Waste marshes shine and glister to the moon
For leagues, then moorland black, then stony ridges;
Great piers and causeways, many noble bridges,
　Connect the town and islet suburbs strewn.

Upon an easy slope it lies at large,
　And scarcely overlaps the long curved crest
Which swells out two leagues from the river marge.
　A trackless wilderness rolls north and west,
Savannahs, savage woods, enormous mountains,
Bleak uplands, black ravines with torrent fountains;
　And eastward rolls the shipless sea's unrest.

The city is not ruinous, although
   Great ruins of an unremembered past,
With others of a few short years ago
   More sad, are found within its precincts vast.
The street-lamps always burn; but scarce a casement
In house or palace front from roof to basement
   Doth glow or gleam athwart the mirk air cast.

The street-lamps burn amidst the baleful glooms,
   Amidst the soundless solitudes immense
Of rangèd mansions dark and still as tombs.
   The silence which benumbs or strains the sense
Fulfils with awe the soul's despair unweeping:
Myriads of habitants are ever sleeping,
   Or dead, or fled from nameless pestilence!

Yet as in some necropolis you find
   Perchance one mourner to a thousand dead,
So there; worn faces that look deaf and blind
   Like tragic masks of stone. With weary tread,
Each wrapt in his own doom, they wander, wander,
Or sit fordone and desolately ponder
   Through sleepless hours with heavy drooping head. . . .

The City is of Night, but not of Sleep;
   There sweet sleep is not for the weary brain;
The pitiless hours like years and ages creep,
   A night seems termless hell. This dreadful strain
Of thought and consciousness which never ceases,
Of which some moments' stupor but increases,
   This, worse than woe, makes wretches there insane.

They leave all hope behind who enter there:
   One certitude while sane they cannot leave,
One anodyne for torture and despair;
   The certitude of Death, which no reprieve

Can put off long; and which, divinely tender,
But waits the outstretched hand to promptly render
That draught whose slumber nothing can bereave.

JAMES THOMSON, from " The City of Dreadful Night "

. . . Is the night chilly and dark?
The night is chilly, but not dark.
The thin gray cloud is spread on high,
It covers but not hides the sky.
The moon is behind, and at the full;
And yet she looks both small and dull.
The night is chill, the cloud is gray:
'Tis a month before the month of May,
And the Spring comes slowly up this way.

The lovely lady, Christabel,
Whom her father loves so well,
What makes her in the wood so late,
A furlong from the castle gate?
She had dreams all yesternight
Of her own betrothèd knight;
And she in the midnight wood will pray
For the weal of her lover that's far away.

She stole along, she nothing spoke,
The sighs she heaved were soft and low,
And naught was green upon the oak
But moss and rarest mistletoe. . . .

SAMUEL TAYLOR COLERIDGE, from " Christabel "

IN DISPRAISE OF THE MOON

I would not be the Moon, the sickly thing,
To summon owls and bats upon the wing;
For when the noble Sun is gone away,
She turns his night into a pallid day.

She hath no air, no radiance of her own,
That world unmusical of earth and stone.
She wakes her dim, uncoloured, voiceless hosts,
Ghost of the Sun, herself the sun of ghosts.

The mortal eyes that gaze too long on her
Of Reason's piercing ray defrauded are.
Light in itself doth feed the living brain;
That light, reflected, but makes darkness plain.

MARY COLERIDGE

TO AMINE

Veil not thy mirror, sweet Amine,
   Till Night shall also veil each star;
   Thou see'st a two-fold marvel there —
The only face as fair as thine,
   The only eyes that near or far
   Can gaze on thine without despair!

JAMES CLARENCE MANGAN

TURN, TURN THY BEAUTEOUS FACE AWAY

Turn, turn thy beauteous face away;
How pale and sickly looks the day,
   In emulation of thy brighter beams!
Oh, envious light, fly, fly, be gone;
Come, night, and piece two breasts as one;
   When what love does we will repeat in dreams.
Yet, thy eyes open, who can day hence fright,
Let but their lids fall, and it will be night.

JOHN FLETCHER

THE MAY–TREE

The May-tree on the hill
  Stands in the night
So fragrant and so still
  So dusky white,

That, stealing from the wood
  In that sweet air,
You'd think Diana stood
  Before you there.

If it be so, her bloom
  Trembles with bliss.
She waits across the gloom
  Her shepherd's kiss.

Touch her. A bird will start
  From these pure snows, —
The dark and fluttering heart
  Endymion knows.

ALFRED NOYES

TO THE EVENING STAR

Thou Fair-haired Angel of the Evening,
Now, whilst the sun rests on the mountains, light
Thy bright torch of love; thy radiant crown
Put on, and smile upon our evening bed!
Smile on our loves, and while thou drawest the
Blue curtains of the sky, scatter thy silver dew
On every flower that shuts its sweet eyes
In timely sleep. Let thy West Wind sleep on
The lake; speak silence with thy glimmering eyes,
And wash the dusk with silver. Soon, full soon,

[161]

Dost thou withdraw; then the wolf rages wide,
And the lion glares thro' the dun forest:
The fleeces of the flocks are covered with
Thy sacred dew: protect them with thy influence.

WILLIAM BLAKE

NIGHTINGALES

Beautiful must be the mountains whence ye come,
And bright in the fruitful valleys the streams, wherefrom
      Ye learn your song:
Where are those starry woods? O might I wander there,
  Among the flowers, which in that heavenly air
      Bloom the year long!

Nay, barren are those mountains and spent the streams:
Our song is the voice of desire, that haunts our dreams,
      A throe of the heart,
Whose pining visions dim, forbidden hopes profound,
  No dying cadence nor long sigh can sound,
      For all our art.

Alone, aloud in the raptured ear of men
We pour our dark nocturnal secret; and then,
      As night is withdrawn
From these sweet-springing meads and bursting boughs of
      May,
Dream, while the innumerable choir of day
      Welcome the dawn.

ROBERT BRIDGES

MOONRISE

I awoke in the Midsummer not to call night, in the white and
  the walk of the morning:
The moon, dwindled and thinned to the fringe of a finger-nail
  held to the candle,

Or paring of paradisaical fruit, lovely in waning but lustreless,
Stepped from the stool, drew back from the barrow, of dark
    Maenefa the mountain;
A cusp still clasped him, a fluke yet fanged him, entangled
    him, not quit utterly.
This was the prized, the desirable sight, unsought, presented
    so easily,
Parted me leaf and leaf, divided me, eyelid and eyelid of
    slumber.

GERARD HOPKINS

TO THE NIGHT

Swiftly walk o'er the western wave,
    Spirit of Night!
Out of the misty eastern cave,
Where, all the long and lone daylight,
Thou wovest dreams of joy and fear,
Which make thee terrible and dear —
    Swift be thy flight!

Wrap thy form in a mantle grey,
    Star-inwrought!
Blind with thine hair the eyes of Day,
Kiss her until she be wearied out,
Then wander o'er city, and sea, and land,
Touching all with thine opiate wand —
    Come, long-sought!

When I arose and saw the dawn,
    I sighed for thee;
When light rode high, and the dew was gone,
And noon lay heavy on flower and tree,
And the weary Day turned to his rest,
Lingering like an unloved guest,
    I sighed for thee.

Thy brother Death came, and cried: —
      " Wouldst thou me? "
Thy sweet child Sleep, the filmy-eyed,
Murmured like a noontide bee: —
" Shall I nestle near thy side?
Wouldst thou me? " — And I replied: —
      No, not thee!

Death will come when thou art dead,
      Soon, too soon!
Sleep will come when thou art fled;
Of neither would I ask the boon
I ask of thee, belovèd Night —
Swift be thine approaching flight,
      Come soon, soon!

PERCY BYSSHE SHELLEY

Waking and Watching

Watchman, what of the night? Watchman, what of the night?
The watchman said, The morning cometh, and also the night . . .

Fall gently, gently and a while him keep
Lost in the civill Wildernesse of sleep.

Waking and Watching

"SHEPHERDS ALL, AND MAIDENS FAIR"

Shepherds all, and maidens fair,
Fold your flocks up; for the air
'Gins to thicken, and the sun
Already his great course hath run.
See the dewdrops how they kiss
Every little flower that is,
Hanging on their velvet heads
Like a rope of crystal beads:
See the heavy clouds low falling,
And bright Hesperus down calling
The dead Night from under ground;
At whose rising, mists unsound,
Damps and vapours fly apace,
Hovering o'er the wanton face
Of these pastures, where they come,
Striking dead both blood and bloom;
Therefore, from such danger lock
Every one his lovèd flock;
And let your dogs lie loose without,
Lest the wolf come as a scout
From the mountain, and, ere day,
Bear a lamb or kid away;
Or the crafty thievish fox
Break upon your simple flocks:
To secure yourself from these,
Be not too secure in ease;

Let one eye his watches keep,
While the t'other eye doth sleep;
So shall you good shepherds prove,
And for ever hold the love
Of our great god. Sweetest slumbers
And soft silence, fall in numbers
On your eye-lids! So, farewell!
Thus I end my evening's knell.

JOHN FLETCHER

HIGH AMONG THE LONELY HILLS

High among the lonely hills,
While I lay beside my sheep,
Rest came down and filled my soul,
From the everlasting deep.

Changeless march the stars above,
Changeless morn succeeds to even;
Still the everlasting hills,
Changeless watch the changeless heaven. . . .

CHARLES KINGSLEY,
from *The Saint's Tragedy, Act I, Scene II*

THE NIGHTINGALE NEAR THE HOUSE

Here is the soundless cypress on the lawn:
It listens, listens. Taller trees beyond
Listen. The moon at the unruffled pond
  Stares. And you sing, you sing.

That star-enchanted song falls through the air
From lawn to lawn down terraces of sound,
Darts in white arrows on the shadowed ground;
  While all the night you sing.

My dreams are flowers to which you are a bee,
As all night long I listen, and my brain
Receives your song, then loses it again
   In moonlight on the lawn.

Now is your voice a marble high and white,
Then like a mist on fields of paradise;
Now is a raging fire, then is like ice,
   Then breaks, and it is dawn.

HAROLD MONRO

NOCTURN

I walk, I only,
Not I only wake;
Nothing is, this sweet night,
But doth couch and wake
For its love's sake;
Everything, this sweet night,
Couches with its mate.
For whom but for the stealthy-visitant sun
Is the naked moon
Tremulous and elate?
The heaven hath the earth
Its own and all apart;
The hushèd pool holdeth
A star to its heart.
You may think the rose sleepeth,
But though she folded is,
The wind doubts her sleeping;
Not all the rose sleeps,
But smiles in her sweet heart
For crafty bliss.

The wind lieth with the rose,
And when he stirs, she stirs in her repose:
The wind hath the rose,
And the rose her kiss. . . .

FRANCIS THOMPSON

SIREN CHORUS

Troop home to silent grots and caves,
    Troop home! and mimic as you go
The mournful winding of the waves
    Which to their dark abysses flow.

At this sweet hour, all things beside
    In amorous pairs to covert creep;
The swans that brush the evening tide
    Homeward in snowy couples keep.

In his green den the murmuring seal
    Close by his sleek companion lies;
While singly we to bedward steal,
    And close in fruitless sleep our eyes.

In bowers of love men take their rest,
    In loveless bowers we sigh alone,
With bosom-friends are others blest, —
    But we have none! but we have none!

GEORGE DARLEY

TO THE NIGHTINGALE

Dear chorister, who from those shadows sends
(Ere that the blushing morn dare show her light)
Such sad lamenting strains, that night attends
Become all ear, stars stay to hear thy plight.

If one whose grief even reach of thought transcends,
Who n'er (not in a dream) did taste delight,
May thee importune who like case pretends,
And seems to joy in woe, in woe's despite?
Tell me (so may thou fortune milder try,
And long long sing) for what thou thus complains?
Sith (winter gone) the sun in dappled sky
Now smiles on meadows, mountains, woods and plains:
  The bird, as if my questions did her move,
  With trembling wings sobbed forth, " I love! I love! "

WILLIAM DRUMMOND

SERENADE

Still is the night breeze! — not a lonely sound
  Steals through the silence of this dreary hour;
O'er these high battlements Sleep reigns profound,
  And sheds on all his sweet oblivious power:

On all but me — I vainly ask his dews
  To steep in short forgetfulness my cares:
The affrighted god still flies when Love pursues,
  Still — still denies the wretched lover's prayers.

ANN RADCLIFFE

Sleep brings no joy to me,
  Remembrance never dies,
My soul is given to mystery,
  And lives in sighs.

Sleep brings no rest to me;
  The shadows of the dead
My wakening eyes may never see
  Surround my bed.

[171]

Sleep brings no hope to me,
   In soundest sleep they come,
And with their doleful imag'ry
   Deepen the gloom.

Sleep brings no strength to me,
   No power renewed to brave;
I only sail a wilder sea,
   A darker wave.

Sleep brings no friend to me
   To soothe and aid to bear;
They all gaze on, how scornfully,
   And I despair.

Sleep brings no wish to fret
   My harassed heart beneath;
My only wish is to forget
   In endless sleep of death.

EMILY BRONTË

Bright star, would I were stedfast as thou art —
   Not in lone splendour hung aloft the night
And watching, with eternal lids apart,
   Like nature's patient, sleepless Eremite,
The moving waters at their priestlike task
   Of pure ablution round earth's human shores,
Or gazing on the new soft-fallen mask
   Of snow upon the mountains and the moors —
No — yet still stedfast, still unchangeable,
   Pillowed upon my fair love's ripening breast,
To feel for ever its soft fall and swell,
   Awake for ever in a sweet unrest,
Still, still to hear her tender-taken breath,
And so live ever — or else swoon to death.

JOHN KEATS

STOPPING BY WOODS ON A SNOWY EVENING

Whose woods these are I think I know.
His house is in the village though;
He will not see me stopping here
To watch his woods fill up with snow.

My little horse must think it queer
To stop without a farmhouse near
Between the woods and frozen lake
The darkest evening of the year.

He gives his harness bells a shake
To ask if there is some mistake.
The only other sound's the sweep
Of easy wind and downy flake.

The woods are lovely, dark and deep.
But I have promises to keep,
And miles to go before I sleep,
And miles to go before I sleep.

ROBERT FROST

THE COUNTRY BEDROOM

My room's a square and candle-lighted boat,
In the surrounding depths of night afloat.
My windows are the portholes, and the seas
The sound of rain on the dark apple-trees.

Sea monster-like beneath, an old horse blows
A snort of darkness from his sleeping nose,
Below, among drowned daisies. Far off, hark!
Far off one owl amidst the waves of dark.

FRANCES CORNFORD

[173]

TENANTS

Suddenly, out of dark and leafy ways,
We came upon the little house asleep
In cold blind stillness, shadowless and deep,
In the white magic of the full moon-blaze:
Strangers without the gate, we stood agaze,
Fearful to break that quiet, and to creep
Into the house that had been ours to keep
Through a long year of happy nights and days.
So unfamiliar in the white moon-gleam,
So old and ghostly like a house of dream
It seemed, that over us there stole the dread
That even as we watched it, side by side,
The ghosts of lovers, who had lived and died
Within its walls, were sleeping in our bed.

WILFRID GIBSON

HOUSE FEAR

Always — I tell you this they learned —
Always at night when they returned
To the lonely house from far away
To lamps unlighted and fire gone gray,
They learned to rattle the lock and key
To give whatever might chance to be
Warning and time to be off in flight:
And preferring the out- to the in-door night,
They learned to leave the house-door wide
Until they had lit the lamp inside.

ROBERT FROST

OUT IN THE DARK

Out in the dark over the snow
The fallow fawns invisible go
With the fallow doe;
And the winds blow
Fast as the stars are slow.

Stealthily the dark haunts round
And, when the lamp goes, without sound
At a swifter bound
Than the swiftest hound,
Arrives, and all else is drowned;

And I and star and wind and deer,
Are in the dark together, — near,
Yet far, — and fear
Drums on my ear
In that sage company drear.

How weak and little is the light,
All the universe of sight,
Love and delight,
Before the might,
If you love it not, of night.

EDWARD THOMAS

"FAR . . ."

Far in a western brookland
  That bred me long ago
The poplars stand and tremble
  By pools I used to know.

There, in the windless night-time,
  The wanderer, marvelling why,
Halts on the bridge to hearken
  How soft the poplars sigh.

[175]

He hears: no more remembered
  In fields where I was known,
Here I lie down in London
  And turn to rest alone.

There, by the starlit fences,
  The wanderer halts and hears
My soul that lingers sighing
  About the glimmering weirs.

A. E. HOUSMAN

SAY NOT 'TIS DARK

Say not 'tis dark! — the night
  Is never dark to me;
Around my couch they come in light —
  Visions I would not see:

Forms I have loved, — as bright
  As in life's joyous years;
Say not 'tis dark! — the murkiest night
  Hath light enough for tears.

CAROLINE NORTON

THE EXILE

In the dead middle of night,
Quiet and cold,
I heard the screwk of Chantecleer:
Three times he called.
It was an angry signature
Upon the silence scrawled.

Thrice at the frozen hour
He cried his crow,
Waking from dreams of what he was
Millenniums ago,

When, in forests of India,
Under a royal sun,
He with his wives, many and meek,
Lived like Solomon.

Some vestiges remain
Of dreams so deep:
Round his insulted heart
Sick humours creep:
And with his crooked crow he signs
The death-warrant of sleep.

GERALD BULLETT

OUR LADIES OF SORROW

The eldest of the three is named *Mater Lachrymarum,* Our Lady of Tears. She it is that night and day raves and moans, calling for vanished faces. . . .

The second Sister is called *Mater Suspiriorum,* Our Lady of Sighs. She never scales the clouds, nor walks abroad upon the winds. She wears no diadem. And her eyes, if they were ever seen, would be neither sweet nor subtle; no man could read their story; they would be found filled with perishing dreams, and with wrecks of forgotten delirium. But she raises not her eyes; her head . . . droops for ever, for ever fastens on the dust. . . . Hers is the meekness that belongs to the hopeless. Murmur she may, but it is in her sleep. Whisper she may, but it is to herself in the twilight. Mutter she does at times, but it is in solitary places that are desolate as she is desolate; in ruined cities, and when the sun has gone down to his rest. . . .

But the third Sister, who is also the youngest! — Hush! whisper while we talk of *her!* Her kingdom is not large, or else no flesh should live; but within that kingdom all powers is hers. Her head, turreted like that of Cybele, rises almost beyond the reach of sight. She droops not; and her eyes rising so high *might* be hidden by distance. But being what they are, they cannot be hidden; through the treble veil of crape which she wears, the fierce light of a blazing misery that rests not for matins or for vespers, for noon of day or noon of night, for ebbing or for flowing tide, may be read from the very ground. She is the defier of God. She also is the mother of lunacies, and the suggestress of suicides. Deep lie the roots of her power; but narrow is the nation that she rules. For she can approach only those in whom a profound nature has been upheaved by central convulsions; in whom the heart trembles and the brain rocks under conspiracies of tempest from without and tempest from within. Madonna moves with uncertain steps, fast or slow, but still with tragic grace. Our Lady of Sighs creeps timidly and stealthily. But this youngest Sister moves with incalculable motions, bounding, and with a tiger's leaps. She carries no key; for, though coming rarely amongst men, she storms all doors at which she is permitted to enter at all. And *her* name is *Mater Tenebrarum*, our Lady of Darkness.

THOMAS DE QUINCEY

Tired Nature's sweet restorer, balmy Sleep!
He, like the world, his ready visit pays
Where Fortune smiles; the wretched he forsakes:
Swift on his downy pinion flies from woe,
And lights on lids unsullied with a tear. . . .
I wake, emerging from a sea of dreams
Tumultuous; where my wrecked desponding thought
From wave to wave of fancied misery
At random drove, her helm of reason lost. . . .
  Night, sable goddess! from her ebon throne,
In rayless majesty now stretches forth
Her leaden sceptre o'er a slumbering world.
Silence how dead! and darkness how profound! . . .
  The bell strikes One. . . .

EDWARD YOUNG

NIGHT AND SLEEP

How strange at night to wake
   And watch, while others sleep,
Till sight and hearing ache
   For objects that may keep
The awful inner sense
   Unroused, lest it should mark
The life that haunts the emptiness
   And horror of the dark!

How strange at night the bay
   Of dogs, how wild the note
Of cocks that scream for day,
   In homesteads far remote;
How strange and wild to hear
   The old and crumbling tower,
Amid the darkness, suddenly
   Take tongue and speak the hour!

If dreams or panic dread
   Reveal the gloom of gloom,
Kiss thou the pillowed head
   By thine, and soft resume
The confident embrace,
   And so each other keep
In the sure league of amity,
   And the safe lap of sleep.

Albeit the love-sick brain
   Affects the dreary moon,
Ill things alone refrain
   From life's nocturnal swoon:
Men melancholy mad,
   Beasts ravenous and sly,
The robber and the murderer,
   Remorse, with lidless eye.

The nightingale is gay,
　For she can vanquish night;
Dreaming, she sings of day
　Notes that make darkness bright;
But when the refluent gloom
　Saddens the gaps of song,
Men charge on her the dolefulness,
　And call her crazed with wrong.

COVENTRY PATMORE

TO HIS SWEET SAVIOUR

Night hath no wings, to him that cannot sleep;
And Time seems then, not for to flie, but creep;
Slowly her chariot drives, as if that she
Had broke her wheele, or crackt her axeltree.
Just so it is with me, who list'ning, pray
The winds, to blow the tedious night away;
That I might see the cheerfull peeping day.
Sick is my heart; O Saviour! do Thou please
To make my bed soft in my sicknesses:
Lighten my candle, so that I beneath
Sleep not for ever in the vaults of death:
Let me Thy voice betimes i' th' morning heare;
Call, and I'le come; say Thou, the when, and where:
Draw me, but first, and after Thee I'le run,
And make no one stop, till my race be done.

ROBERT HERRICK

THE REVIVAL

Unfold, unfold! take in his light,
Who makes thy Cares more short than night.
The Joys, which with his *Day-star* rise,
He deals to all, but drowsy Eyes:

[180]

And what the men of this world miss,
Some *drops* and *dews* of future bliss.
　　Hark! how his *winds* have changed their *note,*
And with warm whispers call thee out.
The *frosts* are past, the *storms* are gone:
And backward *life* at last comes on.
The lofty *groves* in express Joyes
Reply unto the *Turtles* voice,
And here in *dust* and *dirt,* O here
The *Lilies* of his love appear!

HENRY VAUGHAN

THE LARK

Swift through the yielding air I glide
While night's sable shades abide,
Yet in my flight, though ne'er so fast,
I tune and time the wild wind's blast:

And e'er the sun be come about,
Teach the young lark his lesson out;
Who, early as the day is born,
Sings his shrill *Ave* to the rising morn.

Let never mortal lose the pain
To imitate my airy strain,
Whose pitch, too high for human ears,
Was set me by the tuneful spheres.

I carol to the fairy king,
Wake him a-mornings when I sing,
And when the sun stoops to the deep,
Rock him again and his fair queen asleep.

Bed

He that lies at the stock,
Shall have the gold rock;
He that lies at the wall,
Shall have the gold ball;
He that lies in the middle,
Shall have the gold fiddle.

Bed

Moreover to reduce the English people the more unto obedience and awe, he [William the Conqueror] took from them all their armour and weapons. He ordained also that the master of every household about eight of the clock in the evening, should cause his fire to be raked up in ashes, his lights to be put out; and then go to bed. Besides this, to the end that every man might have knowledge of the hour to go to rest, he gave order, that in all cities, towns and villages, where any church was, there should a bell be rung at the said hour, which custom is still used even unto this day, and commonly called by the French word, "Couvre feu," that is, "Rake up the fire."

RAPHAEL HOLINSHED

Every day when the Archbishop [Thomas Becket] arose from dinner, unless more important business prevented him, he always devoted himself to reading the Scripture until the hour of vespers, at the time of sunset. His bed was covered with soft coverlets and cloths of silk, embroidered on the surface with gold wrought therein; and while other people were asleep, he alone used to lie on the bare floor before his bed, repeating psalms and hymns, and never ceasing from prayers, until at last, overcome with fatigue, he would gradually recline his head upon a stone put beneath it in place of a pillow: and thus would his eyes enjoy sleep. . . . His inner garment was of coarse sackcloth made of goat's hair: with which his whole body was covered from the arms down to the knees. But his outer garments were remarkable for their splendour and extreme costliness, to the end that, thus deceiving human eyes, he might please the sight of God. . . .

ROGER DE HOVEDEN

The greatest personages in the land were content with arrangements which would be intolerable in the present day. There must have been cases of overcrowding which would have scandalised modern ideas. Indeed, we know from the minstrel's lays which have survived that it was customary for the whole household, except the lord and lady, not only to eat in the hall, but to use it as a sleeping apartment. If room could not be found in the hall, guests were quite content to sleep in the stables, or indeed anywhere under cover; and it was no particular mark of inferiority, nor in any way an unusual proceeding, for Ivanhoe, when he visited his father's house in disguise, to take his night's rest in the stable. Nor need we sympathise overmuch with Don Quixote when he was relegated to the loft of the inn for his repose. *Autres temps, autres mœurs.* Although the lord had his solar, or private room, it was certainly no more than he wanted, for it served for all purposes not public. It was at once bedroom and audience-chamber. Edward I and his queen were sitting on their bed, attended by the ladies of the court, when they were nearly killed by lightning in the year 1287. Nevertheless, limited as the accommodation was, it was considered enough for the purpose during the three centuries that followed the Conquest. . . .

J. A. GOTCH

. . . Of comfort or privacy in the modern sense these London houses [in the fourteenth century] had little to offer. The living rooms were frequently limited to hall and bower (i.e. bedroom); only the better sort had two chambers; glass was rare; in Paris, which was at least as well-built as London, a well-to-do citizen might well have windows of oiled linen for his bedroom, and even in 1575 a good-sized house at Sheffield contained only sixteen feet of glass altogether. Meanwhile the wooden shutters which did duty for casements were naturally full of chinks; and the inhabitants were exposed during dark night not only to the nuisance and danger of " common listeners at the eaves," against whom medieval town legislation is deservedly severe, but also to the far greater chances of burglary afforded by the frailty of their habitations. It is not infrequently recorded in medieval inquests that the housebreaker found his line of least resistance not through a window or a door, but through the wall itself. . . .

But the worst discomfort of the house, to the modern mind, was the want of privacy. There was generally but one bedroom; for most of the household the house meant simply the hall; and some of those with whom the rest were brought into such close contact might indeed be " gey ill to live wi'." We have seen that, even as a King's squire, Chaucer had not a bed to himself; and sometimes one bed had to accommodate three occupants. This was so ordered, for instance, by the 15th-century statutes of the choir-schools at Wells, which provided minutely for the packing: " two smaller boys with their heads to the head of the bed, and an older one with his head to the foot of the bed and his feet between the others' heads." A distinguished theologian of the same century, narrating a ghost-story of his own, begins quite naturally: " When I was a youth, and lay in a square chamber, which had only a single door well shut from within, together with three more companions in the same bed. . . ." One of these, we presently find, " was of greater age, and a man of some experience. . . ."

G. G. Coulton

. . . There are old men yet [in the reign of Queen Elizabeth] dwelling in the village where I remain which have noted three things to be marvellously altered in England within their sound remembrance. . . .

One is the multitude of chimneys lately erected. . . . The second is the great (though not general) amendment of lodging; for said they, our fathers, yea and we ourselves also, have lain full oft upon straw pallets, or rough mats covered only with a sheet, under coverlets made of dogswain, and a good round log under their heads instead of a bolster or pillow. If it were so that our fathers — or the good man of the house — had within seven years after his marriage purchased a mattress or a flock bed and thereto a sack of chaff to rest his head upon, he thought himself to be as well lodged as the lord of the town that peradventure lay seldom in a bed of down or whole feathers, so well were they contented and with such bare kind of furniture. Pillows (said they) were thought meet only for women. . . . As for servants, if they had any sheet above them it was well, for seldom had they any under their bodies to keep them from the pricking straws that ran oft through the canvas of the pallet and rased their hardened hides.

The third thing they tell of is the exchange of vessel, as of treen platters into pewter and wooden spoons into silver or tin. . . .

WILLIAM HARRISON

The furniture of the great chamber or bedroom was an elaborate affair, the hangings of the bed, walls, and windows often costing a very large sum. The oak or walnut bedsteads, finely carved and inlaid, consisted of a panelled head and corniced tester, supported on two posts at the foot. Occasionally the posts stood on plinths separate from the frame. The bedding, which was carried on a wide criss-cross of ropes, was a pallet of straw or wool underneath two or more feather beds; over the sheets and blankets lay another thin feather bed as a coverlid, with an embroidered quilt; curtains of needlework, tester valances, lower valances called basses, consisting of fine silks interwoven with gold and trimmed with most elaborate fringes, completed a structure that often cost considerably over £1,000 of our money. Some Elizabethan fringes for repairing the hangings of these beds have been reproduced in modern times, and have cost over £5 a yard. . . .

All important beds, small or large, were made more or less on these lines until the beginning of the seventeenth century, when in fashionable households the carved oak posts, tester, and back, were discarded, and the structure was hung with embroidered silk, linen, velvet, cloth, or other material. The bed at Knole, prepared for James I and hung entirely with embroidered cloth-of-gold, cost the Earl of Dorset £8,000 in money of that time. . . . The curtains round standing beds were carefully drawn and often pinned at night; draughty leaded glass, and ill-fitting doors, doubtless made these stuffy precautions necessary. . . .

There were no chests-of-drawers, few washing-tables, and, except in large houses, no regular dressing-tables. The top of a chest, furnished with cushions, served as a couch, and often as an extra bed, and a taller chest held the silver or brass ewer, basin, and other articles of toilet. These were, however, some-times placed an a shelf affixed to the wainscot. . . .

The other furniture of a fine bedroom comprised a hanging cupboard, carved or inlaid with marquetry, two or more carved chests, a small table for the little standing looking-glass, which by the end of the sixteenth century had begun to make its appearance, and silver boxes and jars for the many essences, cosmetics, and paints used by an Elizabethan lady of fashion. Wall mirrors were exceedingly scarce and small. . . .

PERCY MACQUOID

The extravagance in the upholstery of a state bedroom at this time for the child's mother [at her lying-in] is almost incredible. We read in a letter written by John Chamberlaine to Mrs. Alice Carton in 1612 that

"about this day sevenight, the Countess of Salisbury was brought a bed of a daughter, and lyes in very richly, for the hangings of her chamber being white satin embroidered with silver and pearl, is valued at fourteen thousand pounds."

Over fifty thousand pounds of our money seems a great ex-
penditure for the furniture and decoration of a lying-in
chamber, but it must be remembered that such events were
important functions in this extravagant age, and that presents,
receptions, and card parties in the room were considered
necessary for the lady's recovery. This custom of visiting and
making presents, usually of money, to the mother extended
to all classes. . . .

Percy Macquoid

GULLIVER'S BEDROOM IN BROBDINGNAG

. . . The queen commanded her own cabinet-maker to
contrive a box, that might serve me for a bed-chamber, after
the model that Glumdalclitch and I should agree upon. This
man was a most ingenious artist, and according to my directions, in three weeks, finished for me a wooden chamber of
sixteen feet square, and twelve high, with sash-windows, a
door and two closets, like a London bed-chamber. The board
that made the ceiling, was to be lifted up and down by two
hinges, to put in a bed ready furnished by her majesty's up-
holsterer, which Glumdalclitch took out every day to air,
made it with her own hands, and letting it down at night,
locked up the roof over me. A nice workman, who was famous for little curiosities, undertook to make me two chairs,
with backs and frames, of a substance not unlike ivory, and
two tables, with a cabinet to put my things in. The room was
quilted on all sides, as well as the floor and the ceiling, to prevent any accident from the carelessness of those who carried
me, and to break the force of a jolt, when I went in a coach.
I desired a lock for my door, to prevent rats and mice from
coming in. The smith, after several attempts, made the smallest that ever was seen among them, for I have known a larger
at the gate of a gentleman's house in England. I made a shift
to keep the key in a pocket of my own, fearing Glumdalclitch
might lose it. The queen likewise ordered the thinnest silks

that could be gotten, to make me clothes, not much thicker than an English blanket, very cumbersome till I was accustomed to them. They were after the fashion of the kingdom, partly resembling the Persian, and partly the Chinese, and are a very grave and decent habit. . . .

JONATHAN SWIFT

24th October, 1660. — . . . To Mr. Lilly's, where not finding Mr. Spong, I went to Mr. Greatorex, where I met him, and where I bought of him a drawing-pen; and he did show me the manner of the lamp-glasses, which carry the light a great way, good to read in bed by, and I intend to have one of them; and we looked at his wooden jack in his chimney, that goes with the smoke, which is indeed very pretty. . . .

SAMUEL PEPYS

RUSH–LIGHTS

Some address is required in dipping these rushes in the scalding fat or grease; but this knack also is to be attained by practice. The careful wife of an industrious Hampshire labourer obtains all her fat for nothing; for she saves the scummings of her bacon-pot for this use. . . . If men that keep bees will mix a little wax with the grease, it will give it a consistency, and render it more cleanly, and make the rushes burn longer; mutton-suet would have the same effect.

A good rush, which measured in length two feet four inches and a half, being minuted, burnt only three minutes short of an hour; and a rush of still greater length has been known to burn one hour and a quarter.

These rushes give a good clear light. Watch-lights (coated with tallow), it is true, shed a dismal one, " darkness visible "; but then the wick of those have two ribs of the rind, or peel, to support the pith, while the wick of the dipped rush has but one. . . .

GILBERT WHITE

15th August, 1665. — It was dark before I could get home, and so land at Churchyard stairs, where, to my great trouble, I met a dead corpse of the plague, in the narrow alley, just bringing down a little pair of stairs. But I thank God I was not much disturbed at it. However, I shall beware of being late abroad again.

16th. To the Exchange, where I have not been a great while. But, Lord! how sad a sight it is to see the streets empty of people, and very few upon the 'Change! Jealous of every door that one sees shut up, lest it should be the plague; and about us two shops in three, if not more, generally shut up. . . .

19th. Home; and having . . . wrote letters, I by water to Charing Cross, to the post-house, and there the people tell me they are shut up; and so I went to the new post-house, and there got a guide and horses to Hounslow. So to Staines, and there by this time it was dark night, and got a guide, who lost his way in the forest, till, by help of the moon (which recompences me for all the pains I ever took about studying of her motions), I led my guide into the way back again; and so we made a man rise that kept a gate, and so he carried us to Cranborne, where in the dark I perceive an old house new building, with a great deal of rubbish, and was fain to go up a ladder to Sir G. Carteret's chamber. And there in his bed I sat down, and told him all my bad news, which troubled him mightily; but yet we were very merry, and made the best of it; and being myself weary did take leave, and, after having spoken with Mr. Fenn in bed, I to bed in my Lady's chamber that she uses to lie in, where the Duchess of York, that now is, was born. So to sleep; being very well, but weary, and the better by having carried with me a bottle of strong water, whereof now and then a sip did me good.

Samuel Pepys

In the worst inn's worst room, with mat half hung,
The floor of plaster and the walls of dung,

Or once a flock-bed, but repaired with straw,
With tape-tied curtains, never meant to draw,
The George and Garter dangling from that bed,
Where tawdry yellow strove with dirty red,
Great Villiers lies — alas, how changed from him,
That life of pleasure, and that soul of whim!
Gallant and gay in Clivedon's proud alcove,
The bower of wanton Shrewsbury and love:
Or just as gay, at council, in the ring
Of mimic statesmen, and their merry king.
No wit to flatter, left of all his store!
No fool to laugh at, which he valued more.
There, victor of his health, of fortune, friends,
And fame, this lord of useless thousands ends.

ALEXANDER POPE

We went, with Madame Recamier and the Russian Princess
Dalgowski, to La Harpe's house, to hear him repeat some of
his own verses. He lives in a wretched house, and we went up
dirty stairs, through dirty passages, where I wondered how
fine ladies' trains and noses could go, and were received in a
dark, small den by the philosopher, or rather devot, for he
spurns the name of philosopher. He was in a dirty reddish
nightgown, and very dirty nightcap bound round the forehead with a superlatively dirty chocolate-coloured ribbon.
Madame Recamier, the beautiful, the elegant, robed in white
satin, trimmed with white fur, seated herself on the elbow of
his armchair, and besought him to repeat his verses.

MARIA EDGEWORTH to Mrs. Mary Sneyd (1803)

. . . The room, with its old-fashioned bed with faded curtains, was the picture of canopied misery. The sight still
haunts me, in spite of the intervening years. There was not
a book or a newspaper or a hand-bag or an ornament anywhere visible; nothing but the bed, a few chairs, and a table.
I had visited genius on the top floors of dingy houses, in gar-

rets far above the hum and movement of the material world, and yet in these places I had noticed signs of home-like comfort — there were books, an easy-chair, a pet cat or dog, and some one within calling distance. This room filled me with horror. [Verlaine] had alighted here like a bird of passage on a withered tree in the wilderness of Paris. He had come to this place I know not how nor for how long, and I am not sure that he felt the situation one way or the other, or gave himself much trouble about the appearance of the room, the house, or anything in it. I had opened the door of Bohemia, and looked in as we look at a ward in a hospital. . . .

FRANCIS GRIERSON

. . . That night our lodging was a house that stood
Alone, within the valley, at a point
Where, tumbling from aloft, a torrent swelled
The rapid stream whose margin we had trod;
A dreary mansion, large beyond all need,
With high and spacious rooms, deafened and stunned
By noise of waters, making innocent sleep
Lie melancholy among weary bones. . . .

WILLIAM WORDSWORTH,
from *The Prelude, Book VI*

. . . Along the floor
Of the small Cottage in the lonely Dell
A grateful couch was spread for our repose;
Where, in the guise of mountaineers, we lay,
Stretched upon fragrant heath, and lulled by sound
Of far-off torrents charming the still night,
And, to tired limbs and over-busy thoughts,
Inviting sleep and soft forgetfulness.

WILLIAM WORDSWORTH,
from *The Excursion, Book IV*

A DOCTOR'S ADVICE: 1830

(Abridged)

The chamber in which we sleep should always be large, high-roofed, and airy. In modern houses, the bed-rooms resemble closets more than any thing else. The bed itself ought to be large, and not placed near to the wall. The curtains should never be drawn closely together, even in the coldest weather. The mattress, or bed, on which we lie, ought always to be rather hard. Nothing is more injurious to health than soft beds; they effeminate the individual, render his flesh soft and flabby, and incapacitate him from undergoing any privation. The pillow, as well as the bed and mattress, should be pretty hard. When it is too soft, the head soon sinks in it, and becomes very hot and unpleasant. With regard to the covering, there can be no doubt that it is most wholesome to lie between sheets. A common custom prevails, of warming the bed before going to sleep. This, also, except with delicate people, and during very cold seasons, is pernicious. Fires are exceedingly hurtful. The window-shutters ought never to be entirely closed, neither ought they to be kept altogether open. A small portion of the window [should be] drawn down from the top, to promote a circulation of air; but this must be done cautiously. The late Dr. Gregory was in the habit of sleeping with the window drawn slightly down during the whole year. Nothing is so injurious as damp beds. On going to sleep the collar of the night-shirt should be unbuttoned, and the neck-cloth taken off. We should wear a thin cotton or silk night-cap; and this is still better if made of network. Some persons wear worsted, or flannel caps, but these are exceedingly improper. In fact, the chief use of this piece of clothing is to preserve the hair, and prevent it from being disordered and matted together. Sleeping in stockings is a bad and uncleanly habit, which should never be practised. Most people pass the greater part of the night upon the side. According to Dr. A.

Hunter, women who love their husbands generally lie upon their right side. It is more wholesome to sleep single than double. The Chinese recommend brushing the teeth and gums previous to lying down. The practice of sleeping in the open air cannot be too strongly reprobated. It is, at all times, dangerous, especially when carried into effect under a burning sun, or amid the damps of night.

Robert Macnish

On Sleep

Lord! what good hours do we keep!
How quietly we sleep! . . .

On Sleep

Among the innumerable mortifications that waylay human arrogance on every side, may well be reckoned our ignorance of the most common objects and effects, a defect of which we become more sensible, by every attempt to supply it. Vulgar and inactive minds confound familiarity with knowledge, and conceive themselves informed of the whole nature of things, when they are shown their form or told their use; but the speculatist, who is not content with superficial views, harasses himself with fruitless curiosity, and still as he inquires more, perceives only that he knows less.

Sleep is a state in which a great part of every life is passed. No animal has been yet discovered, whose existence is not varied with intervals of insensibility; and some late philosophers have extended the empire of sleep over the vegetable world.

Yet of this change, so frequent, so great, so general, and so necessary, no searcher has yet found either the efficient or final cause; or can tell by what power the mind and body are thus chained down in irresistible stupefaction; or what benefits the animal receives from this alternate suspension of its active powers.

Whatever may be the multiplicity or contrariety of opinions upon this subject, nature has taken sufficient care that theory shall have little influence on practice. The most diligent inquirer is not able long to keep his eyes open; the most eager disputant will begin about midnight to desert his argument; and, once in four-and-twenty hours, the gay and the gloomy,

the witty and the dull, the clamorous and the silent, the busy
and the idle, are all overpowered by the gentle tyrant, and all
lie down in the equality of sleep. . . .

SAMUEL JOHNSON

ANIMAL SLEEP

Although we spend a large fraction of our life in sleep, we
are far from understanding what it precisely means, either for
ourselves or for animals. Sleep is part of an established
rhythm, a state of partial fatigue in the higher nerve-centres,
during which recuperation occurs, probably associated with
the removal of subtle waste-products or *toxins*. It is " natural," we say, that rest should alternate with activity. Yet, as
we repeat this, the difficulty arises in our mind that many animals — most animals, indeed — do not sleep at all; that
many parts of our body, such as heart and lungs, food-canal
and kidneys, go on doing their work while we sleep; that
our spinal cord must be a very light sleeper, and that the
" breathing centre " in our medulla does not seem to need a
rest all the days of our life. The necessity for rest after work
does not carry us far towards an understanding of sleep.

Perhaps there is a flash of light on the problem in the fact
that, with few exceptions, only the higher animals seem to
require sleep. We must exclude mere resting, seen in many
fishes and reptiles; we must exclude hibernation, cold coma,
and animal hypnosis; we must exclude the suspended animation of many of the simple creatures that lie low. Sleep is
different from all these; it is a peculiar state in which all the
everyday functions are continuing; even the muscle-engines
are going, though not in gear; the blinds of the body, notably
the eyelids, are drawn down; only to a slight extent are we
able to " answer the door " to the knockings of the outer
world; except in somnambulism, we have very little power of
moving about without first awakening. In this sense a number of the more intelligent mammals, like horse and dog, are
genuine sleepers. A dog that cannot get a sleep will die in

four or five days. On the other hand, it is said that some of the less intelligent mammals, such as guinea-pigs, never fall asleep. This points to the theory, suggested by Professor Hempelmann, that sleep is a tax on having a really fine forebrain. The less intellectual the animal, the less sleep it needs. We pay for our wits by becoming sleepy.

J. Arthur Thomson

. . . Nothing ought so much to be recommended unto youth as activity and vigilancy. Our life is nothing but motion, I am hardly shaken, and am slow in all things, be it to rise, to goe to bed, or to my meales. Seaven of the clocke in the morning is to me an early houre; and where I may command, I neither dine before eleven, nor sup till after six. I have heretofore imputed the cause of agues or maladies, whereinto I have falne, to the lumpish heavinesse or drowzy dullnesse which my long sleeping had caused me, and ever repented mee to fall asleepe againe in the morning. Plato condemnes more the excesse of sleeping than the surfet of drinking. I love to lie hard and alone, yea and without a woman by me, after the kingly manner; somewhat well and warme covered. I never had my bed warmed, but since I came to be an old man, if need require, I have clothes given me to warme my feete and my stomacke. . . . If there be any curiosity in my behaviour or manner of life, it is rather about my going to bed than any thing else; but if neede bee, I generally yeeld and accommodate my selfe unto necessity, as well and as quietly, as any other whosoever. Sleeping hath possessed a great part of my life; and as old as I am, I can sleepe eight or nine houres together. I doe with profit withdraw my self from this sluggish propension, and evidently finde my selfe better by it. Indeede, I somewhat feele the stroke of alteration, but in three dayes it is past. And I see few that live with lesse (when need is), and that more constantly exercise themselves, nor whom toyling and labour offend lesse. . . .

Montaigne, translated by John Florio

OF THE SLOTHFUL

He takes no less care how to spend time than others how to gain by the expense; and when business importunes him, is more troubled to forethink what he must do, than another to effect it. Summer is out of his favour for nothing but long days that make no haste to their even. He loves still to have the sun witness of his rising, and lies long, more for lothness to dress him than will to sleep; and after some streaking and yawning, calls for dinner unwashed, which having digested with a sleep in his chair, he walks forth to the bench in the market-place, and looks for companions. Whomsoever he meets he stays with idle questions, and lingering discourse; how the days are lengthened, how kindly the weather is, how false the clock, how forward the spring, and ends ever with, What shall we do? It pleases him no less to hinder others than not to work himself. When all the people are gone from church, he is left sleeping in his seat alone. . . . He is so loth to leave his neighbour's fire, that he is fain to walk home in the dark; and if he be not looked to, wears out the night in the chimney-corner, or if not that, lies down in his clothes, to save two labours. He eats and prays himself asleep, and dreams of no other torment but work. This man is a standing pool, and cannot choose but gather corruption. He is descried amongst a thousand neighbours by a dry and nasty hand, that still savours of the sheet, a beard uncut, unkempt, an eye and ear yellow with their excretions, a coat shaken on, ragged, unbrushed, by linen and face striving whether shall excel in uncleanness. For body, he hath a swollen leg, a dusky and swinish eye, a blown cheek, a drawling tongue, an heavy foot, and is nothing but a colder earth moulded with standing water. . . .

JOSEPH HALL

THE SLUGGARD

'Tis the Voice of the Sluggard; I heard him complain,
" You have waked me too soon; I must slumber again; "

As the Door on its Hinges, so he on his Bed,
Turns his Sides, and his Shoulders, and his heavy Head.

" A little more Sleep, and a little more Slumber ";
Thus he wastes half his Days, and his Hours without Number;
And when he gets up, he sits folding his Hands,
Or walks about saunt'ring, or trifling he stands.

I passed by his Garden, and saw the wild Brier
The Thorn and the Thistle grow broader and higher;
The Clothes that hang on him are turning to Rags;
And his Money still wastes, till he starves or he begs.

I made him a Visit, still hoping to find
That he took better Care for improving his Mind;
He told me his Dreams, talked of Eating and Drinking;
But he scarce reads his Bible, and never loves Thinking.

Said I then to my Heart, " Here's a Lesson for me;
That Man's but a Picture of what I might be;
But thanks to my Friends for their Care in my Breeding,
Who taught me betimes to love Working and Reading."

ISAAC WATTS

. . . " In some churches the sidesmen gang about with
staves as in old days they used, when required, whips and
dog-tongs and give every sleeper a good nope."

As waking that hurts, by all means must be avoided, so
sleep, which so much helps, by like ways, " must be procured,
by nature or art, inward or outward medicines, and be protracted longer than ordinary, if it may be, as being an especial
help." It moistens and fattens the body, concocts, and helps
digestion (as we see in dormice, and those Alpine mice that
sleep all winter), which Gesner speaks of, when they are so

found sleeping under the snow in the dead of winter, as fat as butter. It expels cares, pacifies the mind, refresheth the weary limbs after long work. . . .

The chiefest thing in all physic, Paracelsus calls it, *omnia arcana gemmarum superans et metallorum.* The fittest time is " two or three hours after supper, when as the meat is now settled at the bottom of the stomach, and 'tis good to lie on the right side first, because at that site the liver doth rest under the stomach, not molesting any way, but heating him as a fire doth a kettle, that is put to it. After the first sleep 'tis not amiss to lie on the left side, that the meat may the better descend "; and sometimes again on the belly, but never on the back. Seven or eight hours is a competent time for a melancholy man to rest, as Crato thinks; but as some do, to lie in bed and not sleep, a day, or half a day together, to give assent to pleasing conceits and vain imaginations, is many ways pernicious. To procure this sweet moistening sleep, it's best to take away the occasions (if it be possible) that hinder it, and then to use such inward or outward remedies, which may cause it. . . . Many cannot sleep for witches and fascinations, which are too familiar in some places. . . . But the ordinary causes are heat and dryness, which must first be removed: a hot and dry brain never sleeps well: grief, fears, cares, expectations, anxieties, great businesses . . . and all violent perturbations of the mind, must in some sort be qualified, before we can hope for any good repose. He that sleeps in the day time, or is in suspense, fear, any way troubled in mind, or goes to bed upon a full stomach, may never hope for quiet rest in the night; *nec enim meritoria somnos admittunt,* as the poet saith; inns and such like troublesome places are not for sleep; one calls ostler, another tapster, one cries and shouts, another sings, whoops, halloos. . . . Who not accustomed to such noises can sleep amongst them? He that will intend to take his rest must go to bed . . . with a secure and composed mind, in a quiet place . . . and if that will not serve, or may not be obtained, to seek then such means as are requisite. To lie in clean linen and sweet; before he goes to bed, or in

bed, to hear "sweet music" . . . "to read some pleasant
author till he be asleep, to have a bason of water still dropping
by his bedside," or to lie near that pleasant murmur, *lene
sonantis aquae.* Some floodgates, arches, falls of water, like
London Bridge, or some continuate noise which may benumb
the senses, *lenis motus, silentium et tenebra, tum et ipsa vo-
luntas somnos faciunt;* as a gentle noise to some procures
sleep, so . . . silence, in a dark room, and the will itself, is
most available to others. Piso commends frications, Andrew
Borde a good draught of strong drink before one goes to bed;
I say, a nutmeg and ale, or a good draught of muscadine, with
a toast and nutmeg, or a posset of the same, which many use in
a morning, but methinks, for such as have dry brains, are
much more proper at night; some prescribe a sup of vinegar
as they go to bed, a spoonful . . . As for baths, fomentations,
oils, potions, simples or compounds, inwardly taken to this
purpose, I shall speak of them elsewhere. If, in the midst of
the night, when they lie awake, which is usual to toss and
tumble, and not sleep, Ranzovius would have them, if it be
in warm weather, to rise and walk three or four turns (till they
be cold) about the chamber, and then go to bed again. . . .

ROBERT BURTON

. . . There is a fruitful branch of homoeopathic magic
which works by means of the dead; for just as the dead can
neither see nor hear nor speak, so you may on homoeopathic
principles render people blind, deaf, and dumb by the use of
dead men's bones or anything else that is tainted by the infec-
tion of death. Thus among the Galelareese, when a young
man goes a-wooing at night, he takes a little earth from a
grave and strews it on the roof of his sweetheart's house just
above the place where her parents sleep. . . . With the same
intention a Hindoo will strew ashes from a pyre at the door
of the house; Indians of Peru scatter the dust of dead men's
bones; and Ruthenian burglars remove the marrow from a
human shin-bone, pour tallow into it, and having kindled the

tallow, march thrice round the house with this candle burning, which causes the inmates to sleep a death-like sleep. Or
the Ruthenian will make a flute out of a human leg-bone and
play upon it; whereupon all persons within hearing are overcome with drowsiness. . . . In Europe similar properties
were ascribed to the Hand of Glory, which was the dried and
pickled hand of a man who had been hanged. If a candle
made of the fat of a malefactor who had also died on the gallows was lighted and placed in the Hand of Glory as in a
candlestick, it rendered motionless all persons to whom it
was presented; they could not stir a finger any more than if
they were dead. Sometimes the dead man's hand is itself the
candle, or rather bunch of candles, all its withered fingers
being set on fire; but should any member of the household
be awake, one of the fingers will not kindle. Such nefarious
lights can only be extinguished with milk. Often it is prescribed that the thief's candle should be made of the finger
of a new-born or, still better, unborn child; sometimes it is
thought needful that the thief should have one such candle
for every person in the house, for if he has one candle too little
somebody in the house will wake and catch him. Once these
tapers begin to burn, there is nothing but milk that will put
them out. . . .

SIR JAMES GEORGE FRAZER

I mentioned that Lord Monboddo told me, he awaked
every morning at four, and then for his health got up and
walked in his room naked, with the window open, which he
called taking *an air bath;* after which he went to bed again,
and slept two hours more. Johnson, who was always ready to
beat down anything that seemed to be exhibited with dis-
proportionate importance, thus observed: "I suppose, Sir,
there is no more in it than this, he wakes at four, and cannot
sleep till he chills himself, and makes the warmth of the bed a
grateful sensation."

I talked of the difficulty of rising in the morning. Dr. Johnson told me, "that the learned Mrs. Carter, at that period

when she was eager in study, did not awake as early as she wished, and she therefore had a contrivance, that, at a certain hour, her chamber-light should burn a string to which a heavy weight was suspended, which then fell with a strong sudden noise: this roused her from her sleep, and then she had no difficulty in getting up." But I said *that* was my difficulty; and wished there could be some medicine invented which would make one rise without pain, which I never did, unless after lying in bed a very long time. Perhaps there may be something in the stores of nature which could do this. I have thought of a pulley to raise me gradually; but that would give me pain, as it would counteract my internal inclination. I would have something that can dissipate the *vis inertiae,* and give elasticity to the muscles. As I imagine that the human body may be put, by the operation of other substances, into any state in which it has ever been; and as I have experienced a state in which rising from bed was not disagreeable, but easy, nay, sometimes agreeable; I suppose that this state may be produced, if we knew by what. We can heat the body, we can cool it; we can give it tension or relaxation; and surely it is possible to bring it into a state in which rising from bed will not be a pain.

Johnson observed, that "a man should take a sufficient quantity of sleep, which Dr. Mead says is between seven and nine hours." I told him, that Dr. Cullen said to me, that a man should not take more sleep than he can take at once. JOHNSON: "This rule, Sir, cannot hold in all cases; for many people have their sleep broken by sickness; and surely Cullen would not have a man to get up, after having slept but an hour. Such a regimen would soon end in a *long sleep.*"[1]

JAMES BOSWELL

---

[1] This regimen was, however, practised by Bishop Ken, of whom Hawkins (*not* Sir John) in his life of that venerable prelate, p. 4, tells us, "And that neither his study might be the aggressor on his hours of instruction, or what he judged his duty, prevent his improvements; or both, his closest addresses to his GOD; he strictly accustomed himself to but one sleep, which often obliged him to rise at one or two of the clock in the morning, and sometimes sooner; and

His Lordship [Francis Bacon] would often drinke a good draught of strong Beer (March beer) to-bedwards, to lay his working fancy asleep, which otherwise would keep him from sleeping a great part of the night. . . .

JOHN AUBREY

At his Diet he [Thomas Fuller] was very sparing and temperate, but yet he allowed himself the repasts and refreshings of two Meals a day: but no lover of Dainties, or the Inventions of Cookery: solid meats better fitting his strength of Constitution. . . . But his great abstinence of all was from Sleep, and strange it was that one of such a Fleshly and sanguine composition, could over-watch so many heavy propense inclinations to Rest. For this in some sort he was beholden to his care in Diet aforesaid (the full Vapours of a repletion in the Stomack ascending to the Brain, causing that usual Drowsinesse we see in many). . . .

" In Spain I shaved myself over-night, and usually slept five or six hours; sometimes, indeed, only three or four, and sometimes only two. In India I never undressed; it is not the custom there; and for many years in the Peninsula I undressed very seldom; never for the first four years." . . .

" Strange impressions come now and then after a battle; and such came to me after the battle of Assaye in India. I slept in a farm yard; and whenever I awaked, it struck me that I had lost all my friends, so many had I lost in that battle. Again and again, as often as I awaked, did it disturb me. In the morning I inquired anxiously after one and an-

---

grew so habitual, that it continued with him almost till his last illness. And so lively and cheerful was his temper, that he would be very facetious and entertaining to his friends in the evening, even when it was perceived that with difficulty he kept his eyes open, and then seemed to go to rest with no other purpose than the refreshing and enabling him with more vigour and cheerfulness to sing his morning hymn, as he then used to do to his lute before he put on his clothes."

other; nor was I convinced that they were living till I saw
them. . . ."   SAMUEL ROGERS,
from *Recollections of the Duke of Wellington*

. . . *Otho* the Emperour having determined to kill himselfe;
the very same night, after he had given order for his domesti-
cal affaires; shared his monie among his servants, and whetted
the edge of a sword, wherewith he intended to wound himselfe, expecting no other thing, but to know whether all his
friends were gone to rest, fell into so sound a sleepe, that the
groomes of his chamber heard him snort in another roome.
. . . But concerning young *Marius* who committed a greater
errour [even than Augustus — who fell asleep " the instant he
should goe to fight " against *Sextus Pompeius* in *Sicilia*] (for
on the day of his last battell against *Sylla,* after he had mar-
shalled his army, and given the word or signall of the battell)
he lay downe in the shadow under a tree, a while to rest
himselfe, and fell so fast asleep, that he could hardly be
awaked with the rout and flight of his men, having seene no
part of the fight, they say, it was because he was so exceedingly aggravated with travell, and over-tired with wearinesse,
and want of sleep, that nature was overcome, and could no
longer endure. And touching this point, Phisitians may consider; whether sleep be so necessarie, that our life must needs
depend of it: For we finde that *Perseus* King of *Macedon,*
prisoner at *Rome,* being kept from sleep, was made to die; but
Plinie aleageth, that some have lived a long time without any
sleep at all. And *Herodotus* reporteth, *There are Nations,
where men sleep and wake by halfe yeares.* And those that
write the life of *Epimenides* the wise, affirme, *that he slept
the continuale space of seven and fifty yeares.*

MONTAIGNE, translated by John Florio

SOMNOLENCY

A remarkable case of somnolency is described by Major
Elliot, professor of mathematics in the Academy of West
Point, in America. A young lady, of a cultivated mind, re-

covered from an attack of somnolency with the loss of all her acquired knowledge. She immediately began the first elements of education (but what precisely these were, e.g. learning to talk, the recorder does not, alas, relate), and had made a considerable progress, when a second fit of somnolency restored to her the knowledge of which the first had deprived her, but obliterated all recollection of what had taken place during the interval. A third attack left her again in a state of ignorance; and these alternate intellectual conditions occurred during a period of four years, with the extraordinary circumstance that, when in the one state, she retained all her original knowledge, but when in the other she retained only what she had acquired since the first attack. In the interval of health, for example, her penmanship was beautiful; but during the paroxysm she wrote " a poor awkward hand." Persons introduced to her during the healthy interval she recognised only during a subsequent healthy interval, and not during the paroxysm, and *vice versa.*

from *Wilson's Wonderful Characters*

On Sunday evening, the 6th of October, 1823, a lad named George Davis, sixteen and a half years of age, in the service of Mr. Hewson, butcher, of Bridge-road, Lambeth, at about twenty minutes after nine o'clock, bent forward in his chair, and rested his forehead on his hands. In ten minutes he started up, fetched his whip, put on his one spur, and went thence to the stable; not finding his own saddle in the proper place, he returned to the house, and asked for it. Being asked what he wanted with it, he replied, to go his rounds. He returned to the stable, got on the horse without the saddle, and was proceeding to leave the stable; it was with much difficulty and force that Mr. Hewson junior, assisted by the other lad, could remove him from the horse; his strength was great, and it was with difficulty he was brought in doors. Mr. Hewson senior, coming home at this time, sent for Mr. Benjamin Ridge, an eminent practitioner, in Bridge-road, who stood by him for a quarter of an hour, during which time the lad considered himself stopped at the turnpike gate, and took sixpence out of his pocket to be changed; and holding out his hand for the change, the sixpence was returned to him. He immediately observed, " None of your nonsense — that is the sixpence again, give me my change." When threepence half-penny was given to him, he counted it over, and said, " None of your gammon; that is not right, I want a penny more "; making the fourpence halfpenny, which was his proper change. He then said, " give me my *custor* " (meaning his hat), which slang terms he had been in the habit of using, and then began to whip and spur to get his horse on; his pulse at this time was one hundred and thirty-six, full and hard; no change of countenance could be observed, nor any spasmodic affection of the muscles, the eyes remaining closed the whole of the time. His coat was taken off his arm, his shirt sleeve stripped up, and Mr. Ridge bled him to thirty-two ounces; no alteration had taken place in him during the first part of the time the blood was flowing; at about twenty-four ounces, the pulse began to decrease; and when the full quantity named above had been taken, it was at eighty, with a slight perspiration on the forehead. During the time of bleeding Mr. Hewson related the circumstance of a Mr. Harris, optician in Holborn, whose son some years before walked out on the parapet of the house in his sleep. The boy joined the conversation, and observed he lived at the corner of Brownlow-street. After the arm was tied up, he unlaced one boot, and said he would go to bed. In three minutes from this time he awoke, got up, and asked what was the matter (having then been one hour in the trance), not having the slightest recollection of any thing that had passed, and wondered at his arm being tied up, and at the blood, &c. A strong aperient medicine was then administered, he went to bed, slept sound, and the next day appeared perfectly well, excepting debility from the bleeding and operation of the medicine, and had no recollection whatever of what had taken place. None of his family or himself were ever affected in this way before. . . .

from *The Times,* October 1823

[211]

TO HIS BED

My bed, the rest of all my cares,
   The end of toiling pain,
Which bringest ease and solace sweet,
   While darkness doth remain;
My bed, yield to me slumber sweet,
   And trifling dreams repel;
Cause carking care from sobbing breast
   To part, where it doth dwell;
All mockeries of this wretched world
   Put clean from out my mind:
Do these, my bed, and then by thee
   Much comfort shall I find.

AN ANSWER

That I may be a rest of cares,
   An end of toiling pain,
See stomach thine be not surcharged
   When sleep thou wouldest gain.
If sugared sleep (devoid of dreams)
   Thou likest to enjoy,
Then live with little, and beware
   No cares thy head annoy.
And lastly deem thy feathered bed
   Always thy grasping grave:
So rest by me thou shalt obtain,
   And eke much comfort have.

TIMOTHY KENDALL

SWEET ISABELL

Here lies sweet Isabell in bed,
With a night-cap on her head;
Her skin is soft, her face is fair,
And she has very pretty hair;
She and I in bed lies nice,
And undisturbed by rats or mice;
She is disgusted with Mr Worgan,
Though he plays upon the organ.
Her nails are neat, her teeth are white,
Her eyes are very, very bright;
In a conspicuous town she lives,
And to the poor her money gives;
Here ends sweet Isabella's story,
And may it be much to her glory.

MARJORIE FLEMING

THE MAID OF THE MOOR

Maiden in the moor lay,
    In the moor lay,
Sennight full and a day,
What was her meat?
What was her meat?
    The primrose and the violet,
    The primrose and the violet.
What was her drink?
    The cold water of the well-spring,
What was her bower?
    The red rose and the lily flower.

ARYSE ERLY

Aryse erly
Serve god devowtely
And the Worlde beseley
Do thy worke wisely
Yeve thyne almes secretely
Goo by the waye sadly
Answer the people demuerly
Go to thy mete apetitely
Sit thereat discretely
Of thy tunge be not to liberally
Arise therefrom temperally
Go to thy supper soberly
And to thy bed merrely
Be in thy Inne jocundly
Plese thy love duely
And slepe suerly.

ALL'S DONE

All's done.
All's said.
To-night
In a strange bed
Alone
I lie.
So slight
So hid
As in a chrysalid
A butterfly.

"The Drowsy Approaches"

. . . Sleep, downy sleep, come close mine eyes,
Tired with beholding vanities;
Sweet slumbers come and chase away
The toils and follies of the day. . . .

Deeply have I slept.
As one who hath gone down into the Springs
Of his existence and there bathed. . . .
I awaked, and my sleep was sweet to me. . . .

"The Drowsy Approaches"

But the Quincunx of Heaven runs low, and 'tis time to close the five ports of knowledge; We are unwilling to spin out our awaking thoughts into the phantasmes of sleep, which often continueth praecogitations; making Cables of Cobwebbes, and Wildernesses of handsome Groves. Beside *Hippocrates* hath spoke so little and the Oneirocritical Masters have left such frigid Interpretations from plants, that there is little encouragement to dream of Paradise itself. Nor will the sweetest delight of Gardens afford much comfort in sleep; wherein the dulnesse of that sense shakes hands with detectable odours; and though in the Bed of *Cleopatra,* can hardly with any delight raise up the ghost of a Rose.

Night, which Pagan Theology could make the daughter of *Chaos,* affords no advantage to the description of order; Although no lower than that masse can we derive its Genealogy. All things began in order, so shall they end, and so shall they begin again; according to the ordainer of order, and mystical Mathematicks of the City of heaven.

Though *Somnus* in *Homer* be sent to rowse up Agamemnon, I finde no such effects in these drowsy approaches of sleep. To keep our eyes open longer were but to act out *Antipodes.* The Huntsmen are up in *America,* and they are already past their first sleep in *Persia.* But who can be drowsie at that hour which freed us from everlasting sleep? or have slumbring thoughts at that time, when sleep itself must end, and as some conjecture all shall awake again?

Sir Thomas Browne

CAVE OF SOMNUS

Near the Cimmerian land, deep-caverned, lies
A hollow mount, the home of sluggish Sleep;
Where never ray from morn or evening skies
Can enter, but where blackening vapours creep,
And doubtful gloom unbroken sway doth keep.
There never crested bird evokes the dawn,
Nor watchful dogs disturb the silence deep,
Nor wandering beast, nor forest tempest-torn,
Nor harsher sound of human passions born.
Mute quiet reigns; — but from the lowest cave
A spring Lethean rising evermore
Pours through the murmuring rocks a slumberous wave.
The plenteous poppy blossoms at the door,
And countless herbs, of night the drowsy store.

Translated by DIGBY MACKWORTH DOLBEN

FROST AT MIDNIGHT

The Frost performs its secret ministry,
Unhelped by any wind. The owlet's cry
Came loud — and hark, again! loud as before.
The inmates of my cottage, all at rest,
Have left me to that solitude, which suits
Abstruser musings: save that at my side
My cradled infant slumbers peacefully.
'Tis calm indeed! so calm, that it disturbs
And vexes meditation with its strange
And extreme silentness. Sea, hill, and wood, . . .
With all the numberless goings-on of life,
Inaudible as dreams! the thin blue flame
Lies on my low-burnt fire, and quivers not;

Only that film, which fluttered on the grate,
Still flutters there, the sole unquiet thing. . . .

SAMUEL TAYLOR COLERIDGE

Oft, in the stilly night,
 Ere Slumber's chain has bound me,
Fond Memory brings the light
 Of other days around me;
  The smiles, the tears,
  Of boyhood's years,
 The words of love then spoken;
  The eyes that shone,
  Now dimmed and gone,
 The cheerful hearts now broken!
Thus, in the stilly night,
 Ere Slumber's chain has bound me,
Sad Memory brings the light
 Of other days around me.

When I remember all
 The friends, so linked together,
I've seen around me fall,
 Like leaves in wintry weather;
  I feel like one
  Who treads alone
 Some banquet-hall deserted,
  Whose lights are fled,
  Whose garlands dead,
 And all but he departed!
Thus, in the stilly night,
 Ere Slumber's chain has bound me,
Sad Memory brings the light
 Of other days around me.

THOMAS MOORE

SUN OF THE SLEEPLESS!

Sun of the sleepless! melancholy star!
Whose tearful beam glows tremulously far,
That show'st the darkness thou canst not dispel,
How like art thou to joy remembered well!
So gleams the past, the light of other days,
Which shines, but warms not with its powerless rays;
A night-beam Sorrow watcheth to behold,
Distinct, but distant — clear, but oh, how cold!

BYRON

TO SLEEP

Dear fool, be true to me!
I know the poets speak thee fair, and I
Hail thee uncivilly.
O, but I call with a more urgent cry!

I do not prize thee less,
I need thee more, that thou dost love to teach —
Father of foolishness —
The imbecile dreams clear out of wisdom's reach.

Come and release me; bring
My irresponsible mind; come in thy hours.
Draw from my soul the sting
Of wit that trembles, consciousness that cowers.

For if night comes without thee
She is more cruel than day. But thou, fulfil
Thy work, thy gifts about thee —
Liberty, liberty, from this weight of will.

My day-mind can endure
Upright, in hope, all it must undergo.
But O, afraid, unsure,
My night-mind waking lies too low, too low.

[220]

Dear fool, be true to me!
The night is thine, man yields it, it beseems
  Thy ironic dignity.
Make me all night the innocent fool that dreams.

ALICE MEYNELL

Where upon the limber grass
Poppy and mandragoras
With like simples not a few
Hang for ever drops of dew.
Where flows Lethe without coil
Softly like a stream of oil
Hie thee, thither, gentle Sleep.

WILLIAM BROWNE

TO SLEEP

O soft embalmer of the still midnight,
  Shutting, with careful fingers and benign,
Our gloom-pleased eyes, embowered from the light,
  Enshaded in forgetfulness divine:
O soothest Sleep! if so it please thee, close,
  In midst of this thine hymn my willing eyes,
Or wait the "Amen," ere thy poppy throws
  Around my bed it's lulling charities.
Then save me, or the passèd day will shine
Upon my pillow, breeding many woes, —
  Save me from curious Conscience, that still lords
Its strength for darkness, burrowing like a mole;
  Turn the key deftly in the oilèd wards,
And seal the hushed Casket of my Soul.

JOHN KEATS

No sad thought his soul affright;
Sleep it is that maketh night;
Let no murmur nor rude wind
To his slumbers prove unkind;
But a quire of angels make
His dreams of heaven, and let him wake
To as many joys as can
In this world befall a man.

"SLEEP, SILENCE' CHILD"

Sleep, Silence' child, sweet father of soft rest,
Prince whose approach peace to all mortals brings,
Indifferent host to shepherds and to kings,
Sole comforter of minds with grief oppressed;
Lo, by thy charming rod all breathing things
Lie slumbering, with forgetfulness possessed,
And yet o'er me to spread thy drowsy wings
Thou spar'st (alas) who cannot be thy guest.
Since I am thine, O come, but with that face
To inward light, which thou art wont to show,
With feignèd solace ease a true-felt woe;
Or if, deaf god, thou do deny that grace,
　　Come as thou wilt, and what thou wilt bequeath;
　　I long to kiss the image of my death.

WILLIAM DRUMMOND

Sleep, sleep, my soul, let sorrow close thine eyes,
　　Nurse fantasy records her lullabies:
Fold up thine arms and into sighs expire,
　　Deep sighs, the drowsy pages of desire.

My restless heart, whom troublous thoughts molest,
    Shall cradle thee; thy cabin is my breast:
Where neither sun of joy, nor star of light
    Can break the mist of an affected night.

Here sadness rules; and here thy drooping head
    Instead of down shall have a frozen bed:
Love rocks thy panting cradle; and to bring
    Thy thoughts asleep, melancholy shall sing.

And when thou wakest, to appease thy cries,
    Sad grief with tears distilling from mine eyes
Shall feed thy passion, till that bitter food
    Do surfeit it, and in my death conclude.

COME THEN, A SONG

[*Scene: A Garden by Moonlight.*]

Veronica. Come then, a song; a winding, gentle song,
To lead me into sleep. Let it be low
As zephyr, telling secrets to his rose,
For I would hear the murmuring of my mind;
And more of voice than of that other music
That grows around the strings of quivering lutes;
But most of thought; for with my mind I listen,
And when the leaves of sound are shed upon it,
If there's no seed remembrance grows not there.
So life, so death; a song, and then a dream!
Begin before another dewdrop fall
From the soft hold of these disturbèd flowers,
For sleep is filling up my senses fast,
And from these words I sink. . . .

               THOMAS LOVELL BEDDOES,
               from *Torrismond, Act I, Scene III*

"THE NIGHT IS COME"

. . . The night is come, like to the day
Depart not Thou, great God, away.
Let not my sins, black as the night,
Eclipse the lustre of Thy light;
Keep still in my horizon; for to me
The Sun makes not the day, but Thee.
Howe'er I rest, great God, let me
Awake again at last with Thee;
And thus assured, behold I lie
Securely, or to wake or die.
These are my drowsy days; in vain
I do now wake to sleep again;
O come that hour, when I shall never
Sleep again, but wake for ever.

SIR THOMAS BROWNE

THE EVENING–WATCH

A Dialogue between *Body* and *Soul*

Farewell! I go to sleep; but when
The day-star springs, I'le wake again.

Go, sleep in peace; and when thou lyest
Unnumbered in thy dust, when all this frame
Is but one dram, and what thou now descriest
    In several parts shall want a name,
Then may his peace be with thee, and each dust
Writ in his book, who ne'er betrayed man's trust!

Amen! but hark, ere we two stray,
How many hours dost think 'till day?

Ah! go; thou art weak, and sleepy. Heav'n
Is a plain watch, and without figures winds

[224]

All ages up; who drew this Circle even
    He fills it; Days, and hours are *Blinds.*
Yet, this take with thee; The last gasp of time
Is thy first breath, and man's *eternal Prime.*

                                   HENRY VAUGHAN

Close now thine eyes, and rest secure;
Thy soul is safe enough; thy body sure;
   He that loves thee, he that keeps
And guards thee, never slumbers, never sleeps.
The smiling conscience in a sleeping breast
   Has only peace, has only rest:
   The music and the mirth of kings
Are all but very discords, when she sings:
   Then close thine eyes and rest secure;
No sleep so sweet as thine, no rest so sure.

                               FRANCIS QUARLES

      Angel spirits of sleep,
      White-robed, with silver hair,
      In your meadows fair,
      Where the willows weep,
      And the sad moonbeam
      On the gliding stream
      Writes her scattered dream:

        Angel spirits of sleep,
      Dancing to the weir
      In the hollow roar
      Of its waters deep;
      Know ye how men say
      That ye haunt no more
      Isle and grassy shore
      With your moonlit play;

That ye dance not here,
White-robed spirits of sleep,
All the summer night
Threading dances light?

ROBERT BRIDGES

Childhood and Sleep

How many miles to Babylon?
  Three score and ten.
Can I get there by candlelight?
  Ay, and back again.

A boy shut up in dreams, a shadow-catcher. . . .

Dream on! there's nothing but illusion true. . . .

Childhood and Sleep

LULLY, LULLA

Lully, lulla, thou little tiny child,
By by, lully, lullay.

O sisters too,
How may we do
  For to preserve this day
This poor youngling,
For whom we sing,
  By by, lully lullay? . . .

"IN A WINTER NIGHT"

In a winter night ere I wakèd
In my sleep I dreamèd so;
I saw a child mother-naked
New born the mother fro,
All alone as God him makèd;
In the wilderness he did go
Till the governance he takèd
An angel friend, an angel foe. . . .

CRADLE SONG

Sleep, Sleep, beauty bright,
Dreaming o'er the joys of night!
Sleep, Sleep: in thy sleep
Little sorrows sit and weep.

Sweet Babe, in thy face
Soft desires I can trace,
Secret joys and secret smiles,
Little pretty infant wiles.

As thy softest limbs I feel,
Smiles as of the morning steal
O'er thy cheek and o'er thy breast
Where thy little heart does rest.

O, the cunning wiles that creep
In thy little heart asleep!
When thy little heart does wake,
Then the dreadful lightnings break. . . .

WILLIAM BLAKE

BEFORE SLEEPING

Matthew, Mark, Luke, and John,
Bless the bed that I lie on.
Before I lay me down to sleep
I give my soul to Christ to keep.
Four corners to my bed,
Four angels there aspread,
Two to foot, and two to head,
And four to carry me when I'm dead.
I go by sea, I go by land,
The Lord made me with His right hand.
If any danger come to me,
Sweet Jesus Christ deliver me.
He's the branch and I'm the flower,
Pray God send me a happy hour,
And if I die before I wake,
I pray that Christ my soul will take.

THE COTTAGER TO HER INFANT

The days are cold, the nights are long,
The Northwind sings a doleful song;
Then hush again upon my breast;
All merry things are now at rest,
  Save thee, my pretty love!

The kitten sleeps upon the hearth;
The crickets long have ceased their mirth;
There's nothing stirring in the house
Save one wee, hungry, nibbling mouse,
  Then why so busy thou?

Nay! start not at the sparkling light;
'Tis but the moon that shines so bright
On the window-pane bedropped with rain:
There, little darling! sleep again,
  And wake when it is day.

DOROTHY WORDSWORTH

. . . Certainly Adam in Paradise had not more sweet and curious apprehensions of the world, than I when I was a child.

All appeared new, and strange at first, inexpressibly rare and delightful and beautiful. I was a little stranger, which at my entrance into the world was saluted and surrounded with innumerable joys. My knowledge was Divine. I knew by intuition those things which since my Apostasy, I collected again by the highest reason. My very ignorance was advantageous. I seemed as one brought into the Estate of Innocence. All things were spotless and pure and glorious: yea, and infinitely mine, and joyful and precious. I knew not that there were any sins, or complaints or laws. I dreamed not of poverties, contentions or vices. All tears and quarrels were hidden from mine eyes. Everything was at rest, free and im-

mortal. I knew nothing of sickness or death or rents or exac-
tion, either for tribute or bread. In the absence of these I was
entertained like an Angel with the works of God in their
splendour and glory, I saw all in the peace of Eden; Heaven
and Earth did sing my Creator's praises, and could not make
more melody to Adam, than to me. All Time was Eternity,
and a perpetual Sabbath. Is it not strange, that an infant
should be heir of the whole World, and see those mysteries
which the books of the learned never unfold? . . .

Thomas Traherne

THE LAND OF DREAMS

Awake, awake, my little Boy!
Thou wast thy Mother's only joy;
Why dost thou weep in thy gentle sleep?
Awake! thy Father does thee keep.

" O, what land is the Land of Dreams?
What are its Mountains, and what are its Streams?
O Father! I saw my Mother there,
Among the Lillies by waters fair.

" Among the Lambs, clothèd in white,
She walked with her Thomas in sweet delight.
I wept for joy, like a dove I mourn;
O! when shall I again return? "

Dear Child, I also by pleasant Streams
Have wandered all night in the Land of Dreams;
But tho' calm and warm the waters wide,
I could not get to the other side.

" Father, O Father! what do we here
In this Land of unbelief and fear?
The Land of Dreams is better far,
Above the light of the Morning Star."

William Blake

THE LITTLE BOY LOST

" Father! father! where are you going?
O do not walk so fast.
Speak, father, speak to your little boy,
Or else I shall be lost."

The night was dark, no father was there;
The child was wet with dew;
The mire was deep, and the child did weep,
And away the vapour flew.

WILLIAM BLAKE

ENCINTURED

Encintured with a twine of leaves,
That leafy twine his only dress!
A lovely Boy was plucking fruits,
By moonlight, in a wilderness.
The moon was bright, the air was free,
And fruits and flowers together grew
On many a shrub and many a tree:
And all put on a gentle hue,
Hanging in the shadowy air
Like a picture rich and rare.
It was a climate where, they say,
The night is more beloved than day.
But who that beauteous Boy beguiled,
That beauteous Boy to linger here?
Alone, by night, a little child,
In place so silent and so wild —
Has he no friend, no loving mother near?

SAMUEL TAYLOR COLERIDGE

. . . " Kilmeny, Kilmeny, where have you been?
Lang hae we sought baith holt and dean;
By linn, by ford, and green-wood tree,
Yet you are halesome and fair to see.
Where gat you that joup o' the lily schene?
That bonny snood of the birk sae green?
And these roses, the fairest that ever were seen?
Kilmeny, Kilmeny, where have you been? "

Kilmeny looked up with a lovely grace,
But nae smile was seen on Kilmeny's face;
As still was her look, and as still was her ee,
As the stillness that lay on the emerant lea,
Or the mist that sleeps on a waveless sea.
For Kilmeny had been she knew not where,
And Kilmeny had seen what she could not declare;
Kilmeny had been where the cock never crew,
Where the rain never fell, and the wind never blew;
But it seemed as the harp of the sky had rung,
And the airs of heaven played round her tongue,
When she spake of the lovely forms she had seen,
And a land where sin had never been;
A land of love, and a land of light,
Withouten sun, or moon, or night;
Where the river swa'd a living stream,
And the light a pure celestial beam:
The land of vision it would seem,
A still, an everlasting dream. . . .

JAMES HOGG

. . . I was dreadfully alive to nervous terrors. The night-
time solitude, and the dark, were my hell. The sufferings I
endured in this nature would justify the expression. I never
laid my head on my pillow, I suppose, from the fourth to the
seventh or eighth year of my life — so far as memory serves
in things so long ago — without an assurance, which realized

its own prophecy, of seeing some frightful spectre. Be old Stackhouse [author of a " History of the Bible "] then acquitted in part, if I say, that to his picture of the Witch raising up Samuel — (O that old man covered with a mantle!) I owe — not my midnight terrors, the hell of my infancy — but the shape and manner of their visitation. It was he who dressed up for me a hag that nightly sate upon my pillow — a sure bed-fellow, when my aunt or my maid was far from me. All day long, while the book was permitted me, I dreamed waking over his delineation, and at night (if I may use so bold an expression) awoke into sleep, and found the vision true. I durst not, even in the day-light, once enter the chamber where I slept, without my face turned to the window, aversely from the bed where my witch-ridden pillow was. — Parents do not know what they do when they leave tender babes alone to go to sleep in the dark. . . .

CHARLES LAMB

Alone, [in childhood] in a room near the top of this not very friendly house, I seemed to be miles and miles from any human being. There were shut doors, there were many flights of stairs, to deaden effectually any sound I might make. Unless I went out on to the landing and screamed I could not possibly be heard.

The effect of this new state of things upon the darkness was immediate and startling. It was no longer a soft dim curtain hung before the gate of sleep: on the contrary, it drove all my drowsiness away. It had become like a vast rotting body swarming with obscene life. I could hear stealthy movements; I dared not open my eyes, because I knew hideous things were there, waiting, gloating, eager to display before me their half shapeless horror. From what Limbo did they flock to me, like vampires who have marked their prey from afar? These were no dreams, no creations of a child's imagination. . . .

It was all for one's good, I had been assured: I must learn to

conquer this senseless, superstitious cowardice. And an easy
way to conquer it was to remember God was with me in the
dark. He wasn't; he never had been — unless he was a tall
smiling figure with long, pointed, yellow teeth, that I saw one
night standing at the foot of my bed. This, at least, was no
dream. At all events, I was not asleep. If I had the requisite
skill I could draw that face now, as I still half believe I could
have photographed it then. . . .

FORREST REID

"What ails you, my child?" said a mother to her son, as he
lay on a couch under the influence of the dreadful one; "what
ails you? you seem afraid!"

BOY. — And so I am; a dreadful fear is upon me.

MOTHER. — But of what? there is no one can harm you; of
   what are you apprehensive?

BOY. — Of nothing that I can express; I know not what I am
   afraid of, but afraid I am.

MOTHER. — Perhaps you see sights and visions; I knew a lady
   once who was continually thinking that she saw an
   armed man threaten her, but it was only an imagination,
   a phantom of the brain.

BOY. — No armed man threatens me; and 'tis not a thing that
   would cause me any fear. Did an armed man threaten
   me, I would get up and fight him; weak as I am, I would
   wish for nothing better, for then, perhaps, I should lose
   this fear; mine is a dread of I know not what, and there
   the horror lies.

MOTHER. — Your forehead is cool, and your speech collected.
   Do you know where you are?

BOY. — I know where I am, and I see things just as they are;
   you are beside me, and upon the table there is a book
   which was written by a Florentine; all this I see, and
   that there is no ground for being afraid. I am, moreover,
   quite cool, and feel no pain — but, but —

And then there was a burst of " gemiti, sospiri ed alti guai."
Alas, alas, poor child of clay! as the sparks fly upward, so wast
thou born to sorrow — Onward! . . .

GEORGE BORROW

O for that sweet, untroubled rest
  That poets oft have sung! —
The babe upon its mother's breast,
  The bird upon its young,
The heart asleep without a pain —
When shall I know that sleep again?

When shall I be as I have been
  Upon my mother's breast
Sweet Nature's garb of verdant green
  To woo to perfect rest —
Love in the meadow, field, and glen,
And in my native wilds again? . . .

I loved the winds when I was young,
  When life was dear to me;
I loved the song which Nature sung,
  Endearing liberty;
I loved the wood, the vale, the stream,
For there my boyhood used to dream.

There even toil itself was play;
  'Twas pleasure e'en to weep;
'Twas joy to think of dreams by day,
  The beautiful of sleep.
When shall I see the wood and plain,
And dream those happy dreams again?

JOHN CLARE
from " The Sleep of Spring "

STILLNESS

When the words rustle no more,
　　And the last work's done,
When the bolt lies deep in the door,
　　And Fire, our Sun,
Falls on the dark-laned meadows of the floor;

When from the clock's last chime to the next chime
　　Silence beats his drum,
And Space with gaunt grey eyes and her brother Time
　　Wheeling and whispering come,
She with the mould of form and he with the loom of rhyme:

Then twittering out in the night my thought-birds flee,
　　I am emptied of all my dreams:
I only hear Earth turning, only see
　　Ether's long bankless streams,
And only know I should drown if you laid not your hand on
　　me.

JAMES ELROY FLECKER

THE CHIMNEY SWEEPER

When my mother died I was very young,
And my father sold me while yet my tongue
Could scarcely cry " 'weep! 'weep! 'weep! 'weep! "
So your chimneys I sweep, and in soot I sleep.

There's little Tom Dacre, who cried when his head,
That curled like a lamb's back, was shaved: so I said
" Hush, Tom! never mind it, for when your head's bare
You know that the soot cannot spoil your white hair."

And so he was quiet, and that very night,
As Tom was a-sleeping, he had such a sight!
That thousands of sweepers, Dick, Joe, Ned, and Jack,
Were all of them locked up in coffins of black.

[238]

And by came an Angel who had a bright key,
And he opened the coffins and set them all free;
Then down a green plain leaping, laughing, they run,
And wash in a river, and shine in the Sun.

Then naked and white, all their bags left behind,
They rise upon clouds, and sport in the wind;
And the Angel told Tom, if he'd be a good boy,
He'd have God for his father, and never want joy.

And so Tom awoke; and we rose in the dark,
And got with our bags and our brushes to work.
Tho' the morning was cold, Tom was happy and warm;
So if all do their duty they need not fear harm.

WILLIAM BLAKE

THE TOYS

My little Son, who looked from thoughtful eyes
And moved and spoke in quiet grown-up wise,
Having my law the seventh time disobeyed,
I struck him, and dismissed
With hard words and unkissed,
His Mother, who was patient, being dead.
Then, fearing lest his grief should hinder sleep,
I visited his bed,
But found him slumbering deep,
With darkened eyelids, and their lashes yet
From his late sobbing wet.
And I, with moan,
Kissing away his tears, left others of my own;
For, on a table drawn beside his head,
He had put, within his reach,
A box of counters and a red-veined stone,
A piece of glass abraded by the beach,
And six or seven shells,
A bottle with bluebells

And two French copper coins, ranged there with careful art,
To comfort his sad heart.
So when that night I prayed
To God, I wept, and said:
Ah, when at last we lie with trancèd breath,
Not vexing Thee in death,
And Thou rememberest of what toys
We made our joys,
How weakly understood,
Thy great commanded good,
Then, fatherly not less
Than I whom Thou hast moulded from the clay,
Thou'lt leave Thy wrath, and say,
" I will be sorry for their childishness."

COVENTRY PATMORE

ON A CHILD SLEEPING IN CYNTHIA'S LAP

Sleep, happy boy, there sleep, and take thy rest,
Free from the passions which disturb my breast;
Yet know 'tis Innocence that thee has freed,
And lets thee sleep so quiet on this bed.

Thy wearied limbs have sweetly rested here,
If with less sun, in a more happy sphere;
Whilst in despair my soul afflicted lies,
And of mere envy to behold thee, dies.

Dream, thou enjoy'st more true felicity,
Than lavish fortune can bestow on thee;
That thou, amidst such precious gems, art hurled,
Art able to enrich th' insatiate world:

That thou the Phoenix shalt transcend in fame,
Who sleep'st, and risest, in a purer flame;
That thou'rt an Angel, Heaven's that lap I view:
Yet all this while, it is no dream, but true.

PHILIP AYRES

THE REVELATION

An idle poet, here and there,
  Looks round him; but, for all the rest,
The world, unfathomably fair,
  Is duller than a witling's jest.
Love wakes men, once a life-time each;
  They lift their heavy lids, and look;
And, lo, what one sweet page can teach,
  They read with joy, then shut the book.
And some give thanks, and some blaspheme,
  And most forget; but, either way,
That and the Child's unheeded dream
  Is all the light of all their day.

COVENTRY PATMORE

. . . And Him I thank, who can make live again,
  The dust, but not the joy we once profane,
  That I, of ye,
Beautiful habitations, auras of delight,
In childish years and since had sometimes sense and
    sight,
But that ye vanish'd quite,
Even from memory,
Ere I could get my breath, and whisper " See! "
  But did for me
They altogether die,
Those trackless glories glimps'd in upper sky?
Were they of chance, or vain,
Nor good at all again
For curb of heart or fret?
Nay, though, by grace,
Lest, haply, I refuse God to His face,

Their likeness wholly I forget,
Ah, yet,
Often in straits which else for me were ill,
I mind me still
I *did* respire the lonely auras sweet,
I *did* the blest abodes behold, and, at the mountains' feet,
Bathed in the holy Stream by Hermon's thymy hill.

COVENTRY PATMORE
from " Auras of Delight "

SONG

While Morpheus thus does gently lay
   His powerful charge upon each part
Making thy spirits even obey
   The silver charms of his dull art;

I, thy Good Angel, from thy side, —
   As smoke doth from the altar rise,
Making no noise as it doth glide, —
   Will leave thee in this soft surprise;

And from the clouds will fetch thee down
   A holy vision, to express
Thy right unto an earthly crown;
   No power can make this kingdom less.

But gently, gently, lest I bring
   A start in sleep by sudden flight,
Playing aloof, and hovering,
   Till I am lost unto the sight.

This is a motion still and soft;
   So free from noise and cry,
That Jove himself, who hears a thought,
   Knows not when we pass by.

HENRY KILLIGREW

Sleeping

Awake, thou spring of speaking grace,
　Mute rest becomes not thee;
The fayrest women, while they sleepe
　And pictures equall be. . . .

" Let her lie still and dream " . . .

Sleeping

THOU FLOWER OF SUMMER

When in summer thou walkest
   In the meads by the river,
And to thyself talkest,
   Dost thou think of one ever —
A lost and a lorn one
   That adores thee and loves thee?
And when happy morn's gone,
   And nature's calm moves thee,
Leaving thee to thy sleep like an angel at rest,
Does the one who adores thee still live in thy breast?

Does nature e'er give thee
   Love's past happy vision,
And wrap thee and leave thee
   In fancies elysian?
Thy beauty I clung to,
   As leaves to the tree;
When thou fair and young too
   Looked lightly on me,
Till love came upon thee like the sun to the west
And shed its perfuming and bloom on thy breast.

JOHN CLARE

★ *Sleeping* ★

Sweet in her green cell the Flower of Beauty slumbers,
Lulled by the faint breezes sighing through her hair;
Sleeps she, and hears not the melancholy numbers
Breathed to my sad lute amid the lonely air?

Down from the high cliffs the rivulet is teeming,
To wind round the willow banks that lure him from above:
Or that in tears from my rocky prison streaming,
I too could glide to the bower of my love!

Ah! where the woodbines with sleepy arms have wound her,
Opes she her eyelids at the dream of my lay,
Listening like the dove, while the fountains echo round her,
To her lost mate's call in the forests far away?

Come then, my Bird! — for the peace thou ever bearest,
Still heaven's messenger of comfort to me,
Come! — this fond bosom, my faithfullest, my fairest!
Bleeds with its death-wound, but deeper yet for thee.

GEORGE DARLEY

I saw the figure of a lovely Maid
Seated alone beneath a darksome tree,
Whose fondly-overhanging canopy
Set off her brightness with a pleasing shade.
No Spirit was she; *that* my heart betrayed,
For she was one I loved exceedingly;
But while I gazed in tender reverie
(Or was it sleep that with my Fancy played?)
The bright corporeal presence — form and face —
Remaining still distinct grew thin and rare,
Like sunny mist, — at length the golden hair,
Shape, limbs, and heavenly features, keeping pace
Each with the other in a lingering race
Of dissolution, melted into air.

WILLIAM WORDSWORTH

[246]

. . . But in my sleep to you I fly:
 I'm always with you in my sleep!
  The world is all one's own.
But then one wakes, and where am I?
  All, all alone.

Sleep stays not, though a monarch bids:
 So I love to wake ere break of day:
  For though my sleep be gone,
Yet while 'tis dark, one shuts one's lids,
  And still dreams on.

     SAMUEL TAYLOR COLERIDGE

You were glad to-night: and now you've gone away.
Flushed in the dark you put your dreams to bed;
But as you fall asleep I hear you say
Those tired sweet drowsy words we left unsaid.

Sleep well: for I can follow you to bless
And lull your distant beauty where you roam;
And with wild songs of hoarded loveliness
Recall you to these arms that were your home.

SIEGFRIED SASSOON, from "The Heart's Journey"

 See, how like twilight slumber falls
 To obscure the glory of those balls
  And, as she sleeps,
  See how light creeps,
 Through the chinks, and beautifies
 The rayie fringe of her fair eyes.

 Observe Love's feuds, how fast they fly,
 To every heart, from her closed eye,
  What then will she,
  When waking, be?

A glowing light for all to admire,
Such as would set the world on fire.

Then seal her eyelids, gentle Sleep,
While cares of her mine open keep;
   Lock up, I say,
   Those doors of day,
Which with the morn for lustre strive,
That I may look on her, and live.

CHARLES COTTON

The ivory, coral, gold,
Of breast, of lips, of hair,
So lively Sleep doth show to inward sight,
That 'wake I think I hold
No shadow, but my fair:
Myself so to deceive
With long-shut eyes I shun the irksome light.
Such pleasure thus I have,
Delighting in false gleams.
If Death Sleep's brother be,
   And souls relieved of sense have so sweet dreams,
   How could I wish thus still to dream and die!

WILLIAM DRUMMOND

Alas! so all things now do hold their peace;
Heaven and earth disturbèd in no thing:
The beasts, the air, the birds their song do cease;
The nightes chare the stars about doth bring:
Calm is the sea; the waves work less and less:
So am not I, whom love, alas, doth wring,
Bringing before my face the great increase
Of my desires, whereat I weep and sing,
In joy and woe, as in a doubtful ease:

For my sweet thoughts sometime do pleasure bring;
But by and by, the cause of my disease
Gives me a pang, that inwardly doth sting,
   When that I think what grief it is again,
   To live and lack the thing should rid my pain.

HENRY HOWARD, EARL OF SURREY

Come, Sleepe! O Sleepe, the certaine knot of peace,
The baiting-place of wit, the balme of woe,
The poore man's wealth, the prisoner's release,
Th' indifferent judge betweene the high and low;
With shield of proofe shield me from out the prease
Of those fierce darts Despaire at me doth throw:
O make in me those civill warres to cease:
I will good tribute pay, if thou do so.
Take thou of me smooth pillowes, sweetest bed,
A chamber deafe to noise and blind of light,
A rosie garland and a weary hed:
And if these things, as being thine in right,
Move not thy heavy grace, thou shalt in me,
Livelier then else-where, Stella's image see.

SIR PHILIP SIDNEY

DOUBTS

When she sleeps, her soul, I know,
Goes a wanderer on the air,
Wings where I may never go,
Leaves her lying, still and fair,
Waiting, empty, laid aside,
Like a dress upon a chair. . . .
This I know, and yet I know
Doubts that will not be denied.

[249]

For if the soul be not in place,
What has laid trouble in her face?
And, sits there nothing ware and wise
Behind the curtains of her eyes,
What is it, in the self's eclipse,
Shadows, soft and passingly,
About the corners of her lips,
The smile that is essential she?

And if the spirit be not there,
Why is fragrance in the hair?

RUPERT BROOKE

LAY YOUR SLEEPING HEAD

Lay your sleeping head, my love,
Human on my faithless arm;
Time and fevers burn away
Individual beauty from
Thoughtful children, and the grave
Proves the child ephemeral:
But in my arms till break of day
Let the living creature lie,
Mortal, guilty, but to me
The entirely beautiful.

Soul and body have no bounds:
To lovers as they lie upon
Her tolerant enchanted slope
In their ordinary swoon,
Grave the vision Venus sends
Of supernatural sympathy,
Universal love and hope;
While an abstract insight wakes
Among the glaciers and the rocks
The hermit's sensual ecstasy.

Certainty, fidelity
On the stroke of midnight pass
Like vibrations of a bell,
And fashionable madmen raise
Their pedantic boring cry;
Every farthing of the cost,
All the dreaded cards foretell
Shall be paid, but from this night
Not a whisper, not a thought,
Not a kiss nor look be lost.

Beauty, midnight, vision dies:
Let the winds of dawn that blow
Softly round your dreaming head
Such a day of sweetness show
Eye and knocking heart may bless,
Find the mortal world enough;
Noons of dryness see you fed
By the involuntary powers,
Nights of insult let you pass
Watched by every human love.

W. H. AUDEN

THE POOR GIRL'S MEDITATION

I am sitting here
Since the moon rose in the night,
Kindling a fire,
And striving to keep it alight;
The folk of the house are lying
In slumber deep;
The geese will be gabbling soon:
The whole of the land is asleep.

May I never leave this world
Until my ill-luck is gone;

★ *Sleeping* ★

Till I have cows and sheep,
And the lad that I love for my own;
I would not think it long,
The night I would lie at his breast,
And the daughters of spite, after that,
Might say the thing they liked best.

Love takes the place of hate,
If a girl have beauty at all:
On a bed that was narrow and high,
A three-month I lay by the wall:
When I bethought on the lad
That I left on the brow of the hill,
I wept from dark until dark,
And my cheeks have the tear-tracks still.

And, O young lad that I love,
I am no mark for your scorn;
All you can say of me is
Undowered I was born:
And if I've no fortune in hand,
Nor cattle and sheep of my own,
This I can say, O lad,
I am fitted to lie my lone!

Padraic Colum

At midnight, in the month of June,
I stand beneath the mystic moon.
An opiate vapour, dewy, dim,
Exhales from out her golden rim,
And, softly dripping, drop by drop,
Upon the quiet mountain top,
Steals drowsily and musically
Into the universal valley.
The rosemary nods upon the grave;
The lily lolls upon the wave;

Wrapping the fog about its breast,
The ruin moulders into rest;
Looking like Lethe, see! the lake
A conscious slumber seems to take,
And would not, for the world, awake.
All Beauty sleeps! — and lo! where lies
(Her casement open to the skies)
Irene, with her Destinies!

Oh, lady bright! can it be right —
This window open to the night?
The wanton airs, from the tree-top,
Laughingly through the lattice drop —
The bodiless airs, a wizard rout,
Flit through thy chamber in and out,
And wave the curtain canopy
So fitfully — so fearfully —
Above the closed and fringèd lid
'Neath which thy slumb'ring soul lies hid,
That, o'er the floor and down the wall,
Like ghosts the shadows rise and fall!
Oh, lady dear, hast thou no fear?
Why and what art thou dreaming here?
Sure thou art come o'er far-off seas,
A wonder to these garden trees!
Strange is thy pallor! strange thy dress,
Strange, above all, thy length of tress,
And this all-solemn silentness! . . .

EDGAR ALLAN POE

LINES TO AN INDIAN AIR

I arise from dreams of thee
In the first sweet sleep of night,
When the winds are breathing low,
And the stars are shining bright:

I arise from dreams of thee,
And a spirit in my feet
Has led me — who knows how?
To thy chamber window, Sweet!

The wandering airs they faint
On the dark, the silent stream —
The Champak odours fail
Like sweet thoughts in a dream;
The nightingale's complaint,
It dies upon her heart; —
As I must die on thine,
Belovèd as thou art!

O lift me from the grass!
I die, I faint, I fail!
Let thy love in kisses rain
On my lips and eyelids pale.
My cheek is cold and white, alas!
My heart beats loud and fast; —
Oh! press it close to thine again,
Where it will break at last.

PERCY BYSSHE SHELLEY

COME, MY ARABIA

Come, my Arabia,
         to the senses stilled
With night. Your locks are lilies dark with dew
As with rich myrrh the deepest leaves are chilled.
Plantations of the East have leaves like fire
And the dark night dew lies on them and sighs.
So my Arabia lies
Upon my heart that is our Phoenix pyre
Whence all the splendours of Arabia rise.

EDITH SITWELL

★ *Sleeping* ★

Go, nor acquaint the rose
Nor Beauty's household with that grief of thine.
Stand not in wait with those
Who with their knocking trouble the divine.

But thou, let Beauty be,
Dread distance of her chancèd slumbers keep.
If then she follow thee
When thou art treading noiseless from her sleep,

Rose then, and wafted rose,
Like summer past and summer's breath still there,
Shall pay thee all she owes,
More than she ever yielded to thy prayer.

VIVIAN LOCKE ELLIS

"Lullay My Liking, My Dear"

" I am no man, if this dream were not spun
By the very Silkworm, that doth make his shop
In Cupid's tender wing-pit." . . .

Cease, dreams, the images of day-desires,
To model forth the passions of the morrow. . . .

"Lullay My Liking, My Dear"

CHARMS

The last summer, on the day of St. John the Baptist, 1694, I accidentally was walking in the pasture behind Montague house, it was 12 o'clock. I saw there about two or three and twenty young women, most of them well habited, on their knees very busy, as if they had been weeding. I could not presently learn what the matter was; at last a young man told me, that they were looking for a coal under the root of a plantain, to put under their head that night, and they should dream who would be their husbands: It was to be sought for that day and hour. . . .

To know whom one shall marry. You must lie in another county, and knit the left garter about the right legged stocking (let the other garter and stocking alone) and as you rehearse these following verses, at every comma, knit a knot.

This knot I knit,
To know the thing, I know not yet,
That I may see,
The man (woman) that shall my husband (wife) be,
How he goes, and what he wears,
And what he does, all days, and years.

Accordingly in your dream you will see him: if a musician, with a lute or other instrument; if a scholar, with a book or papers.

A gentlewoman that I knew, confessed in my hearing, that she used this method, and dreamt of her husband whom she had never seen; about two or three years after, as she was on Sunday at church (at our Lady's church in Sarum), up pops a young Oxonian in the pulpit: she cries out presently to her sister, this is the very face of the man that I saw in my dream. Sir William Soame's Lady did the like.

Another way, is, to charm the moon thus: at the first appearance of the new moon after new year's day (some say any other new moon is as good), go out in the evening, and stand over the spars of a gate or stile, looking on the moon (in Yorkshire they kneel on a ground-fast stone), and say,

> All hail to the moon, all hail to thee,
> I prithee good moon reveal to me,
> This night, who my husband (wife) must be.

You must presently after go to bed.

I knew two gentlewomen that did thus when they were young maids, and they had dreams of those that married them.

JOHN AUBREY

> New moon, new moon, I pray thee
> Tell me this night who my true love will be.
>
> Now good St. Agnes play thy part,
> And send to me my own sweetheart;
> And shew me such an happy bliss,
> This night of him to have a kiss.
>
> Good St. Thomas do me right,
> And bring my love to me this night,
> That I may look him in the face,
> And in my arms may him embrace.
>
> St. Luke, St. Luke, be kind to me,
> In dreams let me my true love see.
>
> Hemp-seed I sow, hemp-seed I sow,
> And he that must be my true love,
> Come after me and mow.

I'M OWRE YOUNG TO MARRY YET

I am my mammie's ae bairn,
　　Wi' unco folk I weary, Sir;
And lying in a man's bed,
　　I'm fley'd wad mak me eerie, Sir.

　　　I'm owre young, I'm owre young,
　　　　I'm owre young to marry yet;
　　　I'm owre young, 'twad be a sin
　　　　To tak me frae my mammie yet.

My mammie coft me a new gown,
　　The kirk maun hae the gracing o't;
Were I to lie wi' you, kind Sir,
　　I'm fear'd ye'd spoil the lacing o't. . . .

Hallowmas is come and gane,
　　The nights are lang in winter, Sir;
And you an' I in ae bed,
　　In truth I dare na venture, Sir. . . .

Fu' loud and shrill the frosty wind
　　Blaws thro' the leafless timmer, Sir;
But if ye come this gate again,
　　I'll aulder be gin simmer, Sir.

　　　I'm owre young, I'm owre young,
　　　　I'm owre young to marry yet;
　　　I'm owre young, 'twad be a sin
　　　　To tak me frae my mammie yet.

ROBERT BURNS

AYE WAUKIN' O!

O Spring's a pleasant time,
  Flowers o' every colour —
The sweet bird builds her nest,
  And I long for my lover.
    Aye waukin' O,
      Waukin' aye, and weary,
    Sleep can I get nane,
      For thinkin' o' my dearie.

O I'm wat, wat,
  O I'm wat and weary;
Yet fain I'd rise and run
  If I thought to meet my dearie.

When I sleep I dream,
  When I wauk I'm eerie;
Sleep can I get nane,
  For thinkin' o' my dearie.

Lanely night comes on;
  A' the lave are sleeping;
I think on my love,
  And blear my een wi' greeting.

Feather-beds are soft,
  Painted rooms are bonnie;
But a kiss o' my dear love
  Is better far than ony.

O for Friday's night,
  Friday at the gloaming!
O for Friday's night!
  Friday's lang o' coming.
    Aye waukin' O,
      Waukin' aye, and weary,
    Sleep can I get nane,
      For thinkin' o' my dearie.

UPON A DAY

Upon a day, as Love lay sweetly slumb'ring
   all in his mother's lap,
A gentle Bee with his loud trumpet murmuring,
   about him flew by hap:
Whereof when he was wakened with the noise,
   and saw the beast so small:
What's this (quoth he) that gives so great a voice,
   that wakens men withal?
In angry wise he flies about
   and threatens all with courage stout.

To whom his mother closely smiling said,
   'twixt earnest and 'twixt game:
See, thou thyself art little made,
   if thou regard the same.
And yet thou suff'rest neither gods in sky,
   nor men in earth to rest:
But when thou art disposèd cruelly,
   their sleep thou dost molest.
Then either change thy cruelty,
   or give like leave unto the fly. . . .

EDMUND SPENSER

BEAUTY SAT BATHING

Beauty sat bathing by a spring,
   Where fairest shades did hide her;
The winds blew calm, the birds did sing,
   The cool streams ran beside her.
My wanton thoughts enticed mine eye
   To see what was forbidden:

[263]

But better memory said, Fie;
    So vain desire was chidden —
    Hey nonny nonny O!
    Hey nonnie nonnie!

Into a slumber then I fell,
    When fond imagination
Seemèd to see, but could not tell
    Her feature or her fashion:
But even as babes in dreams do smile,
    And sometimes fall a-weeping,
So I awaked, as wise this while
    As when I fell a-sleeping —
    Hey nonny nonny O!
    Hey nonnie nonnie!

ANTHONY MUNDAY

The star that bids the shepherd fold
Now the top of heaven doth hold;
And the gilded car of day
His glowing axle doth allay
In the steep Atlantic stream;
And the slope sun his upward beam
Shoots against the dusky pole,
Pacing toward the other goal
Of his chamber in the east.
Meanwhile, welcome joy and feast,
Midnight shout and revelry,
Tipsy dance and jollity.
Braid your locks with rosy twine,
Dropping odours, dropping wine.
Rigour now is gone to bed;
And Advice with scrupulous head,
Strict Age, and sour Severity,
With their grave saws, in slumber lie.

We, that are of purer fire,
Imitate the starry quire,
Who, in their nightly watchful spheres,
Lead in swift round the months and years.
The sounds, and seas, with all their finny drove,
Now to the moon in wavering morrice move;
And on the tawny sands and shelves
Trip the pert fairies and the dapper elves.
By dimpled brook, and fountain-brim,
The wood-nymphs, decked with daisies trim,
Their merry wakes and pastimes keep:
What hath night to do with sleep?
Night hath better sweets to prove;
Venus now wakes, and wakens love. . . .

JOHN MILTON, from *Comus*

SILVY

On a time the amorous Silvy
Said to her shepherd, " Sweet, how do you?
Kiss me this once, and then God b' wi' you,
        My sweetest dear!
Kiss me this once, and then God b' wi' you,
For now the morning draweth near."

With that, her fairest bosom showing,
Opening her lips, rich perfumes blowing,
She said, " Now kiss me and be going,
        My sweetest dear!
Kiss me this once and then be going,
For now the morning draweth near."

With that the shepherd waked from sleeping,
And, spying where the day was peeping,
He said, " Now take my soul in keeping,
        My sweetest dear!
Kiss me, and take my soul in keeping,
Since I must go, now day is near."

[265]

SWEET BESSIE

It fell on a summer's day,
While sweet Bessie sleeping lay
In her bower, on her bed,
Light with curtains shadowèd,
Jamy came: she him spies,
Opening half her heavy eyes.

Jamy stole in through the door,
She lay slumbering as before;
Softly to her he drew near,
She heard him, yet would not hear,
Bessie vow'd not to speak,
He resolv'd that dump to break.

First a soft kiss he doth take,
She lay still, and would not wake;
Then his hands learn'd to woo,
She dreamt not what he would do,
But still slept, while he smiled
To see love by sleep beguiled.

Jamy then began to play,
Bessie as one buried lay,
Gladly still through this sleight
Deceiv'd in her own deceit,
And since this trance begoon,
She sleeps every afternoon.

THOMAS CAMPION

Give me a kiss from those sweet lips of thine
And make it double by enjoining mine,
Another yet, nay yet and yet another,
And let the first kiss be the second's brother.

Give me a thousand kisses and yet more;
And then repeat those that have gone before;
Let us begin while daylight springs in heaven,
And kiss till night descends into the even,
And when that modest secretary, night,
Discolours all but thy heaven beaming bright,
We will begin revels of hidden love
In that sweet orb where silent pleasures move.
In high new strains, unspeakable delight,
We'll vent the dull hours of the silent night:
Were the bright day no more to visit us,
Oh, then for ever would I hold thee thus,
Naked, enchained, empty of idle fear,
As the first lovers in the garden were. . . .

A KISS

Hark, happy lovers, hark!
This first and last of joys,
This sweet'ner of annoys,
This nectar of the gods
You call a kiss, is with itself at odds;
And half so sweet is not
In equal measure got,
At light of Sun, as it is in the dark:
Hark, happy lovers, hark!

WILLIAM DRUMMOND

WITH LULLAY, LULLAY, LYKE A CHYLDE

With lullay, lullay, lyke a chylde,
Thou slepyst to long; thou art begylde.

" My darlyng dere, my daysy floure,
Let me," quod he, " ly in your lap."

[267]

"Ly styll," quod she, "my paramoure;
  Ly styll hardely, and take a nap."
  Hys hed was hevy, such was his hap,
    All drowsy, dremyng, dround in slepe,
    That of hys loue he toke no kepe.
    With hey lullay, lullay. . . .

With "ba, ba, ba,"[1] and "bas, bas, bas,"[1]
  She cheryshed hym, both cheke and chyn,
That he wyst never where he was;
  He had forgoten all dedely syn.
  He wantyd wyt her love to wyn;
    He trusted her payment and lost all hys pray;
    She left hym slepyng and stale away.
    With hey lullay, lullay. . . .

JOHN SKELTON

. . . Full on this casement shone the wintry moon,
    And threw warm gules on Madeline's fair breast,
    As down she knelt for heaven's grace and boon;
    Rose-bloom fell on her hands, together prest,
    And on her silver cross soft amethyst,
    And on her hair a glory, like a saint:
    She seemed a splendid angel, newly drest,
    Save wings, for heaven: — Porphyro grew faint:
She knelt, so pure a thing, so free from mortal taint.

    Anon his heart revives: her vespers done,
    Of all its wreathèd pearls her hair she frees;
    Unclasps her warmèd jewels one by one;
    Loosens her fragrant boddice; by degrees
    Her rich attire creeps rustling to her knees:
    Half-hidden, like a mermaid in sea-weed,
    Pensive awhile she dreams awake, and sees,
    In fancy, fair St. Agnes in her bed,
But dares not look behind, or all the charm is fled.

[1] Kiss.

Soon, trembling in her soft and chilly nest,
In sort of wakeful swoon, perplexed she lay,
Until the poppied warmth of sleep oppressed
Her soothèd limbs, and soul fatigued away;
Flown, like a thought, until the morrow-day;
Blissfully havened both from joy and pain;
Clasped like a missal where swart Paynims pray;
Blinded alike from sunshine and from rain,
As though a rose should shut, and be a bud again.

JOHN KEATS, from "The Eve of St. Agnes"

THE WAKEFUL NIGHTINGALE

The wakeful nightingale, that takes no rest,
While Cupid warms his little breast;
All night how sweetly he complains,
And makes us fear that love has pains:
No, no, no, no, 'tis no such thing,
For love that makes him wakeful, makes him sing.

THE SISTERS

After hot loveless nights, when cold winds stream
Sprinkling the frost and dew, before the light,
Bored with the foolish things that girls must dream
Because their beds are empty of delight,

Two sisters rise and strip. Out from the night
Their horses run to their low-whistled pleas —
Vast phantom shapes with eyeballs rolling white
That sneeze a fiery steam about their knees:

Through the crisp manes their stealthy prowling hands,
Stronger than curbs, in slow caresses rove,
They gallop down across the milk-white sands
And wade far out into the sleeping cove:

The frost stings sweetly with a burning kiss
As intimate as love, as cold as death:
Their lips, whereon delicious tremors hiss,
Fume with the ghostly pollen of their breath.

Far out on the grey silence of the flood
They watch the dawn in smouldering gyres expand
Beyond them: and the day burns through their blood
Like a white candle through a shuttered hand.

Roy Campbell

THE BROOMFIELD HILL

There was a knight and a lady bright,
   Had a true tryste at the broom;
The ane gaed early in the morning,
   The other in the afternoon.

And ay she sat in her mother's bower door,
   And ay she made her mane:
" O whether should I gang to the Broomfield Hill,
   Or should I stay at hame?

" For if I gang to the Broomfield Hill,
   My maidenhead is gone;
And if I chance to stay at hame,
   My love will ca' me mansworn."

Up then spake a witch-woman,
   Ay from the room aboon:
" O ye may gang to the Broomfield Hill,
   And yet come maiden hame.

" For when ye gang to the Broomfield Hill,
   Ye'll find your love asleep,
With a silver belt about his head,
   And a broom-cow at his feet.

"Take ye the blossom of the broom,
 The blossom it smells sweet,
And strew it at your true-love's head,
 And likewise at his feet.

"Take ye the rings off your fingers,
 Put them on his right hand,
To let him know, when he doth awake,
 His love was at his command."

She pu'd the broom flower on Hive Hill,
 And strewd on's white hals-bane,
And that was to be wittering true
 That maiden she had gane.

"O where were ye, my milk-white steed
 That I hae coft sae dear,
That wadna watch and waken me,
 When there was maiden here?"

"I stamped wi' my foot, master,
 And gar'd my bridle ring,
But na kin thing wald waken ye,
 Till she was past and gane."

"And wae betide ye, my gay goss-hawk,
 That I did love sae dear,
That wadna watch and waken me
 When there was maiden here."

"I clapped wi' my wings, master,
 And aye my bells I rang,
And aye cry'd, Waken, waken, master,
 Before the ladye gang."

"But haste and haste, my gude white steed,
 To come the maiden till,
Or a' the birds of gude green wood
 Of your flesh shall have their fill."

"Ye need na burst your gude white steed
  Wi' racing o'er the howm;
Nae bird flies faster through the wood,
  Than she fled through the broom."

THE GIPSY LADDIE

The gipsies came to our good lord's gate,
  And wow but they sang sweetly!
They sang sae sweet and sae very complete
  That down came the fair lady.

And she came tripping down the stair,
  And a' her maids before her;
As soon as they saw her weel-faured face,
  They coost the glamour o'er her.

"Gae tak frae me this gay mantile,
  And bring to me a plaidie;
For if kith and kin and a' had sworn,
  I'll follow the gipsy laddie.

"Yestreen I lay in a well-made bed,
  And my good lord beside me;
This night I'll lie in a tenant's barn,
  Whatever shall betide me."

"Come to your bed," says Johnnie Faa,
  "Oh come to your bed, my dearie;
For I vow and I swear, by the hilt of the sword,
  That your lord shall nae mair come near ye."

"I'll go to bed to my Johnnie Faa,
  I'll go to bed to my dearie;
For I vow and I swear, by what passed yestreen,
  That my lord shall nae mair come near me.

" I'll mak a hap to my Johnnie Faa,
   And I'll mak a hap to my dearie;
And he's gat a' the coat gaes round,
   And my lord shall nae mair come near me."

And when our lord came hame at een,
   And speired for his fair lady,
The tane she cried, and the other replied,
   " She's away with the gipsy laddie."

" Gae saddle to me the black, black steed,
   Gae saddle and make him ready;
Before that I either eat or sleep,
   I'll gae seek my fair lady."

And we were fifteen well-made men,
   Although we were nae bonnie,
And we were a' put down for ane,
   A fair young wanton lady.

SHALL I COME

Shall I come, sweet Love, to thee,
   When the evening beams are set?
Shall I not excluded be?
   Will you find no feignèd let?
Let me not, for pity, more,
Tell the long hours at your door.

Who can tell what thief or foe,
   In the covert of the night,
For his prey will work my woe,
   Or through wicked foul despite:
So may I die unredressed
Ere my long love be possessed.

[273]

But to let such dangers pass,
   Which a lover's thoughts disdain,
'Tis enough in such a place
   To attend love's joys in vain.
Do not mock me in thy bed,
While these cold nights freeze me dead.

THOMAS CAMPION

WHAN I SLEEP I DREAM

Whan I sleep I dream,
   Whan I wauk I'm eerie,
Sleep I canna get,
   For thinkin' o' my dearie.

Lanely night comes on,
   A' the house are sleeping,
I think on the bonie lad
   That has my heart a keeping.
     Ay waukin O, waukin ay and wearie,
     Sleep I canna get, for thinkin' o' my dearie.

Lanely night comes on,
   A' the house are sleeping,
I think on my bonie lad,
   An' I bleer my een wi' greetin'!
     Ay waukin O, waukin ay and wearie,
     Sleep I canna get, for thinkin' o' my dearie.

ROBERT BURNS

BURD HELEN

There liv'd a lord on yon sea-side,
   And he thought on a wile,
How he would go over the saut sea
   A lady to beguile.

[274]

"O learn to mak your bed, Helen,
   And learn to ly your lane,
For I'm gaun over the saut seas
   A bright bride to bring hame."

"How can I mak my bed," she says,
   "Unless I mak it wide,
Whan I have seven o' your sons
   To lie down by my side?

"And the first o' your seven sons,
   He rides a milk-white steed;
The second o' your seven sons,
   He wears a milk-white weed.

"The third ane o' your seven sons,
   He draws baith ale and wine;
The fourth ane o' your seven sons,
   He serves you when you dine.

"The fifth ane o' your seven sons,
   He can baith read and write;
And the sixth ane o' your seven sons,
   He is a' your heart's delight.

"And the youngest o' your seven sons,
   He sleeps on my breast-bane;
Whan him and I ly down at night,
   For him rest get I nane."

"O wha will bake my bridal bread,
   And brew my bridal ale?
And wha will welcome my gae lady,
   That I bring o'er the dale?

"And sin' ye've ta'en the turn in hand,
   See that ye do it right,
And ilka chimly o' the house,
   That they be dearly dight."

[275]

O a' the day she washed and wrang,
 And a' the night she buik,
And she's awa' to her chamber,
 To gie her young son suck. . . .

"Come here, come here, my eldest son,
 And see what you may see;
For yonder comes your father dear,
 Your mother-in-law side be."

She's ta'en a cake o' the best bread,
 A bottle o' the best wine,
And a' the keys upon her arm,
 And to the yates she's gaen.

"Ye are welcome hame, gay lady," she said,
 "And ay ye are welcome hame;
And sae is a' the gentlewomen
 That's wi' you ridden and gane.

"You are welcome hame, gay lord," she said,
 "And ay ye are welcome hame;
And sae is a' the gentlemen
 That's wi' you ridden and gane."

She saird [2] them up, she saird them down,
 She saird them till and frae;
But when she went behind their backs,
 The tear did blind her ee.

Whan day was gane, and night was come,
 And a' man boun' to bed,
The bridegroom and the bonny bride
 In their chamber was laid.

Burd Helen and her seven sons
 Lay in a bower near by;

. . . .
. . . . . .

[2] Served.

" If my seven sons were seven grey ratts,
 To rin frae wa' to wa',
And I mysell a good grey cat,
 I would bite their back a-twa.

" If my seven sons were seven grey hares,
 And them to rin a race,
And I mysell a good greyhound,
 I would gie them a chace."

Up and spak the bonny bride,
 In chamber where she lay:
" There is a lady in this bower,
 She will gae mad or day."

" Lye still, lye still, my bonny bride,
 Lie still and tak a sleep;
It's but ane o' my wine puncheons;
 Nae langer wad it keep."

" King Henry was my father dear,
 Queen Catherine was my mother,
Lady Anne she was my sister dear,
 And Frederick was my brother.

" And when I was six years of age,
 They ca'd me Mary Mild;
I was stown frae my father's yate,
 Whan I was but a child."

Then up and spak the bonny bride,
 By her lord as she lay:
" Lye down, lye down, my dear sister,
 There's nae ill done for me.

" O seven ships conveyed me here,
 And seven came o'er the main;
And four o' them shall stay wi' you,
 And three convey me hame.

" But when I gae hame to my father's house,
　They will laugh me to scorn,
To come awa' a wedded wife,
　Gae hame a maid the morn."

"BY THIS HE KNEW SHE WEPT"

By this he knew she wept with waking eyes:
That, at his hand's light quiver by her head,
The strange low sobs that shook their common bed
Were called into her with a sharp surprise,
And strangled mute, like little gaping snakes,
Dreadfully venomous to him. She lay
Stone-still, and the long darkness flowed away
With muffled pulses. Then, as midnight makes
Her giant heart of Memory and Tears
Drink the pale drug of silence, and so beat
Sleep's heavy measure, they from head to feet
Were moveless, looking through their dead black years,
By vain regret scrawled over the blank wall.
Like sculptured effigies they might be seen
Upon their marriage-tomb, the sword between;
Each wishing for the sword that severs all. . . .

GEORGE MEREDITH

Go thou that vainly dost mine eyes invite
To taste the softer comforts of the night,
And bid'st me cool the fever of my brain,
In those sweet balmy dews which slumber pain;
Enjoy thine own peace in untroubled sleep,
Whilst my sad thoughts eternal vigils keep.

O couldst thou for a time change breasts with me,
Thou in that broken glass shouldst plainly see,

A heart which wastes in the slow smoth'ring fire
Blown by despair, and fed by false desire,
Can only reap such sleeps as sea-men have,
When fierce winds rock them on the foaming wave.

HENRY KING

. . . Eftsoons they heard a most melodious sound,
   Of all that might delight a dainty ear,
   Such as at once might not on living ground,
   Save in this Paradise, be heard elsewhere:
   Right hard it was, for wight, which did it hear,
   To read, what manner music that might be:
   For all that pleasing is to living ear,
   Was there consorted in one harmony,
Birds, voices, instruments, winds, waters, all agree.

The joyous birds shrouded in cheerful shade,
   Their notes unto the voice attempered sweet;
   The angelical soft trembling voices made
   To the instruments divine respondence meet:
   The silver sounding instruments did meet
   With the base murmur of the waters' fall:
   The waters fall with difference discreet,
   Now soft, now loud, unto the wind did call:
The gentle warbling wind low answerèd to all.

There, whence that Music seemèd heard to be,
   Was the fair Witch her self now solacing,
   With a new Lover, whom through sorcery
   And witchcraft, she from far did thither bring:
   There she had him now laid a-slumbering,
   In secret shade, after long wanton joys:
   Whilst round about them pleasantly did sing
   Many fair Ladies, and lascivious boys,
That ever mixt their song with light licentious toys.

And all that while, right over him she hung,
  With her false eyes fast fixèd in his sight,
  As seeking medicine, whence she was stung,
  Or greedily depasturing delight:
  And oft inclining down with kisses light,
  For fear of waking him, his lips bedewed,
  And through his humid eyes did suck his spright,
  Quite molten into lust and pleasure lewd;
Wherewith she sighèd soft, as if his case she rued. . . .

Upon a bed of Roses she was laid,
  As faint through heat, or dight to pleasant sin,
  And was arrayed, or rather disarrayed,
  All in a veil of silk and silver thin,
  That hid no whit her alabaster skin,
  But rather shewed more white, if more might be:
  More subtile web *Arachne* cannot spin,
  Nor the fine nets, which oft we woven see
Of scorchèd dew, do not in th' air more lightly flee.

Her snowy breast was bare to ready spoil
  Of hungry eyes, which n'ote therewith be filled.
  And yet through languour of her late sweet toil,
  Few drops, more clear than Nectar, forth distilled,
  That like pure Orient pearls adown it trilled,
  And her fair eyes sweet smiling in delight,
  Moistened their fiery beams, with which she thrilled
  Frail hearts, yet quenchèd not; like starry light
Which sparkling on the silent waves, does seem more
  bright. . . .

EDMUND SPENSER,
from *The Faerie Queene*

LA BELLE DAME SANS MERCI

O, what can ail thee, knight at arms,
  Alone and palely loitering?
The sedge is withered from the lake,
  And no birds sing.

O, what can ail thee, knight at arms,
　So haggard and so woe-begone?
The squirrel's granary is full,
　And the harvest's done.

I see a lilly on thy brow,
　With anguish moist and fever dew;
And on thy cheek a fading rose
　Fast withereth too.

I met a lady in the meads,
　Full beautiful, a faery's child;
Her hair was long, her foot was light,
　And her eyes were wild.

I made a garland for her head,
　And bracelets too, and fragrant zone;
She looked at me as she did love,
　And made sweet moan.

I set her on my pacing steed,
　And nothing else saw all day long;
For sideways would she lean, and sing
　A faery's song.

She found me roots of relish sweet,
　And honey wild, and manna dew;
And sure in language strange she said,
　I love thee true.

She took me to her elfin grot,
　And there she gazed and sighed full sore,
And there I shut her wild wild eyes
　With kisses four.

And there she lullèd me asleep,
　And there I dreamed, ah woe betide,
The latest dream I ever dreamed
　On the cold hill side.

I saw pale kings, and princes too,
　　Pale warriors, death-pale were they all;
They cried — " La belle Dame sans merci
　　Hath thee in thrall! "

I saw their starved lips in the gloam
　　With horrid warning gapèd wide,
And I awoke, and found me here
　　On the cold hill side.

And this is why I sojourn here
　　Alone and palely loitering,
Though the sedge is withered from the lake,
　　And no birds sing.

JOHN KEATS

It is not Beauty I demand,
　　A crystal brow, the moon's despair,
Nor the snow's daughter, a white hand,
　　Nor mermaid's yellow pride of hair.

Tell me not of your starry eyes,
　　Your lips that seem on roses fed,
Your breasts, where Cupid trembling lies,
　　Nor sleeps for kissing of his bed. . . .

For crystal brows — there's naught within,
　　They are but empty cells for pride;
He who the Siren's hair would win
　　Is mostly strangled in the tide. . . .

GEORGE DARLEY

THE LOVER IN WINTER PLAINETH FOR THE SPRING

O western wind, when wilt thou blow,
　　[That] the small rain down can rain?
Christ, that my love were in my arms
　　And I in my bed again!

I have lived and I have loved;
I have waked and I have slept;
I have sung and I have danced;
I have smiled and I have wept;
I have won and wasted treasure;
I have had my fill of pleasure;
And all these things were weariness,
And some of them were dreariness.
And all these things — but two things
Were emptiness and pain:
And Love — it was the best of them;
And Sleep — worth all the rest of them.

"That Not Impossible She"

As I lay sleeping
In dreames fleeting
Ever my sweeting
   Is in my mind . . .

Let joy be thy soul's guest,
And care be banished quite,
Since she hath thee expressed
To be her favourite. . . .

But the erl-king's daughter dances still
When the moonlight sleeps on the frosted hill.

"That Not Impossible She"

Dear, why should you command me to my rest,
   When now the night doth summon all to sleep?
Methinks this time becometh lovers best;
Night was ordained together friends to keep:
How happy are all other living things,
Which though the day disjoin by several flight,
The quiet evening yet together brings,
And each returns unto his love at night!
O, thou that art so courteous else to all,
Why shouldst thou, Night, abuse me only thus,
That every creature, to his kind dost call,
And yet 'tis thou dost only sever us?
   Well could I wish it would be ever day,
   If, when night comes, you bid me go away.

MICHAEL DRAYTON

A DREAM

One night, with sleep my senses being opprest,
Fixt on that thought, which still o'er-ruled my breast
In mourning dress, with silence did appear,
She of her sex was to my soul most dear:

" Cynthia," methought, I said, and gazed awhile,
" Where's thy accustomed look, and cheerful smile?
What sad occasion thus disturbs thee now,
And hangs that gloomy sadness on thy brow? "

She only sighed, and offering to depart,
I snatched her hand, and laid it to my heart,
And whilst I in this trembling rapture stand,
She took, and held me by my other hand.

I thought my heart 'twixt joy, and grief would break,
Adding with tears, " My dear, I prithee speak ";
And grasped her fast, she struggling to be gone,
Till waked: but then I found myself alone.

Oft have I grieved to think what this might prove,
And gathered hence ill omens to my Love;
But since I may too soon the mischief find,
I'll strive to chase the fancy from my mind.

PHILIP AYRES

FAIR MOON, WHO WITH THY COLD AND SILVER SHINE

Fair Moon, who with thy cold and silver shine
Makes sweet the horror of the dreadful night,
Delighting the weak eye with smiles divine,
Which Phoebus dazzles with his too much light;
Bright Queen of the first Heaven, if in thy shrine,
By turning oft, and Heaven's eternal might,
Thou hast not yet that once sweet fire of thine,
Endymion, forgot, and lover's plight?
If cause like thine may pity breed in thee,
And pity somewhat else to it obtain,
Since thou hast power of dreams, as well as he
Who paints strange figures in the slumbering brain,
  Now while she sleeps, in doleful guise her show
  These tears, and the black map of all my woe.

WILLIAM DRUMMOND

[288]

THE HAUNTED HOUSE

How loud the storm blew all that bitter night!
The loosened ivy tapping on the pane
Woke me and woke, again and yet again,
Till I was full awake and sat upright.
I listened to the noises of the night,
And presently I heard, disguised yet plain,
A footstep on the stair which mounted light
Towards me, and my heart outbeat the rain.
I knew that it was you. I knew it even
Before the door, which by design ajar
Waited your coming, had disclosed my fate.
I felt a wind upon my face from heaven.
I felt the presence of a life. My hair
Was touched as by a spirit. Insensate
I drew you to my bosom. Ah, too late!
I clutched the darkness. There was nothing there.

WILFRID SCAWEN BLUNT

TO SLEEP

How comes it, Sleep, that thou
Even kisses me affords
Of her (dear her) so far who's absent now?
How did I hear those words,
Which rocks might move, and move the pines to bow?
Ah me! before half day
Why didst thou steal away?
Return, I thine for ever will remain,
If thou wilt bring with thee that guest again.

WILLIAM DRUMMOND

DREAM LAND

When in my dreams thy lovely face
Smiles with unwonted tender grace,
Grudge not the precious seldom cheer:
I know full well, my lady dear,
   It is no boon of thine!

In thy sweet sanctuary of sleep,
If my sad sprite should kneeling weep,
Suffer its speechless worship there:
Thou know'st full well, my lady fair,
   It is no fault of mine!

FRANCES ANNE KEMBLE

Sleep, angry beauty, sleep and fear not me!
   For who a sleeping lion dares provoke?
It shall suffice me here to sit and see
   Those lips shut up that never kindly spoke:
What sight can more content a lover's mind
Than beauty seeming harmless, if not kind?

My words have charmed her, for secure she sleeps,
   Though guilty much of wrong done to my love;
And in her slumber, see! she, closed-eyed, weeps:
   Dreams often more than waking passions move.
Plead, Sleep, my cause, and make her soft like thee,
That she in peace may wake and pity me.

THOMAS CAMPION

ROSE AYLMER

Ah what avails the sceptred race,
   Ah what the form divine!
What every virtue, every grace!
   Rose Aylmer, all were thine.

Rose Aylmer, whom these wakeful eyes
   May weep, but never see,
A night of memories and sighs
   I consecrate to thee.

WALTER SAVAGE LANDOR

I dug, beneath the cypress shade,
   What well might seem an elfin's grave;
And every pledge in earth I laid,
   That erst thy false affection gave.

I pressed them down the sod beneath;
   I placed one mossy stone above;
And twined the rose's fading wreath
   Around the sepulchre of love.

Frail as thy love, the flowers were dead,
   Ere yet the evening sun was set:
But years shall see the cypress spread,
   Immutable as my regret.

THOMAS LOVE PEACOCK

THE TRYST

O luely, luely, cam she in
And luely she lay doun:
I kent her be her caller lips
And her breists sae sma' and roun'.

A' thru the nicht we spak nae word
Nor sinder'd bane frae bane:
A' thru the nicht I heard her hert
Gang soundin' wi' my ain.

It was about the waukrife hour
Whan cocks begin to craw

[291]

That she smool'd saftly thru the mirk
Afore the day wud daw.

Sae luely, luely, cam she in
Sae luely was she gaen;
And wi' her a' my simmer days
Like they had never been.

WILLIAM SOUTAR

Depart, depart, depart!
Alace! I must depart
From her that has my heart,
　　With heart full soir!
Against my will indeed,
And can find no remeid —
I wot the pains of deid
　　Can do no moir.

Now must I go, alace!
From sight of her sweet face,
The ground of all my grace,
　　And sovereign;
What chance that may fall me
Sall I never merry be,
Unto the time I see
　　My sweet again.

I go, and wot not where,
I wander here and there,
I weep and sich right sair,
　　With panes smart:
Now must I pass away, away,
In wilderness and wildsome way —
Alace! this woful day
　　We should depart!

My spirit does quake for dreid,
My thirlèd heart does bleed,
My panès does exceed:
    What should I say?
I, woful wight, alone,
Makand ane piteous moan;
Alace! my heart is gone,
    For ever and ay!

Through languor of my sweet,
So thirlèd is my spreit,
My days are most complete,
    Through her absence:
Christ, sen she knew my smart,
Ingraven in my heart,
Because I must depart
    From her presence!

Adieu, my own sweet thing,
My joy and comforting,
My mirth and solaceing
    Of earthly gloir!
Fare well, my lady bright,
And my remembrance right,
Fare well, and have good night —
    I say no moir.

                  ALEXANDER SCOTT

By day mine eyes, by night my soul desires thee,
  Weary, I lie alone.
Once in a dream it seémed thou wert beside me;
  O far beyond all dreams, if thou wouldst come!

             MS. of Beauvais,
         translated by Helen Waddell

Young and gold haired, fair of face,
  Thou gav'st me tender kisses in my sleep.
If waking I may never look upon thee,
  O Sleep, I pray you, never let me wake!

MS. of St. Remy at Rheims,
translated by Helen Waddell

ECHO

Come to me in the silence of the night;
  Come in the speaking silence of a dream;
Come with soft rounded cheeks and eyes as bright
  As sunlight on a stream;
    Come back in tears,
O memory, hope, love of finished years.

O dream how sweet, too sweet, too bitter sweet,
  Whose wakening should have been in Paradise,
Where souls brimful of love abide and meet;
  Where thirsting longing eyes
    Watch the slow door
That opening, letting in, lets out no more.

Yet come to me in dreams, that I may live
  My very life again though cold in death:
Come back to me in dreams, that I may give
  Pulse for pulse, breath for breath:
    Speak low, lean low,
As long ago, my love, how long ago.

CHRISTINA ROSSETTI

Weary with toil, I haste me to my bed,
The dear repose for limbs with travel tired;
But then begins a journey in my head
To work my mind, when body's work's expired:

For then my thoughts — from far where I abide —
Intend a zealous pilgrimage to thee,
And keep my drooping eyelids open wide,
Looking on darkness which the blind do see:
Save that my soul's imaginary sight
Presents thy shadow to my sightless view,
Which, like a jewel hung in ghastly night,
Makes black night beauteous and her old face new.
  Lo! thus, by day my limbs, by night my mind,
    For thee, and for myself no quiet find.

WILLIAM SHAKESPEARE

When most I wink, then do mine eyes best see,
For all the day they view things unrespected;
But when I sleep, in dreams they look on thee,
And darkly bright, are bright in dark directed.
Then thou, whose shadow shadows doth make bright,
How would thy shadow's form form happy show
To the clear day with thy much clearer light,
When to unseeing eyes thy shade shines so!
How would, I say, mine eyes be blessed made
By looking on thee in the living day,
When in dead night thy fair imperfect shade
Through heavy sleep on sightless eyes doth stay!
  All days are nights to see till I see thee,
    And nights bright days when dreams do show thee me.

WILLIAM SHAKESPEARE

ELEGIE X: THE DREAME

. . . When you are gone, and *Reason* gone with you,
    Then *Fantasie* is Queene and Soule, and all;
  She can present joyes meaner then you do;
    Convenient, and more proportionall.

[295]

So, if I dreame I have you, I have you,
　For, all our joyes are but fantasticall.
And so I scape the paine, for paine is true;
　And sleepe which locks up sense, doth lock out all.
After a such fruition I shall wake,
　And, but the waking, nothing shall repent;
And shall to love more thankfull Sonnets make,
　Then if more *honour, teares,* and *paines* were spent.
But dearest heart, and dearer image stay;
　Alas, true joyes at best are *dreame* enough;
Though you stay here you passe too fast away:
　For even at first life's *Taper* is a snuffe.
Filled with her love, may I be rather grown
Mad with much *heart,* then *ideott* with none.

JOHN DONNE

NOT EVEN IN DREAM

This love is crueller than the other love:
　We had the Dreams for Tryst, we other pair;
But here there is no *we;* — not anywhere
　Returning breaths of sighs about me move.
No wings, even of the stuff which fancy wove,
　Perturb Sleep's air with a responsive flight
When mine sweep into dreams. My soul in fright
　Circles as round its widowed nest a dove.

One shadow but usurps another's place:
　And, though this shadow more enthralling is,
Alas, it hath no lips at all to miss!
　I have not even that former poignant bliss,
That haunting sweetness, that forlorn sad trace,
　The phantom memory of a vanished kiss.

FRANCIS THOMPSON

SAPPHICS

All the night sleep came not upon my eyelids,
Shed not dew, nor shook nor unclosed a feather,
Yet with lips shut close and with eyes of iron
    Stood and beheld me.

Then to me so lying awake a vision
Came without sleep over the seas and touched me,
Softly touched mine eyelids and lips; and I too,
    Full of the vision,

Saw the white implacable Aphrodite,
Saw the hair unbound and the feet unsandalled
Shine as fire of sunset on western waters;
    Saw the reluctant

Feet, the straining plumes of the doves that drew her,
Looking always, looking with necks reverted,
Back to Lesbos, back to the hills whereunder
    Shone Mitylene;

Heard the flying feet of the Loves behind her
Make a sudden thunder upon the waters,
As the thunder flung from the strong unclosing
    Wings of a great wind. . . .

                ALGERNON CHARLES SWINBURNE

" THE DREAME "

Deare love, for nothing lesse than thee
Would I have broke this happy dreame,
    It was a theame
For reason, much too strong for phantasie.
Therefore thou waked'st me wisely; yet
My Dreame thou brok'st not, but continued'st it,

Thou art so true, that thoughts of thee suffice,
To make dreames truths; and fables histories;
Enter these armes, for since thou thoughtst it best,
Not to dreame all my dreame, let's act the rest.

As lightning, or a Taper's light,
Thine eyes, and not thy noise wak'd mee;
   Yet I thought thee
(For thou lovest truth) an Angell, at first sight,
But when I saw thou sawest my heart,
And knew'st my thoughts, beyond an Angel's art,
When thou knew'st what I dreamt, when thou knew'st when
Excesse of joy would wake me, and cam'st then,
I must confesse, it could not chuse but bee
Prophane, to thinke thee any thing but thee.

Comming and staying show'd thee, thee,
But rising makes me doubt, that now,
   Thou art not thou.
That love is weake, where feare's as strong as hee;
'Tis not all spirit, pure, and brave,
If mixture it of *Feare, Shame, Honor,* have.
Perchance as torches which must ready bee,
Men light and put out, so thou deal'st with mee,
Thou cam'st to kindle, goest to come; Then I
Will dreame that hope againe, but else would die.

JOHN DONNE

Dreams Dreamed

"*I dreamed a dream to-night.*"
                    "*And so did I.*"
"*Well, what was yours?*"
                    "*That dreamers often lie.*"
"*In bed asleep, while they do dream things true.*"

"*Last night I looked into a dream; 'twas drawn*
  On the black velvet of a midnight sleep
  And set to woeful thoughts . . ."

"*We rest — a dream has power to poison sleep;*
  We rise — one wandering thought pollutes the days . . ."

Dreams Dreamed

Especially at the close of my experience [the effects of a dose of mescal button (*Anhalomium Leivenii*)] I must, I think, have been for a while in the peculiar interval between the waking state and that of sleep — the " prædormitum " — the time when we are apt to dream half-controlled stories; but as to this I am not very sure. As a rule I was on guard, with every power of observation and reflection in full activity.

My first vivid show of mescal colour effects came quickly. I saw the stars, and then, of a sudden, here and there delicate floating films of colour — usually delightful neutral purples and pinks. These came and went — now here, now there.
. . .

When I opened my eyes all was gone at once. Closing them, I began after a long interval to see for the first time definite objects associated with colours. The stars sparkled and passed away. A white spear of grey stone grew up to huge height, and became a tall, richly finished Gothic tower of very elaborate and definite design, with many rather worn statues standing in the doorways or on stone brackets. As I gazed, every projecting angle, cornice, and even the face of the stones at their joinings were by degrees covered or hung with clusters of what seemed to be huge precious stones, but uncut, some being more like masses of transparent fruit. These were green, purple, red, and orange; never clear yellow and never blue. All seemed to possess an interior light, and to give the faintest idea of the perfectly satisfying intensity and purity of these gorgeous colour-fruits is quite beyond my power. All the colours I have ever beheld are dull as compared to these.

As I looked, and it lasted long, the tower became of a fine mouse hue, and everywhere the vast pendent masses of emerald green, ruby reds, and orange began to drip a slow rain of colours. All this while nothing was at rest a moment. The balls of colour moved tremulously. The tints became dull, and then, at once, past belief vivid; the architectural lines were all active with shifting tints. The figures moving shook the long, hanging lines of living light, and then, in an instant, all was dark.

After an endless display of less beautiful marvels I saw that which deeply impressed me. An edge of a huge cliff seemed to project over a gulf of unseen depth. My viewless enchanter set on the brink a huge bird-claw of stone. Above, from the stem or leg, hung a fragment of some stuff. This began to unroll and float out to a distance which seemed to me to represent Time as well as immensity of Space. Here were miles of rippled purples, half transparent, and of ineffable beauty. Now and then soft golden clouds floated from these folds, or a great shimmer went over the whole of the rolling purples, and things, like green birds, fell from it, fluttering down into the gulf below. Next, I saw clusters of stones hanging in masses from the claw toes, as it seemed to me miles of them, down far below into the underworld of the black gulf.

This was the most distinct of my visions. Incautiously I opened my eyes, and it was gone. . . .

S. WEIR MITCHELL

Both Mr. Galton and M. Maury relate stories of faces seen in the dark; . . . faces seemingly standing off upon the air, and coming and going as with a will and purpose of their own. These I know something about. It is not, perhaps, a very rare experience; but however that may be, I have been familiar with such apparitions for many years.

In my case, as in M. Maury's, these faces [*hallucinations hypnagogiques*] usually appear in the dropping-off-to-sleep time. But they also appear when I wake in the night; and the effect of their coming on either occasion is to dispel the 'tween-sleep-and-waking twilight and fix a critical attention on themselves. Yet they are never seen except when the eyelids are closed, and they have an apparent distance of five or six feet. Though they seem living enough, they look through the darkness as if traced in chalks on a black ground. Colour sometimes they have, but the colour is very faint. Indeed, their general aspect is as if their substance was of pale smoke; and their outlines waver, fade, and revive (with the effect, though not the aspect, of phosphorescent limnings), so that, except for the half of a moment, the whole face is never clearly or completely visible at one time. Always of a strikingly distinctive character, these visionary faces are like none that can be remembered as seen in life or in pictures; indeed, one of their constant and most remarkable characteristics is their convincing *un*likeness. . . .

In all likelihood, Blake's visions were some such phantoms as these, presented to his eyes in broad daylight. I am inclined to think so because his wonderful, dreadful drawing, " The Ghost of a Flea," is precisely such a transcript as I could have made by the score but for lack of his pictorial skill. Under my own eyelids I have seen many a face of the same awful family; and some more dreadful still, being alive and astir with animation. . . .[1]

FREDERICK GREENWOOD

Many years ago I dreamed of having killed a man by throwing him from the verge of an old, unfrequented quay. The murder itself did not come into the dream, which began (according to my waking remembrance) just after I had turned from the scene. It might have been a dream of horror as well as guilt — of horror, the torment of which, we may suspect, is often tempered by the thought of it as punishment that

---

[1] Grief the most despairing, scorn, cunning, pride, hate, malicious inquiry, envious or triumphant mockery — no human face that ever was seen, I am sure, displayed these emotions with a comparable fulness and intensity. It is not the characteristic of all, but it is of some to an almost appalling extent. . . .

atones. But the deed being out of sight, so to speak, in my case horror there was none. The dream was of guilt alone; and whenever I review that vision of myself stealing away through the old streets that bordered the quay (it was early morning and the streets were bathed in a thin clear slanting light), and when I recall my sensations, the whole mind of me an abyss of listening silence, my very footsteps seeming noiseless, and a wide environment of distance standing between me and every passer-by, I believe I really do know the awful solitude a murderer feels, or know it far beyond mere imagining. . . .

The dream . . . is no proof that if I did commit murder I should feel as I felt then; but it was a most impressive, a most terrible and convincing lesson in what a murderer naturally feels when he is not a born assassin. If, beyond the entertainment it affords, there be any use in literature, any use in the novelist's pictures, the poet's revelations, the dramatist's embodiment and display of human feeling, it must be something to have the stage erected in our own breasts, the scene our own lives, the stir of emotion and passion our own in situations of acute trial and intense meaning. . . .

FREDERICK GREENWOOD

. . . A deaf and dumb writer of ability who has precise and highly emotional dreams — which sometimes remind him of the atmosphere of Poe's tales, and are occasionally in organised sequence from night to night — writes: " The enormous reality and vividness of these dreams is their remarkable point. They leave a mark behind. When I come to consider I believe that much that I have written, and many things that I have said and thought and believed, are directly due to these dream-experiences and my ponderings over how they came. Beneath the superficiality of our conscious mind — prim, smug, self-satisfied, owlishly wise — there lies the vast gulf of a subconscious personality that is dark and obscure, seldom seen or even suspected. It is this, I think, that wells up into my dreams. It is always there — always affecting us and modifying us, and bringing about strange and unforeseen new things in us — but in these dreams I peer over the edge of the conscious world into the giant-house and Utgard of the subconscious, lit by one ray of sunset that shows the weltering deeps of it. And the vivid sense of this is responsible for many things in my life ". . . .

HAVELOCK ELLIS

"When man's interior sight is opened, which is that of his spirit, then there appear the things of another life, which cannot possibly be made visible to the bodily sight." . . .

"By the internal sight it has been granted me to see the things that are in the other life, more clearly than I see those that are in the world. From these considerations, it is evident that external vision exists from interior vision, and this from a vision still more interior, and so on." . . .

"There are with every man at least two evil spirits." . . .

"With wicked genii there is also a fluent speech which is harsh and grating. There is also among them a speech which is not fluent, wherein the dissent of the thoughts is perceived as something secretly creeping along within it." . . .

"If evil spirits could perceive that they were associated with man, and yet that they were spirits separate from him, and if they could flow in into the things of his body, they would attempt by a thousand means to destroy him; for they hate man with a deadly hatred." . . .

"Knowing, therefore, that I was a man in the body, they were continually striving to destroy me, not as to the body only, but especially as to the soul; for to destroy any man or spirit is the very delight of the life of all who are in hell; but I have been continually protected by the Lord. Hence it appears how dangerous it is for man to be in a living consort with spirits, unless he be in the good of faith." . . .

EMANUEL SWEDENBORG, quoted by Sheridan le Fanu

And Jacob went out from Beer-Sheba, and went toward Haran. And he lighted upon a certain place, and tarried there all night, because the sun was set; and he took of the stones of that place, and put them for his pillows, and lay down in that place to sleep. And he dreamed, and behold a ladder set up on the earth, and the top of it reached to heaven: and behold the angels of God ascending and descending on it. And, behold, the Lord stood above it and said, I am the Lord God of Abraham thy father, and the God of Isaac: the land whereon thou liest, to thee will I give it, and to thy seed; and thy seed shall be as the dust of the earth, and thou shalt spread abroad to the west, and to the east, and to the north, and to the south: and in thee and in thy seed shall all the families of the earth be blessed. And, behold, I am with thee, and will keep thee in all places whither thou goest, and will bring thee again into this land; for I will not leave thee, until I have done that which I have spoken to thee of.

And Jacob awaked out of his sleep, and he said, Surely the Lord is in this place; and I knew it not. And he was afraid, and said, How dreadful is this place! this is none other than the house of God, and this is the gate of heaven. . . .

THE BOOK OF GENESIS

. . . I once heard a friend, and one not specially fanciful . . . tell how he had been one night tormented by the strangest vision. He was asleep, and on a curtain of darkness there hung before him a beautiful female face; and this face, as if keeping time with the ticks of the watch under his pillow, the beating of his pulse, the systole and diastole of his heart, was alternately beautiful — and a skull. There, on the curtain of darkness, the apparition throbbed in regular and dreadful change. And this strange and regularly recurring antithesis of beauty and horror, with the spiritual meaning and significance under it — for the loveliest face that ever poet sang, or painter painted, or lover kissed, is but a skull beclothed with flesh: we are all naked under our clothes, we are all skeletons under our flesh — was as much out of my prosaic friend's usual way of thinking as crown, sceptre, and robe of state are out of a day labourer's way of life. . . .

ALEXANDER SMITH

THE GRAY SISTERS

Perseus walked across the Ister dry-shod, and away through the moors and fens, day and night, toward the bleak northwest, turning neither to the right hand nor the left, till he came to the Unshapen Land, and the place which has no name.

And seven days he walked through it, on a path which few can tell; for those who have trodden it like least to speak of it, and those who go there again in dreams are glad enough when they awake; till he came to the edge of the everlasting night, where the air was full of feathers, and the soil was hard with ice; and there at last he found the three Gray Sisters, by the shore of the freezing sea, nodding upon a white log of drift-wood, beneath the cold white winter moon; and they chaunted a low song together. . . .

CHARLES KINGSLEY

THE CYPRESS CURTAIN

The cypress curtain of the night is spread,
And over all a silent dew is cast.
The weaker cares by sleep are conquerèd;
But I alone, with hideous grief, aghast,
In spite of Morpheus' charms, a watch do keep
Over thine eyes, to banish careless sleep.

Yet oft my trembling eyes through faintness close,
And then the Map of hell before me stands,
Which Ghosts do see, and I am one of those
Ordained to pine in sorrow's endless bands,

[307]

Since from my wretched soul all hopes are reft
And now no cause of life to me is left.

Grief, seize my soul, for that will still endure,
When my crased body is consumed and gone,
Bear it to thy black den, there keep it sure,
Where thou ten thousand souls dost tyre upon.
But all do not afford such food to thee
As this poor one, the worser part of me.

THOMAS CAMPION

SILENCE

There is a silence where hath been no sound,
   There is a silence where no sound may be,
   In the cold grave — under the deep, deep sea,
Or in wide desert where no life is found,
Which hath been mute, and still must sleep profound;
   No voice is hushed — no life treads silently,
   But clouds and cloudy shadows wander free,
That never spoke, over the idle ground:
But in green ruins, in the desolate walls
   Of antique palaces, where Man hath been,
Though the dun fox, or wild hyaena, calls,
   And owls, that flit continually between,
Shriek to the echo, and the low winds moan,
There the true Silence is, self-conscious and alone.

THOMAS HOOD

A BEAUTIFUL NIGHT

How lovely is the heaven of this night,
How deadly still its earth. The forest brute
Has crept into his cave, and laid himself
Where sleep has made him harmless like the lamb;
The horrid snake, his venom now forgot,
Is still and innocent as the honied flower
Under his head: — and man, in whom are met

Leopard and snake, — and all the gentleness
And beauty of the young lamb and the bud,
Has let his ghost out, put his thoughts aside
And lent his senses unto death himself;
Whereby the King and beggar all lie down
On straw or purple-tissue, are but bones
And air, and blood, equal to one another
And to the unborn and buried: so we go
Placing ourselves among the unconceived
And the old ghosts, wantonly, smilingly,
For sleep is fair and warm. . . .

THOMAS LOVELL BEDDOES

THE PAINS OF SLEEP

Ere on my bed my limbs I lay,
It hath not been my use to pray
With moving lips or bended knees;
But silently, by slow degrees,
My spirit I to Love compose,
In humble trust mine eye-lids close,
With reverential resignation,
No wish conceived, no thought exprest,
Only a sense of supplication;
A sense o'er all my soul imprest
That I am weak, yet not unblest,
Since in me, round me, every where
Eternal Strength and Wisdom are.

But yester-night I prayed aloud
In anguish and in agony,
Up-starting from the fiendish crowd
Of shapes and thoughts that tortured me:
A lurid light, a tramping throng,
Sense of intolerable wrong,
And whom I scorned, those only strong!
Thirst of revenge, the powerless will

Still baffled, and yet burning still!
Desire with loathing strangely mixed
On wild or hateful objects fixed.
Fantastic passions! maddening brawl!
And shame and terror over all!
Deeds to be hid which were not hid,
Which all confused I could not know
Whether I suffered, or I did:
For all seemed guilt, remorse or woe,
My own or others still the same
Life-stifling fear, soul-stifling shame.
So two nights passed: the night's dismay
Saddened and stunned the coming day.
Sleep, the wide blessing, seemed to me
Distemper's worst calamity.
The third night, when my own loud scream
Had waked me from the fiendish dream,
O'ercome with sufferings strange and wild,
I wept as I had been a child;
And having thus by tears subdued
My anguish to a milder mood,
Such punishments, I said, were due
To natures deepliest stained with sin, —
For aye entempesting anew
The unfathomable hell within,
The horror of their deeds to view,
To know and loathe, yet wish and do!
Such griefs with such men well agree,
But wherefore, wherefore fall on me? . . .

SAMUEL TAYLOR COLERIDGE

WOULD GOD IT WERE MORNING

My God, how many times ere I be dead
    Must I the bitterness of dying know?
How often like a corpse upon my bed
    Compose me and surrender me and so

Thro' hateful hours and ill-rememberèd
  Between the twilight and the twilight go
By visions bodiless obscurely led
  Thro' many a wild enormity of woe?
And yet I know not but that this is worst
When with that light, the feeble and the first,
  I start and gaze into the world again,
And gazing find it as of old accurst
And grey and blinded with the stormy burst
  And blank appalling solitude of rain.

FREDERIC MYERS

"THY DREAMS OMINOUS"

Blest is the man that sees and hears
  The shuttles of the eternal weaver,
And shrieks not, sobs not savage tears,
      Burns not with fever.
He is the tree that's finely planted
  Where a plunging cataract blanches,
Spreading there as though enchanted
      His lucky branches.

But what if I, whose different thews
  Scarce bear the dawning light unwincing,
Discovered in some curious clues
      Vision commencing?
I should be driftwood, moon and sun
  In gulping, groaning water-gorges
Sucked down, shot high, and snatched and spun
      Through timeless orgies.

EDMUND BLUNDEN

MY DREAM

Hear now a curious dream I dreamed last night,
Each word whereof is weighed and sifted truth.

I stood beside Euphrates while it swelled
Like overflowing Jordan in its youth:
It waxed and coloured sensibly to sight,
Till out of myriad pregnant waves there welled
Young crocodiles, a gaunt blunt-featured crew,
Fresh-hatched perhaps and daubed with birthday dew.
The rest if I should tell, I fear my friend,
My closest friend, would deem the facts untrue;
And therefore it were wisely left untold;
Yet if you will, why, hear it to the end.

Each crocodile was girt with massive gold
And polished stones that with their wearers grew:
But one there was who waxed beyond the rest,
Wore kinglier girdle and a kingly crown,
Whilst crowns and orbs and sceptres starred his breast.
All gleamed compact and green with scale on scale,
But special burnishment adorned his mail
And special terror weighed upon his frown;
His punier brethren quaked before his tail,
Broad as a rafter, potent as a flail.

So he grew lord and master of his kin:
But who shall tell the tale of all their woes?
An execrable appetite arose,
He battened on them, crunched, and sucked them in.
He knew no law, he feared no binding law,
But ground them with inexorable jaw:
The luscious fat distilled upon his chin,
Exuded from his nostrils and his eyes,
While still like hungry death he fed his maw;
Till every minor crocodile being dead
And buried too, himself gorged to the full,

[312]

He slept with breath oppressed and unstrung claw.
Oh marvel passing strange which next I saw:
In sleep he dwindled to the common size,
And all the empire faded from his coat.
Then from far off a wingèd vessel came,
Swift as a swallow, subtle as a flame:
I know not what it bore of freight or host,
But white it was as an avenging ghost.
It levelled strong Euphrates in its course;
Supreme yet weightless as an idle mote
It seemed to tame the waters without force
Till not a murmur swelled or billow beat:
Lo, as the purple shadow swept the sands,
The prudent crocodile rose on his feet
And shed appropriate tears and wrung his hands.

What can it mean? you ask. I answer not
For meaning, but myself must echo, What?
And tell it as I saw it on the spot.

CHRISTINA ROSSETTI

" Night, but clear with grey light. Part of church in the background with the clock-side towards the spectator. In the churchyard many sheep with good innocent expressions; one especially heavenly. Amid them with full face a Satan-like goat lying, with a kingly look and horns. Three white longish-haired dogs in front confused with the sheep though somewhat smaller than they: one with a flattering face, a second with head almost entirely turned away, but what one sees of the face sensual and abominable. My dream, C.G.R."

CHRISTINA ROSSETTI

[About 1880, some twenty-five years after Christina Rossetti dreamed this dream, she added: " This *real* dream left me with an impression it was my duty to paint the above subject as a picture — contingent duty perhaps. Of course I never became competent."]

SLEEP AT SEA

Sound the deep waters: —
  Who shall sound that deep?
Too short the plummet,
  And the watchmen sleep.
Some dream of effort
  Up a toilsome steep:
Some dream of pasture grounds
  For harmless sheep.

White shapes flit to and fro
  From mast to mast;
They feel the distant tempest
  That nears them fast:
Great rocks are straight ahead,
  Great shoals not past;
They shout to one another
  Upon the blast.

Oh, soft the streams drop music
  Between the hills,
And musical the birds' nests
  Beside those rills:
The nests are types of home
  Love-hidden from ills,
The nests are types of spirits
  Love-music fills.

So dream the sleepers,
  Each man in his place;
The lightning shows the smile
  Upon each face:
The ship is driving, — driving, —
  It drives apace:
And sleepers smile, and spirits
  Bewail their case.

The lightning glares and reddens
　Across the skies;
It seems but sunset
　To those sleeping eyes.
When did the sun go down
　On such a wise?
From such a sunset
　When shall day arise?

" Wake," call the spirits:
　But to heedless ears:
They have forgotten sorrows
　And hopes and fears;
They have forgotten perils
　And smiles and tears;
Their dream has held them long,
　Long years and years.

" Wake," call the spirits again:
　But it would take
A louder summons
　To bid them awake.
Some dream of pleasure
　For another's sake;
Some dream, forgetful
　Of a lifelong ache.

One by one slowly,
　Oh, how sad and slow!
Wailing and praying
　The spirits rise and go:
Clear stainless spirits
　White, as white as snow;
Pale spirits, wailing
　For an overthrow.

One by one flitting,
　Like a mournful bird

Whose song is tired at last
  For no mate heard.
The loving voice is silent,
  The useless word;
One by one flitting
  Sick with hope deferred.

Driving and driving,
  The ship drives amain:
While swift from mast to mast
  Shapes flit again,
Flit silent as the silence
  Where men lie slain;
Their shadow cast upon the sails
  Is like a stain.

No voice to call the sleepers
  No hand to raise:
They sleep to death in dreaming
  Of length of days.
Vanity of vanities,
  The Preacher says:
Vanity is the end
  Of all their ways.

CHRISTINA ROSSETTI

I Nebuchadnezzar was at rest in mine house, and flourishing in my palace: I saw a dream which made me afraid, and the thoughts upon my bed and the visions of my head troubled me. Therefore made I a decree to bring in all the wise men of Babylon before me, that they might make known unto me the interpretation of the dream. Then came in the magicians, the astrologers, the Chaldeans, and the soothsayers: and I told the dream before them; but they did not make known unto me the interpretation thereof. But at the last Daniel came in before me, whose name was Belteshazzar, according to the name of my god, and in whom is the spirit of the holy

gods: and before him I told the dream, saying, O Belteshazzar, master of the magicians, because I know that the spirit of
the holy gods is in thee, and no secret troubleth thee, tell me
the visions of my dream that I have seen, and the interpretation thereof. Thus were the visions of mine head in my bed;
I saw, and behold a tree in the midst of the earth, and the
height thereof was great. The tree grew, and was strong, and
the height thereof reached unto heaven, and the sight thereof
to the end of all the earth: The leaves thereof were fair, and
the fruit thereof much, and in it was meat for all: the beasts
of the field had shadow under it, and the fowls of the heaven
dwelt in the boughs thereof, and all flesh was fed of it. I saw
in the visions of my head upon my bed, and, behold, a watcher
and an holy one came down from heaven; He cried aloud, and
said thus, Hew down the tree, and cut off his branches, shake
off his leaves, and scatter his fruit: let the beasts get away
from under it, and the fowls from his branches: nevertheless
leave the stump of his roots in the earth, even with a band of
iron and brass, in the tender grass of the field; and let it be wet
with the dew of heaven, and let his portion be with the beasts
in the grass of the earth: Let his heart be changed from man's,
and let a beast's heart be given unto him; and let seven times
pass over him. . . . This dream I king Nebuchadnezzar have
seen. Now thou, O Belteshazzar, declare the interpretation
thereof, forasmuch as all the wise men of my kingdom are not
able to make known unto me the interpretation: but thou art
able; for the spirit of the holy gods is in thee.

Then Daniel, whose name was Belteshazzar, was astonied
for one hour, and his thoughts troubled him. The king spake,
and said, Belteshazzar, let not the dream, or the interpretation
thereof, trouble thee. Belteshazzar answered and said. . . .
This is the interpretation, O king, and this is the decree of the
most High, which is come upon my lord the king: that they
shall drive thee from men, and thy dwelling shall be with the
beasts of the field, and they shall make thee to eat grass as
oxen, and they shall wet thee with the dew of heaven, and
seven times shall pass over thee, till thou know that the most

High ruleth in the kingdom of men, and giveth it to whomsoever he will. And whereas they commanded to leave the stump of the tree roots; thy kingdom shall be sure unto thee, after that thou shalt have known that the heavens do rule. Wherefore, O king, let my counsel be acceptable unto thee, and break off thy sins by righteousness, and thine iniquities by shewing mercy to the poor; if it may be a lengthening of thy tranquillity.

All this came upon the king Nebuchadnezzar. At the end of twelve months he walked in the palace of the kingdom of Babylon. The king spoke, and said, Is not this great Babylon, that I have built for the house of the kingdom by the might of my power, and for the honour of my majesty? While the word was in the king's mouth, there fell a voice from heaven, saying, O king Nebuchadnezzar, to thee it is spoken; The kingdom is departed from thee. . . . The same hour was the thing fulfilled upon Nebuchadnezzar: and he was driven from men, and did eat grass as oxen, and his body was wet with the dew of heaven, till his hairs were grown like eagles' feathers, and his nails like birds' claws. . . .

THE BOOK OF DANIEL

. . . Furthermore, there was a certain soothsayer that had given Caesar warning long time afore, to take heed of the day of the Ides of March (which is the fifteenth of the moneth), for on that day he should be in great danger. That day being come, Caesar going unto the Senate-house, and speaking merrily unto the soothsayer, told him, The Ides of March be come: So be they, softly answered the soothsayer, but yet are they not past. And the very day before, Caesar supping with Marcus Lepidus, sealed certain letters as he was wont to do at the board: so talk falling out amongst them, reasoning what death was best: he preventing their opinions, cried out aloud, Death unlooked for. Then going to bed the same night as his manner was, and lying with his wife Calpurnia, all the windows and doors of his chamber flying open, the noise awoke him, and made him afraid when he saw such light: but more, when he heard his wife Calpurnia, being fast asleep, weep and sigh, and put forth many fumbling lamentable speeches. For she dreamed that Caesar was slain, and that she had him in her arms. . . .

SIR THOMAS NORTH, from Plutarch's Lives

. . . And Jesus stood before the governor: and the governor asked him, saying, Art thou the King of the Jews? And Jesus said unto him, Thou sayest. And when he was accused of the chief priests and elders, he answered nothing. Then said Pilate unto him, Hearest thou not how many things they witness against thee? And he answered him to never a word; insomuch that the governor marvelled greatly. . . . When he was set down on the judgment seat, his wife sent unto him, saying, Have thou nothing to do with that just man: for I have suffered many things this day in a dream because of him. . . .

The Gospel according to St. Matthew

A MIDNIGHT VISION

A grey peak, naked as some sharp-edged cloud,
Splintering the smooth breast of a placid sky,
Rough to the hand, it charms the tired eye;
Small tufts of sea-pink round its basement crowd,
A tide beneath, that mounts and tumbles by
In monstrous wrinkles, each ten cubits high.
Around a ship-less, sail-less wilderness,
On high, with arms outstretched as in distress,
Cutting the lone grey sky, one broken cross —

. . . . . .

— Say, long since seen, long-vanished sign of grace,
Man's needs, man's sorrows, why from thy dim height,
Thy most austere, remote, abiding place,
Steal'st thou, grey ghost, to visit me to-night?

EMILY LAWLESS

[319]

And Saul, yet breathing out threatenings and slaughter against the disciples of the Lord, went unto the high priest, and desired of him letters to Damascus to the synagogues, that if he found any of this way, whether they were men or women, he might bring them bound unto Jerusalem. And as he journeyed, he came near Damascus: and suddenly there shined round about him a light from heaven: and he fell to the earth, and heard a voice saying unto him, Saul, Saul, why persecutest thou me? And he said, Who art thou, Lord? And the Lord said, I am Jesus whom thou persecutest: it is hard for thee to kick against the pricks. And he trembling and astonished said, Lord, what wilt thou have me to do? And the Lord said unto him, Arise, and go into the city, and it shall be told thee what thou must do. And the men which journeyed with him stood speechless, hearing a voice, but seeing no man. And Saul arose from the earth; and when his eyes were opened, he saw no man: but they led him by the hand, and brought him into Damascus. And he was three days without sight, and neither did eat nor drink.

And there was a certain disciple at Damascus, named Ananias; and to him said the Lord in a vision, Ananias. And he said, Behold, I am here, Lord. And the Lord said unto him, Arise, and go into the street which is called Straight, and inquire in the house of Judas for one called Saul, of Tarsus: for, behold, he prayeth, and hath seen in a vision a man named Ananias coming in, and putting his hand on him, that he might receive his sight. Then Ananias answered, Lord, I have heard by many of this man, how much evil he hath done to thy saints at Jerusalem: and here he hath authority from the chief priests to bind all that call on thy name. But the Lord said unto him, Go thy way: for he is a chosen vessel unto me, to bear my name before the Gentiles, and kings, and the children of Israel: for I will shew him how great things he must suffer for my name's sake.

And Ananias went his way, and entered into the house; and putting his hands on him said, Brother Saul, the Lord, even Jesus, that appeared unto thee in the way as thou camest,

hath sent me, that thou mightest receive thy sight, and be
filled with the Holy Ghost. And immediately there fell from
his eyes as it had been scales: and he received sight forthwith,
and arose, and was baptized. . . .

The Acts of the Apostles

I was a stricken deer, that left the herd
Long since; with many an arrow deep infixed
My panting side was charged, when I withdrew
To seek a tranquil death in distant shades.
There was I found by one who had himself
Been hurt by the archers. In his side he bore,
And in his hands and feet, the cruel scars.
With gentle force soliciting the darts,
He drew them forth, and healed, and bade me live.
Since then, with few associates, in remote
And silent woods I wander, far from those
My former partners of the peopled scene;
With few associates, and not wishing more.
Here much I ruminate, as much I may,
With other views of men and manners now
Than once, and others of a life to come.
I see that all are wanderers, gone astray
Each in his own delusions; they are lost
In chase of fancied happiness, still wooed
And never won. Dream after dream ensues;
And still they dream that they shall still succeed.
And still are disappointed. Rings the world
With the vain stir. I sum up half mankind,
And add two-thirds of the remaining half,
And find the total of their hopes and fears
Dreams, empty dreams. . . .

WILLIAM COWPER, from *The Task, Book III*

Dreams Feigned

Dream not of other worlds . . . Contented . . .

Black night hath hid the pleasures of the day,
And sheeting darkness overhangs the earth,
And with the black fall of her cloudy robe
Obscures us from the eyesight of the world. . . .

Dreams Feigned

DREAM–PEDLARY

If there were dreams to sell,
  What would you buy?
Some cost a passing bell;
  Some a light sigh,
That shakes from Life's fresh crown
Only a roseleaf down.
If there were dreams to sell,
Merry and sad to tell,
And the crier rung the bell,
  What would you buy?

A cottage lone and still,
  With bowers nigh,
Shadow, my woes to still,
  Until I die.
Such pearl from Life's fresh crown
Fain would I shake me down.
Were dreams to have at will,
This would best heal my ill,
  This would I buy.

But there were dreams to sell
  Ill didst thou buy;
Life is a dream, they tell,
  Waking, to die.
Dreaming — a dream to prize —
Is wishing ghosts to rise;

[325]

And, if I had the spell
To call the buried, well,
    Which one would I?

THOMAS LOVELL BEDDOES

THE ANGEL

I dreamt a Dream! What can it mean?
And that I was a maiden Queen
Guarded by an Angel mild:
Witless woe was ne'er beguiled!

And I wept both night and day,
And he wiped my tears away;
And I wept both day and night,
And hid from him my heart's delight.

So he took his wings and fled;
Then the morn blushed rosy red;
I dried my tears, and armed my fears
With ten thousand shields and spears.

Soon my Angel came again;
I was armed, he came in vain;
For the time of youth was fled,
And grey hairs were on my head.

WILLIAM BLAKE

THE PHOENIX [1]

By feathers green, across Casbeen,
    The pilgrims track the Phoenix flown,
By gems he strewed in waste and wood
    And jewelled plumes at random thrown.

[1] Note by the author: — "I dreamed the whole poem in a dream . . . and wrote it down in the middle of the night on a scrap of paper by my bedside. I have never had a similar experience, and . . . can offer no explanation either of the idea of the poem or its interpretation. . . ."

Till wandering far, by moon and star,
    They stand beside the fruitful pyre,
Whence breaking bright with sanguine light,
    The impulsive bird forgets his sire.

Those ashes shine like ruby wine,
    Like bag of Tyrian murex split;
The claw, the jowl of the flying fowl
    Are with the glorious anguish gilt.

So rare the light, so rich the sight,
    Those pilgrim men, on profit bent,
Drop hands and eyes and merchandise,
    And are with gazing most content.

A. C. BENSON

XANDU

This Citie is three day's journey Northeastward to the Citie Xandu, which the great Chan Cublay now raigning, built; erecting therein a marvellous and artificiall Palace of Marble and other stones, which abutteth on the wall on one side, and the midst of the Citie on the other. He included sixteene miles within the circuit of the wall on that side where the Palace abutteth on the Citie wall, into which none can enter but by the Palace. In this inclosure or Parke are goodly meadowes, springs, rivers, red and fallow Deere. . . . In the middest in a faire Wood hee hath built a royall House on pillars gilded and vernished, on every of which is a Dragon all gilt, which windeth his tayle about the pillar, with his head bearing up the loft, as also with his wings displayed on both sides: the cover also is of Reeds gilt and varnished, so that the rayne can doe it no injurie, the reeds being three handfuls thicke and ten yards long, split from knot to knot. He hath a herd of white Horses, and white Mares, about ten thousand, of the milke whereof none may drinke except hee be of the progenie of Cingis Can, except one family, called Boriat, privileged hereto by Cingis for their valour. . . .

SAMUEL PURCHAS

KUBLA KHAN [2]

In Xanadu did Kubla Khan
A stately pleasure-dome decree:
Where Alph, the sacred river, ran
Through caverns measureless to man
    Down to a sunless sea.
So twice five miles of fertile ground
With walls and towers were girdled round:

[2] *The following fragment is here published at the request of a poet of great and deserved celebrity [Lord Byron], and, as far as the Author's own opinions are concerned, rather as a psychological curiosity, than on the ground of any* supposed *poetic* merits.

In the summer of the year 1797 [1798], the Author, then in ill health, had retired to a lonely farm-house between Porlock and Linton, on the Exmoor confines of Somerset and Devonshire. In consequence of a slight indisposition, an anodyne had been prescribed, from the effects of which he fell asleep in his chair at the moment that he was reading the following sentence, or words of the same substance, in "Purchas's Pilgrimage": "Here the Khan Kubla commanded a palace to be built, and a stately garden thereunto. And thus ten miles of fertile ground were inclosed with a wall." The Author continued for about three hours in a profound sleep, at least of the external senses, during which time he has the most vivid confidence, that he could not have composed less than from two to three hundred lines; if that indeed can be called composition in which all the images rose up before him as things, with a parallel production of the correspondent expressions, without any sensation or consciousness of effort. On awaking he appeared to himself to have a distinct recollection of the whole, and taking his pen, ink, and paper, instantly and eagerly wrote down the lines that are here preserved. At this moment he was unfortunately called out by a person on business from Porlock, and detained by him above an hour, and on his return to his room, found, to his no small surprise and mortification, that though he still retained some vague and dim recollection of the general purport of the vision, yet, with the exception of some eight or ten scattered lines and images, all the rest had passed away like the images on the surface of a stream into which a stone has been cast, but, alas! without the after restoration of the latter!

                    Then all the charm
Is broken — all that phantom-world so fair
Vanishes, and a thousand circlets spread,
And each mis-shape['s] the other. Stay awhile,
Poor youth! who scarcely dar'st lift up thine eyes —
The stream will soon renew its smoothness, soon
The visions will return! And lo, he stays
And soon the fragments dim of lovely forms
Come trembling back, unite, and now once more
The pool becomes a mirror.   *S. T. C.*

And there were gardens bright with sinuous rills,
Where blossomed many an incense-bearing tree;
And here were forests ancient as the hills,
Enfolding sunny spots of greenery.

But oh! that deep romantic chasm which slanted
Down the green hill athwart a cedarn cover!
A savage place! as holy and enchanted
As e'er beneath a waning moon was haunted
By woman wailing for her demon-lover!
And from this chasm, with ceaseless turmoil seething,
As if this earth in fast thick pants were breathing,
A mighty fountain momently was forced:
Amid whose swift half-intermitted burst
Huge fragments vaulted like rebounding hail,
Or chaffy grain beneath the thresher's flail:
And 'mid these dancing rocks at once and ever
It flung up momently the sacred river.
Five miles meandering with a mazy motion
Through wood and dale the sacred river ran,
Then reached the caverns measureless to man,
And sank in tumult to a lifeless ocean:
And 'mid this tumult Kubla heard from far
Ancestral voices prophesying war!
   The shadow of the dome of pleasure
   Floated midway on the waves;
   Where was heard the mingled measure
   From the fountain and the caves.
It was a miracle of rare device,
A sunny pleasure-dome with caves of ice!

   A damsel with a dulcimer
   In a vision once I saw:
   It was an Abyssinian maid,
   And on her dulcimer she played,
   Singing of Mount Abora.
   Could I revive within me

Her symphony and song,
To such a deep delight 'twould win me,
That with music loud and long,
I would build that dome in air,
That sunny dome! those caves of ice!
And all who heard should see them there,
And all should cry, Beware! Beware!
His flashing eyes, his floating hair!
Weave a circle round him thrice,
And close your eyes with holy dread,
For he on honey-dew hath fed,
And drunk the milk of Paradise.

SAMUEL TAYLOR COLERIDGE

I dreamt that I stood (I say *stood*, but one is not conscious of a physical posture — one is just present, omnipresent) by the shore of a lake or inland sea. To my right was a cliff, falling sheer into the lake, whose waters were crystal clear, so clear that I could distinctly see the rocky bed, uneven in surface and mottled in colour. As I stood there I suddenly became aware of a figure floating between the cliff and the lake. It was a naked female form, very lovely; and she held above her, like a horizontal sail, a sheet of golden silk. She floated gracefully down to the surface of the water, into which she fell without a sound or a ripple. The golden sail remained floating on the water, and in the middle of it I then observed a neat coil of rope, such as one sees on a ship or a pier. Below the sail, on the rocky floor of the lake the body of the naked girl was now extended, as if lifeless. I had a distinct impulse to dive into the lake, as if to rescue her from drowning. But as I " registered " this impulse, at the same moment my attention was caught by the floating sail of silk and the superimposed coil of rope; and in the instant that I hesitated another figure ran across the shore and dived into the lake. As he touched the surface, I awoke.

Here is a dream of very striking imagery. From a psychoanalytical point of view it has certain obvious features, but its interpretation is a personal matter of no immediate interest. I am concerned with its literary possibilities. Can I, while the dream is still vividly impressed on my mind, convert it into a poem?

I made the attempt, and this is what I wrote:

Her angel flight from cliff to lake
sustains its poise upon the sheet of silk
she holds above her head.

The air is still in dreams
a clear and plasmic element.
No ripples dim the surface as she falls
the cold distress
of days unknown of days to be.

The lake receives her, the lake her lover.
Her ravished flesh redeems the rocky floor.
Still, as if asleep, she lies
a treasure to be salvaged by who dares
shatter the level mirror of the lake.

I do not dare; defeatist I have seen
the cloth she held relinquished on the lake;
a baldaquin on which reposes
a neatly ravelled coil of rope.

Another runs and dives and I am free
to stay a prisoner in the timeless cell of dreams.

Let me first state, to prevent a misunderstanding, that I consider this poem a failure. It is a failure in a personal sense because it does not nearly express the peculiar vividness and significance of the dream. It is a failure in a general sense because, as a consequence of its personal failure, it cannot possible convey the quality of the dream to other people. But most essentially it is simply a failure as poetry. It might conceivably have been a success as poetry and still not have expressed or conveyed the quality of the dream. But actually it fails both in creation and in communication. The experience has not adequately fused the linguistic symbols: it has not selected them finely enough nor collected them significantly enough.

HERBERT READ

ON THE SUNNY SHORE

Chequered with woven shadows as I lay
Among the grass, blinking the watery gleam —
I saw an Echo-Spirit in his bay,
Most idly floating in the noontide beam.
Slow heaved his filmy skiff, and fell, with sway
Of ocean's giant pulsing, and the Dream,
Buoyed like the young moon on a level stream
Of greenish vapour at decline of day,
Swam airily — watching the distant flocks
Of sea-gulls, whilst a foot in careless sweep
Touched the clear-trembling cool with tiny shocks,
Faint-circling; till at last he dropt asleep,
Lulled by the hush-song of the glittering deep
Lap-lapping drowsily the heated rocks.

WILLIAM ALLINGHAM

THE QUESTION

I dreamed that, as I wandered by the way,
  Bare Winter suddenly was changed to Spring,
And gentle odours led my steps astray,
  Mixed with a sound of waters murmuring
Along a shelving bank of turf, which lay
  Under a copse, and hardly dared to fling
Its green arms round the bosom of the stream,
But kissed it and then fled, as thou mightest in dream.

There grew pied wind-flowers and violets,
   Daisies, those pearled Arcturi of the earth,
The constellated flower that never sets;
   Faint oxlips; tender bluebells, at whose birth
The sod scarce heaved; and that tall flower that wets —
   Like a child, half in tenderness and mirth —
Its mother's face with Heaven's collected tears,
When the low wind, its playmate's voice, it hears.

And in the warm hedge grew lush eglantine,
   Green cowbind and the moonlight-coloured may,
And cherry-blossoms, and white cups, whose wine
   Was the bright dew, yet drained not by the day;
And wild roses, and ivy serpentine,
   With its dark buds and leaves, wandering astray;
And flowers azure, black, and streaked with gold,
Fairer than any wakened eyes behold.

And nearer to the river's trembling edge
   There grew broad flag-flowers, purple prankt with white,
And starry river buds among the sedge,
   And floating water-lilies, broad and bright,
Which lit the oak that overhung the hedge
   With moonlight beams of their own watery light;
And bulrushes, and reeds of such deep green
As soothed the dazzled eye with sober sheen.

Methought that of these visionary flowers
   I made a nosegay, bound in such a way,
That the same hues, which in their natural bowers
   Were mingled or opposed, the like array
Kept these imprisoned children of the Hours
   Within my hand, — and then, elate and gay,
I hastened to the spot whence I had come,
That I might there present it! — oh! to whom?

P. B. SHELLEY

[333]

ODE TO PSYCHE

O Goddess! hear these tuneless numbers, wrung
   By sweet enforcement and remembrance dear,
And pardon that thy secrets should be sung
   Even into thine own soft-conchèd ear:
Surely I dreamt to-day, or did I see
   The wingèd Psyche with awakened eyes?
I wandered in a forest thoughtlessly,
   And, on the sudden, fainting with surprise,
Saw two fair creatures, couchèd side by side
   In deepest grass, beneath the whisp'ring roof
   Of leaves and trembled blossoms, where there ran
     A brooklet, scarce espied:

'Mid hushed, cool-rooted flowers, fragrant-eyed,
   Blue, silver-white, and budded Tyrian,
They lay calm-breathing on the bedded grass;
   Their arms embracèd, and their pinions too;
   Their lips touched not, but had not bade adieu,
And if disjoinèd by soft-handed slumber,
And ready still past kisses to outnumber
   At tender eye-dawn of aurorean love:
     The winged boy I knew;
   But who wast thou, O happy, happy dove?
     His Psyche true!

O latest born and loveliest vision far
   Of all Olympus' faded hierarchy!
Fairer than Phoebe's sapphire-regioned star,
   Or Vesper, amorous glow-worm of the sky;
Fairer than these, though temple thou hast none,
     Nor altar heaped with flowers;
Nor virgin-choir to make delicious moan
     Upon the midnight hours;
No voice, no lute, no pipe, no incense sweet
   From chain-swung censer teeming;

No shrine, no grove, no oracle, no heat
  Of pale-mouthed prophet dreaming.

O brightest! though too late for antique vows,
  Too, too late for the fond believing lyre,
When holy were the haunted forest boughs,
  Holy the air, the water, and the fire;
Yet even in these days so far retired
  From happy pieties, thy lucent fans,
  Fluttering among the faint Olympians,
I see, and sing, by my own eyes inspired.
So let me be thy choir, and make a moan
        Upon the midnight hours;
Thy voice, thy lute, thy pipe, thy incense sweet
  From swinged censer teeming;
Thy shrine, thy grove, thy oracle, thy heat
  Of pale-mouthed prophet dreaming.

Yes, I will be thy priest, and build a fane
  In some untrodden region of my mind,
Where branchèd thoughts, new grown with pleasant pain,
  Instead of pines shall murmur in the wind:
Far, far around shall those dark-clustered trees
  Fledge the wild-ridgèd mountains steep by steep;
And there by zephyrs, streams, and birds, and bees,
  The moss-lain Dryads shall be lulled to sleep;
And in the midst of this wide quietness
A rosy sanctuary will I dress
With the wreathed trellis of a working brain,
  With buds, and bells, and stars without a name,
With all the gardener Fancy e'er could feign,
  Who breeding flowers, will never breed the same:
And there shall be for thee all soft delight
  That shadowy thought can win,
A bright torch, and a casement ope at night,
  To let the warm Love in!

JOHN KEATS

[335]

TO SHEILA PLAYING HAYDN

Oh, when thy fingers touch the notes, I think
The deer go stepping to the brook to drink;
Beneath the level beech-leaves low I peer,
And see again, branch-horned, the crested deer,
The thin-legged doe, the fawn in that green light
On tiptoe following them out of sight.

Most deft adored, thy nimble fingers make
A thousand pictures in my mind awake;
For no young thing of beast or bird or tree
I've seen, but I have seemed to look on thee,
And at thy sound I go remembering
About the woods of every vanished spring.

SYLVIA LYND

DREAM

Meseemed it was a chamber tall
Wherein I stood, and, on the wall,
The glass of pictures in the gloom
Echoed the window round the room.
Far upward wound the cold, white stair;
Far down my spirit wandered there,
As light or shadow on the door,
My errant fancy outward bore,
And, faintly caught, as if they strayed,
Came children's voices in, afraid.

One lay upon the mantled bed,
So still and cold I thought him dead;
But ever thus, in wakeful sleep,
I must my lonely vigil keep,
Until they come — but who or whence
I know not — and shall bear him hence.

JAMES GUTHRIE

SPRING AND DEATH

I had a dream. A wondrous thing:
It seemed an evening in the Spring:
— A little sickness in the air
From too much fragrance everywhere: —
As I walked a stilly wood,
Sudden, Death before me stood:
In a hollow lush and damp,
He seemed a dismal mirky stamp
On the flowers that were seen
His charnelhouse-grate ribs between,
And with coffin-black he barred the green.
" Death," said I " what do you here
At this Spring season of the year? "
" I mark the flowers ere the prime
Which I may tell at Autumn-time."
Ere I had further question made
Death was vanished from the glade.
Then I saw that he had bound
Many trees and flowers round
With a subtle web of black,
And that such a sable track,
Lay along the grasses green
From the spot where he had been.
    But the Spring-tide passed the same;
Summer was as full of flame;
Autumn-time no earlier came.
And the flowers that he had tied,
As I marked not always died
Sooner than their mates; and yet
Their fall was fuller of regret:
    It seemed so hard and dismal thing,
Death, to mark them in the Spring.

GERARD HOPKINS

ULALUME

The skies they were ashen and sober;
  The leaves they were crispèd and sere —
  The leaves they were withering and sere;
It was night in the lonesome October
  Of my most immemorial year;
It was hard by the dim lake of Auber,
  In the misty mid region of Weir —
It was down by the dank tarn of Auber,
  In the ghoul-haunted woodland of Weir.

Here once, through an alley Titanic,
  Of cypress, I roamed with my soul —
  Of cypress, with Psyche, my Soul.
These were days when my heart was volcanic
  As the scoriac rivers that roll —
  As the lavas that restlessly roll
Their sulphurous currents down Yaanek
  In the ultimate climes of the Pole —
That groan as they roll down Mount Yaanek
  In the realms of the boreal pole.

Our talk had been serious and sober,
  But our thoughts they were palsied and sere —
  Our memories were treacherous and sere —
For we knew not the month was October,
  And we marked not the night of the year —
  (Ah, night of all nights in the year!)
We noted not the dim lake of Auber —
  (Though once we had journeyed down here),
Remembered not the dank tarn of Auber,
  Nor the ghoul-haunted woodland of Weir.

And now, as the night was senescent,
  And star-dials pointed to morn —
  As the star-dials hinted of morn —

At the end of our path a liquescent
   And nebulous lustre was born,
Out of which a miraculous crescent
   Arose with a duplicate horn —
Astarte's bediamonded crescent
   Distinct with its duplicate horn.

And I said — " She is warmer than Dian:
   She rolls through an ether of sighs —
   She revels in a region of sighs:
She has seen that the tears are not dry on
   These cheeks, where the worm never dies,
And has come past the stars of the Lion,
   To point us the path to the skies —
   To the Lethean peace of the skies —
Come up, in despite of the Lion,
   To shine on us with her bright eyes —
Come up through the lair of the Lion,
   With love in her luminous eyes."

But Psyche, uplifting her finger,
   Said — " Sadly this star I mistrust —
   Her pallor I strangely mistrust: —
Oh, hasten! — oh, let us not linger!
   Oh, fly! — let us fly! — for we must."
In terror she spoke, letting sink her
   Wings until they trailed in the dust —
In agony sobbed, letting sink her
   Plumes till they trailed in the dust —
   Till they sorrowfully trailed in the dust.

I replied: — " This is nothing but dreaming:
   Let us on by this tremulous light!
   Let us bathe in this crystalline light!
Its Sybilic splendour is beaming
   With Hope and in Beauty to-night: —
   See! — it flickers up the sky through the night!

Ah, we safely may trust to its gleaming,
    And be sure it will lead us aright —
We safely may trust to a gleaming
    That cannot but guide us aright,
    Since it flickers up to Heaven through the night."

Thus I pacified Psyche and kissed her,
    And tempted her out of her gloom —
    And conquered her scruples and gloom;
And we passed to the end of the vista,
    But were stopped by the door of a tomb —
    By the door of a legended tomb;
And I said — " What is written, sweet sister,
    On the door of this legended tomb? "
    She replied — " Ulalume — Ulalume —
    'Tis the vault of thy lost Ulalume! "

Then my heart it grew ashen and sober
    As the leaves that were crispèd and sere —
    As the leaves that were withering and sere —
And I cried — " It was surely October
    On *this* very night of last year
    That I journeyed — I journeyed down here —
    That I brought a dread burden down here —
    On this night of all nights in the year,
    Ah, what demon has tempted me here?
Well I know, now, this dim lake of Auber —
    This misty mid region of Weir —
Well I know, now, this dank tarn of Auber,
    This ghoul-haunted woodland of Weir."

                                EDGAR ALLAN POE

THOMAS. But does your king then need a carpenter?
CAPTAIN. Yes, for he dreamed a dream; and like a man
    Who, having eaten poison, and with all
    Force of his life turned out the crazing drug,

Has only a weak and wrestled nature left
That gives in foolishly to some bad desire
A healthy man would laugh at; so our king
Is left desiring by his venomous dream.
But, being a king, the whole land aches with him.

THOMAS.   What dream was that?

CAPTAIN.   A palace made of souls; —
Ay, there's a folly for a man to dream!
He saw a palace covering all the land,
Big as the day itself, made of a stone
That answered with a better gleam than glass
To the sun's greeting, fashioned like the sound
Of laughter copied into shining shape:
So the king said. And with him in the dream
There was a voice that fleered upon the king:
" This is the man who makes much of himself
For filling the common eyes with palaces
Gorgeously bragging out his royalty:
Whereas he hath not one that seemeth not
In work, in height, in posture on the ground,
A hut, a peasant's dingy shed, to mine.
And all his excellent woods, metals, and stones,
The things he's filcht out of the earth's old pockets
And hoised up into walls and domes; the gold,
Ebony, agate stairs, wainscots of jade,
The windows of jargoon, and heavenly lofts
Of marble, all the stuff he takes to be wealth,
Reckons like savage mud and wattle against
The matter of my building." — And the king,
Gloating upon the white sheen of that palace,
And weeping like a girl ashamed, required
" What is that stone? " And the voice answered him,
" Soul." . . .

LASCELLES ABERCROMBIE
from " The Sale of St. Thomas "

[341]

I followed once a fleet and mighty serpent
Into a cavern in a mountain's side;
And, wading many lakes, descending gulphs,
At last I reached the ruins of a city,
Built not like ours but of another world,
As if the aged earth had loved in youth
The mightiest city of a perished planet,
And kept the image of it in her heart,
So dream-like, shadowy, and spectral was it.
Nought seemed alive there, and the very dead
Were of another world the skeletons.
The mammoth, ribbed like to an arched cathedral,
Lay there, and ruins of great creatures else
More like a shipwrecked fleet, too great they seemed
For all the life that is to animate:
And vegetable rocks, tall sculptured palms,
Pines grown, not hewn, in stone; and giant ferns
Whose earthquake-shaken leaves bore graves for nests. . . .

THOMAS LOVELL BEDDOES,
from *Death's Jest-Book, Act III, Scene I*

[Awake again], I listened doubtingly an instant; detected
the disturber [of my sleep — the branch of a fir tree rasping
against the lattice window], then turned and dozed, and
dreamt again . . . .

This time, I remembered I was lying in the oak closet, and
I heard distinctly the gusty wind, and the driving of the snow;
I heard, also, the fir-bough repeat its teasing sound, and ascribed it to the right cause: but it annoyed me so much, that
I resolved to silence it, if possible; and, I thought, I rose and
endeavoured to unhasp the casement. The hook was soldered
into the staple: a circumstance observed by me when awake,
but forgotten. "I must stop it, nevertheless!" I muttered,
knocking my knuckles through the glass, and stretching an
arm out to seize the importunate branch; instead of which, my

fingers closed on the fingers of a little, ice-cold hand! The intense horror of nightmare came over me: I tried to draw back my arm, but the hand clung to it, and a most melancholy voice sobbed, " Let me in — let me in! " " Who are you? " I asked, struggling, meanwhile, to disengage myself. " Catherine Linton," it replied, shiveringly (why did I think of *Linton?* I had read *Earnshaw* twenty times for Linton). " I'm come home: I'd lost my way on the moor! " As it spoke, I discerned, obscurely, a child's face looking through the window. Terror made me cruel; and, finding it useless to attempt shaking the creature off, I pulled its wrist on to the broken pane, and rubbed it to and fro till the blood ran down and soaked the bedclothes: still it wailed, " Let me in! " and maintained its tenacious gripe, almost maddening me with fear. " How can I! " I said at length. " Let *me* go, if you want me to let you in! " The fingers relaxed, I snatched mine through the hole, hurriedly piled the books up in a pyramid against it, and stopped my ears to exclude the lamentable prayer. I seemed to keep them closed above a quarter of an hour; yet, the instant I listened again, there was the doleful cry moaning on! " Begone! " I shouted, " I'll never let you in, not if you beg for twenty years." " It is twenty years," mourned the voice: " twenty years. I've been a waif for twenty years! "
. . .

EMILY BRONTË, from *Wuthering Heights*

THE CONDEMNED PRISONER

. . . Since his dread sentence, nothing seemed to be
As once it was — he seeing could not see,
Nor hearing, hear aright; — when first I came
Within his view, I fancied there was shame,
I judged resentment; I mistook the air, —
These fainter passions live not with despair;
Or but exist and die: — Hope, fear, and love,
Joy, doubt, and hate, may other spirits move,

But touch not his, who every waking hour
Has one fixed dread, and always feels its power. . . .

Still I behold him, every thought employed
On one dire view! — all others are destroyed. . . .
He takes his tasteless food, and when 'tis done,
Counts up his meals, now lessened by that one;
For expectation is on time intent,
Whether he brings us joy or punishment.

Yes! e'en in sleep the impressions all remain,
He hears the sentence and he feels the chain;
He sees the judge and jury, when he shakes,
And loudly cries, " Not guilty," and awakes:
Then chilling tremblings o'er his body creep,
Till worn-out nature is compelled to sleep.

Now comes the dream again: it shows each scene,
With each small circumstance that comes between —
The call to suffering and the very deed —
There crowds go with him, follow, and precede;
Some heartless shout, some pity, all condemn,
While he in fancied envy looks at them:
He seems the place for that sad act to see,
And dreams the very thirst which then will be:
A priest attends — it seems, the one he knew
In his best days, beneath whose care he grew.

At this his terrors take a sudden flight;
He sees his native village with delight;
The house, the chamber, where he once arrayed
His youthful person; where he knelt and prayed:
Then too the comforts he enjoyed at home,
The days of joy; the joys themselves are come; —
The hours of innocence; — the timid look
Of his loved maid, when first her hand he took,
And told his hope; her trembling joy appears,
Her forced reserve and his retreating fears.

All now is present; — 'tis a moment's gleam
Of former sunshine — stay, delightful dream!
Let him within his pleasant garden walk,
Give him her arm, of blessings let them talk.

Yes! all are with him now, and all the while
Life's early prospects and his Fanny's smile:
Then come his sister and his village-friend,
And he will now the sweetest moments spend
Life has to yield; — No! never will he find
Again on earth such pleasure in his mind:
He goes through shrubbery walks these friends among,
Love in their looks and honour on the tongue:
Nay, there's a charm beyond what nature shows,
The bloom is softer and more sweetly glows; —
Pierced by no crime, and urged by no desire
For more than true and honest hearts require,
They feel the calm delight, and thus proceed
Through the green lane, — Then linger in the mead, —
Stray o'er the heath in all its purple bloom, —
And pluck the blossom where the wild bees hum;
Then through the broomy bound with ease they pass,
And press the sandy sheep-walk's slender grass,
Where dwarfish flowers among the gorse are spread,
And the lamb browses by the linnet's bed;
Then 'cross the bounding brook they make their way
O'er its rough bridge — and there behold the bay! —
The ocean smiling to the fervid sun —
The waves that faintly fall and slowly run —
The ships at distance and the boats at hand;
And now they walk upon the sea-side sand,
Counting the number and what kind they be,
Ships softly sinking in the sleepy sea:
Now arm in arm, now parted, they behold
The glitt'ring waters on the shingles rolled:
The timid girls, half dreaming their design,
Dip the small foot in the retarded brine,

[345]

And search for crimson weeds, which spreading flow,
Or lie like pictures on the sand below:
With all those bright red pebbles, that the sun
Through the small waves so softly shines upon;
And those live lucid jellies which the eye
Delights to trace as they swim glittering by:
Pearl-shells and rubied star-fish they admire,
And will arrange above the parlour-fire, —
Tokens of bliss! —
" Oh! horrible! a wave
Roars as it rises — save me, Edward! save! "
She cries: — Alas! the watchman on his way
Calls, and lets in — truth, terror, and the day!

GEORGE CRABBE,
from " *The Condemned Prisoner* "

CONDEMNED

. . . The chief difficulty in the study of these criminals lay in the fact that their conscious life was wholly resolved into a chaos of confused brooding on matters great and small, on events which had been of critical importance and on daily occurrences of no significance whatever, on what had happened the day before and raised real difficulties, and on the most innocent recollections of childhood or early youth, but always with anguished fear. In this ever shifting chaos it was extremely difficult to discover any fixed or reliable characteristics whatever. In a way the conscious psychic life of these prisoners was as good as meaningless, and also, owing to its diffuseness and lack of cohesion, its shifting and vagueness, it was never possible directly to observe the deeper psychological realities underlying it. It was therefore a considerable time before I clearly recognised that the determining force in their lives from beginning to end was nothing but their sense of insecurity, their cowardice, their terror of life, or, in a word, their complete lack of self-confidence. . . .

. . . At the very beginning of my studies among prisoners under life sentence, I had been struck by the curious way in which they lived in the past, or rather continued mentally the life which superficially had been closed by their crime. All the previous desires, hopes, plans, endeavours, cares, successes, joys, unrestrained vices, lusts, orgies, crimes and despair remained with them not only in memory but as actual, living, psychic realities, whilst life in prison and its daily routine passed over them like a misty dream, whose bearing or significance they were never able to grasp. Not infrequently this was possible by means of gigantic self-deception, whereby they really succeeded in entirely driving out of their consciousness, or at least in reducing in their own minds to the proportions of an insignificant and indifferent inconvenience, the long period of imprisonment before them. The consequence was that whilst in prison they could peacefully occupy their minds with visions of life after their release, much in the same way as a free man who is unfortunately delayed during a journey in a place where there is nothing to awaken his interest, may continue to dwell on his plans of the future. . . .

A. BJERRE, translated by E. Classen

VITTORIA COROMBONA. To pass away the time, I'll tell your
    grace
  A dream I had last night.
BRACHIANO. Most wishedly.
VIT. COR. A foolish idle dream.
    Methought I walked about the mid of night
    Into a church-yard, where a goodly yew-tree
    Spread her large root in ground. Under that yew,
    As I sate sadly leaning on a grave
    Chequered with cross sticks, there came stealing in
    Your duchess and my husband: one of them
    A pick-axe bore, the other a rusty spade,
    And in rough terms they gan to challenge me
    About this yew.

BRACH. That tree?

VIT. COR. This harmless yew:
> They told me my intent was to root up
> That well-grown yew, and plant i' the stead of it
> A withered blackthorn; and for that they vowed
> To bury me alive. My husband straight
> With pick-axe gan to dig, and your fell duchess
> With shovel, like a Fury, voided out
> The earth, and scattered bones. Lord, how, methought,
> I trembled! and yet, for all this terror,
> I could not pray.

FLAMINEO. No; the devil was in your dream.

VIT. COR. When to my rescue there arose, methought,
> A whirlwind, which let fall a massy arm
> From that strong plant;
> And both were struck dead by that sacred yew,
> In that base shallow grave that was their due.

FLAM. Excellent devil! she hath taught him in a dream
> To make away his duchess and her husband. . . .

> JOHN WEBSTER,
> from *The White Devil, Act I, Scene II*

HESPERUS [*starting from his couch*].
> Who speaks? Who whispers there? A light! A light!
> I'll search the room, something hath called me thrice,
> With a low muttering voice of toadish hisses,
> And thrice I slept again. But still it came
> Nearer and nearer, plucked my mantle from me,
> And made mine heart an ear, in which it poured
> Its loathed enticing courtship. Ho! a light.
>> [*Enter* ATTENDANT *with a torch.*
> Thou drowsy snail, thy footsteps are asleep,
> Hold up the torch.

ATTEND.　　　　　　　My lord, you are disturbed.
　Have you seen aught?
HESP.　　　　　　　　I lay upon my bed,
　And something in the air, out-jetting night,
　Converting feeling to intenser vision,
　Featured its ghastly self upon my soul
　Deeper than sight.
ATTEND.　　　　　　This is Delusion surely;
　She's busy with men's thoughts at all night hours,
　And to the waking subtle apprehension
　The darkling chamber's still and sleepy air
　Hath breath and motion oft.
HESP.　Lift up the hangings, mark the doors, the corners;
　Seest nothing yet? No face of fiendlike mirth
　More frightful than the fixed and doggish grin
　Of a dead madman?
ATTEND.　　　　　　Nought I see, my lord,
　Save the long, varied crowd of warlike shapes
　Set in the stitched picture.
HESP.　　　　　　　　Heard ye then?
　There was a sound, as though some marble tongue
　Moved on its rusty hinge, syllabling harshly
　The hoarse death-rattle into speech.
ATTEND.　The wind is high, and through the silent rooms
　Murmurs his burthen, to an heedless ear
　Almost articulate.
HESP.　　　　　　　Thou sleepest, fool,
　A voice has been at my bedside to-night,
　Its breath is burning on my forehead still,
　Still o'er my brain its accents, wildly sweet,
　Hover and fall. Away and dream again.
　I'll watch myself. . . .

　　　　　　　　T. L. BEDDOES
　　　from *The Bride's Tragedy, Act II, Scene V*

THE DREAM OF HENRY VIII

THE KING [*To the* LORDS.] . . . I will put you down,
    masters: come hither, Archbishop; this is the man
    I owe much, by my faith in Almighty God.
    I will nod you to your death before him; I vow
    there shall none of you touch the man the King loves.
                        [*The* LORDS *retire.*
    They are gone; I have saved you awhile; but yet
    this life, lord Archbishop, is a catcher of men,
    aye . . . aye . . . it shall catch you.
             [*The* SKELETON *comes up and sits at*
                  the KING's *feet.*
CRANMER. Sir, I desire no more.
THE KING. Y'are an honest man. Listen: I had a dream.
    I saw a creature run about the world,
    everywhere at all times, that would be caught
    but would not stay for catching, or mayhap
    the thing was still, it was everything else ran by,
    and I ran also, too slowly or too fast;
    sometimes I could see, sometimes I could not see,
    but when I saw I wept for the joy of it —
    a crimson flashing creature, full of power.
    All my life I sought for it, and then I died,
    and it was gone and everything was gone,
    except a voice calling, *Where is the prey,*
    King of England? but I was not the King: it called
    Henry, where is the prey? but I was not Henry.
    In the nothingness, for the creature was not, I stood
    and answered: *I* — and before I added more
    the nothingness broke over me in a peal
    of laughter, all the angels crying *You!* —
    Here is a fellow calls himself I, — and their mirth
    filled me, but I was weeping; there were streams
    of mockery running to misery; and I woke,

the tears upon my cheeks, and the chamberlains trembled
beside me, hearing me roaring in my sleep.
What did I say that was wrong — am I not I?
am I not I myself? what did this mean?
CRANMER. Sir, I do not know.
THE SKELETON.   You will know.
                    [*To the audience*] So will you.

> CHARLES WILLIAMS
> from *Thomas Cranmer of Canterbury*

SERJEANT, WHAT HOUR . . . ?

[*A camp. Enter* CHARLEMONT *in arms, a* MUSKETEER,
and a SERJEANT.]

CHARLEMONT. Serjeant, what hour o' the night is't?
SERJEANT. About one.
CHARL. I would you would relieve me, for I am
    So heavy that I shall ha' much ado
    To stand out my perdu.   [*Thunder and lightning.*
SERJ. I'll e'en but walk
    The round, sir, and then presently return.
SOLDIER. For God's sake, serjeant, relieve me. Above five
    hours together in so foul a stormy night as this!
SERJ. Why, 'tis a music, soldier. Heaven and earth are now in
    consort, when the thunder and the cannon play one to
    another.   [*Exit* SERJEANT.
CHARL. I know not why I should be thus inclined
    To sleep. I feel my disposition pressed
    With a necessity of heaviness.
    Soldier, if thou hast any better eyes,
    I prithee wake me when the serjeant comes.
SOL. Sir, 'tis so dark and stormy that I shall
    Scarce either see or hear him, ere he comes
    Upon me.

CHARL. I cannot force myself to wake. — [*Sleeps.*]
          Enter the GHOST OF MONTFERRERS. . . . [*Exit.*
                        [CHARLEMONT *starts and wakes.*
CHARL. O my affrighted soul, what fearful dream
    Was this that waked me? Dreams are but the raised
    Impressions of premeditated things
    By serious apprehension left upon
    Our minds; or else the imaginary shapes
    Of objects proper to the complexion, or
    The dispositions of our bodies. These
    Can neither of them be the cause why I
    Should dream thus; for my mind has not been moved
    With any one conception of a thought
    To such a purpose; nor my nature wont
    To trouble me with fantasies of terror.
    It must be something that my Genius would
    Inform me of. Now gracious Heaven forbid!
    Oh! let my spirit be deprived of all
    Foresight and knowledge, ere it understand
    That vision acted, or divine that act
    To come. Why should I think so? Left I not
    My worthy father i' the kind regard
    Of a most loving uncle? Soldier, saw'st
    No apparition of a man?
SOL.   You dream,
    Sir. I saw nothing.
CHARL.   Tush! these idle dreams
    Are fabulous. Our boyling fantasies
    Like troubled waters falsify the shapes
    Of things retained in them, and make 'em seem
    Confounded when they are distinguishèd.

                          CYRIL TOURNEUR
              from *The Atheist's Tragedy, Act II, Scene VI.*

DARKNESS

I had a dream, which was not all a dream,
The bright sun was extinguished, and the stars
Did wander darkling in the eternal space,
Rayless, and pathless; and the icy earth
Swung blind and blackening in the moonless air;
Morn came and went — and came, and brought no day,
And men forgot their passions in the dread
Of this their desolation; and all hearts
Were chilled into a selfish prayer for light:
And they did live by watchfires — and the thrones,
The palaces of crowned kings — the huts,
The habitations of all things which dwell,
Were burnt for beacons; cities were consumed,
And men were gathered round their blazing homes
To look once more into each other's face;
Happy were those who dwelt within the eye
Of the volcanoes, and their mountain-torch:
A fearful hope was all the world contained;
Forests were set on fire — but hour by hour
They fell and faded — and the crackling trunks
Extinguished with a crash — and all was black. . . .
　　　　　　　　　No love was left;
All earth was but one thought — and that was death
Immediate and inglorious; and the pang
Of famine fed upon all entrails — men
Died, and their bones were tombless as their flesh. . . .
　　　　　　　　　The world was void,
The populous and the powerful was a lump,
Seasonless, herbless, treeless, manless, lifeless,
A lump of death — a chaos of hard clay.
The rivers, lakes, and ocean all stood still,
And nothing stirred within their silent depths;
Ships sailorless lay rotting on the sea,

And their masts fell down piecemeal; as they dropped,
They slept on the abyss without a surge —
The waves were dead; the tides were in their grave,
The Moon, their mistress, had expired before;
The winds were withered in the stagnant air,
And the clouds perished; Darkness had no need
Of aid from them — She was the Universe!

Byron, from " Darkness "

MACBETH

Macbeth.   If we should fail?
Lady Macbeth.   We fail!
 But screw your courage to the sticking-place,
 And we'll not fail. When Duncan is asleep, —
 Whereto the rather shall his day's hard journey
 Soundly invite him, — his two chamberlains
 Will I with wine and wassail so convince,
 That memory, the warder of the brain,
 Shall be a fume, and the receipt of reason
 A limbec only: when in swinish sleep
 Their drenchèd natures lie as in a death,
 What cannot you and I perform upon
 The unguarded Duncan? what not put upon
 His spongy officers, who shall bear the guilt
 Of our great quell? . . .

❀ ❀ ❀

Macb. Go bid thy mistress, when my drink is ready,
 She strike upon the bell. Get thee to bed.
 Is this a dagger which I see before me, [*He stands at gaze.*
 The handle toward my hand? — Come, let me clutch
  thee.
 I have thee not, and yet I see thee still.
 Art thou not, fatal vision, sensible
 To feeling as to sight? or art thou but
 A dagger of the mind, a false creation,

[354]

Proceeding from the heat-oppressèd brain?
I see thee yet, in form as palpable
As this which now I draw.
Thou marshall'st me the way that I was going; —
And such an instrument I was to use.
Mine eyes are made the fools o' the other senses,
Or else worth all the rest: — I see thee still;
And on thy blade and dudgeon gouts of blood,
Which was not so before. There's no such thing:
It is the bloody business which informs
Thus to mine eyes. — Now o'er the one half-world
Nature seems dead, and wicked dreams abuse
The curtain'd sleep; witchcraft celebrates
Pale Hecate's offerings; and wither'd murder,
Alarum'd by his sentinel, the wolf,
Whose howl's his watch, thus with his stealthy pace,
With Tarquin's ravishing strides, towards his design
Moves like a ghost. . . .

❊   ❊   ❊

MACB. I have done the deed. Didst thou not hear a noise?
LADY M. I heard the owl scream, and the crickets cry. Did
    not you speak?
MACB.   When?
LADY M.   Now.
MACB. As I descended?
LADY M. Ay.
MACB. Hark!
    Who lies i' the second chamber?
LADY M.   Donalbain.
MACB. [*Looking on his hands.*] This is a sorry sight.
LADY M. A foolish thought, to say a sorry sight.
MACB. There's one did laugh in's sleep, and one cried, " Mur-
    der! "
    That they did wake each other: I stood and heard them:
    But they did say their prayers, and address'd them
    Again to sleep.

LADY M. There are two lodg'd together.

MACB. One cried, " God bless us! " and, " Amen," the other:
As they had seen me with these hangman's hands.
Listening their fear, I could not say " Amen,"
When they did say " God bless us! "

LADY M. Consider it not so deeply.

MACB. But wherefore could not I pronounce " Amen "?
I had most need of blessing, and " Amen "
Stuck in my throat.

LADY M. These deeds must not be thought
After these ways; so, it will make us mad.

MACB. Methought I heard a voice cry, " Sleep no more!
Macbeth does murder sleep," — the innocent sleep,
Sleep that knits up the ravell'd sleave of care,
The death of each day's life, sore labour's bath,
Balm of hurt minds, great nature's second course,
Chief nourisher in life's feast, —

LADY M.   What do you mean?

MACB. Still it cried, " Sleep no more! " to all the house:
" Glamis hath murder'd sleep, and therefore Cawdor
Shall sleep no more, Macbeth shall sleep no more! " . . .

✻   ✻   ✻

WAITING-GENTLEWOMAN. Lo you, here she comes! This is
her very guise; and, upon my life, fast asleep. Observe
her; stand close.

DOCTOR. How came she by that light?

GEN. Why, it stood by her: she has light by her continually; 'tis her command.

DOCT. You see, her eyes are open.

GEN. Ay, but their sense is shut.

DOCT. What is it she does now? Look, how she rubs her
hands.

GEN. It is an accustomed action with her, to seem thus washing her hands. I have known her to continue in this a
quarter of an hour.

LADY MACBETH. Yet here's a spot . . . Out, damned spot! out, I say! One, two: why, then, 'tis time to do't. Hell is murky! Fie, my lord, fie! a soldier, and afeard? What need we fear who knows it, when none can call our power to account? Yet who would have thought the old man to have had so much blood in him? . . . The thane of Fife had a wife: where is she now? What! will these hands ne'er be clean? No more o' that, my lord, no more o' that: you mar all with this starting. . . . Here's the smell of the blood still: all the perfumes of Arabia will not sweeten this little hand. Oh! oh! oh! . . . Wash your hands, put on your nightgown; look not so pale. I tell you yet again, Banquo's buried; he cannot come out on's grave. . . . To bed, to bed: there's knocking at the gate. Come, come, come, come, give me your hand. What's done cannot be undone. To bed, to bed, to bed. . . .

WILLIAM SHAKESPEARE
from *Macbeth, Act I, Scene II; Act II, Scene I–II;*
Act V, Scene I

. . . O sleep! it is a gentle thing,
Beloved from pole to pole!
To Mary Queen the praise be given!
She sent the gentle sleep from Heaven,
That slid into my soul.

The silly buckets on the deck,
That had so long remained,
I dreamt that they were filled with dew;
And when I awoke, it rained.

My lips were wet, my throat was cold,
My garments all were dank;
Sure I had drunken in my dreams,
And still my body drank.

I moved, and could not feel my limbs:
I was so light — almost
I thought that I had died in sleep,
And was a blessèd ghost.

And soon I heard a roaring wind:
It did not come anear;
But with its sound it shook the sails,
That were so thin and sere.

The upper air burst into life!
And a hundred fire-flags sheen,
To and fro they were hurried about!
And to and fro, and in and out,
The wan stars danced between.

And the coming wind did roar more loud,
And the sails did sigh like sedge;
And the rain poured down from one black cloud;
The Moon was at its edge.

The thick black cloud was cleft, and still
The Moon was at its side:
Like waters shot from some high crag,
The lightning fell with never a jag,
A river steep and wide.

The loud wind never reached the ship,
Yet now the ship moved on!
Beneath the lightning and the Moon
The dead men gave a groan.

They groaned, they stirred, they all uprose,
Nor spake, nor moved their eyes;
It had been strange, even in a dream,
To have seen those dead men rise.

The helmsman steered, the ship moved on;
Yet never a breeze up-blew;

The mariners all 'gan work the ropes,
Where they were wont to do;
They raised their limbs like lifeless tools —
We were a ghastly crew.

The body of my brother's son
Stood by me, knee to knee:
The body and I pulled at one rope,
But he said nought to me.

" I fear thee, ancient Mariner! "
Be calm, thou Wedding-Guest!
'Twas not those souls that fled in pain,
Which to their corses came again,
But a troop of spirits blest:

For when it dawned — they dropped their arms,
And clustered round the mast;
Sweet sounds rose slowly through their mouths,
And from their bodies passed.

Around, around, flew each sweet sound,
Then darted to the Sun;
Slowly the sounds came back again,
Now mixed, now one by one.

Sometimes a-dropping from the sky
I heard the sky-lark sing;
Sometimes all little birds that are,
How they seemed to fill the sea and air
With their sweet jargoning!

And now 'twas like all instruments,
Now like a lonely flute;
And now it is an angel's song,
That makes the heavens be mute.

It ceased; yet still the sails made on
A pleasant noise till noon,

A noise like of a hidden brook
In the leafy month of June,
That to the sleeping woods all night
Singeth a quiet tune. . . .

SAMUEL TAYLOR COLERIDGE
from " The Rime of the Ancient Mariner "

As I walked through the wilderness of this world, I lighted
on a certain place, where was a Den; and I laid me down in
that place to sleep: and as I slept I dreamed a dream. I
dreamed, and behold I saw a man clothed with rags, standing
in a certain place, with his face from his own house, a book in
his hand, and a great burden upon his back. I looked, and
saw him open the book, and read therein; and as he read, he
wept and trembled: and not being able longer to contain, he
broke out with a lamentable cry; saying; " What shall I do? "
In this plight, therefore, he went home, and refrained himself as long as he could, that his wife and children should not
perceive his distress; but he could not be silent long, because
that his trouble increased: wherefore at length he brake his
mind to his wife and children; and thus he began to talk to
them, O my dear wife, said he, and you the children of my
bowels, I your dear friend am in myself undone by reason of a
burden that lieth hard upon me: moreover, I am for certain informed, that this our city will be burned with fire from
heaven, in which fearful overthrow, both myself, with thee,
my wife, and you, my sweet babes, shall miserably come to
ruin; except (the which, yet I see not) some way of escape
can be found, whereby we may be delivered. At this his relations were sore amazed; not for that they believed, that what
he had said to them was true, but because they thought that
some frenzy distemper had got into his head: therefore, it
drawing towards night, and they hoping that sleep might
settle his brains, with all haste they got him to bed; but the
night was as troublesome to him as the day: wherefore instead of sleeping, he spent it in sighs and tears. So when the

morning was come, they would know how he did; he told them, Worse and worse. He also set to talking to them again, but they began to be hardened; they also thought to drive away his distemper by harsh and surly carriages to him: sometimes they would deride, sometimes they would chide, and sometimes they would quite neglect him: wherefore he began to retire himself to his chamber to pray for, and pity them; and also to condole his own misery: he would also walk solitarily in the fields, sometimes reading, and sometimes praying: and thus for some days he spent his time.

Now, I saw upon a time, when he was walking in the fields, that he was (as he was wont) reading in his book, and greatly distressed in his mind; and as he read, he burst out, as he had done before, crying, " What shall I do to be saved? "

I saw also that he looked this way, and that way, as if he would run; yet he stood still, because as I perceived, he could not tell which way to go. I looked then, and saw a man named Evangelist coming to him, who asked, Wherefore dost thou cry? . . .

JOHN BUNYAN

In the middle of the journey of our life, I found myself in a dark wood; for the straight way was lost. Ah! how hard a thing it is to tell what a wild, and rough, and stubborn wood this was, which in my thought renews the fear: so bitter is it, that scarcely more is death. But to treat of the good that I there found, I will relate the other things that I discerned.

I cannot rightly tell how I entered it, so full of sleep was I about the moment that I left the true way. But after I had reached the foot of a Hill there, where that valley ended, which had pierced my heart with fear, I looked up and saw its shoulders already clothed with the rays of the Planet that leads men straight on every road. Then the fear was somewhat calmed, which had continued in the lake of my heart the night that I passed so piteously. And as he, who with panting breath has escaped from the deep sea to the shore, turns to the dangerous water and gazes; so my mind, which still was fleeing, turned back to see the pass that no one ever left alive.

After I had rested my weary body, I took the way again along the desert strand, so that the firm foot always was the lower.

And behold, almost at the commencement of the steep, a Leopard, light and very nimble, which was covered with a spotted skin: and it went not from before my face; nay, so impeded my way, that I had often turned to go back.

The time was at the beginning of the morning; and the Sun was mounting up with those stars, which were with him when Divine Love first moved those fair things: so that the gay skin of that animal, the hour of time, and the sweet season, were causes to me of good hope; yet not so, but that I feared at the sight, which appeared to me, of a Lion.

He seemed coming upon me with head erect, and furious hunger; so that the air seemed to quake thereat. And a She-wolf, that looked full of all cravings in her leanness; and has ere now made many live in sorrow: She brought such heaviness upon me with the terror of her aspect, that I lost the hope of ascending. And as one who is eager in gaining, and, when the time arrives that makes him lose, weeps and afflicts himself in all his thoughts; such that restless beast made me, which coming against me, by little and little drove me back to where the Sun is silent. . . .

> DANTE, from *The Divine Comedy*
> translated by John Aitken Carlyle

Lo! I will tell you the fairest of dreams, that came to me at midnight when mortal men abode in sleep. It seemed to me that I beheld a beauteous tree uplifted in the air, enwreathed with light, brightest of beams. All that beacon was enwrought with gold. Four jewels lay upon the earth, and five were at the crossing of the arms. All the winsome angels of the Lord gazed upon it through the firmament. Nor was that the cross indeed of any evil-doer, but holy spirits looked upon it, men on earth, and all the bright creation. Wondrous was that victor-tree, and I was stained with sin and wounded with my wickedness. I beheld the cross of glory shining in splendour, graced with hangings and adorned with gold. Worthily had jewels covered all that forest tree.

Yet through the gold might I perceive the olden woe of wretched souls, when on the right side it began to bleed. In my sorrow I was greatly troubled, smitten of fear, before that winsome vision. I saw that beacon swiftly change in hangings and in hue; whiles was it all bedewed with moisture, with flowing blood befouled; and whiles adorned with treasure. Natheless, lying there a weary while, I gazed upon the Saviour's cross with rueful heart, till that I heard how it addressed me; that fairest of all trees began to speak:

"Many years have gone — yet still I have it in remembrance — since I was felled upon a forest's edge and wakened from my slumbers. Strange foes seized hold upon me and wrought me to a pageant and bade me lift aloft their wretched men. Men bore me on their shoulders, till that they set me on a hill; enough of foes forsooth, fastened me there. Then I beheld the Lord of men hasting with mighty, steadfast heart, for He would fain ascend upon me. Yet might I not bow down nor break, against the word of God, what time I saw the compass of the earth tremble and shake. All those foes might I lay low; yet firm I stood.

"The Hero young — He was Almighty God — did off His raiment, steadfast, stout of heart. With valour, in the sight of many men, He mounted up upon the lofty gallows, when He would fain redeem mankind. I trembled when the Hero clasped me. Yet dared I not incline unto the ground, nor fall upon the face of earth, but I must needs stand firm. As a cross was I lifted up; bore aloft the righteous King, the Lord of heaven; I dared not bow me down.

"They pierced me through with darksome nails; on me the scars are manifest, the open, woeful wounds. Yet dared I not work harm to any one of them. They mocked us both together. All bedewed with blood was I, gushing from the Hero's side, when He had yielded up His spirit. Many a dire affliction I bode upon that mount; beheld the Lord of hosts stretched out grievously. Darkness had compassed about with clouds the body of the wielding God, that lustrous radiance. Wan under heaven shadows went forth. And all creation wept, wailing the slaughter of its King. Christ was on the cross.

"Yet souls hasted from afar unto the Prince; I beheld it all. Sorely was I smit with sorrow, yet in lowliness, with enduring heart, I yielded to the hands of men. Then they took Almighty God and lifted Him from off His woeful torment; those war-wolves left me standing, overspread with blood; all wounded was I with their darts. There they laid Him down, weary of limb, and at His body's head they stood and gazed upon the Lord of heaven. And for a little time He rested there, feeble after His great strife. These men began, in the sight of His slayers, to dig a sepulchre; out of the gleaming rock they carved it. And there they laid the God of victory. In the even-tide with woeful hearts they sang a dirge. Full soon must they depart again, soul-weary, from their mighty Prince. So with a little band He rested there. . . .

"Now bliss is come, so that men revere me far and wide throughout the earth, and all the great Creation prayeth to this beacon. On me the Son of God suffered a little time; wherefore in glory now I tower up beneath the sky; and I may bring healing unto every one of those that have regard for me." . . .

CYNEWULF, from *The Dream of the Rood*
translated by Charles W. Kennedy

A VISION OF PARADISE

Now when we were past all these places and sights aforesaid, and had gone a good space more inward, and ever grew to us more and more joy and fairness of places: also at the last we saw afar a full glorious wall of crystal, whose height no

man might see, and length no man might consider: and when
we came thither I saw withinforth a full fair bright shining
gate, that stood open, save it was signed and laid over with
a cross. Truly thither came flockmeal the multitude of those
blessed souls that were next to it, and would come in at that
fair gate. . . .

That glorious shining light was bright and smooth, and
so ravished a man that beheld it, that it bare a man above himself by the great brightness of light, in so mickle that whatsoever I saw before, it was as nothing, methought, in comparison of it. That brightness, though it were inestimable,
nevertheless it dulled not a man's sight; it rather sharped it.
Soothly it shone full marvellously, but more inestimably it delighted a man that beheld it, and wonderfully coupled a man's
sight to see it. And withinforth nothing I might see but light
and the wall of crystal through the which we came in. And
also from the ground up to top of that wall were greces ordained and disposed fair and marvellously, by the which the
joyful company that was come in at the foresaid gate gladly
ascended up. There was no labour, there was no difficulty,
there was no tarrying in their ascending, and the higher they
went the gladder they were.

Soothly I stood beneath on the ground, and long time I saw
and beheld how they that came in at the gate ascended up by
the same greces. And at the last, as I looked up higher, I saw
in a throne of joy sitting our blessed Lord and Saviour Jesus
Christ, in likeness of man; and about Him, as it seemed to me,
were a five hundred souls, the which late had stied up to that
glorious throne; and so they came to our Lord and worshipped Him, and thanked Him for His great mercy and grace
showed and done to them: and some were seen on the upper
parts of the wall as they had walked hither and thither. Truly
I knew for certain that this place, where I saw our Lord sitting in a throne, was not the high Heaven of Heavens where
the blessed spirits of angels and the holy souls of righteous
men joy in the sight of God. . . . For no man may come to
it, the which no mortal man seeth, neither may see. Soothly.

He is seen only of holy spirits that be pure and clean, the which be not grieved by no corruption of body, neither of soul. And in this vision that I saw, so mickle I conceived in my soul of joy and gladness, that whatsoever may be said of it by man's mouth, full little it is, and insufficient to express the joy of my heart that I had there.

Therefore when I had seen all these sights above said, and many other innumerable, my lord Saint Nicholas, that held me by the hand, said shortly this to me: " Lo, son," he said, " now a part after thy petition and great desire thou hast seen and beholden the state of the world that is to come as it might be to possible. . . . And now thou must go again to thyself and to thine [own], and to the world's fighting. Truly thou shalt have and perceive the joys that thou hast seen, and mickle more, if thou continue and persevere in the dread of God." And when he had said this to me he brought me forth through the same gate that we came in: wherefore full heavy and sorry was I, and more than a man may suppose: for well I knew that I must turn again from that heavenly bliss to this world's wretchedness. . . .

And while the holy confessor, Saint Nicholas, this wise spake yet with me, suddenly I heard there a solemn peal and a ringing of a marvellous sweetness, and as all the bells in the world, or whatsoever is of sounding, had been rung together at once. Truly in this peal and ringing brake out also a marvellous sweetness, and a variant meddling of melody sounded withal. And I wot not whether the greatness of melody or the sweetness of sounding of bells was more to be wondered [at]. And to so great a noise I took good heed, and full greatly my mind was suspended to hear it. Soothly, anon as that great and marvellous sounding and noise was ceased, suddenly I saw myself departed from the sweet fellowship of my duke and leader, Saint Nicholas. Then was I returned to myself again, and anon I heard the voices of my brethren that stood about our bed.

WILLIAM DE MACHLINIA

How and Why?

. . . *Men mark when they hit, and never mark when they miss;
as they do generally.*

*Wade not too far, my boy, in waves so deep:
The feeble eyes of our aspiring thoughts
Behold things present, and record things past;
But things to come exceed our human reach
And are not painted yet in angels' eyes. . . .*

How and Why?

A BRIEF MEMORANDUM

Now, seeing we cannot agree together in the manner of expounding or interpreting the sense of the Virgilian lots, let us bend our course another way, and try a new sort of divination."

" Of what kind? " asked Panurge.

" Of a good, ancient, and authentic fashion," answered Pantagruel; " it is by dreams. For in dreaming, such circumstances and conditions being thereto adhibited, as are clearly enough described by Hippocrates . . . by Plato, Plotinus, Iamblicus, Synesius, Aristotle, Xenophon, Galen, Plutarch, Artemidorus, Daldianus, Herophilus, Q. Calaber, Theocritus, Pliny, Athenaeus, and others,[1] the soul doth oftentimes foresee what is to come. . . ."

RABELAIS

Half our days we pass in the shadow of the earth; and the brother of death exacteth a third part of our lives. A good part of our sleep is peered out with visions and fantastical objects, wherein we are confessedly deceived. The day supplieth us with truths; the night with fictions and falsehoods, which uncomfortably divide the natural account of our beings. And, therefore, having passed the day in sober la-

[1] Others being: Democritus, Epicurus, Lucretius, Zeno, Dicaearchus, Poseidonius, Ennius, Strabo, Epictetus, Porphyry, Lucian, Dion Cassius, Lactantius, Josephus, Cyprian, St. Basil, St. Bernard, Thomas Aquinas, etc., etc., and a multitude of writers since and in recent times.

bours and rational enquiries of truth, we are fain to betake ourselves unto such a state of being, wherein the soberest heads have acted all the monstrosities of melancholy, and which unto open eyes are no better than folly and madness. . . .

SIR THOMAS BROWNE

Dreams look like the relaxations and amusements of the soul when she is disencumbered of her machine, her sports and recreations when she has laid her charge asleep. . . .

What I would here remark is that wonderful power in the soul of producing her own company [in dreams]. She converses with numberless beings of her own creation, and is transported into ten thousand scenes of her own raising. She is herself the theatre, the actors, and the beholder. This puts me in mind of a saying which I am infinitely pleased with and which Plutarch ascribes to Heraclitus, "That all men whilst they are awake are in one common world; but that each of them, when he is asleep, is in a world of his own."

JOSEPH ADDISON

A MERRY HEART

DON PEDRO. In faith, lady, you have a merry heart.

BEATRICE. Yea, my lord; I thank it, poor fool, it keeps on the windy side of care. . . . I was born to speak all mirth and no matter.

D. PEDRO. Your silence most offends me, and to be merry best becomes you; for, out of question, you were born in a merry hour.

BEAT. No, sure, my lord, my mother cried; but then there was a star danced, and under that was I born. Cousins, God give you joy! . . .

[370]

LEONATO. There's little of the melancholy element in her, my
  lord: she is never sad but when she sleeps; and not ever
  sad then, for I have heard my daughter say, she hath
  often dreamed of unhappiness and waked herself with
  laughing.

WILLIAM SHAKESPEARE
from *Much Ado About Nothing, Act II, Scene I*

THE ISLE

CALIBAN. Art thou afeard?
STEPHANO. No, monster, not I.
CAL. Be not afraid: the isle is full of noises,
  Sounds and sweet airs, that give delight, and hurt not.
  Sometimes a thousand twangling instruments
  Will hum about mine ears; and sometimes voices,
  That, if I then had waked after long sleep,
  Will make me sleep again: and then, in dreaming,
  The clouds methought would open and show riches
  Ready to drop upon me; that, when I waked
  I cried to dream again.

WILLIAM SHAKESPEARE
from *The Tempest, Act III, Scene II*

BOTTOM'S DREAM

TITANIA. What, wilt thou hear some music, my sweet love?
BOTTOM. I have a reasonable good ear in music: let us have
  the tongs and the bones.
TITA. Or say, sweet love, what thou desir'st to eat.
BOT. Truly, a peck of provender: I could munch your good
  dry oats. Methinks I have a great desire to a bottle of
  hay: good hay, sweet hay, hath no fellow.
TITA. I have a venturous fairy that shall seek
  The squirrel's hoard, and fetch thee thence new nuts.

Bot. I had rather have a handful or two of dried pease. But,
I pray you, let none of your people stir me; I have an
exposition of sleep come upon me.

Tita. Sleep thou, and I will wind thee in my arms.
Fairies, be gone, and be all ways away. . . .
So doth the woodbine the sweet honeysuckle
Gently entwist; the female ivy so
Enrings the barky fingers of the elm.
Oh! how I love thee; how I dote on thee! . . .

[*They sleep.*

Bot. [*Awaking.*] When my cue comes, call me, and I will answer: my next is, " Most fair Pyramus." Heigh-ho! Peter
Quince! Flute, the bellows-mender! Snout, the tinker!
Starveling! God's my life! stolen hence, and left me
asleep! I have had a most rare vision. I have had a
dream, past the wit of man to say what dream it was:
man is but an ass, if he go about to expound this dream.
Methought I was, — and methought I had, — but man
is but a patched fool, if he will offer to say what methought I had. The eye of man hath not heard, the ear
of man hath not seen, man's hand is not able to taste,
his tongue to conceive, nor his heart to report, what my
dream was. I will get Peter Quince to write a ballad of
this dream: it shall be called Bottom's Dream, because it
hath no bottom; and I will sing it in the latter end of a
play, before the duke: peradventure, to make it the more
gracious, I shall sing it at her death.

WILLIAM SHAKESPEARE
from *A Midsummer-Night's Dream, Act IV, Scene I*

Mrs. Otter. Is Master Truewit gone?

Sir Dauphine Eugekie. Yes, lady, there is some unfortunate
business fallen out.

Mrs. Ott. So I adjudged by the physiognomy of the fellow
that came in; and I had a dream last night too of the new
pageant, and my lady mayoress, which is always very
ominous to me. I told it my Lady Haughty t'other day,

when her honour came hither to see some China stuffs; and she expounded it out of Artemidorus, and I have found it since very true. It has done me many affronts.

CLERMONT. Your dream, lady?

MRS. OTT. Yes, sir, anything I do but dream of the city. It stained me a damask table-cloth, cost me eighteen pound at one time; and burnt me a black satin gown, as I stood by the fire at my lady Centaure's chamber in the college, another time. A third time, at the lords' masque, it dropt all my wire and my ruff with wax candle, that I could not go up to the banquet. A fourth time, as I was taking coach to go to Ware, to meet a friend, it dashed me a new suit all over (a crimson satin doublet, and black velvet skirts) with a brewer's horse, that I was fain to go in and shift me, and kept my chamber a leash of days for the anguish of it.

DAUP. These were dire mischances, lady.

CLER. I would not dwell in the city, an 'twere so fatal to me.

MRS. OTT. Yes, sir; but I do take advice of my doctor to dream of it as little as I can.

DAUP. You do well, Mistress Otter.

BEN JONSON,
from *The Silent Woman, Act III, Scene I*

. . . Some Dreams I confess may admit of easie and feminine Exposition; he who dreamed that he could not see his right Shoulder, might easily fear to lose the Sight of his right Eye; he that before a Journey dreamed that his Feet were cut off, had a plain Warning not to undertake his intended Journey. But why to dream of Lettuce should presage some ensuing Disease, why to eat Figs should signifie foolish Talk, why to eat Eggs great Trouble, and to dream of Blindness should be so highly commended, according to the *Oneirocritical* Verses of *Astrampsychus* and *Nicephorus,* I shall leave unto your Divination. . . .

SIR THOMAS BROWNE

It is unquestionably true that dreams are somtimes evoked by sensory stimuli which almost immediately awake the dreamer. But the supposition that this fairly common fact involves an extraordinary acceleration of the rapidity with which mental images are formed is due to a failure to comprehend the conditions under which psychic activity in sleep takes place. If the sleeper were wide awake, and were suddenly startled by a mysterious voice at the window or the door, he would arrive at a theory of the sound, and even form a plan of action, with at least as much rapidity as when the stimulus occurs during sleep. The difference is that in sleep the ordinary mental associations are more or less in abeyance, and the way is therefore easily open to new associations. These new associations, when we look back at them from the standpoint of waking life, seem to us so bizarre, so far-fetched, that we think it must have required a long time to imagine them. We fail to realise that, under the conditions of dream thought, they have come about as automatically and as instantaneously as the ordinary psychic concomitants of external stimulation in waking life. . . .

Clavière showed by experiments with an alarum clock which struck twice with an interval of twenty-two seconds that speech dreams at all events take place merely with normal rapidity, or are even slightly slower than under waking conditions. The imagery of sleep, Clavière concluded, is not more rapid than the imagery of waking life, though to the dreamer it may seem to last for hours or days. It is often slackened rather than accelerated, says Piéron, who refers to the corresponding illusion under the influence of drugs like hashisch, though in some cases he finds that there is really a slight acceleration. The illusion is simply due, Foucault thinks, to the dreamer's belief that the events of his dream occupy the same time as real events. This illusion of time, concludes Dr. Justine Tobolowska, in her Paris thesis on this subject, is simply the necessary and constant result of the form assumed by psychic life during sleep. . . .

Havelock Ellis

. . . Dreams may be "nothing more than the common vibrations of terrestrial media acting upon a corporeal vibratorium." Now they arise from the firing of a gun, the ringing of a bell, a breath of cold air upon a naked foot, or some other disturbance from without; and now " perturbation in the richly-nerved digestive organs send vibrating and startling messages from within to the mental centres," and then we have another sort of dream. And thus the whole thing is explained. Dreams are " a purely physical phase of life. They are " all explainable on physical grounds," and there is no mystery about them to any one who has a fair portion of the knowledge that may be gained in a dissecting-room.

That this account of the matter has something explanatory in it is obvious; but it is so little as to be of no importance. In like manner, and to about the same degree, the alphabet is an explanation of Shakespeare's plays. . . .

. . . We all agree that when the vibratory sounds of a bell pierce through the mufflings of sleep, and act upon the vibratorium in our skulls, but yet not so as to wake us, mind begins to dream. But what happens when the noise is loud enough to wake us quite? Why, then, and as a consequence of the same vibratory action in the vibratorium, we begin to think. The thought may be so trivial that it does not abide with us in any sense or to any purpose, even for a moment; and the dream may be so unimpressive that it passes just as quickly away. But whether they are of that common character, or whether the dream is full of meaning and the thought an inspiration (we are used to calling thoughts " inspired "), they both take shape by operation of the mind, and were started by the same agency in the same manner. . . .

. . . The physiological explanation of dreams is almost if not entirely worthless; so far does it fall short of its pretensions. At best it is no more explanatory of what it is supposed to expound than the following account of the writing of a book would be: — "A man takes into his hand an instrument called a pen; he dips one end of it into a fluid (usually black) called ink; and with the ink at the end of the pen he makes a variety of marks on white or blue-tinted paper. And there is no more to be said about the writing of a book: the explanation is simple and complete." . . .

FREDERICK GREENWOOD

. . . Doctors tell of dreams which embody intimations of physical disorder while it is yet so obscure and undeveloped as to be quite unknown to the dreamer in his waking state, and entirely unsuspected by everybody else. It is evident that dreams of that kind have a speciality which distinguishes them from those in which mental processes are carried on; as when, to quote an unimpeachable authority, "a scholar engaged in a work of imagination, thinking himself to sleep at the junction of cross-roads of thought, has often arisen in the morning well advanced on one of them, and inspired to write as fast as his pen would let him a passage or a poem." Here we have examples of two distinct sorts of dreaming — the one reflective, the other constructive; and both are quite unlike the rambling inconsequential nonsense which dreaming often is — without, however, being more nonsensical than a good deal that runs on in the same minds in their waking hours. . . .

Now whenever some latent malady is so revealed in sleep, it is not likely to be done in the language of a medical practitioner stating a case. . . . Parable is their means of expression. Fable mounted as a sort of stage-play in the mind is what meaning dreams always are. Then what more likely than that they should be mistaken for mere vapourish, haphazard phantasms? The fable is unrecognised, uninterpreted, and dismissed as the usual nonsense; all in ignorant contempt of a very serviceable function of mind. This consideration places us on one line of thought. The other leads straight to what has been suggested as the grand terminal point of the whole enquiry, and the one that should be always kept in view. For every such dream is evidence that the mind is capable of exhibiting in sleep finer powers of detection, comprehension, interpretation, that it is conscious of in its waking state. It can receive and record in the one condition sensations of which it is unaware in the other. . . .

FREDERICK GREENWOOD

. . . Galen's third [dream] more worthy of being called a miracle, was, when being twice admonished in his sleep, to cut the artery that lies between the fore finger and the thumb, and doing it accordingly, he was freed from a continual daily pain with which he was afflicted in that part where the liver is joined to the midriff; and this he has testified at the end of his book of Venesection. 'Tis certainly a very great example, when a man so great as he was in the medicinal art, put so much confidence in a dream as to try experiments upon himself; where he was to run the risque of his life, in his own very art. I cannot help but admire his probity in the next place, that where he might have arrogated the merit of the invention to himself, and placed it wholly to the account of the subtility and penetration of his own genius, he attributed it to God, to whom it was due. In this alone did the man well deserve to purchase an immortality to his name and his writings. . . .

Mrs. Cl—, of S—, in the county of S—, had a beloved daughter, who had been a long time ill, and received no benefit from her physicians. She dreamed that a friend of hers deceased, told her, that if she gave her daughter a drench of yew pounded, that she would recover; she gave her the drench, and it killed her. Whereupon she grew almost distracted: her chamber maid to complement her, and mitigate her grief, said surely that could not kill her, she would adventure to take the same herself; she did so, and died also. This was about the year 1670, or 1671. I knew the family. . . .

. . . When Sir Christopher Wren was at Paris, about 1671, he was ill and feverish, made but little water, and had a pain

in his reins. He sent for a physician, who advised him to be
let blood, thinking he had a plurisy: but bleeding much dis-
agreeing with his constitution, he would defer it a day longer:
that night he dreamt, that he was in a place where palm-trees
grew, (suppose Ægypt) and that a woman in a romantic
habit, reached him dates. The next day he sent for dates
which cured him of the pain of his reins. Since, I have
learned that dates [i.e. the stones " pulverized and searced "],
are an admirable medicine for the stone, from old Captain
Tooke of K—. . . .

JOHN AUBREY

" He [Jean Louis Agassiz] had been for two weeks striving
to decipher the somewhat obscure impression of a fossil fish
on the stone slab in which it was preserved. Weary and perplexed, he put his work aside at last, and tried to dismiss it
from his mind. Shortly after, he waked one night persuaded
that while asleep he had seen his fish with all the missing
features perfectly restored. But when he tried to hold and
make fast the image it escaped him. Nevertheless, he went
early to the Jardin des Plantes, thinking that on looking anew
at the impression he should see something which would put
him on the track of his vision. In vain — the blurred record
was as blank as ever. The next night he saw the fish again,
but with no more satisfactory result. When he awoke it disappeared from his memory as before. Hoping that the same
experience might be repeated, on the third night he placed a
pencil and paper beside his bed before going to sleep.

" Accordingly, towards morning the fish reappeared in his
dream, confusedly at first, but at last with such distinctness
that he had no longer any doubt as to its zoological characters.
Still half dreaming, in perfect darkness, he traced these
characters on the sheet of paper at his bedside. In the morning he was surprised to see in his nocturnal sketch features
which he thought it impossible the fossil itself should reveal.
He hastened to the Jardin des Plantes, and, with his drawing
as a guide, succeeded in chiselling away the surface of the

stone under which portions of the fish proved to be hidden. When wholly exposed it corresponded with his dream and his drawing, and he succeeded in classifying it with ease."

MME AGASSIZ: quoted by Dr. John Bigelow in
"The Mystery of Sleep"

MOSCOW, 1887.

I have just read your "Karelin's Dream," and am now much occupied by the question of how far the dream you describe really is a dream. It seems to me that the workings of the brain and the general condition of a person asleep are described with physiological truth and remarkable art. I remember reading about two or three years ago a French story (I do not remember the name of the author, but the title, I believe, was "Cherrie") in which the author, in describing a Cabinet Minister's daughter — probably without suspecting it himself — gave a correct clinical picture of hysteria. It occurred to me then that the flair of an artist is sometimes worth the brains of a scientist, that both have the same objects, the same nature, and that perhaps, in time, with perfected methods they are destined to fuse into a gigantic, stupendous force, which now it is difficult even to imagine. . . . "Karelin's dream" led me to similar thoughts, and to-day I willingly believe Buckle, who saw in Hamlet's reflections on clay and the dust of Alexander the Great, Shakespeare's knowledge of the law of transmutation of matter — that is, the artist's power to get ahead of the men of science. . . . A dream is a subjective phenomenon and its inner bearing one can observe in oneself. But, as the process of dreaming is the same in all people, then it seems to me that every reader can measure "Karelin" by his own measure, and every critic is bound to be subjective. Personally, following my own measure, I can thus formulate my impression.

First of all, you describe the sensation of cold with remarkable subtlety. When at night my blanket falls off, I begin to see in my dream huge, slippery stones, cold autumnal water, naked shores — all this dimly, in a mist, without a scrap of blue sky. In dismay and anguish, like one lost, I look at the stones and somehow feel it is inevitable I must cross a deep river; I see at that time small tugs drawing huge boats, floating logs. . . . All this is infinitely forbidding, dismal and damp. . . . When I run away from the river, I find on my way broken-down cemetery gates, a funeral, my schoolmasters. . . . And at the time a heavy, nightmare-like cold penetrates me, unthinkable when awake and felt only by those who sleep. . . .

It seems to me that had I been born in Petersburg and lived permanently there I should always dream about the banks of the Neva, about the Senate Square, about massive masonry.

When I feel cold in my sleep, I see people. . . . One always dreams of unattractive people. For instance, when feeling cold I always dream of my scripture master, a learned and good-looking priest, who once insulted my mother when I was a boy; I dream of wicked, implacable, intriguing people who smile spitefully, such as one does not see when awake. Laughter at the windows of the carriage is a characteristic symptom of Karelin's nightmare. When in sleep one feels the pressure of an evil will, the inevitable ruin caused by someone else's will, one always hears something like that laughter. One also dreams of people one loves, but they usually appear to suffer together with the dreamer.

But when my body gets accustomed to the cold or one of my family covers me, the sensation of cold, of loneliness, and of an oppressive wicked will gradually disappears. With the warmth I begin to feel that I am walking on soft carpets or on grass, I see the sun, women, children. . . . The scenes change gradually, but more sharply than in wakefulness, so that on waking it is difficult to remember the gradations from one scene to another. That sharpness comes out well in your story, and it strengthens the impression of the dream.

The eye is also keenly struck by a natural fact observed by you; those who dream express their emotions by acute outbursts, with childish sincerity, like Karelin. Everyone knows that sleepers weep and cry out much more frequently than those who are awake. . . .

Of myself I can say little good. I write not what I want to write, and to write as you advised I have neither the energy nor the solitude. .. . . A great many good themes knock about in my head — and that is all. Meanwhile, I feed myself with hopes for the future, and watch the present fruitlessly gliding away.

ANTON TCHEKHOV, to D. V. Grigorovich

Professor Sigmund Freud's *Die Traumdeutung* (first edition, 1900), may be said to belong to the introspective class, though to a special division which Freud himself terms psycho-analytic. This is undoubtedly the most original, the most daring, the most challenging of recent books on dreams, and is now the text-book of a whole school of investigators. It is not a book to be neglected, for it is written by one of the profoundest of living investigators into the obscure depths of the human soul. Even if one rejects Freud's methods as unsatisfactory and his facts as unproved, the work of one so bold and so sincere cannot fail to be helpful and stimulating in the highest degree. If it is not the truth it will at least help us to reach the truth. . . .

HAVELOCK ELLIS

. . . His followers, however, and to a large extent Freud himself, have become so engrossed with the cruder side of sexual life that their works might often be taken for contributions to pornography rather than to medicine. In some of Freud's followers this absorption in the sexual has gone to such lengths that perverse tendencies and prurient ideas are scented in every thought, waking or sleeping, of the patients who come under their care. To a certain extent this excess is a reaction from the timidity and prudery of the great mass of the medical profession in relation to sexual matters, and is a protest against the ignorance of this side of life which so often exists. The mistake which is now being made by many is to

[381]

regard this excess as a necessary part of the Freudian scheme instead of an unfortunate excrescence. . . . There are even those who are so obsessed by the sexual aspect of Freud's psychology that they regard sexuality as its basic principle, and have fallen into a state of mind which wholly blinds them to its merits. . . .

W. H. R. RIVERS

Professor Freud, in describing the results of his life-work, says that he has been unable to detect any difference between pleasure arising from bodily functions and the " merely affective and friendly impulses to which usage applies the exceedingly ambiguous word ' love.' " The carnal mind, or mortality, which is the only mind that psycho-analysis can touch, can provide no other form of love for dissection, and the account of it is just. Will the future show that the disinterested devotion of a lifetime has indeed exposed the nature of an illusion, but one which the searcher has failed to identify? Will time prove that research has without doubt laid bare the dream, but a dream to which the researcher has been blind? Should this be the case, the sincere search for truth will be rewarded in unsought ways. Reality will shine through appearance and psycho-analysis may mark the end of an epoch. . . .

MARGARET H. BULLEY

. . . Dreams, it is argued, are inevitably transformed in our hands; what we are studying is not our dreams, but only our waking, and probably altogether false, impressions of our dreams. There is a certain element of truth in this objection. It is very difficult, indeed impossible, to recall exactly, and in their proper order, even the details of a real adventure which has only just happened to us. It is, obviously, incomparably more difficult to recall an experience which took place, under such shadowy conditions, in a world so remote from the world of waking life. There is, further, the very definite difficulty that we only catch our dreams for a moment by the light, as it were, of the open door as we are emerging from sleep. In other words, our waking consciousness is for a moment observing and interpreting a process in another kind of consciousness, or even if we assert that it is the same consciousness it is still a consciousness that has been working under quite different conditions from waking consciousness, and accepting data which in the waking state it would not accept. For the student of dreams it must ever be a serious question how far the facts become inevitably distorted in this process. Sleeping or waking, it is probable, our consciousness never embraces the whole of the possible psychic field within us. There are, when we are dreaming as well as when we are awake . . . subconscious, or imperfectly conscious, states just below our consciousness, and exerting an influence upon it. Our latent psychic possessions, among which dreams move, would seem to be by no means always at the same depth; the specific gravity of consciousness, as it were, varies, and these latent elements rise or fall, becoming nearer to the conscious surface or falling further away from it. But the greatest change must take place when the waking surface is reached and the outer world breaks on sleeping consciousness. In that change there is doubtless a process of necessary and automatic transformation and interpretation. . . .

HAVELOCK ELLIS

Cryptomnesia [subconscious memory] may also appear in dreams.

The classical case of Delbœuf is quite characteristic in this respect: in a complicated dream he saw, among other things, a plant with its botanical name, *Asplenium ruta muraria.* Now Delbœuf was totally ignorant of this name, or thought he was. After long search he found that two years before he had turned over the leaves of a botanical album and there had seen both the plant and the name, of which he had not thought again. . . .

Sometimes the subject . . . shows knowledge totally for-

[383]

gotten, such as a language learned in childhood. Pitres cites the case of a patient, Albertine M., who thus used the *patois* of Saintonge, which she had only spoken in childhood. During this regressional delirium, says Pitres, " she expressed herself in *patois,* and if we begged her to speak in French, she invariably answered always in *patois,* that she did not know the talk of the townspeople." . . .

The entire subconscious memory seems, therefore, to be independent of cerebral contingencies. Cases have even been quoted in which it has reappeared by flashes, in spite of the loss of normal memory through injuries to the brain. Such is the case of Mr. Hanna, a very characteristic one in this respect. Mr. Hanna, by reason of a fall on his head, forgot entirely the whole of his past life, all his knowledge and all his acquirements, and returned to the psychological state of a new-born babe who has everything to learn. But curiously enough, though the memory had disappeared, the capacity to learn was intact. Now during this process of re-education, M. Flournoy records, " he had dreams and visions, incomprehensible to himself, which he described with astonishment to his relations, and in which they recognised very exact recollections of places where the patient had been before his accident." There was, therefore, a latent memory, also clearly shown by his power of very rapid learning. . . .

GUSTAVE GELEY, translated by Stanley de Brath

Dreams, dreams that mock us with their flitting shadows,
They come not from the temples of the gods,
They send them not, the powers of the air.
Each man makes his own dreams. The body lies
Quiet in sleep, what time the mind set free
Follows in darkness what it sought by day.
He who makes kingdoms quake for fear and sends
Unhappy cities ruining in fire,
Sees hurtling blows and broken fighting ranks

And death of kings and sodden battle fields.
The lawyer sees the judge, the crowded court,
The miser hides his coin, digs buried treasure,
The hunter shakes the forests with his hounds,
The sailor rescues from the sea his ship,
Or drowning, clings to it. Mistress to lover
Writes a love-letter: the adulteress
Yields in her sleep, and in his sleep the hound
Is hot upon the traces of the hare.
The wounds of the unhappy in the night
Do but prolong their pain.

Petronius Arbiter,
translated by Helen Waddell

The Stuff of Dreams

Dreams are rough copies of the waking mind.

By these gates entering, which cloudy show,
I from the touching lustful world did go;
And, faring on — need none, the way to ask —
Saw in a water, there, my face sans mask. . . .

Let not your prophets and your diviners deceive you. . . .

The Stuff of Dreams

The Imagination is ever busie, and (as far as I can perceive) never *Sleeps;* the *Judgment* or *Reason* for the most part, is impedited from acting, especially after its common way or outward Fashion, when a man sleeps. The *Memory* sometimes is more, and sometimes less clouded and obstructed, according to the nature of the fumes sent up; and hence it comes to pass, that we have sometimes a clearer, sometimes a more confused, and sometimes scarce any Apprehension or Remembrance of our *Dreams* when we awake. . . .

T. TRYON

. . . All men dream, and the most common experience of the phenomenon is the sort of double existence which it entails. The life of the night is usually very different from the life of the day. And these strange spectres and shapes of slumber do not perish; they live in some obscure ante-room or limbo of memory, and reappear at times in the most singular fashion. Most people have been startled by this reappearance. Something of importance to you has happened quite new, quite unexpected; you are sitting in a strange railway-station waiting for the train; you have gone to see a friend in a distant part of the country, and in your solitary evening stroll you come on a pool of water, with three pollard willows, such as you see in old engravings, growing beside it, and above the willows an orange sunset through which a string of rooks are flying; and all at once this new thing which has happened wears the face of an old experience; the strange railway-station becomes familiar; and the pool, the willows, the sunset with the undulating line of rooks, seem to have been witnessed *not* for the first time. This curious feeling is gone almost as swiftly as it has come; but you are perplexed with the sense of a double identity, with the emergence as of a former existence. The feeling alluded to is so swift and intangible that often you cannot arrest it; you cannot pin it down for inspection as you would a butterfly on a card; but when you *can,* you find that what has startled you with familiarity is simply a vagrant dream — that from the obscure limbo of the memory some occult law of association has called a wandering wraith of sleep, and that for a moment it has flitted betwixt you and the sunshine of consciousness, dimming it as it flits. . . .

ALEXANDER SMITH

. . . The soul of a sleeper is supposed [by certain primitive races] to wander away from his body and actually to visit the places, to see the persons, and to perform the acts of which he dreams. For example, when an Indian of Brazil or Guiana wakes up from a sound sleep, he is firmly convinced that his soul has really been away hunting, fishing, felling trees, or whatever else he has dreamed of doing, while all the time his body has been lying motionless in his hammock. . . .

Now the absence of the soul in sleep has its dangers, for if from any cause the soul should be permanently detained away from the body, the person thus deprived of the vital principle must die. There is a German belief that the soul escapes from the sleeper's mouth in the form of a white mouse or a little bird, and that to prevent the return of the bird or animal would be fatal to the sleeper. Hence in Transylvania they say that you should not let a child sleep with its mouth open, or its soul will slip out in the shape of a mouse, and the child will never wake. . . .

Still more dangerous is it in the opinion of primitive man to move a sleeper or alter his appearance, for if this were done the soul on its return might not be able to find or recognise its body, and so the person would die. . . .

SIR JAMES GEORGE FRAZER

The Australian natives hold that the soul quits the body during sleep; while the Arab regards its absence as a great danger, never awakening a sleeper without an invocation to God to recall the errant soul. The Eskimo thinks that his spirit goes a-hunting while he lies asleep or in a trance. If the soul of the Solomon Islander fails to return by morning, the man dies; but on reaching the mouth of Panoi, or Hades, the soul may be " hustled back " by the other ghosts and so returned to the sleeper or sick person. Tylor cited the Dyaks, the Zulu, the Khond, and the Turanian, as holding similar beliefs; and takes occasion to compare them with the later cases of Socrates and Jerome Cardan. Noting the popular expression of " beside one's self " as " crystallizing this idea in language," he adds, " that the mere evolution of the idea of the soul from a concrete, substantial image of the person (*eidolon*) to the tenuous, spiritualized abstraction used at present, is the result of gradual development from the conception of primitive, savage animism."

That early and deeply rooted conviction that the soul could leave its owner, has a vital bearing on the present discussion. In all the words and works of the mystics its persistence is revealed. Whatever meanings the theorist has attached to these words and works, whatever transcendental web he has tried to spin from them, — when all the threads are carefully unwound, this one fact alone will be found lying at the heart. The early mystic is impregnated with this conviction of the wandering soul; it underlies his experience; it is the real basis of his belief in mysticism. If we turn to the great passages upon which mysticism is founded, what do we find? Richard of St. Victor's famous statement is on close analysis, seen to be only this, — that he believed his soul could be " away." Augustin's reliance is, after all, but upon that great " *if* " the soul might be " away." The texts cited by Dante, in the letter to Can Grande, serve to show his appreciation of the fact that the soul can be " away." " It seems to the ecstatic," writes Teresa, " that he is transported to a region wholly different from that where we find ourselves ordinarily." And if we ask them to define, to separate, and determine this conviction, what is their response? One and all, without a single important exception, dwell on the significant fact that their soul may not remember what has happened to it during its absence. Paul, even, " heard unspeakable words which it is not lawful for a man to utter." Angela da Foligno says, " I know not how to speak of it, nor to offer any similitude." This failure of memory is not capricious and accidental; it is a fundamental characteristic of the mystical experience, and taken by the subject to be the confirmation of its Divine nature. . . .

ANNA ROBESON BURR

Our life is twofold: Sleep hath its own world,
A boundary between the things misnamed
Death and existence: Sleep hath its own world,
And a wide realm of wild reality.
And dreams in their development have breath,
And tears, and tortures, and the touch of joy;
They leave a weight upon our waking thoughts,
They take a weight from off our waking toils,
They do divide our being; they become
A portion of ourselves as of our time,
And look like heralds of eternity;
They pass like spirits of the past, — they speak
Like sibyls of the future; they have power —
The tyranny of pleasure and of pain:
They make us what we were not — what they will,
And shake us with the vision that's gone by,
The dread of vanished shadows — are they so?
Is not the past all shadow? — What are they?
Creations of the mind? — The mind can make
Substance, and people planets of its own
With beings brighter than have been, and give
A breath to forms which can outlive all flesh. . . .

BYRON, from " The Dream "

"So, I repeat," [says the Dreaming to the Waking Self,] "I differ from you precisely in that I do nothing. The effort that you give without cessation I simply abstain from giving. In place of attaching myself to life, I detach myself from it. Everything has become indifferent to me. I have become disinterested in everything. To sleep is to become disinterested. One sleeps to the exact extent to which one becomes disinterested. A mother who sleeps by the side of her child will not stir at the sound of thunder, but the sigh of the child will wake her. Does she really sleep in regard to her child? We do not sleep in regard to what continues to interest us.

"You ask me what it is that I do when I dream? I will tell you what you do when you are awake. You take me, the me of dreams, me the totality of your past, and you force me, by making me smaller and smaller, to fit into the little circle that you trace around your present action. That is what it is to be awake. That is what it is to live the normal psychical life. It is to battle. It is to will. As for the dream, have you really any need that I should explain it? It is the state into which you naturally fall when you let yourself go, when you no longer have the power to concentrate yourself upon a single point, when you have ceased to will. What needs much more to be explained is the marvellous mechanism by which at any moment your will obtains instantly, and almost unconsciously, the concentration of all that you have within you upon one and the same point, the point that interests you. But to explain this is the task of normal psychology, of the psychology of waking, for willing and waking are one and the same thing."

This is what the dreaming ego would say. And it would tell us a great many other things still if we could let it talk freely. But let us sum up briefly the essential difference which separates a dream from the waking state. In the dream the same faculties are exercised as during waking, but they are in a state of tension in the one case, and of relaxation in the other. The dream consists of the entire mental life minus the tension, the effort, and the bodily movement. We perceive still, we remember still, we reason still. All this can abound in the dream; for abundance, in the domain of the mind, does not mean effort. What requires an effort is the precision of adjustment. To connect the sound of a barking dog with the memory of a crowd that murmurs and shouts requires no effort. But in order that this sound should be perceived as the barking of a dog, a positive effort must be made. It is this force that the dreamer lacks. It is by that, and by that alone, that he is distinguished from the waking man. . . .

HENRI BERGSON, translated by Edwin E. Slosson

. . . No day-dream compares for intensity, vividness, force, wildness, with dreams of the night, and this difference seems to arise entirely from the fact that in one case imagination possesses the mind much more exclusively than in the other. It is seen at work in a condition of freedom and domination unknown to us in any other mood when awake, and in that condition it transcends all it is capable of when working in harness with the other faculties. . . .

FREDERICK GREENWOOD

. . . I know not whether my reader is aware that many children have a power of painting, as it were, upon the darkness all sorts of phantoms; in some that power is simply a mechanic affection of the eye; others have a voluntary or semi-voluntary power to dismiss or summon such phantoms; or, as a child once said to me, when I questioned him on the matter, "I can tell them to go, and they go; but sometimes they come when I don't tell them to come." He had by one-half as unlimited a command over apparitions as a Roman centurion over his soldiers. In the middle of 1817 this faculty became increasingly distressing to me: at night, when I lay awake in bed, vast processions moved along continually in mournful pomp; friezes of never-ending stories, that to my feelings were as sad and solemn as stories drawn from times before Œdipus or Priam, before Tyre, before Memphis. And, concurrently with this, a corresponding change took place in my dreams; a theatre seemed suddenly opened and lighted up within my brain, which presented nightly spectacles of more than earthly splendour. And the four following facts may be mentioned, as noticeable at this time: —

1. That, as the creative state of the eye increased, a sympathy seemed to arise between the waking and the dreaming states of the brain in one point — that whatsoever I happened to call up and to trace by a voluntary act upon the darkness was very apt to transfer itself to my dreams; and at length I feared to exercise this faculty. . . .

2. This and all other changes in my dreams were accompanied by deep-seated anxiety and funereal melancholy, such as are wholly incommunicable by words. I seemed every night to descend — not metaphorically, but literally to descend — into chasms and sunless abysses, depths below depths, from which it seemed hopeless that I could ever re-ascend. Nor did I, by waking, feel that I *had* re-ascended. Why should I dwell upon this? For indeed the state of gloom which attended these gorgeous spectacles, amounting at last to utter darkness, as of some suicidal despondency, cannot be approached by words.

3. The sense of space, and in the end the sense of time, were both powerfully affected. . . . Space swelled, and was amplified to an extent of unutterable and self-repeating infinity. This disturbed me very much less than the vast expansion of time. Sometimes I seemed to have lived for seventy or a hundred years in one night; nay, sometimes had feelings representative of a duration far beyond the limits of any human experience.

4. The minutest incidents of childhood, or forgotten scenes of later years, were often revived. I could not be said to recollect them; for, if I had been told of them when waking, I should not have been able to acknowledge them as parts of my past experience. But placed as they were before me, in dreams like intuitions, and clothed in all their evanescent circumstances and accompanying feelings, I *recognised* them in-

stantaneously. I was once told by a near relative of mine, that having in her childhood fallen into a river, and being on the very verge of death . . . she saw in a moment her whole life, clothed in its forgotten incidents, arrayed before her as in a mirror, not successively, but simultaneously; and she had a faculty developed as suddenly for comprehending the whole and every part. . . .

THOMAS DE QUINCEY

There are hours claimed by Sleep, but refused to him. None the less are they his by some state within the mind, which answers rhythmically and punctually to that claim. Awake and at work, without drowsiness, without languor, and without gloom, the night mind of man is yet not his day mind; he has night-powers of feeling which are at their highest in dreams, but are night's as well as sleep's. The powers of the mind in dream, which are inexplicable, are not altogether baffled because the mind is awake; it is the hour of their return as it is the hour of a tide's, and they do return.

In sleep they have their free way. Night then has nothing to hamper her influence, and she draws the emotion, the senses, and the nerves of the sleeper. She urges him upon those extremities of anger and love, contempt and terror, to which not only can no event of the real day persuade him, but for which, awake, he has perhaps not even the capacity. This increase of capacity, which is the dream's, is punctual to the night, even though sleep and the dream be kept at arm's length. . . .

Never to have had a brilliant dream, and never to have had any delirium, would be to live too much in the day; and hardly less would be the loss of him who had not exercised his waking thought under the influence of the hours claimed by dreams. And as to choosing between day and night, or guessing whether the state of day or dark is the truer and the more natural, he would be rash who should make too sure. . . .

It is in the hours of sleep that the mind, by some divine

paradox, has the extremest sense of light. Almost the most shining lines in English poetry — lines that cast sunrise shadows — are those of Blake, written confessedly from the side of night, the side of sorrow and dreams, and those dreams the dreams of little chimney-sweepers; all is as dark as he can make it with the "bags of soot"; but the boy's dream of the green plain and the river is too bright for day. So, indeed, is another brightness of Blake's, which is also, in his poem, a child's dream, and was certainly conceived by him in the hours of sleep, in which he woke to write the Songs of Innocence. . . .

ALICE MEYNELL

. . . We have before demonstrated, that during the sleep of the Body, the Soul is as it were already Separated, and in Eternity, so that both Joy and Sorrow is essential unto it, and the Soul does really enjoy either pleasure or pain. For this cause both good and evil Angels and Spirits can most easily and familiarly communicate with the Souls of men in sleep; for then the Soul is near unto their *Ubi* or Being, and there is a great affinity between them; but when the Body is awake, and all its sally-ports of the Senses wide open, to let in outward material Objects, the Soul is clothed with a dark, heavy, earthy, sensual vesture, which does as it were wholly captivate and chain this incorporeal Essence; and as those Communications, Revelations, Sights, or whatever else does happen to the Soul in Dreams and Visions, seems as nothing to the Body and Senses after waking (which is one main cause so many slight Dreams), so what is translated through the Senses, or in the outward material World is nothing to the Soul in Dreams; but the Beggar has as lofty Representations, as the King, and the poor Captive as free Enjoyments as his Judge; therefore we should consider the vast difference between the internal and external principles, and their respective Inhabitants, and that the external Eye can see only into its own Birth or Original; that is, into the Things and Light of this outward material World, as receiving its Light from thence, for nothing can see further than its own principle whence it proceeded.

For this cause no mortal man can see and communicate with Angels and Spirits by sight, and under the perfect Exercise of their outward Senses; therefore when the holy Prophets and Antients received Visions, and the good Angels and Spirits Communicated their Secrets unto them, it was always in Dreams, Ecstacies or Raptures. . . .

T. Tryon

Dreams have not yet had their due in the systems either of moralists or psychologists. Life is divided into states of action and perception. The waking condition is almost exclusively the time of action, though not altogether so. St. Augustine notes, for example, that it is sometimes possible, in dreams, for a man who is habitually watchful over himself to resist the movements of the senses, and to refuse the consent of the will to the tempting imagery aroused by them in sleep. But, as a rule, the will is wholly passive in dreams and irresponsible for all that passes in them. Inasmuch, then, as a man is his will, and becomes more or less a man by compelling it to good or abandoning it to evil, his waking and active hours are most real. But it is in dreams, or in what the world regards as of little more substance and consequence — those waking moments of perception and emotion which come and go like dreams, those " visionary gleams " that cease for most persons with the times of childhood and virginal love — that we find ourselves in contact with another kind of reality which, little as moralists have dwelt on the fact, is the essential complement of the major reality of action. . . . The man who remembers, reverences, and often dwells upon the heaven which " lies about us in our infancy," which transfigured soul and sense in the time of his howsoever " foolish " first-love, and of which the poignant rays have probably never shone with such splendour as in the few and far-between visitations of angelic power, in sleep, will find in such experience an aid to rectitude and beauty of life of quite incalculable price;

and only second in power to these sweet lures to righteousness will he find those moments of reasonable or unreasonable, waking or sleeping, suffering and terror, which also come to all men and reveal to them capacities and future possibilities of suffering far beyond those which arise from physical pain, the death of beloved persons, or any of the other ordinary calamities of life. . . .

COVENTRY PATMORE

FRENCH PEASANTS

These going home at dusk
Along the lane,
After the day's warm work,
Do not complain.

Were you to say to them,
" What does it mean?
What is it all about,
This troubled dream? "

They would not understand,
They'd go their way,
Or, if they spoke at all,
They'd surely say,

" Dawn is the time to rise,
Days are to earn
Bread and the mid-day rest,
Dusk to return;

" To be content, to pray.
To hear songs sung,
Or to make wayside love,
If one is young.

" All from the good God comes,
All then is good;
Sorrow is known to Him,
And understood."

[399]

One who had questioned all,
And was not wise,
Might be ashamed to meet
Their quiet eyes.

All is so clear to them,
All is so plain,
These who go home at dusk,
Along the lane.

MONK GIBBON

You deceive yourself, Claire, in thinking there are none so wretched as yourself! All who are unfortunate make the same assertion. I have known those who were out of all comparison more wretched; — that mentally and bodily have endured such tortures, that I would rather suffer all you have suffered during your life — than what they endured hourly. — I have not only seen a considerable portion of the world — and played a part — but I have looked into it with an experienced and thinking eye, — it is full of misery — I have sometimes thought that the planet we are dwelling in is Hell — and that we are suffering the penalty for sins we have committed in some anterior state of existence in some other planet; do we not all suffer here? — disproportionately I allow — but you have learnt to brood and dwell exclusively on your own sufferings till you fancy you are alone suffering. . . .

EDWARD TRELAWNY, to Claire Clairmont

. . . Most souls, 'tis true, but peep out once an age,
Dull, sullen prisoners in the body's cage;
Dim lights of life, that burn a length of years,
Useless, unseen, as lamps in sepulchres;
Like eastern kings, a lazy state they keep,
And close confined to their own palace, sleep. . . .

ALEXANDER POPE

[400]

. . . Men act in sleep with some conformity unto their awaked senses; and consolations or discouragements may be drawn from dreams which intimately tell us ourselves. Luther was not like to fear a spirit in the night, when such an apparition would not terrify him in the day. . . .

Death alone, not sleep, is able to put an end unto sin; and there may be a night-book of our iniquities; for beside the transgressions of the day, casuists will tell us of mortal sins in dreams, arising from evil precogitations; meanwhile human law regards not noctambulos; and if a night-walker should break his neck, or kill a man, takes no notice of it. . . .

If some have swooned, they may also have died in dreams, since death is but a confirmed swooning. Whether Plato died in a dream, as some deliver, he must rise again to inform us. That some have never dreamed, is as improbable as that some have never laughed. That children dream not the first half-year; that men dream not in some countries, with many more, are unto me sick men's dreams; dreams out of the ivory gate, and visions before midnight.

SIR THOMAS BROWNE

". . . Certain of the unnecessary pleasure and appetites I conceive to be unlawful; every one appears to have them, but in some persons they are controlled by the laws and by reason, and the better desires prevail over them — either they are wholly banished or they become few and weak; while in the case of others they are stronger, and there are more of them."

" Which appetites do you mean? "

" I mean those which are awake when the reasoning and human and ruling power is asleep; then the wild beast within us, gorged with meat or drink, starts up and having shaken off sleep, goes forth to satisfy his desires; and there is no conceivable folly or crime — not excepting incest or any other unnatural union, or parricide, or the eating of forbidden food — which at such a time, when he has parted company with all shame and sense, a man may not be ready to commit."

"Most true," he said.

"But when a man's pulse is healthy and temperate, and when before going to sleep he has awakened his rational powers, and fed them on noble thoughts and enquiries, collecting himself in meditation; after having first indulged his appetites neither too much nor too little, but just enough to lay them to sleep, and prevent them and their enjoyments and pains from interfering with the higher principle — which he leaves in the solitude of pure abstraction, free to contemplate and aspire to the knowledge of the unknown, whether in past, present, or future: when again he has allayed the passionate element, if he has a quarrel against any one — I say, when, after pacifying the two irrational principles, he rouses up the third, which is reason, before he takes his rest, then, as you know, he attains truth most nearly, and is least likely to be the sport of fantastic and lawless visions."

PLATO, translated by Benjamin Jowett

There are no good and no bad men if we take the sum of everybody's existence into account, their nights as well as their days, and allow as much reality to their dreams as to their waking hours. The unfulfilled desires of the virtuous are evil; the unfulfilled desires of the vicious are good: and conduct is not, as Matthew Arnold said, three-fourths of life; it is not even three-fourths of conduct. The desires which I do not express I must live with for ever, and endure their development, growth, transformation and degeneration within myself if I do not throw them out into the world. What dreams Marcus Aurelius must have had! Every night he must have been a sort of Tiberius. The faces of men tell us less than they should, because sleep as well as action traces lines upon them. The heads of men like Caesar Borgia, who are known to have been cruel and conscienceless, have sometimes had an exalted and ethereal beauty which has astonished all men, and have preserved even in waking a strange look of tranquillity, as if they were frozen in some delightful dream. The faces of the worst murderers can be paralleled in ugliness by the faces of the most blameless saints.

Edwin Muir

With respect to dreams in particular I desire simply to state here that they are induced on man by spirits. Thus dreams by which the future is revealed, and also truths, are caused by the spirits of God-Messiah [i.e. by angels], but other dreams by spirits that are not of God-Messiah; those dreams, however, by which men are deceived are induced by evil spirits, and thus by the devil's crew. They express themselves either by the living voice, or, most frequently by representations, of which there are innumerable kinds; and unless a person know these kinds, it is impossible for him to know the signification of representative dreams. For they are representations of things from heaven, by means of such things chiefly as are seen upon earth, and thus by the things of nature. . . . I need not mention here visions which are altogether similar to dreams; nor representations which are like them, and which sometimes appear as in clear daylight to the life in a state of wakefulness, before and after sleep. . . . Fantastical dreams . . . have a different origin.

Emanuel Swedenborg, translated by R. L. Tafel

. . . To refuse to give to dreams the weight they deserve as being often among the most impressive and even life-affecting parts of man's experience, is stupidity too great to be argued with. If to dream is to dwell in unrealities, not knowing them for such, what is the life of many but an uninterrupted dream? The wise, however, will own, with Goethe, "They are not shadows which produce a dream. I know they are eternal, for they ARE." He who has known, even once in his life, the *somnus Endymionis*, in which the Queen of Purity has visited him as being also the Queen of Love,

[403]

lifting his ideal, if not his way of life, for ever after, and convincing him that the felicity of the spirit and its senses is as far above the best of the waking life of the body as the electric light is above that of a smoky torch, will have discarded the ignorant distinction between realities and dreams, and will understand how

> Real are the dreams of gods, and smoothly pass
> Their pleasure in a long immortal dream.

COVENTRY PATMORE

The authorship of these surpassing dreams — dreams that surpass all that we can believe ourselves capable of planning and informing with so much meaning, beauty, terror — must either be our own or else must come from without. The Spirit of the Age forbids belief in exterior influences as mere superstition. But fancy is free, and we are at liberty to please ourselves with the conjecture that when our mental faculties are discharged of their duty in sleep, resting like harps from which the hand has been withdrawn, some spiritual influence may come in and take possession, turning them to its own uses. It is at least a pretty poetical kind of notion, fruitful of pleasure as flowers are or a song, of which none can make a meal. And the physiologist himself is bound to support it from his knife-and-scalpel knowledge. An honest man, he will admit that the supposed spiritual intelligence need not break in like a thief. He knows his nerve-systems, and his nerve-centres in the brain of a man, which is the study, workshop, and theatre of mind; and he will say that so little violence is needed to stir imagination, or to move and direct the springs of thought, that they will answer to a touch light as the passing of a shadow over the harp-strings of our simile. Just so light, then, may be the touch of the spiritual intelligence. But if, nevertheless, this fancy and all such must be dismissed, we are forced back upon the first alternative. The authorship of these dreams is all our own; in which case the human mind has powers which it cannot recognise as pertaining to itself, neither can it comprehend them. . . .

FREDERICK GREENWOOD

Daily experience teaches us that, during sleep, the body is at rest, and the mind is not distracted by external objects; hence, therefore, the latter can more readily and more successfully execute its operations. In dreaming, it not unfrequently happens that *many things become to us clear and exposed, which were previously concealed, things long forgotten occur to the memory, and powers which Nature often seemed to have denied to us, are developed during sleep, when the mind is reinstated in its rights.* Thus it has frequently happened to myself, who possess no natural genius for poetry, to have composed and recited very elegant Latin verses, in proper order and series, of which I could still remember some when awake. And who is so ignorant of sacred literature as not to know that God has revealed the most important matters in dreams, for no other reason than that the mind, during sleep, is more attentive, and more capable of apprehending those things which are revealed?

FREDERICK HOFFMANN

It has been objected that the soul is in our sleep either inactive (as when we do not so much as dream), or acteth irregularly and irrationally, according to the fortuitous motion of the spirits; *ergo,* it is no incorporeal, immortal substance.

To this I answer (1) that I suppose the soul is never totally inactive. I never awaked since I had the use of memory, but I found myself coming out of a dream. And I suppose they that think they dream not, think so because they forget their dreams. (2) Many a time my reason hath acted for a time as regularly, and much more forcibly, than it doth when I am awake, which showeth what it can do, though it be not ordinary.

(3) This objection is no better than another which I have

before answered; where I told you, that it argueth not that I am a horse, or no wiser than my horse, because I ride but according to his pace when he halteth or is tired. Nor doth it prove that, when I alight, I cannot go on foot. He is hard of understanding that believeth that all the glorious parts of the world above us have no nobler intellectual natures than man. Suppose there be angels, and suppose one of them should be united to a body, as our souls are, we cannot imagine but that he would actuate it, and operate in it according to its nature; as I write amiss when my pen is bad. The same I say of persons lethargick, apoplectick, delirant, etc. . . .

Richard Baxter

. . . Those who have reflected upon the experience of dreams must have become aware that the distinction of the corporeal and spirited senses is not a mere doctrine but a manifest fact. It is the " spiritual body " that enjoys and suffers in dreams. Time, again, in dreams, is not the time of nature; but it exists and is measured, as St. Thomas Aquinas says that it exists and is measured in eternity: that is, as and by the succession of perceptions. What, in waking moments, would be centuries of agony or felicity is sometimes actually endured and appears as the duration of centuries in a minute of sleep. . . .

Coventry Patmore

. . . There are many who taste in dreams a happiness they never know when awake. In the waking moments of our complex civilised life we are ever in a state of suspense which makes all great conclusions impossible; the multiplicity of the facts of life, always present to consciousness, restrains the free play of logic (except for that happy dreamer, the mathematician), and surrounds most of our pains and nearly all our pleasures with infinite qualifications; we are tied down to a sober tameness. In our dreams the fetters of civilisation are loosened, and we know the fearful joy of freedom.

In this way the Paradise of dreams has been a reservoir from which men have always drawn consolation and sweet memory and hope, even belief, the imagination and gratification of desires that the world restrained, the promise and proof of the dearest and deepest aspirations. . . .

HAVELOCK ELLIS

. . . There is surely a piece of Divinity in us, something that was before the Elements, and owes no homage unto the Sun. Nature tells me I am the Image of God, as well as Scripture. . . . In brief, I am content, and what should providence add more? Surely this is it we call happiness, and this do I enjoy; with this I am happy in a dream, and as content to enjoy a happiness in a fancy, as others in a more apparent truth and reality. There is surely a nearer apprehension of any thing that delights us in our dreams, than in our waked senses; without this I were unhappy: for my awaked judgment discontents me, ever whispering unto me, that I am from my friend; but my friendly dreams in night requite me, and make me think I am within his arms. I thank God for my happy dreams, as I do for my good rest, for there is a satisfaction in them unto reasonable desires, and such as can be content with a fit of happiness. And surely it is not a melancholy conceit to think we are all asleep in this World, and that the conceits of this life are as mere dreams to those of the next, as the Phantasms of the night, to the conceits of the day. There is an equal delusion in both, and the one doth but seem to be the emblem or picture of the other; we are somewhat more than our selves in our sleeps, and the slumber of the body seems to be but the waking of the soul. . . .

SIR THOMAS BROWNE

. . . Thus in Dreams the soul enjoys a more compleat and unmixed pleasure and delight, than is possible for any person to enjoy when awake, and in the use of the perfectest Senses; for then in the height of his Complacency, fears and appre-

[407]

hensions of losing the pleasing objects, or jealousies of others sharing with him therein, or one thing or other is apt to crowd in and interrupt his Joy. But in many *Dreams* the *Horizon is all Light,* and clear, no Cloud to be seen, and the whole seems to be so real, that nothing we possess in this world can for the time be more; insomuch, that these Joys, and delightful Transports do oft times awaken the sensitive power of the outward Nature, the thoughts and Considerations thereof is very delightful to the mind even after the waking of the Body. . . .

T. TRYON

. . . The great naturalist, Linnæus, once said that he could spend a lifetime in studying as much of the earth as he could cover with his hand. However small the patch we investigate, it will lead us back to the sun at last. There is nothing too minute or too trivial. I have often remembered with a pang, how, long years ago, I once gave pain by saying, with the arrogance of boyhood, that it was foolish to tell one's dreams. I have done penance for that remark since. " Il faut cultiver notre jardin," said the wise philosopher of the eighteenth century. I have cultivated, so far as I care to, my garden of dreams, and it scarcely seems to me that it is a large garden. Yet every path of it, I sometimes think, might lead at last to the heart of the universe.

HAVELOCK ELLIS

Apparition: Hallucination: Chance?

Strange was that dream. If it was more than dream I cannot
*   tell. . . .*

Her eyes were open, but she still beheld,
Now wide awake, the vision of her sleep. . . .

Deep into that darkness peering, long I stood there, wondering,
*   fearing. . . .*

> *" O come you from the earth? " she said,*
> *   " Or come you from the skye? "*
> *" Oh, I am from yonder churchyard,*
> *   Where my crumbling relicks lie."*

Apparition: Hallucination: Chance?

It chanced [says St. Augustine in his *De Cura pro Mortuis Habenda*,] at Carthage that the rhetorician Eulogius, who had been my disciple in that art, being (as he himself, after our return to Africa, told us the story) in course of lecturing to his disciples on Cicero's rhetorical books, as he looked over the portion of reading which he was to deliver on the following day, fell upon a certain passage, and not being able to understand it, was scarce able to sleep for the trouble of his mind: in which night, as he dreamed, I expounded to him that which he did not understand; nay, not I, but my likeness, while I was unconscious of the thing and far away beyond sea, it might be doing, or it might be dreaming, some other thing, and not in the least caring for his cares. In what way these things come about I know not; but in what way soever they come, why do we not believe it comes in the same way for a person in a dream to see a dead man, as it comes that he sees a living man? both, no doubt, neither knowing nor caring who dreams of their images, or where or when.

"Like dreams, moreover, are some visions of persons awake, who have had their senses troubled, such as phrenetic persons, or those who are mad in any way, for they, too, talk to themselves just as though they were speaking to people verily present, and as well with absent men as with present, whose images they perceive whether persons living or dead. But just as they who live are unconscious that they are seen of them and talk with them (for indeed they are not really themselves present, or themselves make speeches, but through troubled senses these persons are wrought upon by such like imaginary visions), just so they also who have departed this

[411]

life, to persons thus affected appear as present while they be absent, and are themselves utterly unconscious whether any man sees them in regard of their image."

. . . That men may sleep without being aware of it, even while walking abroad; that we may drift, while we think ourselves awake, into a semi-somnolent state for a period of time perhaps almost imperceptible is certain enough. Now, the peculiarity of sleep is to expand or contract time, as we may choose to put the case. Alfred Maury, the well-known writer on Greek religion, dreamed a long, vivid dream of the Reign of Terror, of his own trial before a Revolutionary Tribunal, and of his execution, in the moment of time during which he was awakened by the accidental fall of a rod in the canopy of his bed, which touched him on the neck. Thus even a prolonged interview with a ghost may *conceivably* be, in real time, a less than momentary dream occupying an imperceptible tenth of a second of somnolence, the sleeper not realising that he has been asleep. . . .

This theory, that apparitions come in an infinitesimal moment of sleep, while a man is conscious of his surroundings and believes himself to be awake was the current explanation of ghosts in the eighteenth century. Any educated man who " saw a ghost " or " had a hallucination " called it a " dream," as Lord Brougham and Lord Lyttelton did. But, if the death of the person seen coincided with his appearance to them, they illogically argued that, out of the innumerable multitude of dreams, some *must* coincide, accidentally, with facts. They strove to forget that though dreams in sleep are universal and countless, " dreams " in waking hours are extremely rare — unique, for instance, in Lord Brougham's own experience. Therefore, the odds against chance coincidence are very great.

Dreams only form subjects of good dream-stories when the vision coincides with and adequately represents an *unknown* event in the past, the present, or the future. . . .

ANDREW LANG

[412]

This view [namely, that a " ghost " may be a reflection of a dead man's dream] will become less difficult to understand if we ask ourselves what natural thing most resembles the common idea of a ghost. You are reading alone at night, let us say, the door opens and a human figure glides into the room. To you it pays no manner of attention; it does not answer if you speak; it may trifle with some object in the chamber and then steal quietly out again. *It is the House-maid walking in her Sleep.*

This perfectly accountable appearance, in its aimlessness, its unconsciousness, its irresponsiveness, is undeniably just like the common notion of a ghost. Now, if ordinary ghosts are not of flesh and blood, like the sleep-walking house-maid, yet are as irresponsive, as unconscious, and as vaguely wandering as she, then (if the dead are somewhat) a ghost *may* be a hallucination produced in the living by the *unconscious* action of the mind of the dreaming dead. The conception is at least conceivable. . . .

Andrew Lang

From thence we went to the Lady Honor O'Brien's, a lady that went for a maid, but few believed it; she was the youngest daughter of the Earl of Thomond. There we stayed three nights. The first of which I was surprised by being laid in a chamber, when, about one o'clock, I heard a voice that wakened me. I drew the curtain, and, in the casement of the window, I saw, by the light of the moon, a woman leaning into the window, through the casement, in white, with red hair and pale and ghastly complexion: she spoke loud, and in a tone I had never heard, thrice, " a horse "; and then, with a sigh more like the wind than breath, she vanished, and to me her body looked more like a thick cloud than substance. I was so much frightened, that my hair stood on end, and my night clothes fell off. I pulled and pinched your father, who never woke during the disorder I was in; but at last was much surprised to see me in this fright, and more so when I related the story and showed him the window opened. Neither of us slept any more that night, but he entertained me with telling me how much more these apparitions were usual in this country than in England; and we concluded the cause to be the great superstition of the Irish, and the want of that knowing faith, which should defend them from the power of the Devil, which he exercises among them very much. About five o'clock the lady of the house came to see us, saying she had not been in bed all night, because a cousin O'Brien of hers, whose ancestors had owned that house, had desired her to stay with him in his chamber, and that he died at two o'clock, and she said, " I wish you to have had no disturbance, for 'tis the custom of the place, that, when any of the family are dying, the shape of a woman appears in the window every night till they be dead. This woman was many ages ago got with child by the owner of this place, who murdered her in his garden, and flung her into the river under the window, but truly I thought not of it when I lodged you here, it being the best room in the house." We made little reply to her speech, but disposed ourselves to be gone suddenly.

LADY FANSHAWE

AN APPARITION OF MILTON

What would you give to have such a dream about Milton, as I had about a week since? I dreamed that, being in a house in the city, and with much company, looking towards the lower end of the room from the upper end of it, I descried a figure, which I immediately knew to be Milton's. He was very gravely, but very neatly attired in the fashion of his day, and had a countenance which filled me with those feelings that an affectionate child has for a beloved father. . . . My first thought was wonder, where he could have been concealed so many years; my second, a transport of joy to find him still alive; my third, another transport to find myself in his company; and my fourth, a resolution to accost him. I did so, and he received me with a complacence, in which I saw equal sweetness and dignity. I spoke of his Paradise Lost, as every man must, who is worthy to speak of it at all, and told him a long story of the manner in which it affected me, when I first discovered it, being at that time a schoolboy. He answered me by a smile, and a gentle inclination of his head. He then grasped my hand affectionately, and with a smile that charmed me said, " Well, you for your part will do well also." At last recollecting his great age (for I understood him to be two hundred years old,) I feared that I might fatigue him by much talking; I took my leave, and he took his with an air of the most perfect good breeding. His person, his features, his manner, were all so perfectly characteristic, that I am persuaded an apparition of him could not represent him more completely.

WILLIAM COWPER

Sometimes I am rewarded for fretting myself so much about present matters by a quite unasked-for pleasant dream. I mean when I am asleep. This dream is as it were a present of an architectural peep-show. I see some beautiful and noble building new made, as it were for the occasion, as clearly as if I were awake; not vaguely or absurdly, as often happens in dreams, but with all the detail clear and reasonable. Some Elizabethan house with its scrap of earlier fourteenth-century building, and its later degradations of Queen Anne and Silly Billy and Victoria, marring but not destroying it, in an old village once a clearing amid the sandy woodlands of Sussex. Or an old and unusually curious church, much churchwardened, and beside it a fragment of fifteenth-century domestic architecture amongst the not unpicturesque lath and plaster of an Essex farm, and looking natural enough among the sleepy elms and the meditative hens scratching about in the litter of the farmyard, whose trodden yellow straw comes up to the very jambs of the richly carved Norman doorway of the church. Or sometimes 'tis a splendid collegiate church, untouched by restoring parson and architect, standing amid an island of shapely trees and flower-beset cottages of thatched grey stone and cob, amidst the narrow stretch of bright green water-meadows that wind between the sweeping Wiltshire downs, so well beloved of William Cobbett. Or some new-seen and yet familiar cluster of houses in a grey village of the upper Thames overtopped by the delicate tracery of a four-teenth-century church; or even sometimes the very buildings of the past untouched by the degradation of the sordid utili-tarianism that cares not and knows not of beauty and history: as once, when I was journeying (in a dream of the night) down the well-remembered reaches of the Thames betwixt Streatley and Wallingford, where the foot-hills of the White Horse fall back from the broad stream, I came upon a clear-seen mediaeval town standing up with roof and tower and spire within its walls, grey and ancient, but untouched from the days of its builders of old. All this I have seen in the dreams of the night clearer than I can force myself to see them in dreams of the day. So that it would have been nothing new to me the other night to fall into an architectural dream if that were all, and yet I have to tell of things strange and new that befell me after I had fallen asleep. . . .

WILLIAM MORRIS, from *A Dream of John Ball*

Many years ago, when I was looking over Piranesi's " An-tiquities of Rome," Coleridge, then standing by, described to me a set of plates from that artist, called his " Dreams," and which record the scenery of his own visions during the delirium of a fever. Some of these (I describe only from memory of Coleridge's account) represented vast Gothic halls; on the floor of which stood mighty engines and ma-chinery, wheels, cables, catapults, &c., expressive of enormous power put forth, or resistance overcome. Creeping along the sides of the walls, you perceived a staircase; and upon this, groping his way upwards, was Piranesi himself. Follow the stairs a little farther, and you perceive them reaching an ab-rupt termination, without any balustrade, and allowing no step onwards to him who should reach the extremity, except into the depths below. Whatever is to become of poor Piranesi, at least you suppose that his labours must now in some way terminate. But raise your eyes, and behold a second flight of stairs still higher, on which again Piranesi is perceived, by this time standing on the very brink of the abyss. Once again elevate your eye, and a still more aerial flight of stairs is described; and there, again, is the delirious Piranesi, busy on his aspiring labours: and so on, until the unfinished stairs and the hopeless Piranesi both are lost in the upper gloom of the hall. With the same power of endless growth and self-reproduction did my architecture proceed in dreams. In the early stages of the malady, the splendours of my dreams were indeed chiefly architectural; and I beheld such pomp of cities and palaces as never yet was beheld by the waking eye, unless in the clouds.

THOMAS DE QUINCEY

The following dream, to which . . . a predisposition must always have existed in my mind . . . having been once roused, . . . never left me, and split into a thousand fantastic variations, which often suddenly re-combined; locked back into startling unity, and restored the original dream.

I thought that it was a Sunday morning in May; that it was Easter Sunday, and as yet very early in the morning. I was standing, as it seemed to me, at the door of my own cottage. Right before me lay the very scene which could really be commanded from that situation, but exalted, as was usual, and solemnised by the power of dreams. There were the same mountains, and the same lovely valley at their feet; but the mountains were raised to more than Alpine height, and there was interspace far larger between them of savannahs and forest lawns; the hedges were rich with white roses; and no living creature was to be seen, excepting that in the green churchyard there were cattle tranquilly reposing upon the verdant graves, and particularly round about the grave of a child whom I had once tenderly loved, just as I had really beheld them, a little before sunrise, in the same summer when that child died. I gazed upon the well-known scene, and I said to myself, "It yet wants much of sunrise; and it is Easter Sunday; and that is the day on which they celebrate the first-fruits of Resurrection. I will walk abroad; old griefs shall be forgotten to-day: for the air is cool and still, and the hills are high, and stretch away to heaven; and the churchyard is as verdant as the forest lawns, and the forest lawns are as quiet as the churchyard; and with the dew I can wash the fever from my forehead; and then I shall be unhappy no longer." I turned, as if to open my garden gate, and immediately I saw upon the left a scene far different; but which yet the power of dreams had reconciled into harmony. The scene was an oriental one; and there also it was Easter Sunday, and very early in the morning. And at a vast distance were visible, as a stain upon the horizon, the domes and cupolas of a great city — an image or faint abstraction, caught perhaps in childhood from some picture of Jerusalem. And not a bow-shot from me, upon a stone, shaded by Judaean palms, there sat a woman; and I looked, and it was — Ann! She fixed her eyes upon me earnestly; and I said to her at length, " So, then, I have found you at last." I waited; but she answered me not a word. Her face was the same as when I saw it last; the same, and yet, again, how different! Seventeen years ago, when the lamp-light of mighty London fell upon her face, as for the last time I kissed her lips, . . . her eyes were streaming with tears. The tears were now no longer seen. Sometimes she seemed altered; yet again sometimes *not* altered; and hardly older. Her looks were tranquil, but with unusual solemnity of expression, and I now gazed upon her with some awe. Suddenly her countenance grew dim; and, turning to the mountains, I perceived vapours rolling between us; in a moment all had vanished; thick darkness came on; and in the twinkling of an eye I was far away from mountains, and by lamp-light in London, walking again with Ann — just as we had walked, when both children, eighteen years before, along the endless terraces of Oxford Street.

Then suddenly would come a dream of far different character — a tumultuous dream — commencing with a music

such as now I often heard in sleep — music of preparation
and of awakening suspense. The undulations of fast-gather-
ing tumults were like the opening of the Coronation Anthem;
and, like *that*, gave the feeling of a multitudinous movement,
of infinite cavalcades filing off, and the tread of innumerable
armies. The morning was come of a mighty day — a day of
crisis and of ultimate hope for human nature, then suffering
mysterious eclipse, and labouring in some dread extremity.
Somewhere, but I knew not where — somehow, but I knew
not how — by some beings, but I knew not by whom — a
battle, a strife, an agony, was travelling through all its stages
— was evolving itself, like the catastrophe of some mighty
drama, with which my sympathy was the more insupportable,
from deepening confusion as to its local scene, its cause, its
nature, and its undecipherable issue. I (as is usual in dreams
where, of necessity, we make ourselves central to every movement) had the power, and yet had not the power, to decide
it. I had the power, if I could raise myself to will it; and yet
again had not the power, for the weight of twenty Atlantics
was upon me, or the oppression of inexpiable guilt. " Deeper
than ever plummet sounded," I lay inactive. Then, like a
chorus, the passion deepened. Some greater interest was at
stake, some mightier cause, than ever yet the sword had
pleaded, or trumpet had proclaimed. Then came sudden
alarms; hurryings to and fro; trepidations of innumerable
fugitives; I knew not whether from the good cause or the bad;
darkness and lights; tempest and human faces; and at last,
with the sense that all was lost, female forms, and the features
that were worth all the world to me; and but a moment allowed — and clasped hands, with heart-breaking partings,
and then — everlasting farewells! and, with a sigh such as the
caves of hell sighed when the incestuous mother uttered the
abhorred name of Death, the sound was reverberated — everlasting farewells! and again, and yet again reverberated —
everlasting farewells!

THOMAS DE QUINCEY
from *Confessions of an English Opium Eater*

[In 1612, when John Donne was in his thirty-ninth year, he accompanied his friend, Sir Robert Drury, and Lord Hay, on an embassy to France — much against the desire of his wife who was then with child, and in ill health. " Her divining soul boded her some ill in his absence "; however, Donne was persuaded. The journey to Paris was completed on the twelfth day].

" Two days," Izaac Walton records, " after their arrival there, Mr. Donne was left alone in that room, in which Sir Robert, and he, and some other friends had dined together. To this place Sir Robert returned within half an hour; and as he left, so he found, Mr. Donne alone; but in such an ecstasy, and so altered as to his looks, as amazed Sir Robert to behold him; insomuch that he earnestly desired Mr. Donne to declare what had befallen him in the short time of his absence. To which Mr. Donne was not able to make a present answer: but, after a long and perplexed pause, did at last say, ' I have seen a dreadful vision since I saw you: I have seen my dear wife pass twice by me through this room, with her hair hanging about her shoulders, and a dead child in her arms: this I have seen since I saw you.' To which Sir Robert replied, ' Sure, Sir, you have slept since I saw you; and this is the result of some melancholy dream, which I desire you to forget, for you are now awake.' To which Mr. Donne's reply was: ' I cannot be surer that I now live, than that I have not slept since I saw you: and am as sure, that at her second appearing, she stopped, and looked me in the face, and vanished.' " . . .

[Rest and sleep only confirmed his confidence. A servant was immediately sent to England. On his return, he informed Donne] " that he found and left Mrs. Donne very sad, and sick in her bed; and that, after a long and dangerous labour, she had been delivered of a dead child. And, upon examination, the abortion proved to be the same day, and about the very hour, that Mr. Donne affirmed he saw her pass by him in his chamber.

" This is a relation that will beget some wonder, and it well may; for most of our world are at present possessed with an opinion, that Visions and Miracles are ceased. And, though it is most certain, that two lutes being both strung and tuned to an equal pitch, and then one played upon, the other, that is not touched, being laid upon a table at a fit distance, will — like an echo to a trumpet — warble a faint audible harmony in answer to the same tune; yet many will not believe there is any such thing as a sympathy of souls; and I am well pleased, that every Reader do enjoy his own opinion." . . .

IZAAC WALTON

. . . Mr. Edmund Halley, R.S.S., was carried on with a strong impulse to take a voyage to St. Hellens, to make observations of the southern constellations, being then about twenty-four years old. Before he undertook his voyage, he dreamt that he was at sea, sailing towards that place, and saw the prospect of it from the ship in his dream, which he declared to the Royal Society, to be the perfect representation of that island, even as he had it really when he approached to it. . . .

JOHN AUBREY

In 1898, when I was staying at an hotel in Sussex, I dreamed, one night, that I was having an argument with one of the waiters as to what was the current time. I asserted that it was half-past four in the afternoon: he maintained that it was half-past four in the middle of the night. With the apparent illogicality peculiar to all dreams, I concluded that my watch must have stopped; and, on extracting that instrument from my waistcoat pocket, I saw, looking down on it, that this was precisely the case. It had stopped — with the hands at half-past four. With that I awoke.

The dream had been a peculiar one (in ways which have nothing to do with this book), and the net result of it all was that I lit a match to see whether the watch had really stopped. To my surprise it was not, as it usually is, by my bedside. I got out of bed, hunted round, and found it lying on the chest

[421]

of drawers. Sure enough, it *had* stopped, and the hands stood at half-past four.

The solution seemed perfectly obvious. The watch must have stopped during the previous afternoon. I must have noticed this, forgotten it, and remembered it in my dream. Satisfied on that point, I rewound the instrument, but, not knowing the real time, I left the hands as they were.

On coming downstairs next morning, I made straight for the nearest clock, with the object of setting the watch right. For if, as I supposed, it had stopped during the previous afternoon, and had merely been rewound at some unknown hour of the night, it was likely to be out by several hours.[1]

To my absolute amazement I found that the hands had lost only some two or three minutes — *about the amount of time which had elapsed between my waking from the dream and rewinding the watch.*

This suggested, of course, that the watch had stopped at the actual moment of the dream.[2] The latter was probably brought about by my missing the accustomed ticking. But — how did I come to see, in that dream, that the hands stood, as they actually did, at half-past four?

If anyone else had told me such a tale I should probably have replied that he had dreamed the whole episode, from beginning to end, including the getting up and re-winding. But that was an answer I could not give to myself. I *knew* that I had been awake when I had risen and looked at the watch lying on the chest of drawers. Yet, what was the alternative? "Clairvoyance" — seeing across space through darkness and closed eyelids? Even supposing that there existed unknown rays which could effect that sort of pene-

---

[1] In other words, it was extremely unlikely that I should have dreamed of half-past four at precisely half-past four. A correspondent, Mr. C. G. Newland, points out that I should make this more clear since the question was essentially one of probability.

[2] The improbability of my having dreamed of half-past four *at* half-past four must be multiplied by the improbability of my having been bothered by a stopped watch on the previous afternoon without retaining the faintest recollection of such a fact.

tration, and then produce vision — which I did not believe — the watch had been lying at a level above that of my eyes. What sort of rays could these be which bent round corners? . . .[3]

J. W. DUNNE

The most important ceremony in which I was officially concerned was the Coronation of King Edward [VII]. By this time all the Departments of State were thoroughly accustomed to large ceremonies, which they had not been in 1887; and, as they received long notice through the postponement of the ceremony until the Autumn, owing to the serious illness of H.M., everything was more or less easy and eventually went off without a hitch.

Before the Coronation I had a remarkable dream. The State coach had to pass through the Arch at the Horse Guards on the way to Westminster Abbey. I dreamed that it stuck in the Arch, and that some of the Life Guards on duty were compelled to hew off the Crown upon the coach before it could be freed. When I told the Crown Equerry, Colonel Ewart, he laughed and said, " What do dreams matter? " " At all events," I replied, " let us have the coach and Arch measured." So this was done, and, to my astonishment, we found that the Arch was nearly two feet too low to allow the coach to pass through. I returned to Colonel Ewart in triumph, and said, " What do you think of dreams now? " " I think it's damned fortunate you had one," he replied. It appears that the State coach had not been driven through the Arch for some time, and that the level of the road had since been raised during repairs. So I am not sorry that my dinner disagreed with me that night; and I only wish all nightmares were as useful.

WILLIAM CAVENDISH-BENTINCK,
DUKE OF PORTLAND

[3 This is but one of many curious and remarkable dreams related by Mr. J. W. Dunne in *An Experiment with Time*, and in its sequels. These he maintains to have been of a prophetic or precognitive nature, and on their evidence he in part bases his theory of " serial Time ".]

One night I dreamt that, making a call on some matter of business I was shown into a fine great drawing-room and asked to wait. Accordingly, I went over to the fire-place in the usual English way, proposing to wait there. And there, after the same fashion, I lounged with my arm upon the mantel-piece; but only for a few moments. For feeling that my fingers had rested on something strangely cold, I looked, and saw that they lay on a dead hand: a woman's hand newly cut from the wrist.

Though I woke in horror on the instant, this dream was quite forgotten — at any rate for the time — when I did next day make a call on some unimportant matter of business, was shown into a pretty little room adorned with various knick-knacks, and then was asked to wait. Glancing by chance toward the mantel-piece (the dream of the previous night still forgotten), what should I see upon it but the hand of a mummy, broken from the wrist. It was a very little hand, and on it was a ring that would have been a " gem ring " if the dull red stone in it had been genuinely precious. Wherefore I concluded that it was a woman's hand.

Coincidence. The dream certainly taught nothing, and had no discernible purpose. Yet visions of severed hands on mantel-pieces are not common, and, with or without previous dreaming of it, few men have actually seen one, even when taken from a mummy case, in that precise situation. Now had I myself rifled the tomb where she reposed from whom the relic was torn, or had I by any means acquired that poor little brown hand to make bric-a-brac of it, my dream would have been pertinent enough. Then it would have made a pretty tale, with a moral that is not unneeded, perhaps. But, as it is, we can make nothing better of it than a dream gone astray.

FREDERICK GREENWOOD

The belief that the gods revealed themselves and declared their will to mankind in dreams was widespread in antiquity;

and accordingly people resorted to temples and other sacred spots for the purpose of sleeping there and holding converse with the higher powers in visions of the night, for they naturally supposed that the deities or the deified spirits of the dead would be most likely to manifest themselves in places specially dedicated to their worship. For example, at Oropus in Attica there was a sanctuary of the dead soothsayer Amphiaraus, where inquirers used to sacrifice rams to him and to other divine beings, whose names were inscribed on the altar; and having offered the sacrifice they spread the skins of the rams on the ground and slept on them, expecting revelations in dreams. . . .

A wild, romantic, densely wooded glen leads down to the ruins of the ancient Epidaurus, beautifully situated on a rocky promontory, which juts out into the sea from a plain covered with lemon groves and backed by high wooded mountains. Patients who had slept in the sanctuary of Aesculapius at Epidaurus, and had been healed of their infirmities through the revelations accorded to them in dreams, used to commemorate the cures on tablets, which were set up in the holy place as eloquent testimonies to the restorative powers of the god and to the saving faith of those who put their trust in him. The sacred precinct was crowded with such tablets in antiquity, and some of them have been discovered in modern times. The inscriptions shed a curious light on institutions which in some respects answered to the hospitals of modern times. . . .

Another ancient and revered Italian oracle was that of Faunus, and the mode of consulting him was similar. The inquirer sacrificed a sheep, spread out its skin on the ground, and sleeping on it received an answer in a dream. If the seat of the oracle was, as there is reason to think, in a sacred grove beside the cascade at Tibur, the solemn shade of the trees and the roar of the tumbling waters might well inspire the pilgrim with religious awe and mingle with his dreams. The little circular shrine, which still overhangs the waterfall, may have been the very spot where the rustic god was believed to whisper in the ears of his slumbering votaries. . . .

SIR JAMES GEORGE FRAZER

To the query: Is divination through dreams unlawful? St. Thomas Aquinas replied: The whole question consists in determining the cause of dreams, and examining whether the same may be the cause of future events, or at least come to the actual knowledge of them. Dreams come sometimes from internal, and sometimes from external, causes. Two kinds of internal causes influence our dreams: one animal, inasmuch as such images remain in a sleeping man's fantasy as were dwelt upon by him while awake; the other found in the body: it is indeed a well-known fact that the actual disposition of the body causes a reaction on the fantasy. Now it is self-evident that neither of these causes has any influence on individual future events. Our dreams may likewise be the effects of a two-fold external cause. This is corporeal when exterior agencies, such as the atmospheric conditions or others, act on the imagination of the sleeper. Finally dreams may be caused by spiritual agencies, such as God, directly or indirectly through his angels, and the devil. It is easy to conclude thence what chances there are to know the future from dreams, and when divination will be lawful or unlawful. . . .

"The Bourne..."

My soul, sit thou a patient looker-on,
Judge not the play until the play is done,
Her plot hath many changes; every day
Speaks a new scene; the last act crowns the play. . . .

I seemed to move among a world of ghosts
  And feel myself the shadow of a dream. . . .

"The Bourne..."

DEATH AND THE WOODMAN

A poor old Woodman with a leafy load,
 Both with his faggots and his years bowed down,
Groaning, with heavy steps along the road
Laboured to reach his hovel smoked and brown.
At last, with toil and pain exhausted quite,
He dropt the boughs to muse upon his plight.
What pleasure had he known since he was born?
In th' whole round world was any more forlorn?
Often no bread, never an hour of rest:
His wife, his children, soldiers foraging,
Forced labour, debt, the taxes for the King —
The finished picture of a life unblest!
He called on Death, who instantly stood by,
And asked of him, " What is't you lack? "
" I wanted you," was the reply,
" To help me load this wood upon my back."

Death can take all ills away;
But here we are, and here would stay.
Better to suffer than to die
Is Everyman's philosophy.

JEAN DE LA FONTAINE,
translated by Sir Edward Marsh

. . . When thou hast lived to that Age thou desirest, or one of *Plato's* Years, so soon as the last of thy Days riseth above thy Horizon, thou wilt then, as now, demand longer Respite, and expect more to come. The oldest are most unwilling to die. It is Hope of long Life that maketh Life seem short. Heaven foreknowing imminent Harms, taketh those which it loves to itself before they fall forth. Death in Youth is like the leaving a superfluous Feast before the drunken Cups be presented. Life is a Journey in a dusty Way, the furthest Rest is Death, in this some go more heavily burdened than others: Swift and active Pilgrims come to the End of it in the Morning or at Noon, which Tortoise-paced Wretches, clogged with the fragmentary Rubbish of this World, scarce with great Travel crawl unto at Midnight. Days are not to be esteemed after the Number of them, but after the Goodness. More Compass maketh not a Sphere more compleat, but as round is a little as a large Ring; nor is that Musician most praiseworthy who hath longest played, but he in measured Accents who hath made sweetest Melody.

WILLIAM DRUMMOND

. . . Upon an everlasting tide
    Into the silent seas we go;
But verdure laughs along the side,
    And roses on the margin blow.

Nor life, nor death, nor aught they hold,
    Rate thou above their natural height;
Yet learn that all our eyes behold,
    Has value, if we mete it right.

Pluck then the flowers that line the stream,
    Instead of fighting with its power;
But pluck as flowers, not gems, nor deem
    That they will bloom beyond their hour.

Whate'er betides, from day to day,
 An even pulse and spirit keep;
And like a child, worn out with play,
 When wearied with existence, sleep.

SIR FRANCIS HASTINGS DOYLE,
from " The Epicurean "

Come, cheerful day, part of my life, to me:
For while thou view'st me with thy fading light,
Part of my life doth still depart with thee,
And I still onward haste to my last night.
 Time's fatal wings do ever forward fly,
 So every day we live a day we die.

But, O ye nights, ordained for barren rest,
How are my days deprived of life in you,
When heavy sleep my soul hath dispossest,
By feignèd death life sweetly to renew!
 Part of my life that, you life deny:
 So every day we live a day we die.

THOMAS CAMPION

When first I stept into the alluring maze
 To tread this world's mysterious ways,
  Alas! I had nor guide, nor clue,
 No Ariadne lent her hand,
Not one of Virtue's guards did bid me stand,
 Or asked me what I meant to do,
  Or whither I would go:
This labyrinth so pleasant did appear,
 I lost myself with much content,
  Infinite hazards underwent,
 Out-straggled Homer's crafty wanderer,

[431]

And ten years more than he in fruitless travels spent;
   The one half of my life is gone,
   The shadow the meridian past;
   Death's dismal evening drawing on,
Which must with damps and mists be overcast,
   An evening that will surely come,
'Tis time, high time to give myself the welcome home. . . .

      Thomas Flatman, from "The Review"

    Night, and the wisdom of eternal loss,
      and down the straight road, far as I can spy,
      a form goes plodding, and that form is I,
    a fated stone that cannot gather moss.

    But faintly through the darkness he hears come
      the echo of another's feet, and squares
      his shoulders 'neath the burden that he bears,
    steps out — and empty is the dark and dumb.

              Charles Williams

UP–HILL

Does the road wind up-hill all the way?
   Yes, to the very end.
Will the day's journey take the whole long day?
   From morn to night, my friend.

But is there for the night a resting-place?
   A roof for when the slow dark hours begin.
May not the darkness hide it from my face?
   You cannot miss that inn.

Shall I meet other wayfarers at night?
   Those who have gone before.
Then must I knock, or call when just in sight?
   They will not keep you standing at that door.

Shall I find comfort, travel-sore and weak?
   Of labour you shall find the sum.
Will there be beds for me and all who seek?
   Yea, beds for all who come.

CHRISTINA ROSSETTI

They are all gone into the world of light!
   And I alone sit ling'ring here;
Their very memory is fair and bright,
   And my sad thoughts doth clear.

It glows and glitters in my cloudy brest
   Like stars upon some gloomy grove,
Or those faint beams in which this hill is drest,
   After the Sun's remove.

I see them walking in an Air of glory,
   Whose light doth trample on my days:
My days, which are best but dull and hoary,
   Meer glimering and decays.

O holy hope! and high humility,
   High as the Heavens above!
These are your walks, and you have shewed them me
   To kindle my cold love,

Dear, beauteous death! the Jewel of the Just,
   Shining no where, but in the dark;
What mysteries do lie beyond thy dust;
   Could man outlook that mark!

He that hath found some fledged bird's nest, may know
   At first sight, if the bird be flown;
But what fair Well, or Grove he sings in now,
   That is to him unknown.

[433]

And yet, as Angels in some brighter dreams
    Call to the soul, when man doth sleep:
So some strange thoughts transcend our wonted theams,
    And into glory peep. . . .

HENRY VAUGHAN

We saw a scraggy-looking fellow, nearly black, and wearing nothing but a cloth round the loins: he was tending flocks. Afterwards I came up with another of these goatherds, whose helpmate was with him. They gave us some goat's milk, a welcome present. I pitied the poor devil of a goatherd for having such a very plain wife. I spend an enormous quantity of pity upon that particular form of human misery.

About mid-day I began to examine my map, and to question my guide. He at first tried to elude inquiry, then suddenly fell on his knees, and confessed that he knew nothing of the country. I was thus thrown upon my own resources, and calculating that, on the preceding day, we had nearly performed a two days' journey, I concluded that the Dead Sea must be near. In this I was right; for at about three or four o'clock in the afternoon I caught a first sight of its dismal face.

I went on, and came near to those waters of Death; they stretched deeply into the southern desert, and before me, and all around, as far away as the eye could follow, blank hills piled high over hills, pale, yellow, and naked, walled up in her tomb for ever the dead and damned Gomorrah. There was no fly that hummed in the forbidden air, but, instead, a deep stillness — no grass grew from the earth — no weed peered through the void sand; but, in mockery of all life, there were trees borne down by Jordan in some ancient flood, and these, grotesquely planted upon the forlorn shore, spread out their grim skeleton arms all scorched, and charred to blackness, by the heats of the long, silent years. . . .

A. W. KINGLAKE

. . . Sleep is, in a way, a happier, more peaceful state than waking and, in a way, death may be said to be better than life, but it is in a very small way. We feel such talk to be blasphemy against good life and, whatever we may say in death's favour, so long as we do not blow our brains out we show that we do not mean to be taken seriously. To know good, other than as a heavy sleeper, we must know vice also. There cannot, as Bacon said, be a " Hold fast that which is good " without a " Prove all things " going before it. There is no knowledge of good without a knowledge of evil also, and this is why all nations have devils as well as gods, and regard them with sneaking kindness. . . .

SAMUEL BUTLER

DEATH

'Tis of all sleeps the sweetest;
Children begin it to us, strong men seek it,
And kings from heights of all their painted glories
Fall, like spent exhalations, to this centre:
And those are fools that fear it, or imagine
A few unhandsome pleasures, or life's profits,
Can recompense this place; and mad that stay it,
Till age blow out their lights, or rotten humours
Bring them dispersèd to the earth. . . .

JOHN FLETCHER

Like to the falling of a star,
Or as the flights of eagles are;
Or like the fresh spring's gaudy hue,
Or silver drops of morning dew;
Or like a wind that chafes the flood,
Or bubbles which on water stood:

[435]

Even such is man, whose borrowed light
Is straight called in, and paid to night.
The wind blows out; the bubble dies;
The spring entombed in autumn lies;
The dew dries up; the star is shot;
The flight is past; and man forgot.

HENRY KING

DUKE. How strange it is that I can live to-day;
    Nay look like other men, who have been sleeping
    On quiet pillows and not dreamt! Methinks
    The look of the world's a lie, a face made up
    O'er graves and fiery depths; and nothing's true
    But what is horrible. — Luckless man
    Avoids the miserable bodkin's point,
    And, flinching from the insect's little sting,
    In pitiful security keeps watch,
    While 'twixt him and that hypocrite the sun,
    To which he prays, comes windless pestilence,
    Transparent as a glass of poisoned water
    Through which the drinker sees his murderer smiling;
    She stirs no dust, and makes no grass to nod,
    Yet every footstep is a thousand graves,
    And every breath of hers as full of ghosts
    As a sunbeam with motes. . . .

THOMAS LOVELL BEDDOES,
from *Death's Jest-Book, Act IV, Scene I*

VALUES

Till darkness lays a hand on these gray eyes
And out of man my ghost is sent alone,
It is my chance to know that force and size
Are nothing but by answered undertone.

No beauty even of absolute perfection
Dominates here — the glance, the pause, the guess
Must be my amulets of resurrection;
Raindrops may murder, lightnings may caress.

There I was tortured, but I cannot grieve;
There crowned and palaced — visibles deceive.
That storm of belfried cities in my mind
Leaves me my vespers cool and eglantined.
From love's wide-flowering mountain-side I chose
This sprig of green, in which an angel shows.

EDMUND BLUNDEN

GIGANTIC DOCTOR

Gigantic doctor, stalking visibly
Out of the freezing north, cadaver calm,
Energic, Death, thy stature takes earth, sky,
And sea with resolution, steady balm
And satisfying, anaesthetic end
Of struggle, white, inexorable friend!

Mirror which flatters not, essential need
Which, expurgating, blesses, architect
Of brains and systems into one square creed
Osseous, subterranean, dissect
My frenzied grief, or petrify the skull
With one drop of thy kindly balsam dull!

E. H. W. MEYERSTEIN

BEDTIME

And now the Day which in the Morne was thine,
Poor Heart, is gone, and can returne no more:
Bury'd in this dark ev'n it goes before,
And tells Me it the next Night may be mine,

Nay why not this? A surer thing is Death
By far than sleep: That nightly drowsy Mist
Which climbs into thy Braine to give Thee Rest,
May by the way obstruct thy feeble Breath.

The Day is gone; and well, if only gone,
Is it not lost? Cast up thy scorn and know
Art so much neerer Heaven as Thou art to
Thy Death; or did thy life without Thee run?

Alas it ran, and for me would not stay,
Who waited on my fruitlesse Vanities.
I might have travl'd far since I did rise,
In praying and in studying hard to-day.

Great Lord of Life and Time, reprieve me still,
Whom My owne Sentence hath condemn'd; That I
May learne to live my Life before I die,
And teach my owne, to follow Thy Sweet Will.

JOSEPH BEAUMONT

To die is only to be as we were before we were born; yet
no one feels any remorse, or regret, or repugnance, in contemplating this last idea. It is rather a relief and disburthen-
ing of the mind; it seems to have been holiday-time with us
then; we were not called to appear upon the stage of life, to
wear robes or tatters, to laugh or cry, be hooted or applauded;
we had lain *perdus* all this while, snug, out of harm's way; and
had slept out our thousands of centuries without wanting to
be waked up; at peace and free from care, in a long nonage,
in a sleep deeper and calmer than that of infancy, wrapped in
the softest and finest dust. And the worst that we dread is,
after a short, fretful, feverish being, after vain hopes and idle
fears, to sink to final repose again, and forget the troubled
dream of life. . . .

WILLIAM HAZLITT

Death is a thing that every one suffers, even persons of the lowest resolution, of the meanest vertue, of no breeding, of no discourse. Take away but the pomps of death, the disguises and solemn bug-bears, the tinsell, and the actings by candle-light, and proper and phantastic ceremonies, the minstrels and the noise-makers, the women and the weepers, the swoonings and the shrikings, the Nurses and the Physicians, the dark room and the Ministers, the Kinred and the Watchers, and then to die is easie, ready and quitted from its troublesome circumstances. It is the same harmelesse thing, that a poor shepherd suffered yesterday, or a maid servant to day; and at the same time in which you die, in that very night, a thousand creatures die with you, some wise men, and many fools; and the wisdom of the first will not quit him, and the folly of the latter does not make him unable to die.

JEREMY TAYLOR

. . . It is therefore Death alone that can suddenly make man to know himselfe. He tells the proud and insolent, that they are but Abjects, and humbles them at the instant; makes them crie, complaine, and repent, yea, even to hate their fore-passed happinesse. He takes the account of the rich, and proves him a beggar; a naked beggar, which hath interest in nothing, but in the gravell that fills his mouth. He holds a glasse before the eyes of the most beautifull, and makes them see therein their deformitie and rottennesse, and they acknowledge it.

O eloquent, just, and mighty Death! whom none could advise, thou hast perswaded; what none hath dared thou hast done; and whom all the world hath flattered, thou only hast cast out of the world and despised: thou hast drawne together all the farre-stretched greatnesse, all the pride, crueltie, and ambition of man, and covered it all over with these two narrow words, *Hic jacet.*

SIR WALTER RALEIGH

PLAINT

Dark, deep, and cold the current flows
Unto the sea where no wind blows,
Seeking the land which no one knows. . . .

Though myriads go with him who goes,
Alone he goes where no wind blows,
Unto the land which no one knows.

For all must go where no wind blows,
And none can go for him who goes,
None, none return whence no one knows. . . .

O shoreless Deep, where no wind blows!
And, thou, O Land which no one knows! —
That God is All, His shadow shows!

EBENEZER ELLIOT

TO HIS SOUL

Poor little, pretty, fluttering thing,
   Must we no longer live together?
And dost thou prune thy trembling wing,
   To take thy flight thou know'st not whither?

Thy humorous vein, thy pleasing folly,
   Lies all neglected, all forgot:
And pensive, wavering, melancholy,
   Thou dread'st and hop'st thou know'st not what.

MATTHEW PRIOR

"That Glassy Interval"

Oh, that I could take
So sound a sleep that I might never wake. . . .

The night grows horrible, and all about me like
my black purpose. . . .

Death is the veil which those who live call life;
They sleep, and it is lifted.

"That Glassy Interval"

THE DREAME

By Dream I saw, one of the three
Sisters of Fate appeare to me.
Close to my Beds side she did stand
Shewing me there a fire brand;
She told me too, as that did spend,
So drew my life unto an end.
Three quarters were consumed of it;
Onely remained a little bit,
Which will be burnt up by and by,
Then *Julia* weep, for I must dy.

ROBERT HERRICK

EUTHANASIA

When Time, or soon or late, shall bring
   The dreamless sleep that lulls the dead,
Oblivion! may thy languid wing
   Wave gently o'er my dying bed!

No band of friends or heirs be there,
   To weep, or wish, the coming blow;
No maiden with dishevelled hair,
   To feel, or feign, decorous woe.

But silent let me sink to earth,
   With no officious mourners near:
I would not mar one hour of mirth,
   Nor startle friendship with a tear.

Yet Love, if Love in such an hour
   Could nobly check its useless sighs,
Might then exert its latest power
   In her who lives, and him who dies.

'Twere sweet, my Psyche, to the last
   Thy features still serene to see:
Forgetful of its struggles past,
   E'en Pain itself should smile on thee.

But vain the wish — for Beauty still
   Will shrink, as shrinks the ebbing breath;
And women's tears, produced at will,
   Deceive in life, unman in death.

Then lonely be my latest hour,
   Without regret, without a groan;
For thousands Death hath ceased to lower,
   And pain been transient or unknown.

"Ay, but to die, and go," alas!
   Where all have gone, and all must go!
To be the nothing that I was
   Ere born to life and living woe!

Count o'er the joys thine hours have seen,
   Count o'er thy days from anguish free,
And know, whatever thou has been,
   'Tis something better not to be.

BYRON

AT LAST

When on my day of life the night is falling,
　And, in the winds from unsunned spaces blown,
I hear far voices out of darkness calling
　My feet to paths unknown,

Thou who hast made my home of life so pleasant,
　Leave not its tenant when its walls decay;
O Love Divine, O Helper ever present,
　Be Thou my strength and stay!

Be near me when all else is from me drifting:
　Earth, sky, home's pictures, days of shade and shine,
And kindly faces to my own uplifting
　The love which answers mine. . . .

J OHN G REENLEAF W HITTIER

O Death, rock me a sleep,
　Bring me to quiet rest,
Let pass my weary guiltless ghost
　Out of my careful breast.
Toll on the passing bell;
Ring out my doleful knell;
Thy sound my death abroad will tell,
　For I must die. . . .

　　Let him lean
Against his life, that glassy interval
'Twixt us and nothing; and, upon the ground
Of his own slippery breath, draw hueless dreams,
And gaze on frost-work hopes. Uncourteous Death
Knuckles the pane and . . .

T HOMAS L OVELL B EDDOES

[445]

Oh, the sad day!
When friends shall shake their heads, and say
    Of miserable me —
" Hark, how he groans, look how he pants for breath,
See how he struggles with the pangs of death! "
    When they shall say of these poor eyes —
    " How hollow and how dim they be!
    Mark how his breast does swell and rise
    Against his potent enemy! "
When some old friend shall step to my bedside,
Touch my chill face, and then shall gently slide,
    And — when his next companions say
" How does he do? What hopes? " — shall turn away,
    Answering only, with a lift-up hand —
      " Who can his fate withstand? "
    Then shall a gasp or two do more
    Than e'er my rhetoric could before:
Persuade the peevish world to trouble me no more!

Thomas Flatman

. . . The seas are quiet, when the winds give o'er;
So calm are we, when passions are no more:
For then we know how vain it was to boast
Of fleeting things, so certain to be lost.
Clouds of affection from our younger eyes
Conceal that emptiness, which age descries.

The soul's dark cottage, battered and decayed,
Lets in new light through chinks that Time has made.
Stronger by weakness, wiser, men become
As they draw near to their eternal home:
Leaving the old, both worlds at once they view
That stand upon the threshold of the new.

Edmund Waller

HIS LETANIE, TO THE HOLY SPIRIT

In the houre of my distresse,
When temptations me oppresse,
And when I my sins confesse,
    Sweet Spirit comfort me!

When I lie within my bed,
Sick in heart, and sick in head,
And with doubts discomforted,
    Sweet Spirit comfort me!

When the house doth sigh and weep,
And the world is drowned in sleep,
Yet mine eyes the watch do keep;
    Sweet Spirit comfort me! . . .

When the passing-bell doth tole,
And the Furies in a shole
Come to fright a parting soule;
    Sweet Spirit comfort me!

When the tapers now burne blew,
And the comforters are few,
And that number more then true;
    Sweet Spirit comfort me!

When the Priest his last hath praid,
And I nod to what is said,
'Cause my speech is now decaid;
    Sweet Spirit comfort me!

When (God knows) I'm tost about
Either with despaire, or doubt;
Yet, before the glasse be out,
    Sweet Spirit comfort me! . . .

When the Judgment is reveal'd,
And that opened which was sealed,
When to Thee I have appealed;
    Sweet Spirit comfort me!

ROBERT HERRICK

Because I do not hope to turn again
Because I do not hope
Because I do not hope to turn
Desiring this man's gift and that man's scope
I no longer strive to strive towards such things
(Why should the agèd eagle stretch its wings?)
Why should I mourn
The vanished power of the usual reign?

Because I do not hope to know again
The infirm glory of the positive hour
Because I do not think
Because I know I shall not know
The one veritable transitory power
Because I cannot drink
There, where trees flower, and springs flow, for there is noth-
    ing again

Because I know that time is always time
And place is always and only place
And what is actual is actual only for one time
And only for one place
I rejoice that things are as they are and
I renounce the blessèd face
And renounce the voice
Because I cannot hope to turn again
Consequently I rejoice, having to construct something
Upon which to rejoice

And pray to God to have mercy upon us
And I pray that I may forget
These matters that with myself I too much discuss
Too much explain
Because I do not hope to turn again
Let these words answer
For what is done, not to be done again
May the judgement not be too heavy upon us

Because these wings are no longer wings to fly
But merely vans to beat the air
The air which is now thoroughly small and dry
Smaller and dryer than the will
Teach us to care and not to care
Teach us to sit still.

Pray for us sinners now and at the hour of our death
Pray for us now and at the hour of our death. . . .

T. S. ELIOT, from *Ash-Wednesday*

DOMINUS ILLUMINATIO MEA

In the hour of death, after this life's whim,
When the heart beats low, and the eyes grow dim,
And pain has exhausted every limb —
    The lover of the Lord shall trust in Him.

When the will has forgotten the lifelong aim,
And the mind can only disgrace its fame,
And a man is uncertain of his own name —
    The power of the Lord shall fill this frame.

When the last sigh is heaved, and the last tear shed,
And the coffin is waiting beside the bed,
And the widow and child forsake the dead —
    The angel of the Lord shall lift this head.

[449]

For even the purest delight may pall,
And power must fail, and the pride must fall,
And the love of the dearest friends grow small —
    But the glory of the Lord is all in all.

RICHARD DODDRIDGE BLACKMORE

LAST PRAYER

Before the beginning Thou hast foreknown the end,
    Before the birthday the death-bed was seen of Thee:
Cleanse what I cannot cleanse, mend what I cannot mend,
    O Lord All-Merciful, be merciful to me.

While the end is drawing near I know not mine end;
    Birth I recall not, my death I cannot foresee:
O God, arise to defend, arise to befriend,
    O Lord All-Merciful, be merciful to me.

CHRISTINA ROSSETTI

IN TIME OF PESTILENCE

Adieu! Farewell earth's bliss!
This world uncertain is:
Fond are life's lustful joys,
Death proves them all but toys.
None from his darts can fly:
I am sick, I must die —
    Lord, have mercy on us!

Rich men, trust not in wealth,
Gold cannot buy you health;
Physic himself must fade;
All things to end are made;
The plague full swift goes by:
I am sick, I must die —
    Lord, have mercy on us!

[450]

Beauty is but a flower
Which wrinkles will devour:
Brightness falls from the air;
Queens have died young and fair;
Dust hath closed Helen's eye:
I am sick, I must die —
  Lord, have mercy on us!

Strength stoops unto the grave;
Worms feed on Hector brave;
Swords may not fight with fate;
Earth still holds ope her gate;
Come! come! the bells do cry:
I am sick, I must die —
  Lord, have mercy on us!

Wit with his wantonness,
Tasteth death's bitterness;
Hell's executioner
Hath no ears for to hear
What vain art can reply.
I am sick, I must die —
  Lord, have mercy on us!

Haste, therefore, each degree
To welcome destiny!
Heaven is our heritage;
Earth but a player's stage.
Mount we unto the sky!
I am sick, I must die —
  Lord, have mercy on us!

THOMAS NASH

DEATH

Death stands above me, whispering low
  I know not what into my ear:
Of his strange language all I know
  Is, there is not a word of fear.

WALTER SAVAGE LANDOR

NEXT OF KIN

The shadows gather round me, while you are in the sun:
My day is almost ended, but yours is just begun:
The winds are singing to us both and the streams are singing
    still,
And they fill your heart with music, but mine they cannot
    fill.

Your home is built in sunlight, mine in another day:
Your home is close at hand, sweet friend, but mine is far away:
Your bark is in the haven where you fain would be:
I must launch out into the deep, across the unknown sea.

You, white as dove or lily or spirit of the light:
I, stained and cold and glad to hide in the cold dark night:
You, joy to many a loving heart and light to many eyes:
I, lonely in the knowledge earth is full of vanities.

Yet when your day is over, as mine is nearly done,
And when your race is finished, as mine is almost run,
You, like me, shall cross your hands and bow your graceful
    head:
Yea, we twain shall sleep together in an equal bed.

CHRISTINA ROSSETTI

THE DEATH-BED

We watched her breathing through the night.
    Her breathing soft and low,
As in her breast the wave of life
    Kept heaving to and fro.

So silently we seemed to speak,
    So slowly moved about,
As we had lent her half our powers
    To eke her living out.

Our very hopes belied our fears,
    Our fears our hopes belied —
We thought her dying when she slept,
    And sleeping when she died.

★ *"That Glassy Interval"* ★

For when the morn came dim and sad
  And chill with early showers,
Her quiet eyelids closed — she had
  Another morn than ours.

Thomas Hood

HUSH

She sleeps so lightly, that in trembling fear
  Beside her, where she lies asleep, I kneel,
The rush of thought and supplication staying,
Lest by some inward sense she see and hear,
  If I too clearly think, too loudly feel,
And break her rest by praying.

Mary Coleridge

BESIDE THE BED

Someone has shut the shining eyes, straightened and folded
  The wandering hands quietly covering the unquiet breast:
So smoothed and silenced you lie, like a child, not again to be
    questioned or scolded;
  But, for you, not one of us believes that this is rest.

Not so to close the windows down can cloud and deaden
  The blue beyond: or to screen the wavering flame subdue
    its breath:
Why, if I lay my cheek to your cheek, your gray lips, like
    dawn, would quiver and redden,
  Breaking into the old odd smile at this fraud of death!

Because all night you have not turned to us or spoken,
  It is time for you to wake; your dreams were never very
    deep:
I, for one, have seen the thin bright twisted threads of them
    dimmed suddenly and broken,
  This is only a most piteous pretence of sleep!

Charlotte Mew

[453]

FIN DE FÊTE

Sweetheart, for such a day
    One mustn't grudge the score;
Here, then, it's all to pay,
    It's Good-night at the door.

Good-night and good dreams to you, —
    Do you remember the picture-book thieves
Who left two children sleeping in a wood the
        long night through,
And how the birds came down and covered
        them with leaves?

So you and I should have slept, — But now,
    Oh, what a lonely head!
With just the shadow of a waving bough
    In the moonlight over your bed.

CHARLOTTE MEW

THE CLOSING OF THE EYES

THE MOTHER: All country folk know, if the dying close their eyes themselves, and you don't have to do it for them, it means they are at peace.

When they keep their eyes open, that means they're not happy, and they'll come and fetch someone to keep them company.

That's why it's best to close their eyes as soon as they die, before they know it. Then they do not come back.

But I — I wanted him to come back for me — I wanted to go with him: and now he has closed his eyes himself. He loved me too much; he never wanted me hurt: forbade me even to go out into the yard when it was cold.

Oh, come back and fetch me. I'll be so good to you, better than ever I was.

You never left me before; don't, don't leave me now here alone. We have been together all the way, how can I go on now; however shall I be able to die without you: there's that last bit to travel, how can I face it alone. You have been with me always, you ought to have waited for me; oh, come back and take me with you!

But no, I know he won't come: he loved me too much on earth.

DENIS SAURAT

. . . I will close with another experience of forty years later. I was watching a dying woman, and I noted in her face the ravages of disease. She was unconscious, and in her last moments of consciousness had said to me, " There must be no sense of hurry. There may be something to be seen or done even now." I was standing at the foot of her bed, and I turned and gazed at a portrait of her taken when she was a young woman. I could not help contrasting its clear beauty with the stricken face on the pillow. Then I looked back again, and the face on the pillow was infinitely — yes, infinitely — the most beautiful I have seen. And I thought: " This is what she was meant to be. This is what she really is."

It was an intuition that completed all else: that in the life of men, their actual bodily life here, without disregarding anything that men call evil, there is a beauty inexpressible and this inexpressible beauty is the truth of human existence.

A. ALLEN BROCKINGTON

WOLFRAM'S DIRGE

If thou wilt ease thine heart
Of love and all its smart,
   Then sleep, dear, sleep;
And not a sorrow
   Hang any tear on your eyelashes;
    Lie still and deep,

[455]

Sad soul, until the sea-wave washes
The rim o' th' sun to-morrow,
   In eastern sky.

But wilt thou cure thy heart
Of love and all its smart,
   Then die, dear, die;
'Tis deeper, sweeter,
  Than on a rose-bank to lie dreaming
    With folded eye;
  And there alone, amid the beaming
Of Love's stars, thou'lt meet her
   In eastern sky.

THOMAS LOVELL BEDDOES

FOR ANNIE

Thank Heaven! the crisis —
  The danger is past,
And the lingering illness
  Is over at last —
And the fever called "Living"
  Is conquered at last.

Sadly, I know
  I am shorn of my strength,
And no muscle I move
  As I lie at full length —
But no matter! — I feel
  I am better at length.

And I rest so composedly,
  Now, in my bed,
That any beholder
  Might fancy me dead —
Might start at beholding me,
  Thinking me dead.

The moaning and groaning,
  The sighing and sobbing,
Are quieted now,
  With that horrible throbbing
At heart: — ah, that horrible,
  Horrible throbbing!

The sickness — the nausea —
  The pitiless pain —
Have ceased, with the fever
  That maddened my brain —
With the fever called "Living"
  That burned in my brain.

And oh! of all tortures
  That torture the worst
Has abated — the terrible
  Torture of thirst
For the naphthaline river
  Of Passion accurst: —
I have drunk of a water
  That quenches all thirst: —

Of a water that flows,
  With a lullaby sound,
From a spring but a very few
  Feet under ground —
From a cavern not very far
  Down under ground.

And ah! let it never
  Be foolishly said
That my room it is gloomy
  And narrow my bed;
For man never slept
  In a different bed —
And, *to sleep,* you must slumber
  In just such a bed.

[457]

My tantalized spirit
  Here blandly reposes;
Forgetting, or never
  Regretting its roses —
Its old agitations
  Of myrtles and roses;

For now, while so quietly
  Lying, it fancies
A holier odour
  About it, of pansies —
A rosemary odour,
  Commingled with pansies —
With rue and the beautiful
  Puritan pansies.

And so it lies happily,
  Bathing in many
A dream of the truth
  And the beauty of Annie —
Drowned in a bath
  Of the tresses of Annie.

She tenderly kissed me,
  She fondly caressed,
And then I fell gently
  To sleep on her breast —
Deeply to sleep
  From the heaven of her breast.

When the light was extinguished
  She covered me warm,
And she prayed to the angels
  To keep me from harm —
To the queen of the angels
  To shield me from harm.

[458]

And I lie so composedly,
   Now, in my bed,
(Knowing her love)
   That you fancy me dead —
And I rest so contentedly,
   Now, in my bed,
(With her love at my breast)
   That you fancy me dead —
That you shudder to look at me,
   Thinking me dead; —

But my heart it is brighter
   Than all of the many
Stars in the sky,
   For it sparkles with Annie —
It glows with the light
   Of the love of my Annie —
With the thought of the light
   Of the eyes of my Annie.

EDGAR ALLAN POE

VILLENEUVE.   [Sees himself in the glass as he passes.]
Unfortunate Villeneuve! — whom fate has marked
To suffer for too firm a faithfulness. —
An Emperor's chide is a command to die. —
By him accursed, forsaken by my friend,
Awhile stern England's prisoner, then unloosed
Like some poor dolt unworth captivity,
Time serves me now for ceasing. Why not cease? . . .
When, as Shades whisper in the chasmal night,
"Better, far better, no percipience here." —
O happy lack, that I should have no child
To come into my hideous heritage,
And groan beneath the burden of my name!

SPIRIT OF THE YEARS.

I'll speak. His mood is ripe for such a parle.

[Sending a voice into VILLENEUVE's ear.]
Thou dost divine the hour!

VILLENEUVE.   But those stern Nays,

That heretofore were audible to me
At each unhappy time I strove to pass?

SPIRIT OF THE YEARS.

Have been annulled. The Will grants exit freely;
Yea, It says " Now." Therefore make now thy time.

SPIRIT OF THE PITIES.

May his sad sunken soul merge into nought
Meekly and gently as a breeze at eve!

VILLENEUVE.

From skies above me and the air around
Those callings which so long have circled me
At last do whisper " Now." Now it shall be!

[He seals a letter, and addresses it to his wife; then takes a
dagger from his accoutrements that are hanging alongside,
and, lying down upon his back on the bed, stabs himself de-
terminedly in many places, leaving the weapon in the last
wound.]

Ungrateful Master; generous foes; Farewell! . . .

[The Scene darkens.]

THOMAS HARDY, from *The Dynasts,*
Part I, Act V, Scene VI

WOLFRAM.   Dar'st die?

A grave-deep question. Answer it religiously.

SIBYLLA. With him I loved, I dared.

WOLFR.   With me and for me.

I am a ghost. Tremble not; fear not me.
The dead are ever good and innocent,
And love the living. They are cheerful creatures,
And quiet as the sunbeams, and most like,
In grace and patient love and spotless beauty,

The new-born of mankind. 'Tis better too
To die, as thou art, young, in the first grace
And full of beauty, and so be remembered
As one chosen from the earth to be an angel;
Not left to droop and wither; and be borne
Down by the breath of time. Come then, Sibylla,
For I am Wolfram!

SIBYL.   Thou art come to fetch me!
It is indeed a proof of boundless love,
That thou hadst need of me even in thy bliss.
I go with thee. O Death! I am thy friend,
I struggle not with thee, I love thy state:
Thou canst be sweet and gentle, be so now;
And let me pass praying away into thee,
As twilight still does into starry night. . . .

THOMAS LOVELL BEDDOES,
from *Death's Jest-Book, Act IV, Scene II*

CLAUDIO.   Death is a fearful thing.
ISABELLA. And shamèd life a hateful.
CLAUD. Ay, but to die, and go we know not where;
To lie in cold obstruction and to rot;
This sensible warm motion to become
A kneaded clod; and the delighted spirit
To bathe in fiery floods, or to reside
In thrilling region of thick-ribbèd ice;
To be imprisoned in the viewless winds,
And blown with restless violence round about
The pendant world; or to be worse than worst
Of those that lawless and incertain thoughts
Imagine howling: 'tis too horrible!
The weariest and most loathèd worldly life
That age, ache, penury and imprisonment
Can lay on nature is a paradise
To what we fear of death. . . .

[461]

CAESAR. Cowards die many times before their deaths;
    The valiant never taste of death but once.
    Of all the wonders that I yet have heard,
    It seems to me most strange that men should fear;
    Seeing that death, a necessary end,
    Will come when it will come.

WILLIAM SHAKESPEARE
from *Measure for Measure, Act III, Scene I:*
Julius Caesar, Act II, Scene II

BRAKENBURY. Why looks your Grace so heavily to-day?

CLARENCE. O, I have passed a miserable night,
    So full of ugly sights, of ghastly dreams,
    That, as I am a Christian faithful man,
    I would not spend another such a night,
    Though 'twere to buy a world of happy days,
    So full of dismal terror was the time.

BRAK. What was your dream, my lord? I pray you, tell me.

CLAR. Methought that I had broken from the Tower,
    And was embarked to cross to Burgundy;
    And in my company my brother Gloucester,
    Who from my cabin tempted me to walk
    Upon the hatches: thence we looked toward England,
    And cited up a thousand heavy times,
    During the wars of York and Lancaster,
    That had befall'n us. As we paced along
    Upon the giddy footing of the hatches,
    Methought that Gloucester stumbled; and, in falling,
    Struck me, that thought to stay him, overboard,
    Into the tumbling billows of the main.
    Lord, Lord! methought what pain it was to drown:
    What dreadful noise of water in mine ears!
    What sights of ugly death within mine eyes!
    Methought I saw a thousand fearful wracks;
    A thousand men that fishes gnawed upon;

Wedges of gold, great anchors, heaps of pearl,
Inestimable stones, unvalued jewels,
All scattered in the bottom of the sea.
Some lay in dead men's skulls; and in those holes
Where eyes did once inhabit, there were crept,
As 'twere in scorn of eyes, reflecting gems,
That wooed the slimy bottom of the deep,
And mocked the dead bones that lay scattered by.

BRAK. Had you such leisure in the time of death
    To gaze upon those secrets of the deep?

CLAR. Methought I had: and often did I strive
    To yield the ghost; but still the envious flood
    Stopt in my soul, and would not let it forth
    To find the empty, vast, and wandering air;
    But smothered it within my panting bulk,
    Which almost burst to belch it in the sea.

BRAK. Awaked you not with this sore agony?

CLAR. No, no, my dream was lengthened after life;
    O! then began the tempest to my soul.
    I passed, methought, the melancholy flood,
    With that grim ferryman which poets write of,
    Unto the kingdom of perpetual night.
    The first that there did greet my stranger soul,
    Was my great father-in-law, renownèd Warwick;
    Who cried aloud, "What scourge for perjury
    Can this dark monarchy afford false Clarence?"
    And so he vanished: then came wandering by
    A shadow like an angel, with bright hair
    Dabbled in blood; and he shrieked out aloud,
    "Clarence is come, — false, fleeting, perjured Clarence,
    That stabb'd me in the field by Tewkesbury; —
    Seize on him! Furies, take him unto torment!"
    With that, methought, a legion of foul fiends
    Environed me, and howlèd in mine ears
    Such hideous cries, that, with the very noise
    I trembling waked, and, for a season after

[463]

Could not believe but that I was in hell,
Such terrible impression made my dream.

BRAK. No marvel, lord, though it affrighted you;
I am afraid, methinks, to hear you tell it. . . .

WILLIAM SHAKESPEARE
from *King Richard the Third, Act I, Scene IV*

DREAM OF DYING

Shivering in fever, weak, and parched to sand,
My ears, those entrances of word-dressed thoughts,
My pictured eyes, and my assuring touch,
Fell from me, and my body turned me forth
From its beloved abode: then I was dead;
And in my grave beside my corpse I sat,
In vain attempting to return: meantime
There came the untimely spectres of two babes,
And played in my abandoned body's ruins;
They went away; and, one by one, by snakes
My limbs were swallowed; and, at last, I sat
With only one, blue-eyed, curled round my ribs,
Eating the last remainder of my heart,
And hissing to himself. O sleep, thou fiend!
Thou blackness of the night! how sad and frightful
Are these thy dreams!

THOMAS LOVELL BEDDOES

KING EDWARD. Who's there? what light is that? wherefore
    com'st thou?

LIGHTBORN. To comfort you, and bring you joyful news.

K. EDW. Small comfort finds poor Edward in thy looks.
    Villain, I know thou com'st to murder me.

LIGHT. To murder you, my most gracious lord!
    Far is it from my heart to do you harm.

The queen sent me to see how you were used,
For she relents at this your misery:
And what eyes can refrain from shedding tears,
To see a king in this most piteous state?

K. EDW. Weep'st thou already? list awhile to me
And then thy heart, were it as Gurney's is,
Or as Matrevis', hewn from the Caucasus,
Yet will it melt, ere I have done my tale.
This dungeon where they keep me is the sink
Wherein the filth of all the castle falls.

LIGHT. O villains!

K. EDW. And there in mire and puddle have I stood
This ten days' space; and, lest that I should sleep,
One plays continually upon a drum.
They give me bread and water, being a king;
So that, for want of sleep and sustenance,
My mind's distempered, and my body's numbed,
And whether I have limbs or no I know not.
O, would my blood dropped out from every vein,
As doth this water from my tattered robes.
Tell Isabel, the queen, I looked not thus,
When for her sake I ran at tilt in France,
And there unhorsed the Duke of Cleremont.

LIGHT. O speak no more, my lord! this breaks my heart.
Lie on this bed, and rest yourself awhile.

K. EDW. These looks of thine can harbour nought but death:
I see my tragedy written in thy brows.
Yet stay; awhile forbear thy bloody hand,
And let me see the stroke before it comes,
That even then when I shall lose my life,
My mind may be more steadfast on my God.

LIGHT. What means your highness to mistrust me thus?

K. EDW. What mean'st thou to dissemble with me thus?

LIGHT. These hands were never stained with innocent blood,
Nor shall they now be tainted with a king's.

[465]

K. EDW. Forgive my thought for having such a thought.
One jewel have I left; receive thou this.

[*Giving jewel.*

Still fear I, and I know not what's the cause,
But every joint shakes as I give it thee.
O, if thou harbourest murder in thy heart,
Let this gift change thy mind, and save thy soul!
Know that I am a king: O, at that name
I feel a hell of grief! where is my crown?
Gone, gone! and do I remain alive?

LIGHT. You're overwatched, my lord; lie down and rest.

K. EDW. But that grief keeps me waking, I should sleep;
For not these ten days have these eyes' lids closed.
Now as I speak they fall, and yet with fear
Open again. O wherefore sitt'st thou here?

LIGHT. If you mistrust me, I'll be gone, my lord.

K. EDW. No, no, for if thou mean'st to murder me,
Thou wilt return again, and therefore stay.   [*Sleeps.*

LIGHT. He sleeps.

K. EDW. [*Waking.*] O let me not die yet: stay, O stay a while!

LIGHT. How now, my lord?

K. EDW. Something still buzzeth in mine ears,
And tells me if I sleep I never wake;
This fear is that which makes me tremble thus;
And therefore tell me, wherefore art thou come?

LIGHT. To rid thee of thy life. — Matrevis, come! . . .

CHRISTOPHER MARLOWE
from *Edward the Second, Act V, Scene V*

Enter EXECUTIONERS, *with a coffin, cords, and a bell.*

BOSOLA. Here is a present from your princely brothers;
And may it arrive welcome, for it brings
Last benefit, last sorrow.

DUCHESS. Let me see it:
I have so much obedience in my blood,
I wish it in their veins to do them good.

[466]

Bos. This is your last presence-chamber.

Cariola. O my sweet lady!

Duch. Peace; it affrights not me.

Bos. I am the common bellman,
    That usually is sent to condemnèd persons
    The night before they suffer.

Duch.   Even now thou said'st
    Thou wast a tomb-maker.

Bos.   'Twas to bring you
    By degrees to mortification. Listen.
        Hark, now everything is still
        The screech-owl and the whistler shrill
        Call upon our dame aloud,
        And bid her quickly don her shroud!
        Much you had of land and rent;
        Your length in clay's now competent:
        A long war disturbed your mind;
        Here your perfect peace is signed.
        Of what is't fools make such vain keeping?
        Sin their conception, their birth weeping,
        Their life a general mist of error,
        Their death a hideous storm of terror.
        Strew your hair with powders sweet,
        Don clean linen, bathe your feet,
        And (the foul fiend more to check)
        A crucifix let bless your neck:
        'Tis now full tide 'tween night and day;
        End your groan, and come away.

Cari. Hence, villains, tyrants, murderers! alas!
    What will you do with my lady? — Call for help.

Duch. To whom? to our next neighbours? they are mad-folks.

Bos. Remove that noise.

Duch. Farewell, Cariola.
    In my last will I have not much to give:
    A many hungry guests have fed upon me;
    Thine will be a poor reversion.

CARI. I will die with her.

DUCH. I pray thee, look thou giv'st my little boy
　　Some syrup for his cold, and let the girl
　　Say her prayers ere she sleep.

> [CARIOLA *is forced out by the* EXECUTIONERS.

　　　　　　　　　　　　　Now what you please:
　　What death?

BOS. Strangling; here are your executioners.

DUCH. I forgive them:
　　The apoplexy, catarrh, or cough o' the lungs,
　　Would do as much as they do.

BOS. Doth not death fright you?

DUCH. Who would be afraid on't,
　　Knowing to meet such excellent company
　　In the other world?

BOS. Yet, methinks,
　　The manner of your death should much afflict you:
　　This cord should terrify you.

DUCH. Not a whit:
　　What would it pleasure me to have my throat cut
　　With diamonds? or to be smotherèd
　　With cassia? or to be shot to death with pearls?
　　I know death hath ten thousand several doors
　　For men to take their exits; and 'tis found
　　They go on such strange geometrical hinges,
　　You may open them both ways; any way, for Heaven
　　　　sake,
　　So I were out of your whispering. Tell my brothers
　　That I perceive death, now I am well awake,
　　Best gift is they can give or I can take.
　　I would fain put off my last woman's fault,
　　I'd not be tedious to you.

1ST EXECUT. We are ready.

DUCH. Dispose my breath how please you; but my body
　　Bestow upon my women, will you?

1ST EXECUT. Yes.

DUCH. Pull, and pull strongly, for your able strength

Must pull down Heaven upon me: —
Yet stay; Heaven-gates are not so highly arched
As princes' palaces; they that enter there
Must go upon their knees. [*Kneels.*] — Come, violent
  death,
Serve for mandragora to make me sleep! —
Go tell my brothers, when I am laid out,
They then may feed in quiet. . . .

JOHN WEBSTER, from *The Duchess of Malfi,*
Act IV, Scene II

THE RETREAT FROM MOSCOW

The Open Country between Smorgoni and Wilna

The winter is more merciless, and snow continues to fall
upon a deserted expanse of unenclosed land in Lithuania.
Some scattered birch bushes merge in a forest in the background.

It is growing dark, though nothing distinguishes where the
sun sets. There is no sound except that of a shuffling of feet
in the direction of a bivouac. Here are gathered tattered men
like skeletons. Their noses and ears are frost-bitten, and pus
is oozing from their eyes.

These stricken shades in a limbo of gloom are among the
last survivors of the French army. Few of them carry arms.
One squad, ploughing through snow above their knees, and
with icicles dangling from their hair that clink like glass-
lustres as they walk, go into the birch wood, and are heard
chopping. They bring back boughs, with which they make a
screen on the windward side, and contrive to light a fire.
With their swords they cut rashers from a dead horse, and
grill them in the flames, using gunpowder for salt to eat them
with. Two others return from a search, with a dead rat and
some candle-ends. Their meal shared, some try to repair their
gaping shoes and to tie up their feet, that are chilblained to
the bone. . . .

[469]

Exhausted, they again crouch round the fire. Officers and privates press together for warmth. Other stragglers arrive, and sit at the backs of the first. With the progress of the night the stars come out in unusual brilliancy, Sirius and those in Orion flashing like stilettos; and the frost stiffens.

The fire sinks and goes out; but the Frenchmen do not move. The day dawns, and still they sit on.

In the background enter some light horse of the Russian army, followed by KUTÚZOF himself and a few of his staff. He presents a terrible appearance now — bravely serving though slowly dying, his face puffed with the intense cold, his one eye staring out as he sits in a heap in the saddle, his head sunk into his shoulders. The whole detachment pauses at the sight of the French asleep. They shout; but the bivouackers give no sign.

KUTÚZOF. Go, stir them up! We slay not sleeping men.

[*The Russians advance and prod the French with their lances.*]

RUSSIAN OFFICER.
  Prince, here's a curious picture. They are dead.

KUTÚZOF [*With indifference*].
  Oh, naturally. After the snow was down
  I marked a sharpening of the air last night.
  We shall be stumbling on such frost-baked meats
  Most of the way to Wilna.

OFFICER [*Examining the bodies*].   They all sit
  As they were living still, but stiff as horns;
  And even the colour has not left their cheeks,
  Whereon the tears remain in strings of ice. —
  It was a marvel they were not consumed:
  Their clothes are cindered by the fire in front,
  While at their back the frost has caked them hard.

KUTÚZOF. 'Tis well. So perish Russia's enemies!

Exeunt . . . and with the advance of day the snow resumes its fall, slowly burying the dead bivouackers.

THOMAS HARDY, from *The Dynasts*,
Part III, Act I, Scene XI

[470]

"TEMPT ME NO MORE"

Tempt me no more; for I
Have known the lightning's hour,
The poet's inward pride,
The certainty of power.

Bayonets are closing round.
I shrink; yet I must wring
A living from despair
And out of steel a song.

Though song, though breath be short,
I'll share not the disgrace
Of those that ran away
Or never left the base.

Comrades, my tongue can speak
No comfortable words,
Calls to a forlorn hope,
Gives work and not rewards.

Oh keep the sickle sharp
And follow still the plough:
Others may reap, though some
See not the winter through.

Father, who endest all,
Pity our broken sleep;
For we lie down with tears
And waken but to weep.

And if our blood alone
Will melt this iron earth,
Take it. It is well spent
Easing a saviour's birth.

CECIL DAY LEWIS

THE TWA CORBIES

As I was walking all alane,
I heard twa corbies making a mane;
The tane unto the t'other say,
"Where sall we gang and dine to-day?"

"In behint yon auld fail dyke,
I wot there lies a new-slain knight;
And naebody kens that he lies there,
But his hawk, his hound, and lady fair.

"His hound is to the hunting gane,
His hawk to fetch the wild-fowl hame,
His lady's ta'en another mate,
So we may mak our dinner sweet.

"Ye'll sit on his white hause-bane,
And I'll pike out his bonny blue een;
Wi' ae lock o' his gowden hair
We'll theek our nest when it grows bare.

"Mony a one for him makes mane,
But nane sall ken where he is gane;
O'er his white banes, when they are bare,
The wind sall blaw for evermair."

"Why dost thou lament my death, or call me miserable that
am much more happy than thyself? what misfortune is befallen me? Is it because I am not so bald, crooked, old, rotten,
as thou art? What have I lost — some of your good cheer,
gay clothes, music, singing, dancing, kissing, merry-meetings,
thalami lubentias, etc., is that it? Is it not much better not to
hunger at all than to eat: not to thirst than to drink to satisfy
thirst: not to be cold than to put on clothes to drive away cold?

You had more need rejoice that I am freed from diseases, agues, cares, anxieties, liver, love, covetousness, hatred, envy, malice, that I fear no more thieves, tyrants, enemies, as you do." . . .

ROBERT BURTON

A LYKE–WAKE DIRGE

This ae nighte, this ae nighte,
  Every nighte and alle,
Fire, and fleet, and candle-lighte,
  And Christe receive thy saule.

When thou from hence away art passed,
  Every nighte and alle,
To Whinny-muir thou com'st at last;
  And Christe receive thy saule.

If ever thou gavest hosen and shoon,
  Every nighte and alle,
Sit thee down and put them on;
  And Christe receive thy saule.

If hosen and shoon thou ne'er gav'st nane,
  Every nighte and alle,
The whinnes sall prick thee to the bare bane;
  And Christe receive thy saule.

From Whinny-muir when thou may'st pass,
  Every nighte and alle,
To Brigg o' Dread thou com'st at last,
  And Christe receive thy saule.

From Brigg o' Dread when thou may'st pass,
  Every nighte and alle,
To Purgatory fire thou com'st at last,
  And Christe receive thy saule.

[473]

If ever thou gavest meat or drink,
  Every nighte and alle,
The fire sall never make thee shrink;
  And Christe receive thy saule.

If meat or drink thou ne'er gav'st nane,
  Every nighte and alle,
The fire will burn thee to the bare bane;
  And Christe receive thy saule.

This ae nighte, this ae nighte,
  — Every nighte and alle,
Fire, and fleet and candle-lighte,
  And Christe receive thy saule.

LULLY, LULLEY

Lully, lulley, lully, lulley,
The faucon hath borne my make away.

He bare him up, he bare him down,
He bare him into an orchard brown.

In that orchard there was an halle,
That was hanged with purpill and pall.

And in that hall there was a bede,
It was hanged with gold so rede.

And in that bede there lithe a knight,
His woundes bleding day and night.

By that bede side kneleth a may,
And she wepeth both night and day.

And by that bede side there stondeth a stone,
Corpus Christi wreten there on.

[474]

"The Turning of the Tide"

Do you think a man who has known how to live honourably for eighty years, does not know how to die for a quarter of an hour?

Did'st thou ever see a lark in a cage?
Such is the soul in the body. . . .

"The Turning of the Tide"

BARDOLPH. Would I were with him, wheresome'er he is, either in heaven or in hell!

HOSTESS. Nay, sure, he's not in hell: he's in Arthur's bosom, if ever man went to Arthur's bosom. A' made a finer end and went away an it had been any christom child; a' parted even just between twelve and one, even at the turning o' the tide: for after I saw him fumble with the sheets and play with flowers and smile upon his fingers' ends, I knew there was but one way; for his nose was as sharp as a pen, and a' babbled of green fields. "How now, Sir John!" quoth I: "what, man! be of good cheer." So a' cried out "God, God, God!" three or four times. Now I, to comfort him, bid him a' should not think of God, I hoped there was no need to trouble himself with any such thoughts yet. So a' bade me lay more clothes on his feet: I put my hand into the bed and felt them, and they were as cold as any stone; then I felt to his knees, and so upward, and upward, and all was as cold as any stone.

WILLIAM SHAKESPEARE,
from *King Henry the Fifth, Act II, Scene III*

ECHECRATES. What was the manner of his death, Phaedo? What was said or done? And which of his friends were with him? . . .

PHAEDO. I had a singular feeling at being in his company. For I could hardly believe that I was present at the death of a friend, and therefore I did not pity him, Echecrates; he died so fearlessly, and his words and bearing were so noble and gracious, that to me he appeared blessed. I thought that in going to the other world he could not be without a divine call, and that he would be happy, if any man ever was, when he arrived there; and therefore I did not pity him as might have seemed natural at such an hour. But I had not the pleasure which I usually feel in philosophical discourse. . . . I was pleased, but in the pleasure there was also a strange admixture of pain; for I reflected that he was soon to die, and this double feeling was shared by us all; we were laughing and weeping by turns, especially the excitable Apollodorus. . . .

Crito made a sign to the servant, who was standing by; and he went out, and having been absent for some time returned with the jailer carrying the cup of poison. Socrates said: You, my good friend, who are experienced in these matters, shall give me directions how I am to proceed. The man answered: You have only to walk about until your legs are heavy, and then to lie down, and the poison will act. At the same time he handed the cup to Socrates, who in the easiest and gentlest manner, without the least fear or change of colour or feature, looking at the man with all his eyes, Echecrates, as his manner was, took the cup and said: What do you say about making a libation out of this cup to any god? May I, or not? The man answered: We only prepare, Socrates, just so much as we deem enough. I understand, he said: but I may and must ask the gods to prosper my journey from this to the other world — even so — and so be it according to my prayer. Then raising the cup to his lips, quite readily and cheerfully he drank off the poison. . . .

And he walked about until, as he said, his legs began to fail, and then he lay on his back, according to the directions, and the man who gave him the poison now and then looked at his feet and legs; and after a while he pressed his feet hard, and asked him if he could feel; and he said, No; and then his legs, and so upwards and upwards, and showed us that he was cold and stiff. And he felt them himself, and said: When the poison reaches the heart, that will be the end. He was beginning to grow cold about the groin, when he uncovered his face, for he had covered himself up, and said — they were his last words — he said: Crito, I owe a cock to Asclepius;

will you remember to pay the debt? The debt shall be paid, said Crito; is there anything else? There was no answer to this question; but in a minute or two a movement was heard, and the attendants uncovered him; his eyes were set, and Crito closed his eyes and mouth.

Such was the end, Echecrates, of our friend; concerning whom I may truly say, that of all the men of his time whom I have known, he was the wisest and justest and best.

PLATO, translated by Benjamin Jowett

Towards the evening of the 3rd of October she [Saint Teresa] asked for Holy Viaticum. . . . The saint prayed, and as they were a little time before bringing the Holy Viaticum she stopped for a moment, and looking round at all the nuns kneeling before her, she stretched out her hands imploringly to them, and said: "Forgive me the bad example I have given you, my daughters. Do not imitate my example, for I am a great sinner, but keep well your Rule and your Constitutions. Obey your superior, I beg of you, for the love of God." . . .

Fr. Anthony, fearing that she would exhaust herself, told her to cease speaking. She was instantly silent, and relapsed into prayer and recollection, leaving her daughters deeply moved. . . .

The rest of the night was spent in intense suffering. At times the sound of the name of Jesus rose to her lips, or she called on God to help her, or repeated her constant prayer: "A contrite and humble heart, O God, Thou wilt not despise."

Sister Anne of St. Bartholomew changed all her linen at early dawn, even to her sleeves and coif. The holy mother thanked her with a smile; they were the garments she was to wear at her heavenly espousals. A little later Fr. Anthony sent Sister Anne to take some food. Teresa, not knowing what had become of her, sought her with her eyes, and appeared to have no rest till she returned. Then, motioning her to her side, she took her hands, and leant her head on the shoulder of her dear infirmarian, her grateful heart wishing to show her by signs, when her lips were no longer able to speak, all she felt for the thirteen years' devoted service which Sister Anne had lavished on her.

At seven o'clock in the morning the saint turned on her left side, and, with a crucifix in her hand, she became absorbed in a profound contemplation, in which she neither spoke, nor saw, nor gave any further attention to outward things. Her agony began without groans, or sighs, or sufferings, joyous as if rapt in ecstasy, she lay in her Saviour's arms, waiting for the moment when Heaven should open to receive her. Her daughters, kneeling round their mother, contemplated her with an admiration which stopped their tears. The little cell had become a place of paradise. An ever-increasing brightness dwelt on the saint's countenance, and lit up Sister Anne's face, who supported her. Her features were invested with a supernatural beauty; the brilliancy of youth was united to the majesty of death and old age. The rays of light which encircled her forehead, the crimson on her cheeks, the unutterable joy of her expression, were all divine. . . . Towards nine in the evening three gentle sighs escaped her, so light that they were scarcely heard, so soft that they resembled rather those made by a person absorbed in prayer, than one in her agony, and she gave up her soul to God.

From *A Carmelite Nun*, translated by Alice Lady Lovat

"THERE, ON THE DARKENED DEATHBED, DIES THE BRAIN"

There, on the darkened deathbed, dies the brain
That flared three several times in seventy years.
It cannot lift the silly hand again,
Nor speak, nor sing, it neither sees nor hears;
And muffled mourners put it in the ground
And then go home, and in the earth it lies
Too dark for vision and too deep for sound,
The million cells that made a good man wise.

Yet for a few short years an influence stirs,
A sense or wraith or essence of him dead,
Which makes insensate things its ministers
To those beloved, his spirit's daily bread;
Then that, too, fades; in book or deed a spark
Lingers, then that, too, fades; then all is dark.

JOHN MASEFIELD

THE GARDEN OF PROSERPINE

Here, where the world is quiet;
　　Here, where all trouble seems
Dead winds' and spent waves' riot
　　In doubtful dreams of dreams;
I watch the green field growing
For reaping folk and sowing,
For harvest-time and mowing,
　　A sleepy world of streams.

I am tired of tears and laughter,
　　And men that laugh and weep;
Of what may come hereafter
　　For men that sow to reap:
I am weary of days and hours,
Blown buds of barren flowers,
Desires and dreams and powers
　　And everything but sleep. . . .

We are not sure of sorrow,
　　And joy was never sure;
To-day will die to-morrow;
　　Time stoops to no man's lure;
And Love, grown faint and fretful,
With lips but half regretful
Sighs, and with eyes forgetful
　　Weeps that no loves endure.

[481]

From too much love of living,
  From hope and fear set free,
We thank with brief thanksgiving
  Whatever gods may be
That no life lives for ever;
That dead men rise up never;
That even the weariest river
  Winds somewhere safe to sea.

Then star nor sun shall waken,
  Nor any charge of light:
Nor sound of waters shaken,
  Nor any sound or sight:
Nor wintry leaves nor vernal,
Nor days nor things diurnal;
Only the sleep eternal
  In an eternal night.

ALGERNON CHARLES SWINBURNE

FRANCISCO DE MEDICI. How now, my noble cousin! what, in
    black!
GIOVANNI. Yes, uncle, I was taught to imitate you
    In virtue, and you must imitate me
    In colours of your garments. My sweet mother
    Is —
FRAN. DE MED. How! where?
GIOV. Is there; no, yonder: indeed, sir, I'll not tell you,
    For I shall make you weep.
FRAN. DE MED. Is dead?
GIOV. Do not blame me now,
    I did not tell you so.
LODOVICO. She's dead, my lord.
FRAN. DE MED. Dead! . . .
GIOV. What do the dead do, uncle? do they eat,
    Hear music, go a hunting, and be merry,
    As we that live?

FRAN. DE MED. No, coz; they sleep.

GIOV. Lord, Lord, that I were dead!
 I have not slept these six nights. — When do they wake?

FRAN. DE MED. When God shall please.

GIOV. Good God, let her sleep ever!
 For I have known her wake an hundred nights,
 When all the pillow where she laid her head
 Was brine-wet with her tears. I am to complain to you,
  sir;
 I'll tell you how they have used her now she's dead:
 They wrapped her in a cruel fold of lead,
 And would not let me kiss her.

FRAN. DE MED. Thou didst love her.

GIOV. I have often heard her say she gave me suck,
 And it should seem by that she dearly loved me,
 Since princes seldom do it.

FRAN. DE MED. O, all of my poor sister that remains! —
 Take him away, for God's sake! . . .

JOHN WEBSTER,
from *The White Devil, Act III, Scene I*

WARNING AND REPLY

In the earth — the earth — thou shalt be laid,
 A grey stone standing over thee;
Black mould beneath thee spread,
 And black mould to cover thee.

" Well — there is rest there,
 So fast come thy prophecy:
The time when my sunny hair
 Shall with grass roots entwinèd be! "

But cold — cold is that resting-place,
 Shut out from joy and liberty,
And all who loved thy living face
 Will shrink from it shudderingly.

[483]

"Not so. Here the world is chill,
   And sworn friends fall from me;
But there — they will own me still,
   And prize my memory."

Farewell, then, all that love,
   All that deep sympathy;
Sleep on: Heaven laughs above,
   Earth never misses thee.

Turf-sod and tombstone drear
   Part human company:
One heart breaks only — here,
   But that heart was worthy thee!

                EMILY BRONTË

MARY'S DREAM

The moon had climbed the highest hill,
   Which rises o'er the source of Dee;
And from the eastern summit shed
   Her silver light on tower and tree;
When MARY laid her down to sleep,
   Her thoughts on SANDY far at sea;
When soft and low a voice was heard,
   Saying, "MARY! weep no more for me!"

She from her pillow gently raised
   Her head, to ask, "Who there might be?"
She saw young SANDY shivering stand,
   With visage pale and hollow eye.
"O, MARY, dear! cold is my clay!
   It lies beneath a stormy sea!
Far, far from thee, I sleep in death;
   So, MARY! weep no more for me! . . .

LOWLANDS A–RAY

I dreamt a dream the other night:
Lowlands, hurrah, my John:
I dreamt a dream the other night:
My Lowlands a-ray.

I dreamt I saw my own true love:
Lowlands, hurrah, my John:
I dreamt I saw my own true love:
My Lowlands a-ray.

He was green and wet with weeds so cold:
Lowlands, hurrah, my John:
He was green and wet with weeds so cold:
My Lowlands a-ray.

"I am drowned in the Lowland seas," he said:
Lowlands, hurrah, my John:
"I am drowned in the Lowland seas," he said:
My Lowlands a-ray.

"I shall never kiss you again," he said:
Lowlands, hurrah, my John:
"I shall never kiss you again," he said:
My Lowlands a-ray.

I will cut away my bonny hair:
Lowlands, hurrah, my John:
I will cut away my bonny hair:
My Lowlands a-ray.

No other man shall think me fair:
Lowlands, hurrah, my John:
No other man shall think me fair:
My Lowlands a-ray.

[485]

O my love lies drowned in the windy Lowlands:
Lowlands, hurrah, my John:
O my love lies drowned in the windy Lowlands:
My Lowlands a-ray.

But as when some kind nurse doth sometime keep
Her pretty babe at suck, whom fallen asleep,
She lays down in his cradle, stints his cry
With many a sweet and pleasing lullaby;
Whilst the sweet child, not troubled with the shock,
As sweetly slumbers, as his nurse doth rock:
So lay the maid, th' amazèd swain sat weeping,
And Death in her was dispossessed by sleeping.
The roaring voice of winds, the billows' raves,
Nor all the muttering of the silent waves
Could once disquiet, or her slumber stir;
But lulled her more asleep than wakened her.

WILLIAM BROWNE

SIBYLLA. . . . If he were dead I should indeed despair.
Can a man die? Ay, as the sun doth set:
It is the earth that falls away from light;
Fixed in the heavens, although unseen by us,
The immortal life and light remains triumphant.
And therefore you shall never see me wail,
Or drop base waters of an ebbing sorrow;
No wringing hands, no sighings, no despair,
No mourning weeds will I betake me to;
But keep my thought of him that is no more,
As secret as great nature keeps his soul,
From all the world; and consecrate my being
To that divinest hope, which none can know of
Who have not laid their dearest in the grave. . . .

THOMAS LOVELL BEDDOES
from *Death's Jest-Book, Act II, Scene II*

[486]

CLERK SANDERS

Clark Sanders and May Margret
  Walkt ower yon graveld green,
And sad and heavy was the love,
  I wat, it fell this twa between.

"A bed, a bed," Clark Sanders said,
  "A bed, a bed for you and I;"
"Fye no, fye no," the lady said,
  "Until the day we married be.

"For in it will come my seven brothers,
  And a' their torches burning bright;
They'll say, We hae but ae sister,
  And here her lying wi a knight."

"Ye'l take the sourde fray my scabbord,
  And lowly, lowly lift the gin,
And you may say, your oth to save,
  You never let Clark Sanders in.

"Ye'l take a napken in your hand,
  And ye'l ty up baith your een,
An ye may say, your oth to save,
  That ye saw na Sandy sen late yestreen.

"Ye'l take me in your armes twa,
  Ye'l carrey me ben into your bed,
And ye may say, your oth to save,
  In your bower-floor I never tread."

She has taen the sourde fray his scabbord,
  And lowly, lowly lifted the gin;
She was to swear, her oth to save,
  She never let Clark Sanders in.

[487]

She has tain a napkin in her hand,
    And she has ty'd up baith her een;
She was to swear, her oth to save,
    She saw na him sene late yestreen.

She has taen him in her armes twa,
    And carried him ben into her bed;
She was to swear, her oth to save,
    He never in her bower-floor tread.

In and came her seven brothers,
    And all their torches burning bright;
Says thay, We hae but ae sister,
    And see there her lying wi a knight.

Out and speaks the first of them,
    " A wat they hay been lovers dear; "
Out and speaks the next of them,
    " They hay been in love this many a year."

Out and speaks the third of them,
    " It wear great sin this twa to twain; "
Out and speaks the fourth of them,
    " It wear a sin to kill a sleeping man."

Out and speaks the fifth of them,
    " A wat they'll near be twained by me; "
Out and speaks the sixt of them,
    " We'l tak our leave an gae our way."

Out and speaks the seventh of them,
    "Altho there wear no a man but me,

      .   .   .   .   .   .

I bear the brand, I'le gar him die."

Out he has taen a bright long brand,
    And he has striped it throw the straw,
And throw and throw Clarke Sanders' body
    A wat he has gard cold iron gae.

Sanders he started, an Margret she lapt,
  Intill his arms whare she lay,
And well and wellsome was the night,
  A wat it was between these twa.

And they lay still, and sleepèd sound,
  Untill the day began to daw;
And kindly till him she did say
  " It's time, trew-love, ye wear awa."

They lay still, and sleepèd sound,
  Untill the sun began to shine;
She lookt between her and the wa,
  And dull and heavy was his een.

She thought it had been a loathsome sweat,
  A wat it had fallen this twa between;
But it was the blood of his fair body,
  A wat his life days wair na lang. . . .

GANE WERE BUT THE WINTER CAULD

Gane were but the winter cauld,
  And gane were but the snaw,
I could sleep in the wild woods
  Whare primroses blaw.

Cauld's the snaw at my head,
  And cauld at my feet,
And the finger o' death's at my een,
  Closing them to sleep.

Let nane tell my father,
  Or my mither sae dear:
I'll meet them baith in heaven,
  At the spring o' the year.

ALLAN CUNNINGHAM

[489]

THE UNQUIET GRAVE

" The wind doth blow today, my love,
    And a few small drops of rain;
I never had but one true-love,
    In cold grave she was lain.

" I'll do as much for my true-love
    As any young man may;
I'll sit and mourn all at her grave
    For a twelvemonth and a day."

The twelvemonth and a day being up,
    The dead began to speak:
" Oh, who sits weeping on my grave,
    And will not let me sleep? "

" 'Tis I, my love, sits on your grave,
    And will not let you sleep;
For I crave one kiss of your clay-cold lips,
    And that is all I seek."

" You crave one kiss of my clay-cold lips;
    But my breath smells earthy strong;
If you have one kiss of my clay-cold lips,
    Your time will not be long.

" 'Tis down in yonder garden green,
    Love, where we used to walk;
The finest flower that ere was seen
    Is withered to a stalk.

" The stalk is withered dry, my love,
    So will our hearts decay;
So make yourself content, my love,
    Till God calls you away."

"WEEP YOU NO MORE, SAD FOUNTAINS"

Weep you no more, sad fountains;
　What need you flow so fast?
Look how the snowy mountains
　Heaven's sun doth gently waste!
But my Sun's heavenly eyes
　View not your weeping,
　That now lies sleeping
Softly, now softly lies
　　　Sleeping.

Sleep is a reconciling,
　A rest that peace begets;
Doth not the sun rise smiling
　When fair at eve he sets?
Rest you then, rest, sad eyes!
　Melt not in weeping,
　While she lies sleeping
Softly, now softly lies
　　　Sleeping.

. . . Weep no more, woful shepherds, weep no more,
For Lycidas, your sorrow, is not dead,
Sunk though he be beneath the watery floor.
So sinks the day-star in the ocean bed,
And yet anon repairs his drooping head,
And tricks his beams, and with new-spangled ore
Flames in the forehead of the morning sky:
So Lycidas sunk low, but mounted high,
Through the dear might of Him that walked the waves,
Where, other groves and other streams along,

With nectar pure his oozy locks he laves,
And hears the unexpressive nuptial song,
In the blest kingdoms meek of joy and love.
There entertain him all the Saints above,
In solemn troops, and sweet societies,
That sing, and singing in their glory move,
And wipe the tears for ever from his eyes. . . .

JOHN MILTON, from *Lycidas*

. . . Weep not for me when I am gone,
    Dear tender one, but hope and smile:
    Or, if you cannot choose but weep,
        A little while weep on,
        Only a little while.

CHRISTINA ROSSETTI,
from " The Summer is ended "

        Listen to the Lyre!
Listen to the knelling of its sweet-toned ditty!
Shrilly now as Pain resounds the various wire,
        Now as soft as Pity!
        Soft as Pity!

        Will the Dreamer know,
Who upon the melancholy harp loves weeping —
Dreamer, it is I that tell the tale of woe,
        Still while thou art sleeping,
        Thou art sleeping? . . .

        I was called above,
But I found no happiness in lone, lone Heaven;
So because I would not, could not, cease to love,
        Earthward I was driven,
        I was driven!

Like a wingèd dream
Here amid the bowers of my youth I hover,
Wailing o'er my sorrows to the deep, chill stream
   Where I lost my lover,
      Lost my lover!

In his oozy bed
Coffinless he slumbers, with the wild flood rolling!
Mermen are his ringers and his dirge is dread,
   Still for ever tolling!
      Ever tolling!

Hearken to the knell!
Hear it through the booming of the loud-voiced billows!
Hear it how it dingles like a clear death-bell,
   Underneath the willows,
      'Neath the willows!

In the desert hours,
Lyrist of thy visions, all my woes repeating,
With my tears for jewels do I fill the flowers,
   While the stars are fleeting,
      Stars are fleeting!

Thou wilt doubt the tale,
Wilt not still believe my woes: thy harp bear token.
See, its very bosom-strings with this deep wail,
   All, like mine, are broken!
      Mine are broken!

GEORGE DARLEY,
from " The Enchanted Lyre "

A JACOBITE EXILE

The weary day rins down and dies,
   The weary night wears through:
And never an hour is fair wi' flower,
   And never a flower wi' dew.

I would the day were night for me,
　I would the night were day:
For then would I stand in my ain fair land,
　As now in dreams I may.

O lordly flow the Loire and Seine,
　And loud the dark Durance:
But bonnier shine the braes of Tyne
　Than a' the fields of France;
And the waves of Till that speak sae still
　Gleam goodlier where they glance.

O weel were they that fell fighting
　On dark Drumossie's day:
They keep their hame ayont the faem,
　And we die far away.

O sound they sleep, and saft, and deep,
　But night and day wake we;
And ever between the sea-banks green
　Sounds loud the sundering sea. . . .

But O gin I were there again,
　Afar ayont the faem,
Cauld and dead in the sweet saft bed
　That haps my sires at hame!

We'll see nae mair the sea-banks fair,
　And the sweet grey gleaming sky,
And the lordly strand of Northumberland,
　And the goodly towers thereby:
And none shall know but the winds that blow
　The graves wherein we lie.

ALGERNON CHARLES SWINBURNE

Large are the treasures of oblivion, and heaps of things in
a state next to nothing almost numberless; much more is

buried in silence than recorded, and the largest volumes are but epitomes of what hath been. The account of time began with night, and darkness still attendeth it. Some things never come to light; many have been delivered; but more have been swallowed in obscurity and the caverns of oblivion. How much is as it were *in vacuo,* and will never be cleared up, of those long living times when men could scarce remember themselves young; and men seem to us not ancient but antiquities, when they [lived] longer in their lives than we can now hope to do in our memories. . . .

SIR THOMAS BROWNE

PROSPERO. Our revels now are ended. These our actors,
    As I foretold you, were all spirits and
    Are melted into air, into thin air:
    And, like the baseless fabric of this vision,
    The cloud-capped towers, the gorgeous palaces,
    The solemn temples, the great globe itself,
    Yea, all which it inherit, shall dissolve
    And, like this insubstantial pageant faded,
    Leave not a rack behind. We are such stuff
    As dreams are made on, and our little life
    Is rounded with a sleep. . . .

WILLIAM SHAKESPEARE,
from *The Tempest, Act IV, Scene I*

THE END

After the blast of lightning from the East,
The flourish of loud clouds, the Chariot Throne;
After the drums of Time have rolled and ceased,
And by the bronze west long retreat is blown,
Shall Life renew these bodies? Of a truth
All death will he annul, all tears assuage? —
Fill the void veins of Life again with youth,
And wash, with an immortal water, Age?

[495]

When I do ask white Age, he saith, " Not so:
My head hangs weighed with snow."
And when I hearken to the Earth, she saith:
" My fiery heart shrinks aching. It is death.
Mine ancient scars shall not be glorified,
Nor my titanic tears, the seas, be dried."

WILFRED OWEN

The Phoenix

Don't you remember sweet Alice, Ben Bolt —
  Sweet Alice whose hair was so brown,
Who wept with delight when you gave her a smile,
  And trembled with fear at your frown?
In the old churchyard in the valley, Ben Bolt,
  In a corner obscure and alone,
They have fitted a slab of the granite so gray,
  And Alice lies under the stone. . . .

The Phoenix

THE OLD WOMAN

A Morality Play in Two Parts

I

DOCTOR.	There is an old woman Who ought to die —
DEACON.	And nobody knows But what she's dead —
DOCTOR.	The air will be cleaner When she's gone —
DEACON.	But we dare not bury her Till she's dead.
LANDLADY.	Come, young doctor From the first floor front, Come, dusty deacon From the fourth floor back. You take her heels And I'll take her head —
DOCTOR AND DEACON.	We'll carry her And bury her — If she's dead!
HOUSE.	They roll her up In her old red quilt, They carry her down At a horizontal tilt. She doesn't say, " Yes! " And she doesn't say, " No! "

She doesn't say, " Gentlemen,
Where do you go? "

DOCTOR. Out in the lot
Where the ash-cans die,
There, old woman,
There shall you lie!

DEACON. Let's hurry away,
And never look behind
To see if her eyes
Are dead and blind,
To see if the quilt
Lies over her face.
Perhaps she'll groan,
Or move in her place —

HOUSE. The room is empty
Where the old woman lay,
And I no longer
Smell like a tomb —

LANDLADY. Doctor, deacon,
Can you say
Who'll pay the rent
For the old woman's room?

II

HOUSE. The room is empty
Down the hall;
There are mice in the closet,
Ghosts in the wall.
A pretty little lady
Comes to see —

WOMAN. Oh, what a dark room!
Not for me!

LANDLADY. The room is large
And the rent is low;
There's a deacon above,
And a doctor below.

[500]

DEACON.   When the little mice squeak
           I will pray —
DOCTOR.   I'll psycho-analyze
           The ghosts away.
LANDLADY. The bed is large
           And the mattress deep;
           Wrapped in a featherbed
           You shall sleep.
WOMAN.   But here's the door
           Without a key —
           An unlocked room
           Won't do for me!
DOCTOR.   Here's a bolt —
DEACON.   And here's a bar —
LANDLADY. You'll sleep safely
           Where you are!
WOMAN.   Good-night, gentlemen,
           It's growing late.
           Good-night, landlady,
           Pray don't wait!
           I'm going to bed —
           I'll bolt the door
           And sleep more soundly
           Than ever before!
DEACON.   Good-night, madam,
           I'll steal away —
DOCTOR.   Glad a pretty lady
           Has come to stay!
HOUSE.   She lights a candle —
           What do I see?
           That cloak looks like
           A quilt to me!
           She climbs into bed
           Where long she's lain;
           She's come back home —
           She won't leave again.
           She's found once more

Her rightful place —
Same old lady
With a pretty new face.
Let the deacon pray
And the doctor talk —
The mice will squeak
And the ghosts will walk.
There's a crafty smile
On the landlady's face —
The old woman's gone
And she's filled her place!

LANDLADY. It's nothing to me
If the old woman's dead —
I've somebody sleeping
In every bed!

MARJORIE ALLEN SEIFFERT

. . . They followed Yeobright upstairs to the landing, where there was a candle burning, which Yeobright took in his hand, and with it led the way into an adjoining room. Here he went to the bedside and folded back the sheet.

They stood silently looking upon Eustacia, who, as she lay there still in death, eclipsed all her living phases. Pallor did not include all the quality of her complexion, which seemed more than whiteness; it was almost light. The expression of her finely carved mouth was pleasant, as if a sense of dignity had just compelled her to leave off speaking. Eternal rigidity had seized upon it in a momentary transition between fervour and resignation. Her black hair was looser than either of them had ever seen it before, and surrounded her brow like a forest. . . .

THOMAS HARDY

. . . In the . . . terrible shipwreck of Italian emigrants
near Gibraltar (March 17, 1891), in which three hundred persons perished, amongst the corpses which were found on the
beach the following morning was that of a woman with a dead
infant clasped to her bosom. Neither the death agony nor
the tempestuous waves which had dashed these corpses on the
shore had sufficed to relax the last embrace, to separate the
mother from her little one.

Most affecting instances of the death rigor were found by
Professor Rossbach on the battle-fields of Beaumont and
Sedan during the campaign of 1870. . . .

The bursting of a shell killed a whole company of soldiers
who had sought shelter in a trench in order to take breakfast
in peace. Of one of these, says Rossbach, one might be certain that he was telling some merry tale, so lively was the expression of pleasure on his countenance, although he had
been killed by a terrible wound in the head. . . . A touching
case of rigor mortis described by Rossbach is that of a German soldier shot in the breast, who on feeling the approach of
death wished once more to look on the portrait of his wife
or sweetheart. He was lying on his side, supporting himself
on one arm, whilst with hand raised and rigid he held before
his eyes the picture which he appeared still to be contemplating in death. . . .

A. Mosso, translated by M. and W. B. Drummond

EPITAPH

Sir, you should notice me: I am the Man;
I am Good Fortune: I am satisfied.
All I desired, more than I could desire,
I have: everything has gone right with me.
Life was a hiding-place that played me false;
I croucht ashamed, and still was seen and scorned:
But now I am not seen. I was a fool,
And now I know what wisdom dare not know:

For I know Nothing. I was a slave, and now
I have ungoverned freedom and the wealth
That cannot be conceived: for I have Nothing.
I lookt for beauty and I longed for rest,
And now I have perfection: nay, I am
Perfection: I am Nothing, I am dead.

LASCELLES ABERCROMBIE

AN OLD SONG ENDED

" *How should I your true love know*
   From another one? "
" *By his cockle-hat and staff*
   And his sandal-shoon. "

" And what signs have told you now
   That he hastens home? "
" Lo! the spring is nearly gone,
   He is nearly come. "

" For a token is there nought,
   Say, that he should bring? "
" He will bear a ring I gave
   And another ring. "

" How may I, when he shall ask,
   Tell him who lies there? "
" Nay, but leave my face unveiled
   And unbound my hair. "

" Can you say to me some word
   I shall say to him? "
" Say I'm looking in his eyes
   Though my eyes are dim. "

DANTE GABRIEL ROSSETTI

. . . Gentlemen, there are cemeteries which destroy and cemeteries which preserve: in the first the bodies are rapidly got rid of; they are preserved for an indefinite time in the second. . . . When there has been poisoning by arsenic, preservation of the corpse is the rule. One of the women poisoned by Pel was found, four years after death, in the exact condition in which she was when put into her coffin. . . .

Five or six years ago the body of a female servant, who had disappeared nine months before, was discovered under a closed brick outhouse at the bottom of a garden belonging to a medical man living in the suburbs of Nantes.

M. Audouard was commissioned to examine the body. The skin was like parchment, shrivelled, and of a buff colour. When it was tapped with the back of a knife, it resounded like cardboard. The body had become very light. M. Audouard found also that the skin was perforated by an infinite number of holes, like a colander, and that dust from within escaped through these little holes. He sent me a thigh and a leg, which weighed one-third of the normal, as is the rule in cases of mummification of adult bodies. I showed the fragments of the body which M. Audouard sent me to M. Mégnin, who has devoted great attention to the study of the natural history of the " labourers of Death." M. Mégnin was enabled to determine the time at which the woman had died, and the conditions under which her death had occurred. How did this female, eighteen or nineteen years of age, become mummified? M. Audouard attributed it to the dryness of the chamber in which the body had been placed, the time at which death had occurred (early in the summer), and, lastly, to the layer of wheat and oat straw under which the body had been buried, and which had absorbed all the moisture of the body. It is quite possible. M. Mégnin made the discovery that the body had been devoured by mites, which had somehow or other eaten all the tissues of this woman. In the leg and thigh, which were in my possession, there remained only the aponeuroses and meshes of cellular tissue. All the muscles had vanished. The dust which escaped in clouds from the perforations in the skin was composed of the excretions and *débris* of the antennae, etc., of the mites. . . .

P. Brouardel, translated by F. Lucas Benham

Great Nature clothes the soul, which is but thin,
With fleshly garments, which the Fates do spin;
And when these garments are grown old and bare,
With sickness torn, Death takes them off with care,
And folds them up in peace and quiet rest,
And lays them safe within an earthly chest:
Then scours them well and makes them sweet and clean,
Fit for the soul to wear those clothes again.

Margaret, Duchess of Newcastle

AN EPITAPH

A house she hathe, it's made
    Of such good fashione
The tenant shall ne'er paye
    For repparatione.

Nor will her landlord ever
    Raise her rente
Or turne her out of doors
    For non paymente.

From chimney money too
    This cell is free,
To such a house who would
    Not tenante be?

AN EPITAPH UPON A VIRGIN

Here a solemne Fast we keepe,
While all beauty lyes asleep
Husht be all things; (no noyse here)
But the toning of a teare:
Or a sigh of such as bring
Cowslips for her covering.

ROBERT HERRICK

ON THE TOMBS IN WESTMINSTER

Mortality, behold and fear!
What a change of flesh is here!
Think how many royal bones
Sleep within this heap of stones;
Here they lie, had realms and lands,
Who now want strength to stir their hands;
Where from their pulpits sealed with dust
They preach: — " In greatness is no trust."
Here's an acre sown indeed
With the richest, royallest seed
That the earth did e'er suck in,
Since the first man died for sin:
Here the bones of birth have cried: —
" Though gods they were, as men they died."
Here are sands, ignoble things,
Dropt from the ruined sides of kings.
Here's a world of pomp and state,
Buried in dust, once dead by fate.

FRANCIS BEAUMONT

The names of those old Londoners I knew,
And others lately dead,
Well as the stones
That in the greying twilight hid from view
(God rest their bones!) . . .

But those, in the path that ran
Outside, in the high-walled way,
Those two, where the ivy's cloak
Fell darkliest, who were they?
Night-hooded, girl and man,
In whispers hushed they spoke,
And had no thought of death at all,
Or the mournful waves
Of the sighing wind that broke
Death-cold over the graves.
But there, by the shielding cliff of the wall,
As quiet they stood
As monuments having no part
In the mounting flood,
The flowing tide of the heart,
The quick distemper of blood:
Unknown lovers, by Love,
Sculptor of perfect art,
Lulled, enchanted above
Change, illusion, decay, —
So quiet they,
On a sudden, it seemed, by their fixed will
The season dreamed and Time stood still. . . .

GEORGE ROSTREVOR HAMILTON,
from " Unknown Lovers "

Oblivion is not to be hired. The greater part must be content to be as though they had not been, to be found in the register of God, not in the record of man. Twenty-seven names make up the first story before the flood, and the recorded names ever since contain not one living century. The number of the dead long exceedeth all that shall live. The night of time far surpasseth the day, and who knows when was the equinox? Every hour adds unto that current arithmetick, which scarce stands one moment. And since death must be the *Lucina* of life, and even Pagans could doubt, whether thus to live were to die; since our longest sun sets at right descensions, and makes but winter arches, and therefore it cannot be long before we lie down in darkness, and have our light in ashes;[1] since the brother of death daily haunts us with dying mementos, and time that grows old in itself, bids us hope no long duration; — diuturnity is a dream and folly of expectation.

SIR THOMAS BROWNE

IDLE CHARON

The shores of Styx are lone for evermore,
   And not one shadowy form upon the steep
   Looms through the dusk, as far as eyes can sweep,
To call the ferry over as of yore;
But tintless rushes, all about the shore,
   Have hemmed the old boat in, where, locked in sleep,
   Hoar-bearded Charon lies; while pale weeds creep
With tightening grasp all round the unused oar.

For now in the world of Life strange rumours run
   That now the Soul departs not with the breath,
But that the Body and the Soul are one;
   And in the loved one's mouth, now, after death,
The widow puts no obol, nor the son,
   To pay the ferry in the world beneath.

EUGENE LEE-HAMILTON

[1] The Jews place a lighted wax-candle in a pot of ashes by the corpse.

My Dear Heart,[2] — My sad parting was so far from making me forget you, that I scarce thought upon myself since, but wholly upon you. Those dear embraces which I yet feel, and shall never lose, being the faithful testimonies of an indulgent husband, have charmed my soul to such a reverence of your remembrance, that were it possible, I would, with my own blood, cement your dead limbs to live again, and (with reverence) think it no sin to rob Heaven a little longer of a martyr. Oh! my dear, you must now pardon my passion, this being my last (oh, fatal word!) that ever you will receive from me; and know, that until the last minute that I can imagine you shall live, I shall sacrifice the prayers of a Christian, and the groans of an afflicted wife. And when you are not (which sure by sympathy I shall know), I shall wish my own dissolution with you, that so we may go hand in hand to Heaven. 'Tis too late to tell you what I have, or rather have not done for you; how being turned out of doors because I came to beg mercy; the Lord lay not your blood to their charge.

I would fain discourse longer with you, but dare not; passion begins to drown my reason, and will rob me of my devoirs, which is all I have left to serve you. Adieu, therefore, ten thousand times, my dearest dear; and since I must never see you more, take this prayer, — May your faith be so strengthened that your constancy may continue; and then I know Heaven will receive you; whither grief and love will in a short time (I hope) translate,

My dear,

Your sad, but constant wife, even to love your ashes when dead,

Arundel Penruddock

May the 3rd, 1655, eleven o'clock at night. Your children beg your blessing, and present their duties to you.

[2] *This was Arundel Penruddock's last letter to her husband — a Wiltshire gentleman of the Royalist party who was beheaded by Cromwell's orders in 1655, at Exeter, for taking part in an insurrection there.*

. . . Dear loss! since thy untimely fate,
My task hath been to meditate
On thee, on thee: thou art the book,
The library, whereon I look,
Though almost blind. For thee (loved clay)
I languish out, not live, the day . . .
Thou hast benighted me; thy set
This eve of blackness did beget,
Who wast my day (though overcast,
Before thou hadst thy noontide past),
And I remember must in tears
Thou scarce hadst seen so many years
As day tell hours. By thy clear sun
My love and fortune first did run;
But thou wilt never more appear
Folded within my hemisphere,
Since both thy light and motion,
Like a fled star, is fallen and gone,
And 'twixt me and my soul's dear wish
The earth now interposèd is,
Which such a strange eclipse doth make,
As ne'er was read in almanack. . . .

Sleep on, my Love, in thy cold bed,
Never to be disquieted!
My last good night! Thou wilt not wake,
Till I thy fate shall overtake:
Till age, or grief, or sickness, must
Marry my body to that dust
It so much loves; and fill the room
My heart keeps empty in thy tomb.
Stay for me there; I will not fail
To meet thee in that hollow vale:
And think not much of my delay;
I am already on the way,

And follow thee with all the speed
Desire can make, or sorrows breed.
Each minute is a short degree,
And every hour a step towards thee.
At night when I betake to rest,
Next morn I rise nearer my West
Of life, almost by eight hours' sail,
Than when sleep breathed his drowsy gale. . . .
 Hark! my pulse, like a soft drum,
Beats my approach, tells thee I come;
And slow howe'er my marches be
I shall at last sit down by thee.
The thought of this bids me go on,
And wait my dissolution
With hope and comfort. Dear (forgive
The crime), I am content to live
Divided, with but half a heart,
Till we shall meet and never part.

 HENRY KING, from " Exequy on his Wife"

A NOCTURNALL UPON S. LUCIES DAY,
BEING THE SHORTEST DAY

Tis the yeares midnight, and it is the dayes,
Lucies, who scarce seaven houres herself unmaskes,
 The Sunne is spent, and now his flasks
 Send forth light squibs, no constant rayes;
 The worlds whole sap is sunke:
The generall balme th' hydroptique earth hath drunk,
Whither, as to the beds-feet, life is shrunke,
Dead and enterred; yet all these seeme to laugh,
Compared with mee, who am their Epitaph.

Study me then, you who shall lovers bee
At the next world, that is, at the next Spring:
 For I am every dead thing,
 In whom love wrought new Alchimie.

For his art did expresse
A quintessence even from nothingnesse,
From dull privations, and leane emptinesse:
He ruined mee, and I am re-begot
Of absence, darknesse, death; things which are not.

All others, from all things, draw all that's good,
Life, soule, forme, spirit, whence they beeing have;
  I, by loves limbecke, am the grave
  Of all, that's nothing. Oft a flood
    Have wee two wept, and so
Drownd the whole world, us two; oft did we grow
To be two Chaosses, when we did show
Care to ought else; and often absences
Withdrew our soules, and made us carcasses.

But I am by her death, (which word wrongs her)
Of the first nothing, the Elixer grown;
  Were I a man, that I were one,
  I needs must know; I should preferre,
    If I were any beast,
Some ends, some means; Yea plants, yea stones detest,
And love; All, all some properties invest;
If I an ordinary nothing were,
As shadow, a light, and body must be here.

But I am None; nor will my Sunne renew.
You lovers, for whose sake, the lesser Sunne
  At this time to the Goat is runne
  To fetch new lust, and give it you,
    Enjoy your summer all;
Since shee enjoyes her long nights festivall,
Let mee prepare towards her, and let mee call
This houre her Vigill, and her Eve, since this
Both the yeares, and the dayes deep midnight is.

JOHN DONNE

Oh, no more, no more! too late
   Sighs are spent; the burning tapers
Of a life as chaste as fate,
   Pure as are unwritten papers,
Are burnt out: no heat, no light
Now remains; 'tis ever night.

Love is dead; let lovers' eyes,
   Locked in endless dreams,
The extremes of all extremes,
Ope no more, for now Love dies.
   Now Love dies, — implying
Love's martyrs must be ever, ever dying.

JOHN FORD

REST

O earth, lie heavily upon her eyes;
   Seal her sweet eyes weary of watching, Earth;
   Lie close around her; leave no room for mirth
With its harsh laughter, nor for sound of sighs.
She hath no questions, she hath no replies,
   Hushed in and curtained with a blessed dearth
   Of all that irked her from the hour of birth;
With stillness that is almost Paradise.
Darkness more clear than noonday holdeth her,
   Silence more musical than any song;
Even her very heart has ceased to stir:
Until the morning of Eternity
Her rest shall not begin nor end, but be;
   And when she wakes she will not think it long.

CHRISTINA ROSSETTI

AN EPITAPH UPON A YOUNG MARRIED COUPLE

Dead and buried together

To these, whom Death again did wed,
This grave's their second marriage-bed;
For though the hand of Fate could force
'Twixt soul and body a divorce,
It could not sunder man and wife,
Because they both lived but one life.
Peace, good Reader, do not weep.
Peace, the lovers are asleep.
They, sweet turtles, folded lie
In the last knot Love could tie.
And though they lie as they were dead,
Their pillow stone, their sheets of lead,
(Pillow hard, and sheets not warm)
Love made the bed; they'll take no harm.
Let them sleep: let them sleep on,
Till this stormy night be gone,
Till the eternal morrow dawn;
Then the curtains will be drawn
And they wake into a light,
Whose day shall never die in night.

RICHARD CRASHAW

DIRGE FOR FIDELE

Fear no more the heat o' the sun,
　Nor the furious winter's rages;
Thou thy wordly task hast done,
　Home art gone, and ta'en thy wages;
Golden lads and girls all must,
As chimney-sweepers, come to dust.

Fear no more the frown o' the great,
   Thou art past the tyrant's stroke:
Care no more to clothe and eat;
   To thee the reed is as the oak:
The sceptre, learning, physic, must
All follow this, and come to dust.

Fear no more the lightning-flash,
   Nor the all-dreaded thunder-stone;
Fear not slander, censure rash;
   Thou hast finished joy and moan:
All lovers young, all lovers must
Consign to thee, and come to dust.

No exorciser harm thee!
   Nor no witchcraft charm thee!
Ghost unlaid forbear thee!
   Nothing ill come near thee!
Quiet consummation have;
And renownèd be thy grave!

WILLIAM SHAKESPEARE

THE BURIED CHILD

He is not dead nor liveth
The little child in the grave,
And men have known for ever
That he walketh again;
They hear him November evenings,
When acorns fall with the rain.

Deep in the hearts of men
Within his tomb he lieth,
And when the heart is desolate
He desolate sigheth.

Teach me then the heart of the dead child,
Who, holding a tulip, goeth
Up the stairs in his little grave-shift,
Sitting down in his little chair
By his biscuit and orange,
In the nursery he knoweth.

Teach me all that the child who knew life
And the quiet of death,
To the croon of the cradle-song
By his brother's crib
In the deeps of the nursery dusk
To his mother saith.

DOROTHY WELLESLEY

THE WIFE OF USHER'S WELL

There lived a wife at Usher's Well,
   And a wealthy wife was she;
She had three stout and stalwart sons,
   And sent them o'er the sea.

They hadna been a week from her,
   A week but hardly ane,
Whan word came to the carline wife
   That her three sons were gane.

They hadna been a week from her,
   A week but barely three,
Whan word came to the carline wife
   That her sons she'd never see.

" I wish the wind may never cease,
   Nor fashes in the flood,
Till my three sons come hame to me,
   In earthly flesh and blood."

It fell about the Martinmass,
　　When nights are lang and mirk,
The carline wife's three sons came hame,
　　And their hats were o' the birk.

It neither grew in syke nor ditch,
　　Nor yet in ony sheugh;
But at the gates o' Paradise,
　　That birk grew fair eneugh. . . .

" Blow up the fire, my maidens,
　　Bring water from the well;
For a' my house shall feast this night,
　　Since my three sons are well."

And she has made to them a bed,
　　She's made it large and wide,
And she's ta'en her mantle her about,
　　Sat down at the bed-side. . . .

Up then crew the red, red cock,
　　And up and crew the gray;
The eldest to the youngest said,
　　'Tis time we were away.

The cock he hadna crawd but once,
　　And clapped his wings at a',
When the youngest to the eldest said,
　　Brother, we must awa.

" The cock doth craw, the day doth daw,
　　The channerin worm doth chide;
Gin we be mist out o' our place,
　　A sair pain we maun bide.

" Fare ye weel, my mother dear!
　　Fareweel to barn and byre!
And fare ye weel, the bonny lass
　　That kindles my mother's fire! "

FUTILITY

Move him into the sun —
Gently its touch awoke him once,
At home, whispering of fields unsown.
Always it woke him, even in France,
Until this morning and this snow.
If anything might rouse him now
The kind old sun will know.

Think how it wakes the seeds,
Woke, once, the clays of a cold star.
Are limbs, so dear-achieved, are sides,
Full-nerved — still warm, — too hard to stir?
Was it for this the clay grew tall?
— O what made fatuous sunbeams toil
To break earth's sleep at all?

WILFRED OWEN

THE WHITEWASHED WALL

Why does she turn in that shy soft way
  Whenever she stirs the fire,
And kiss to the chimney-corner wall,
  As if entranced to admire
Its whitewashed bareness more than the sight
  Of a rose in richest green?
I have known her long, but this raptured rite
  I never before have seen.

— Well, once when her son cast his shadow there,
  A friend took a pencil and drew him
Upon that flame-lit wall. And the lines
  Had a life-like semblance to him.

[519]

And there long stayed his familiar look;
    But one day, ere she knew,
The whitener came to cleanse the nook,
    And covered the face from view.

" Yes," he said: " My brush goes on with a rush,
    And the draught is buried under;
When you have to whiten old cots and brighten,
    What else can you do, I wonder? "
But she knows he's there. And when she yearns
    For him, deep in the labouring night,
She sees him as close at hand, and turns
    To him under his sheet of white.

THOMAS HARDY

. . . To that high Capital, where kingly Death
    Keeps his pale court in beauty and decay,
    He came; and bought, with price of purest breath,
    A grave among the eternal. — Come away!
    Haste, while the vault of blue Italian day
    Is yet his fitting charnel-roof! while still
    He lies, as if in dewy sleep he lay;
    Awake him not! surely he takes his fill
Of deep and liquid rest, forgetful of all ill.

He will awake no more, oh, never more! —
    Within the twilight chamber spreads apace
    The shadow of white Death, and at the door
    Invisible Corruption waits to trace
    His extreme way to her dim dwelling-place;
    The eternal Hunger sits, but pity and awe
    Soothe her pale rage, nor dares she to deface
    So fair a prey, till darkness, and the law
Of change, shall o'er his sleep the mortal curtain draw.

[520]

O, weep for Adonais! — The quick Dreams,
The passion-wingèd Ministers of thought,
Who were his flocks, whom near the living streams
Of his young spirit he fed, and whom he taught
The love which was its music, wander not, —
Wander no more, from kindling brain to brain,
But droop there, whence they sprung; and mourn their lot
Round the cold heart, where, after their sweet pain,
They ne'er will gather strength, nor find a home again. . . .

PERCY BYSSHE SHELLEY, from "Adonais"

. . . Alas, but though my flying song flies after,
　　O sweet strange elder singer, thy more fleet
　　Singing, and footprints of thy fleeter feet,
Some dim derision of mysterious laughter
　　From the blind tongueless warders of the dead,
　　Some gainless glimpse of Proserpine's veiled head,
Some little sound of unregarded tears
　　Wept by effaced unprofitable eyes,
　　And from pale mouths some cadence of dead sighs —
These only, these the hearkening spirit hears,
　　Sees only such things rise.

Thou art far too far for wings of words to follow,
　　Far too far off for thought or any prayer.
　　What ails us with thee, who art wind and air?
What ails us gazing where all seen is hollow?
　　Yet with some fancy, yet with some desire,
　　Dreams pursue death as winds a flying fire,
Our dreams pursue our dead and do not find.
　　Still, and more swift than they, the thin flame flies,
　　The low light fails us in elusive skies,
Still the foiled earnest ear is deaf, and blind
　　Are still the eluded eyes. . . .

[521]

For thee, O now a silent soul, my brother,
　　Take at my hands this garland, and farewell.
　　Thin is the leaf, and chill the wintry smell,
And chill the solemn earth, a fatal mother,
　　With sadder than the Niobean womb,
　　And in the hollow of her breasts a tomb.
Content thee, howsoe'er, whose days are done;
　　There lies not any troublous thing before,
　　Nor sight nor sound to war against thee more,
For whom all winds are quiet as the sun,
　　All waters as the shore.

ALGERNON CHARLES SWINBURNE,
from " Ave Atque Vale "
In memory of Charles Beaudelaire

LORENZO'S BAS RELIEF FOR
A FLORENTINE CHEST

Lust is the oldest lion of them all,
And he shall have first place;
With a malignant growl satirical
To curve in foliations prodigal
Round and around his face,
Extending till the echoes interlace
With Pride and Prudence, two cranes gaunt and tall.

Four lesser lions crouch and malign the cranes.
Cursing and gossiping, they shake their manes,
While from their long tongues leak
Drops of thin venom as they speak.
The cranes, unmoved, peck grapes and grains
From a huge cornucopia, which rains
A plenteous meal from its antique
Interior — a note quite curiously Greek.

And nine long serpents twist
And twine, twist and twine —
A riotously beautiful design
Whose elements consist
Of eloquent spirals, fair and fine,
Embracing cranes and lions, who exist
Seemingly free, yet tangled in that living vine.

And in this chest shall be
Two cubic metres of space —
Enough to hold all memory
Of you and me. . . .
And this shall be the place
Where silence shall embrace
Our bodies, and obliterate the trace
Our souls made on the purity
Of night. . . .
    Now lock the chest, for we
Are dead, and lose the key!

      M ARJORIE A LLEN S EIFFERT

THE RUIN

Gone are the coloured princes, gone echo, gone laughter:
Drips the blank roof: and the moss creeps after.

Dead is the crumbled chimney: all mellowed to rotting
The wall-tints, and the floor-tints, from the spotting
Of the rain, from the wind and slow appetite
Of patient mould: and of the worms that bite
At beauty all their innumerable lives.

— But the sudden nip of knives,
The lady aching for her stiffening lord,
The passionate-fearful bride,
And beaded Pallor clamped to the torment-board,

[523]

Leave they no ghosts, no memories by the stairs?
No sheeted glimmer treading floorless ways?
No haunting melody of lovers' airs,
Nor stealthy chill upon the noon of days?

No: for the dead and senseless walls have long forgotten
What passionate hearts beneath the grass lie rotten.

Only from roofs and chimneys pleasantly sliding
Tumbles the rain in the early hours:
Patters its thousand feet on the flowers,
Cools its small grey feet in the grasses.

RICHARD HUGHES

So I came down the steps to Lenin.
With a herd of peasants before
And behind me, I saw
A room stained scarlet, and there
A small wax man in a small glass case.
Two sentinels at his feet, and one at his head,
Two little hands on his breast:
Pious spinster asleep; and I said
"Many warrants these delicate hands have signed."
A lamp shone, red,
An aureole over him, on his red hair;
His uniform clothed him still.

Greedy of detail I saw,
In those two minutes allowed,
The man was not wax, as they said,
But a corpse, for a thumb nail was black;
The thing was Lenin.

Then a woman beside me cried
With a strange voice, foreign, loud.
And I, who fear not life nor death, and those who have died

Only a little, was inwardly shaken with fear,
For I stood in the presence of God;
The voice I heard was the voice of all generations
Acclaiming new faiths, horrible, beautiful faiths;
I knew that the woman wailed as women wailed long ago
For Christ in the sepulchre laid.
Chirst was a wax man too,
When they carried Him down to the grave. . . .

DOROTHY WELLESLEY, from " Lenin "

THE SKELETON OF THE FUTURE

(*At Lenin's Tomb*)

Red granite and black diorite, with the blue
Of the labradorite crystals gleaming like precious stones
In the light reflected from the snow; and behind them
The eternal lightning of Lenin's bones.

HUGH McDIARMID

" FULL FATHOM FIVE "

Full fathom five thy father lies;
   Of his bones are coral made:
Those are pearls that were his eyes:
   Nothing of him that doth fade,
But doth suffer a sea-change
Into something rich and strange.
Sea-nymphs hourly ring his knell:
     Ding-dong.
Hark! now I hear them, — ding-dong, bell.

WILLIAM SHAKESPEARE

[525]

. . . But O how near
that Other Life to this!
I go in daily hope, in daily fear:
when shall I see? when shall I hear?
For all this world is but a mist
that hides the lip of the supreme Abyss,
and all things that exist
the Metaphor of Being. When shall I
see the thing meant in the thing seen,
and know what ocean, earth and sky,
what living and what dying mean?

In daily hope, in daily fear I go.
When, with a hushed premonitory shock,
shall I hear Echo from her wooded rock
cry back a name I did not cry?
or run to meet my friend —
to meet, upon my running's end,
one whom I never knew — whom yet I know
more nearly than the beating of my heart?
When will the rounded hill, the hollow dale,
the solid mountain sweeping to its snow,
grow flat and tremble like a veil . . .
and like the temple-curtain suddenly
be rent apart
to show. . . .

Eye hath not seen, ear hath not heard!
And thinking hath no thought and speech no word!
And I . . . ?
In daily fear, in daily hope I go.
     J. REDWOOD ANDERSON, from " Intimations "

AT THE GRAVE OF HENRY VAUGHAN

Above the voiceful windings of a river
An old green slab of simply graven stone
Shuns notice, overshadowed by a yew.
Here Vaughan lies dead, whose name flows on for ever
Through pastures of the spirit washed with dew
And starlit with eternities unknown.

Here sleeps the Silurist; the loved physician;
The face that left no portraiture behind;
The skull that housed white angels and had vision
Of daybreak through the gateways of the mind.
  Here faith and mercy, wisdom and humility
  (Whose influence shall prevail for evermore)
  Shine. And this lowly grave tells Heaven's
    tranquillity.
And here stand I, a suppliant at the door.

                    SIEGFRIED SASSOON

EL DESDICHADO

 · I am that dark, that disinherited,
    That all-dishonoured Prince of Aquitaine,
    The Star upon my scutcheon long hath fled;
  A black sun on my lute doth yet remain!
  Oh, thou that didst console me not in vain
    Within the tomb, among the midnight dead,
    Show me Italian seas, and blossoms wed,
  The rose, the vine-leaf, and the golden grain.

  Say, am I love or Phoebus? Have I been
  Or Lusignan or Biron? By a Queen
    Caressed within the Mermaid's haunt I lay,

And twice I crossed the unpermitted stream,
And touched on Orpheus' lyre as in a dream,
  Sighs of a Saint, and laughter of a Fay!

    GERARD DE NERVAL, translated by Andrew Lang

    O blest unfabled Incense Tree,
    That burns in glorious Araby,
    With red scent chalicing the air,
    Till earth-life grow Elysian there!

    Half buried to her flaming breast
    In this bright tree, she makes her nest,
    Hundred-sunned Phoenix! when she must
    Crumble at length to hoary dust.

    Her gorgeous death-bed! her rich pyre
    Burnt up with aromatic fire!
    Her urn, sight high from spoiler men!
    Her birthplace, when self-born, again!

    The mountainless green wilds among,
    Here ends she her unechoing song!
    With amber tears and odorous sighs
    Mourned by the desert where she dies! . . .

      GEORGE DARLEY, from " The Phoenix "

" DEATH BE NOT PROUD "

Death be not proud, though some have callèd thee
Mighty and dreadfull, for, thou art not soe,
For, those, whom thou think'st, thou dost overthrow,
Die not, poore death, nor yet canst thou kill mee.
From rest and sleepe, which but thy pictures bee,
Much pleasure, then from thee, much more must flow,
And soonest our best men with thee doe goe,
Rest of their bones, and soules deliverie.

[528]

Thou art slave to Fate, Chance, kings, and desperate men,
And dost with poyson, warre, and sicknesse dwell,
And poppie, or charmes can make us sleepe as well,
And better than thy stroake; why swell'st thou then?
One short sleepe past, wee wake eternally,
And death shall be no more; death, thou shalt die.

JOHN DONNE

"The Life of Things"

On the idle hill of summer
  Sleepy with the flow of streams
Far I hear the steady drummer
  Drumming like a noise in dreams. . . .

Art thou real, Earth? Am I?
In whose dream do we exist? . . .

"The Life of Things"

L ife, one might say, is the daughter of the sun. The rays
whose waves fall upon the chlorophyll in the leaves of
plants, produce a chemical action which man has been unable
to obtain by the synthetic methods which are now at the service of science. The living energy of the sun is absorbed and
transformed: his potential energy goes to sleep, if it is permis-
sible so to express it, in the leaves, in the seeds of the plants,
in the albuminoid substances which are produced in vegetable cells. . . .

A. Mosso

The microscopic animalculæ luxuriating near [my] study
window, in a bowl of growing ferns, which is surmounted by
a dome-shaped glass shade, doubtless regard the graceful
herbage as composing a tract of vegetation so vast as infinitely
to exceed, by comparison, any forest that we could even conceive. Merely to switch on or off the electric light is, as we
well know, not only to constitute for myriads of these tiny
creatures an irregular night and day, but actually to provide
them with a climatic change with each movement. To consider their aspect, their conduct, their lives, in comparison
with our own, is, in the main, an impossibility, but certainly
we could not believe that their understanding of the world,
still less of the universe, could be of any moment whatever.

If the earth and the moon were connected by a pole, the
one orb held stationary and the other swung around it, the
circle described would be considerably less in diameter than
is the sun. Our light-giver, as every schoolboy knows, is,
roughly, a million and a half times larger than the earth; but

Sirius is 2,000 times larger than the sun, three thousand million times larger than the earth. Imagine a sphere of that size peopled with creatures who were proportionate in stature to their planet as we are to ours — i.e., 3,000,000,000 times greater — suppose they had brains and years equally in proportion, how would they contemplate us? We know of creatures this much smaller, why not allow for others that much larger?

J. W. FLAVELL

In any case, to destroy the objection [that although any close observation of flowers and insects reveals marvels apparently of their own creation, yet that these marvels remain eternally the same and are not the outcome of " intelligence "], it would be enough to establish one act of intelligent progress, were it but for a single occasion, outside mankind. But, apart from the pleasure which one takes in refuting an over-vain and out-of-date argument, how little importance, when all is said, attaches to this question of the personal intelligence of the flowers, the insects or the birds! Suppose that we say, speaking of the Orchid and the bee alike, that it is nature and not the plant or the insect that calculates, that combines, that adorns, invents and thinks: what interest can this distinction have for us? A much loftier question and one much worthier of our eager attention towers over these details. What we have to do is to grasp the character, the quality, the habits and perhaps the object of the general intelligence whence emanate all the intelligent acts performed upon this earth. It is from this point of view that the study of those creatures — the ants and the bees, among others — in which, outside the human form, the proceedings and the ideal of that genius are most clearly manifested becomes one of the most curious that we can undertake. It is clear, after all that we have shown, that those tendencies, those intellectual methods must be at least as complex, as advanced, as startling in the Orchids as in the gregarious

Hymenopteræ. Let us add that a large number of the motives and a portion of the logic of these restless insects, so difficult of observation, still escape us, whereas we can grasp with ease all the silent motives, all the wise and stable arguments of the peaceful flower. . . .

MAURICE MAETERLINCK, translated
by Alexander Teixeira de Mattos

Has any one of us ever *seen* a Tree? I certainly do not think that I have — except most superficially. That very penetrating observer and naturalist, Henry D. Thoreau, tells us he would often make an appointment to visit a certain tree, miles away — but what or whom he saw when he got there, he does not say. Walt Whitman, also a keen observer . . . mentions that, in a dream trance he actually once saw his " favourite trees step out and promenade up, down and around, *very curiously.*" Once the present writer seemed to have a partial vision of a tree. It was a beech, standing somewhat isolated, and still leafless in quite early Spring. Suddenly I was aware of its skyward-reaching arms and upturned finger-tips, as if some vivid life (or electricity) was streaming through them far into the spaces of heaven, and of its roots plunged in the earth and drawing the same energies from below. The day was quite still and there was no movement in the branches, but in that moment the tree was no longer a separate or separable organism, but a vast being ramifying far into space, sharing and uniting the life of Earth and Sky, and full of most amazing activity. . . .

EDWARD CARPENTER

One morning when I was in the wood something happened which was nothing less than a transformation of myself and the world, although I " believed " nothing new. I was looking at a great, spreading, bursting oak. The first tinge from the greenish-yellow buds was just visible. It seemed to be no longer a tree away from me and apart from me. The enclos-

[535]

ing barriers of consciousness were removed and the text came into my mind, "Thou in me and I in Thee." The distinction of self and not-self was an illusion. I could feel the rising sap; in me also sprang the fountain of life uprushing from its roots, and the joy of its outbreak at the extremity of each twig right up to the summit was my own: that which kept me apart was nothing. . . .

MARK RUTHERFORD

It was not, I think, till my eighth year that I began to be distinctly conscious of something more than this mere childish delight in nature. It may have been there all the time from infancy — I don't know; but when I began to know it consciously it was as if some hand had surreptitiously dropped something into the honeyed cup which gave it at certain times a new flavour. . . . I would go out of my way to meet it, and I used to steal out of the house alone when the moon was at its full, to stand, silent and motionless, near some group of large trees, gazing at the dusky green foliage silvered by the beams; and at such times the sense of mystery would grow until a sensation of delight would change to fear, and the fear increase until it was no longer to be borne, and I would hastily escape to recover the sense of reality and safety indoors, where there was light and company. Yet on the very next night I would steal out again and go to the spot where the effect was strongest, which was usually among . . . the white acacia trees, which gave the name of Las Acacias to our place. The loose feathery foliage on moonlight nights had a peculiar hoary aspect that made this tree seem more intensely alive than others, more conscious of my presence and watchful of me. . . .

W. H. HUDSON

The forest absorbed us; as one's attention would be challenged and drawn by the casual regard, never noticeably direct, but never withdrawn, of a being superior and mys-

terious, so I was drawn to watch the still and intent stature
of the jungle, waiting for it to become vocal, for some re-
laxing of its static form. Nothing ever happened. I never
discovered it. Rigid, watchful, enigmatic, its presence was
constant, but without so much as one blossom in all its green
vacuity to show the least friendly familiarity to one who had
found flowers and woodland kind. It had nothing that I knew.
It remained securely aloof and indifferent, till I thought
hostility was implied, as the sea implies its impartial hostility,
in a constant presence which experience could not fathom,
nor interest soften, nor courage intimidate. We sank gradually deeper inwards towards its central fastnesses. . . .

H. M. TOMLINSON

It is an isle 'twixt Heaven, Air, Earth, and Sea,
Cradled, and hung in clear tranquillity . . .
And from the sea there rise, and from the sky
There fall, clear exhalations, soft and bright,
Veil after veil, each hiding some delight,
Which Sun or Moon or zephyr draw aside,
Till the isle's beauty, like a naked bride
Glowing at once with love and loveliness,
Blushes and trembles at its own excess:
Yet, like a buried lamp, a Soul no less
Burns in the heart of this delicious isle,
An atom of th' Eternal, whose own smile
Unfolds itself, and may be felt, not seen
O'er the gray rocks, blue waves, and forests green,
Filling their bare and void interstices. —
But the chief marvel of the wilderness
Is a lone dwelling, built by whom or how
None of the rustic island-people know:
'Tis not a tower of strength, though with its height
It overtops the woods; but, for delight,
Some wise and tender Ocean-King, ere crime
Had been invented, in the world's young prime,
Reared it, a wonder of that simple time,

[537]

An envy of the isles, a pleasure-house
Made sacred to his sister and his spouse.
It scarce seems now a wreck of human art,
But, as it were Titanic; in the heart
Of Earth having assumed its form, then grown
Out of the mountains, from the living stone,
Lifting itself in caverns light and high:
For all the antique and learnèd imagery
Has been erased, and in the place of it
The ivy and the wild vine interknit
The volumes of their many-twining stems;
Parasite flowers illume with dewy gems
The lampless halls, and when they fade, the sky
Peeps through their winter-roof of tracery
With moonlight patches, or star atoms keen,
Or fragments of the day's intense serene; —
Working mosaic on their Parian floors.
And, day and night, aloof, from the high towers
And terraces, the Earth and Ocean seem
To sleep in one another's arms, and dream
Of waves, flowers, clouds, woods, rocks, and all
    that we
Read in their smiles, and call reality. . . .

        P. B. SHELLEY, from *Epipsychidion*

One summer afternoon, you find
Some lonely trees. Persuade your mind
To drowse. Then, as your eyelids close,
And you still hover into those
Three stages of a darkening doze,
This side the barrier of sleep,
Pause. In that last clear moment open quick
Your sight toward where the green is bright and thick.
Be sure that everything you keep
To dream with is made out of trees.

[538]

Grip hard, become a root, so drive
Your muscles through the ground alive
That you'll be breaking from above your knees
Out into branches. Let your manhood be
Forgotten, your whole purpose seem
The purpose of a simple tree
Rooted in a quiet dream. . . .

It is a dangerous journey. If you go
Think carefully of this, which now I know. —
Tree-life is like a corridor between
The Seen and the Unseen.
Trees are like sentinels that keep
The passage of a gate
From this sleep to that other sleep:
Between two worlds they wait.
If they discover you, you cannot hide.
Run backward. They are stern.
You may be driven out that other side,
And not return. . . .

HAROLD MONRO, from "Trees"

ROOTS

I've known days when a passing sight
Was window to the infinite.
There is a place where a cart track
Cuts deep into a green down's back,
As wire cuts cheese, and you may walk
In shade between two walls of chalk,
Save at sun's height. Once in noon glare
I came on sudden shadow there,
And looking up I saw on high
A tree whose branches brushed the sky
Sprouting from the cliff-edge and, wonder!
A tree inverted, branching under

Into the chalk. It was as if
Twin seeds had struck root on the cliff,
And one grown skyward and one thirled
His fingers to the underworld;
But those down-delving limbs and shoots
Were that same lofty giant's roots.

Through the cleft ridge the pathway led
Down to a vale with trees o'erspread,
But for a while I scarce could see
In all that vale a single tree,
Only roots, roots. . . . Then the path wound
Upwards; I footed open ground
And shadowless grass, but I was 'ware
Of a power moving in the air,
A ferment underneath the green,
Under each tree a tree unseen.
And when a scared bird rose to fly,
His outspread wings against the sky
Seemed roots. Methought, all Nature bruits
A mystery. O what the roots
And on what stem eternal grows
Earth's evanescent sunset rose?
And when the crimson fades in gloom
Darkness bursts into starry bloom,
And globèd buds the heavens fill
Rooted more deep than Igdrasil.

THOMAS SHARP

PRIMROSE

So is the primrose-breath a far-off sweetness.
  Moon draws through pools of day
A like unsearchable gleam; immortal lovers
  Have trod this mortal way.
The darkness is a nameless hand laid lightly

On trembling lids of sleep.
A kindly hand, that with the darkness gathers
The odours of the deep.

Root of an earthly glade, O deathly primrose,
Thy flower, thy deathless part,
Untasted Spring upon a grave of Autumn,
Is heaped against my heart.

VIVIAN LOCKE ELLIS

It was a memorable night! I will name it the Night of the Great Peacock. Who does not know this superb moth, the largest of all our European butterflies, with its livery of chestnut velvet and its collar of white fur? . . .

On the morning of the 6th of May a female emerged from her cocoon in my presence on my laboratory table. I cloistered her immediately, all damp with the moisture of metamorphosis, in a cover of wire gauze. I had no particular intentions regarding her; I imprisoned her from mere habit; the habit of an observer always on the alert for what may happen.

I was richly rewarded. About nine o'clock that evening, when the household was going to bed, there was a sudden hubbub in the room next to mine. Little Paul, half undressed, was rushing to and fro, running, jumping, stamping, and overturning the chairs as if possessed. I heard him call me. I ran. . . .

Candle in hand, we entered the room. What we saw is unforgettable. With a soft *flic-flac* the great night-moths were flying round the wire-gauze cover, alighting, taking flight, returning, mounting to the ceiling, re-descending. They rushed at the candle and extinguished it with a flap of the wing; they fluttered on our shoulders, clung to our clothing, grazed our faces. My study had become a cave of a necromancer, the darkness alive with creatures of the night! . . .

The weather was stormy; the sky heavily clouded; the darkness was so profound that out of doors, in the garden and away from the trees, one could scarcely see one's hand before one's face.

In addition to such darkness as this there were certain difficulties of access. The house is hidden by great plane-trees; an alley densely bordered with lilacs and rose-trees makes a kind of outer vestibule to the entrance; it is protected from the *mistral* by groups of pines and screens of cypress. A thicket of evergreen shrubs forms a rampart at a few paces from the door. It was across this maze of leafage, and in absolute darkness, that the butterflies had to find their way in order to attain the end of their pilgrimage.

Under such conditions the screech-owl would not dare to forsake its hollow in the olive-tree. The butterfly, better endowed with its faceted eyes than the owl with its single pupils, goes forward without hesitation, and threads the obstacles without contact. So well it directs its tortuous flight that, in spite of all the obstacles to be evaded, it arrives in a state of perfect freshness, its great wings intact, without the slightest flaw. The darkness is light enough.[1] . . .

J. H. FABRE, translated by Bernard Miall

I must describe another occurrence which took place during our observation because it bears upon the theory of the organic unity of the termitary.

While we were watching the queen, a fairly large piece of hard clay became detached from the edge of the roof of the cell and fell down, dealing the queen a somewhat hard blow. Immediately a series of extraordinary occurrences took place. The only effect which the shock had on the queen herself, was that she began moving her head to and fro in a rhythmic fashion. The workers immediately ceased all work within the cell and wandered round in aimless groups. The circle of

---

[1] [There are many similar mysteries connected with the night hours, in nature and in man. The "migration fever," for example, burns in a wild bird, at a certain season of the year, between midnight and dawn, even when it has been confined in the darkest of cages. At 2 a.m. the vitality of the human body is said to be at its lowest ebb, when, that is, it is sunken into its "deepest" nocturnal sleep. Newcomers to this world enter it more frequently during the night than during the day; and we are a little more likely to make our departure from it in the dark hours than by daylight.]

bodyguards broke up at once and most of them vanished down the passages behind the palace cavity. Then we saw masses of tiny workers thronging into the palace cavity and cell. They swarmed over the queen in order to suck the fluid through her skin, in exactly the same way as the masseurs had done in normal circumstances. The king greedily took part in this draining of his mate. They succeeded so well that within a few minutes the skin of the queen was hanging in loose folds.

In the meantime we visited far outlying parts of the nest, where the termites had been very active just before the accident. Even in the farthest parts all work had ceased. The large soldiers and workers gathered in great excitement in different parts of the nest. There appeared to be a tendency to collect in groups. There was not the least doubt the shock to the queen was felt in the outermost parts of the termitary within a few minutes. Recovery began in the same place where the first and greatest disturbance took place. Slowly the destructive workers stopped their assault on the queen. The bodyguard took up their positions in a circle and the queen ceased the rhythmic movements of her head. She appeared to be recovering from the shock. So quickly that it was barely possible for me to follow all the stages, normal activity began anew. The only difference in conduct which I could notice was that the workers appeared to be speeding up the feeding of the queen, and before long her body had resumed its usual gigantic size. The following day all activity in the outermost parts of the termitary was in full swing. . . .

Eugene N. Marais, translated by Winifred de Kok

The Goldfinch (or Thistlefinch) is every where in England well known, and highly esteemed both for Singing and for the Elegancy of its Colours, being certainly the most beautiful and the finest-feathered of all Cage-Birds. . . .

They are of a mild and gentle Nature, as may even thence appear, that presently after they are caught, without using any Art or Care, they will fall to their Meat and Drink; nor are they so affrighted at the Presence of a Man as most other Birds are wont to be, nor very much troubled at their Imprisonment in a Cage; for, if they have continued there a good while, they like it so well, that though you let them loose, they will not fly away; but when scared, fly directly to their Cage for Shelter, as I have proved by Experience.

They are called in some places, *Draw-Waters*, from their Aptness to learn to draw their Water when they want to drink, in a little Ivory Bucket, fastened to a small Chain, made for that Purpose: 'tis a pretty Sight to see with what Dexterity these little Creatures will pull up their Bucket, drink, and throw it down again; and lift up the Lid of a small Box, or Bin, with their Bill, to come at their Meat, etc. They are wonderfully delighted with viewing themselves in a Glass, fixed to the Back of their Bucket-Board, where they will sit upon their Perch, pruning and dressing themselves with the greatest Care imaginable, often looking in the Glass, and placing every Feather in the nicest Order; no Lady can take greater Pleasure, or be more nice in dressing herself, than this little beautiful Bird is in rectifying all Disorders in his Plume, not suffering a Feather to lay amiss.

ELEAZAR ALBIN

THE COMMON QUESTION

Behind us at our evening meal
    The grey bird ate his fill,
Swung downward by a single claw
    And wiped his hookèd bill.

He shook his wings and crimson tail,
    And set his head aslant,
And, in his sharp, impatient way,
    Asked, " What does Charlie want? "

" Fie, silly bird! " I answered, " tuck
    Your head beneath your wing,

And go to sleep; " — but o'er and o'er
   He asked the self-same thing. . . .

He shook his wings and crimson tail,
   And set his head aslant,
And, in his sharp, impatient way,
   Asked, " What does Charlie want? "

JOHN GREENLEAF WHITTIER

ONE WHO KNOWS HIS SEA–GULLS

Two sea-gulls carved of ivory
Stand by the early morning-sea.

One has a head, and one has none,
His clean white breast-feathers run
Up and over and do not stop,
There is no sign of that large drop
Of dark fire, round as sky,
That could be called a sea-gull's eye.

One sea-gull has a head, and one
Sea-gulls stands there white with none.

Yet one who knows his sea-gulls knows
There is a head hid in the snows
Of the feathers on the back
Of the headless one, and black
Beads of life are sheathed there sound,
Ready to build a world around
The circle of a sea-gull's head
At the lightest alien tread.

A sea-gull's beak is made to slide
Between his wings in back and hide,
His head is made exactly right
To go between his wings for night.

ROBERT P. TRISTRAM COFFIN

[545]

. . . O let your strong imagination turn
The great wheel backward, until Troy unburn,
And then unbuild, and seven Troys below
Rise out of death, and dwindle, and outflow,
Till all have passed, and none has yet been there:
Back, ever back. Our birds still crossed the air;
Beyond our myriad changing generations
Still built, unchanged, their known inhabitations.
A million years before Atlantis was
Our lark sprang from some hollow in the grass,
Some old soft hoof-print in a tussock's shade;
And the wood-pigeon's smooth snow-white eggs were
　　laid
High, amid green pines' sunset-coloured shafts,
And rooks their villages of twiggy rafts
Set on the tops of elms, where elms grew then,
And still the thumbling tit and perky wren
Popped through the tiny doors of cosy balls
And the blackbird lined with moss his high-built walls;
A round mud cottage held the thrush's young,
And straws from the untidy sparrow's hung.
And, skimming forktailed in the evening air,
When man first was were not the martens there?
Did not those birds some human shelter crave,
And stow beneath the cornice of his cave
Their dry tight cups of clay? And from each door
Peeped on a morning wiseheads three or four.

Yes, daw and owl, curlew and crested hern,
Kingfisher, mallard, water-rail and tern,
Chaffinch and greenfinch, wagtail, stonechat, ruff,
Whitethroat and robin, fly-catcher and chough,
Missel-thrush, magpie, sparrow-hawk, and jay,
Built, those far ages gone, in this year's way.
And the first man who walked the cliffs of Rame,
As I this year, looked down and saw the same

Blotches of rusty red on ledge and cleft
With grey-green spots on them, while right and left
A dizzying tangle of gulls were floating and flying,
Wheeling and crossing and darting, crying and crying,
Circling and crying, over and over and over,
Crying with swoop and hover and fall and recover.
And below on a rock against the grey sea fretted,
Pipe-necked and stationary and silhouetted,
Cormorants stood in a wise, black, equal row
Above the nests and long blue eggs we know.

O delicate chain over all the ages stretched,
O dumb tradition from what far darkness fetched:
Each little architect with its one design
Perpetual, fixed and right in stuff and line,
Each little ministrant who knows one thing,
One learnèd rite to celebrate the spring.
Whatever alters else on sea or shore,
These are unchanging: man must still explore.

J. C. SQUIRE, from "The Birds"

THE NIGHTJAR

We loved our Nightjar, but she would not stay with us.
We had found her lying as dead, but soft and warm,
Under the apple tree beside the old thatched wall.
Two days we kept her in a basket by the fire,
Fed her, and thought she well might live — till suddenly
In the very moment of most confiding hope
She raised herself all tense, quivered, and drooped, and died.
Tears sprang into my eyes — why not? the heart of man
Soon sets itself to love a living companion,
The more so if by chance it asks some care of him.
And this one had the kind of loveliness that goes
Far deeper than the optic nerve — full fathom five

To the soul's ocean cave, where Wonder and Reason
Tell their alternate dreams of how the world was made.
So wonderful she was — her wings the wings of night
But powdered here and there with tiny golden clouds
And wave-line markings like sea-ripples on the sand.
O how I wish I might never forget that bird —
Never! — but even now, like all beauty of earth
She is fading from me into the dusk of Time.

SIR HENRY NEWBOLT

. . . That blessed mood,
In which the burthen of the mystery,
In which the heavy and the weary weight
Of all this unintelligible world,
Is lightened: — that serene and blessed mood,
In which the affections gently lead us on, —
Until, the breath of this corporeal frame
And even the motion of our human blood
Almost suspended, we are laid asleep
In body, and become a living soul:
While with an eye made quiet by the power
Of harmony, and the deep power of joy,
We see into the life of things. . . .

WILLIAM WORDSWORTH, from
" Lines composed a few miles above Tintern Abbey"

THE SEED SHOP

Here in a quiet and dusty room they lie,
Faded as crumbled stone or shifting sand,
Forlorn as ashes, shrivelled, scentless, dry —
Meadows and gardens running through my hand.

In this brown husk a dale of hawthorn dreams,
A cedar in this narrow cell is thrust;

It will drink deeply of a century's streams,
These lilies shall make summer on my dust.

Here in their safe and simple house of death,
Sealed in their shells a million roses leap;
Here I can blow a garden with my breath,
And in my hand a forest lies asleep.

MURIEL STUART

FIRST FAUN. Canst thou imagine where those spirits live
　　Which make such delicate music in the woods?
　　We haunt within the least frequented caves
　　And closest coverts, and we know these wilds,
　　Yet never meet them, though we hear them oft:
　　Where may they hide themselves?
SECOND FAUN.　　　　　　　　'Tis hard to tell:
　　I have heard those more skilled in spirits say,
　　The bubbles, which the enchantment of the sun
　　Sucks from the pale faint water-flowers that pave
　　The oozy bottom of clear lakes and pools,
　　Are the pavilions where such dwell and float
　　Under the green and golden atmosphere
　　Which noontide kindles thro' the woven leaves;
　　And when these burst, and the thin fiery air,
　　The which they breathed within those lucent domes,
　　Ascends to flow like meteors thro' the night,
　　They ride on them, and rein their headlong speed,
　　And bow their burning crests, and glide in fire
　　Under the waters of the earth again.
FIRST F. If such live thus, have others other lives,
　　Under pink blossoms or within the bells
　　Of meadow flowers, or folded violets deep,
　　Or on their dying odours, when they die,
　　Or on the sunlight of the spherèd dew?
SECOND F. Ay, many more which we may well divine.
　　But, should we stay to speak, noontide would come,

And thwart Silenus find his goats undrawn,
And grudge to sing those wise and lovely songs
Of Fate, and Chance, and God, and Chaos old,
And Love, and the chained Titan's woeful dooms,
And how he shall be loosed, and make the earth
One brotherhood; delightful strains which cheer
Our solitary twilights, and which charm
To silence the unenvying nightingales.

PERCY BYSSHE SHELLEY,
from *Prometheus Unbound, Act II, Scene II*

TREE PURGE

I, driven, deeper driven in the glade,
As one from blood-guilt (Lord have mercy!)
Flying, seeking sanctuary,
From Fear the Avenger flying to green shade. . . .

Your strength, O trees, your stature,
Not by these,
O not by these alone
From the crimson shadow,
From my tormented nature,
Save me, O trees!

I, inward have I known,
Beneath rough bark,
The pulse of the sap, the life-blood in the dark
Pounding, pounding up
From the blind-nurtured root:
Felt those streams course
Through giant trunk and bough with passionless force —
No passion and no fever and no lust —
To where miraculous the green leaves shoot
Skyward, from dust.

I, therefore, to that flood,
I fugitive cry,
Let my tumultuous blood,
Red rivulet in spate
Pricking with lust and turbulent with hate,
A tributary run:
To sink itself and so again be found,
In life not mine washed, overwhelmed and drowned,
All lost,
All won,
Crimson no more, and I no longer I,
In that great channel sucked toward the sun.

GEORGE ROSTREVOR HAMILTON

"The Silent Pool"

Lakes that endlessly outspread
Their lone waters. . . .
Shrouded forms that start and sigh
As they pass the wanderer by. . . .

"The Silent Pool"

Look downward in the silent pool:
    The weeds cling to the ground they love;
They live so quietly, are so cool;
They do not need to think, or move.

Look down in the unconscious mind:
There everything is quiet too
And deep and cool, and you will find
Calm growth and nothing hard to do,
And nothing that need trouble you.

HAROLD MONRO

FRUTTA DI MARE

I am a sea-shell flung
Up from the ancient sea;
Now I lie here, among
Roots of a tamarisk tree;
No one listens to me.

I sing to myself all day
In a husky voice, quite low,
Things the great fishes say
And you must need to know;
All night I sing just so.

But lift me from the ground,
And hearken at my rim,

Only your sorrow's sound
Amazed, perplexed and dim,
Comes coiling to the brim;

For what the wise whales ponder
Awaking out from sleep,
The key to all your wonder,
The answers of the deep,
These to myself I keep.

GEOFFREY SCOTT

MEN FADE LIKE ROCKS

Rock-like the souls of men
    Fade, fade in time.
Falls on worn surfaces,
    Slow chime on chime,

Sense, like a murmuring dew,
    Soft sculpturing rain,
Or the wind that blows hollowing
    In every lane.

Smooth as the stones that lie
    Dimmed, water-worn,
Worn of the night and day,
    In sense forlorn,

Rock-like the souls of men
    Fade, fade in time;
Smoother than river-rain
    Falls chime on chime.

W. J. TURNER

THE POET

Mine is a still small cry
a pipe with one stop,
one tune or two maybe
run in my song
backwards and forwards
crying and calling
like a lost girl
in a wood of fauns.

There is no woman
can touch on abundance
in the teeming world
of moons and suns
save in the threaded womb
that with a silver
net draws down thought
to the hidden children.

Our lovers must bring us
news of the mountains,
redden with their songs
our quiet mouths.
They will not remember
what thoughts, what horizons
they drew down to themselves
out of our silence.

PAMELA TRAVERS

ABNORMAL PSYCHOLOGY

I am, they say, a darkling pool
Where huge and cunning lurks a fool
Childish and monstrous, untaught of time,
Still wallowing in primeval slime.

[557]

All powerful he with fang and claw
To fill his red capacious maw,
And not a thousand thousand years
Have eased his belly, stilled his fears.
But ever with dim consuming fire
Swirl the slow eddies of desire
About his sprawling limbs, and lull
The torments of his brutish skull.
He is most merciless, lone, and proud,
There in the scaly darkness bowed,
And sleeps, and eats, and lusts, and cries,
And never lives, and never dies.

Nay, but above this stagnant night
The lovely highways of the light
Sweep on with winds and dawning flowers
And stoop to touch its midnight hours.
If I am he, I'm also one
With all that's brave beneath the sun,
With lovers' singing, and tall great trees,
And the white glory of morning seas.
What of this silence, so there stay
Child's laughter to the end of day?
And what of dark, if on the hill
Eve is a burning opal still?

BARRINGTON GATES

Beware of blindly trusting
To outward art,
And specious sheen;
For vice is oft
The hollow heart
Within unseen.

See that black pool below thee!
There heaven sleeps
In golden fire.
Yet whatso'er it show thee,
The mirror's deeps
Are slime and mire.

JAMES CLARENCE MANGAN

THE UNABSOLVED

The thing he did that haunts him most,
　　The worst, the darkest wrong,
That sin against the Holy Ghost
　　He would redeem with song,
Grieves in his sleep from room to room
Along the mind's black catacomb.

No thought that shames the words once said
　　Goes utterly out of mind;
Strangle the cry of the betrayed,
　　Cripple and crush and blind
The memory of it, yet it will
Break from the dungeon, loud and shrill.

There is no penance, no remorse,
　　Purgation or escape
Enough for him who has dared force
　　On his own soul a rape;
Not all earth's waters cleanse him shall,
Nor poetry's confessional.

EDWARD DAVISON

LOSS

Like the dark germs across the filter clean
So in the clear day of a thousand years
This dusty cloud is creeping to our eyes,

Here, as we grow, and are as we have been
Or living give for life some morning tears
The flowering hour bent and unconscious lies.

As in Vienna now, the wounded walls
Silently speak, as deep in Austria
The battered shape of man is without shade

So, time in metaphor, tomorrow falls
On Europe, Asia and America,
And houses vanish, even as they were made,

For yesterday is always sad, its nature
Darker than love would wish in every feature.

CHARLES MADGE

My brain, methinks, is like an hour-glass,
Wherein my imaginations run like sands,
Filling up time; but then are turned and turned.
So that I know not what to stay upon,
And less to put in act. . . .

BEN JONSON

1ST DOCTOR. How does your grace now feel yourself?
THIERRY. What's *that*?
1ST DOCTOR. Nothing at all, sir, but your fancy.
THIERRY. 　　　　　　Tell me,
Can ever these eyes more, shut up in slumbers,
Assure my soul there is sleep? is there night
And rest for human labours? do not you
And all the world, as I do, out-stare Time,
And live, like funeral lamps, never extinguished?
Is there a grave? (and do not flatter me,

Nor fear to tell the truth,) and in that grave
Is there a hope I shall sleep? can I die?
Are not my miseries immortal? Oh,
The happiness of him that drinks his water,
After his weary day, and sleeps for ever! . . .
                    The eyes of Heaven
See but their certain motions, and then sleep:
The rages of the ocean have their slumbers
And quiet silver calms; each violence
Crowns in his end a peace; but my fixed fires
Shall never, never set. . . .

JOHN FLETCHER, from
Thierry and Theodoret, Act V, Scene II

HÖLDERLIN'S JOURNEY

When Hölderlin started from Bordeaux
   He was not mad but lost in mind,
For time and space had fled away
   With her he had to find.

" The morning bells rang over France
   From tower to tower. At noon I came
Into a maze of little hills,
   Head-high and every hill the same.

" A little world of emerald hills,
   And at their heart a faint bell tolled;
Wedding or burial, who could say?
   For death, unseen, is bold.

" Too small to climb, too tall to show
   More than themselves, the hills lay round.
Nearer to her, or farther? They
   Might have stretched to the world's bound.

[561]

" A shallow candour was their all,
   And the mean riddle, How to tally
Reality with such appearance,
   When in the nearest valley

" Perhaps already she I sought,
   She, sought and seeker, had gone by,
And each of us in turn was trapped
   By simple treachery.

" The evening brought a field, a wood.
   I left behind the hills of lies,
And watched beside a mouldering gate
   A deer with its rock-crystal eyes.

" On either pillar of the gate
   A deer's head watched within the stone.
The living deer with quiet look
   Seemed to be gazing on

" Its pictured death — and suddenly
   I knew, Diotima was dead,
As if a single thought had sprung
   From the cold and the living head.

" That image held me and I saw
   All moving things so still and sad,
But till I came into the mountains
   I know I was not mad.

" What made the change? The hills and towers
   Stood otherwise than they should stand,
And without fear the lawless roads
   Ran wrong through all the land.

" Upon the swarming towns of iron
   The bells hailed down their iron peals,
Above the iron bell the swallows
   Glided on iron wheels.

" And there I watched in one confounded
   The living and the unliving head.
Why should it be? For now I know
   Diotima was dead

" Before I left the starting place;
   Empty the course, the garland gone,
And all that race as motionless
   As these two heads of stone."

So Hölderlin mused for thirty years
   On a green hill by Tübingen,
Dragging in pain a broken mind
   And giving thanks to God and men.

EDWIN MUIR

   . . . " Then there was myself; for what was I born? Are not all things born to be forgotten? That's incomprehensible: yet is it not so? Those butterflies fall and are forgotten. In what is man better than a butterfly? All then is born to be forgotten. Ah! that was a pang indeed; 'tis at such a moment that a man wishes to die. The wise king of Jerusalem, who sat in his shady arbours beside his sunny fishpools, saying so many fine things, wished to die, when he saw that not only all was vanity, but that he himself was vanity. Will a time come when all will be forgotten that now is beneath the sun? If so, of what profit is life? . . .

   " ' Would I had never been born! ' I said to myself; and a thought would occasionally intrude. But was I ever born? Is not all that I see a lie — a deceitful phantom? Is there a world, and earth, and sky? . . ."

GEORGE BORROW

I AM

I am: yet what I am who cares or knows,
   My friends forsake me like a memory lost;
I am the self-consumer of my woes,

They rise and vanish — an oblivious host,
Shadows of life, whose very soul is lost,
And yet I am — I live — though I am tossed

Into the nothingness of scorn and noise,
  Into the living sea of waking dream;
Where there is neither sense of life, nor joys,
  But the huge shipwreck of my own esteem,
And all that's dear. Even those I loved the best
Are strange — nay, they are stranger than the rest.

I long for scenes where man has never trod;
  For scenes where woman never smiled or wept;
There to abide with my Creator, God,
  And sleep as I in childhood sweetly slept:
Full of high thoughts, unborn. So let me lie, —
The grass below; above, the vaulted sky.

JOHN CLARE

TO AN UNBORN PAUPER CHILD

Breathe not, hid Heart: cease silently,
And though thy birth-hour beckons thee,
    Sleep the long sleep:
    The Doomsters heap
Travails and teens around us here,
And Time-wraiths turn our songsingings to fear.

Hark, how the peoples surge and sigh,
And laughters fail, and greetings die:
    Hopes dwindle; yea,
    Faiths waste away,
Affections and enthusiasms numb;
Thou canst not mend these things if thou dost come.

Had I the ear of wombèd souls
Ere their terrestrial chart unrolls,
　　And thou wert free
　　To cease, or be,
Then would I tell thee all I know,
And put it to thee: Wilt thou take Life so?

Vain vow! No hint of mine may hence
To theeward fly: to thy locked sense
　　Explain none can
　　Life's pending plan:
Thou wilt thy ignorant entry make
Though skies spout fire and blood and nations quake.

Fain would I, dear, find some shut plot
Of earth's wide wold for thee, where not
　　One tear, one qualm,
　　Should break the calm.
But I am weak as thou and bare;
No man can change the common lot to rare.

Must come and bide. And such are we —
Unreasoning, sanguine, visionary —
　　That I can hope
　　Health, love, friends, scope
In full for thee; can dream thou wilt find
Joys seldom yet attained by humankind!

THOMAS HARDY

. . . Man hath still either toys, or Care,
He hath no root, nor to one place is tied,
But ever restless and Irregular
　About this Earth doth run and ride,
He knows he hath a home, but scarce knows where,
　He says it is so far
That he hath quite forgot how to go there.

[565]

He knocks at all doors, strays and roams,
Nay hath not so much wit as some stones have
Which in the darkest nights point to their homes,
    By some hid sense their Maker gave;
Man is the shuttle, to whose winding quest
    And passage through these looms
God ordered motion, but ordained no rest.

                    HENRY VAUGHAN, from "Man"

COMPANIONSHIP

The men and women round thee, what are they?
    Frail as the flowers, less lasting than the snow.
If there be angels flitting in the day,
    Who knows those angels? Who shall ever know?
Let them alone and go thou on thy way!
    They came like dreams; like dreams they come and go.

Nay, the companions of thy timeless hours
    Are dreams dreamt first for thee by them of old,
That thou might'st dream them after! These are powers
    Unending and unaging — never cold —
White as the driven snow, fair as the flowers.
    These be thy verities, to have, to hold!

                    MARY COLERIDGE

. . . "The eye — it cannot choose but see;
    We cannot bid the ear be still;
    Our bodies feel, where'er they be,
    Against or with our will.

"Nor less I deem that there are Powers
    Which of themselves our minds impress;
    That we can feed this mind of ours
    In a wise passiveness.

" Think you, 'mid all this mighty sum
Of things for ever speaking,
That nothing of itself will come,
But we must still be seeking?

"— Then ask not wherefore, here, alone,
Conversing as I may,
I sit upon this old grey stone,
And dream my time away."

WILLIAM WORDSWORTH,
from "Expostulation and Reply"

. . . Wise men in tracing Nature's laws
Ascend unto the highest Cause;
Shepherds with humble fearfulness
Walk safely, though their Light be Life:
Though wise men better know the way
It seems no honest heart can stray.

There is no merit in the wise
But Love, (the shepherd's sacrifice);
Wise men, all ways of knowledge past,
To the shepherds' wonder come at last:
To know can only wonder breed,
And not to know is wonder's seed. . . .

SIDNEY GODOLPHIN, from "Hymn"

THEME

The golden eve is all astir,
The tides of sunset flood on us
— Incredible, miraculous —
We look with adoration on
Beauty coming, beauty gone,
That waits not any looking on.

Thoughts will bubble up, and break,
Spilling a sea, a limpid lake,
Into the soul; and, as they go
— Lightning visitors! we know
A lattice opened, and the mind
Poised for all that is behind
The lattice, and the poising mind.

Could the memory but hold!
— All the sunsets, flushed with gold,
Are streaming in it!

All the store
Of all that ever was before
Is teeming in it!

All the wit
Of holy living, holy writ,
Waiting till we remember it,
Is dreaming in it!

JAMES STEPHENS

LIFE OF LIFE

What's that, which, ere I spake, was gone:
   So joyful and intense a spark
That, whilst o'erhead the wonder shone,
   The day, before but dull, grew dark?
I do not know; but this I know,
   That, had the splendour lived a year,
The truth that I some heavenly show
   Did see, could not be now more clear.
This know I too: might mortal breath
   Express the passion then inspired,
Evil would die a natural death,
   And nothing transient be desired;

And error from the soul would pass,
   And leave the senses pure and strong
As sunbeams. But the best, alas,
   Has neither memory nor tongue!

COVENTRY PATMORE

SPIRIT OF THE YEARS.
     Something of difference animates your quiring,
     O half-convinced Compassionates and fond,
     From chords consistent with our spectacle!
     You almost charm my long philosophy
     Out of my strong-built thought, and bear me back
     To when I thanksgave thus . . . Ay, start not,
        Shades;
     In the Foregone I knew what dreaming was,
     And could let raptures rule! But not so now.
     Yea, I psalmed thus and thus . . . But no so now!

SEMICHORUS I OF THE YEARS (*Aerial music*).
     O Immanence, That reasonest not
     In putting forth all things begot,
     Thou build'st Thy house in space — for what?

SEMICHORUS II. O Loveless, Hateless! — past the sense
     O kindly eyed benevolence,
     To what tune danceth this Immense?

SPIRIT IRONIC. For one I cannot answer. But I know
     'Tis handsome of our Pities so to sing
     The praises of the dreaming, dark, dumb Thing
     That turns the handle of this idle Show!

     As once a Greek asked I would fain ask too,
     Who knows if all the Spectacle be true,
     Or an illusion of the gods (the Will,
     To wit) some hocus-pocus to fulfil?

SEMICHORUS I OF THE YEARS (*Aerial music*).
     Last as first the question rings
     Of the Will's long travailings;

[569]

Why the All-mover,
Why the All-prover
Ever urges on and measures out the chordless
chime of Things.

SEMICHORUS II.　　Heaving dumbly
As we deem,
Moulding numbly
As in dream,
Apprehending not how fare the sentient subjects
of Its scheme.

SEMICHORUS I OF THE PITIES.
Nay; — shall not Its blindness break?
Yes, must not Its heart awake,
Promptly tending
To Its mending
In a genial germing purpose, and for loving-
kindness' sake?

SEMICHORUS II.　　Should It never
Curb or cure
Aught whatever
Those endure
Whom It quickens, let them darkle to extinction
swift and sure.

CHORUS.　　But — a stirring thrills the air
Like the sounds of joyance there
That the rages
Of the ages
Shall be cancelled, and deliverance offered from
the darts that were,
Consciousness the Will informing, till It fashion
all things fair!

THOMAS HARDY,
[from *The Dynasts, Part III, After Scene*]

[570]

EARL HENRY. "Oh! there is joy above the name of pleasure,
Deep self-possession, an intense repose."

SANDOVAL (*With a sarcastic smile*).
"No other than as eastern sages paint,
The God, who floats upon a Lotos leaf,
Dreams for a thousand ages; then awaking,
Creates a world, and smiling at the bubble,
Relapses into bliss."

SAMUEL TAYLOR COLERIDGE,
from "The Night-Scene"

The first range of hills, that encircles the scanty vale of human life, is the horizon for the majority of its inhabitants. On *its* ridges the common sun is born and departs. From *them* the stars rise, and touching *them* they vanish. By the many, even this range, the natural limit and bulwark of the vale, is but imperfectly known. Its highest ascents are too often hidden by mists and clouds from uncultivated swamps, which few have courage or curiosity to penetrate. To the multitude below these vapours appear, now as the dark haunts of terrific agents, on which none may intrude with impunity; and now all *a-glow,* with colours not their own, they are gazed at as the splendid palaces of happiness and power. But in all ages there have been a few, who measuring and sounding the rivers of the vale at the feet of their farthest inaccessible falls have learned that the sources must be far higher and far inward; a few, who even in the level streams have detected elements which neither the vale itself nor the surrounding mountains contained or could supply. How and whence to these thoughts, these strong probabilities, the ascertaining vision, the intuitive knowledge may finally supervene, can be learnt only by the fact. . . .

SAMUEL TAYLOR COLERIDGE

Reason and Imagination

. . . There is a figure with a down-turned torch
Carved on a pillar in an olden time,
A calm and lovely boy
That comes not to destroy
But to lead age back to its golden prime. . . .

By his own handiwork has man been misled, or
led away into curious valleys of vision. . . .

Reason and Imagination

OF ELUTROPIA

Elutropia is a Gemme, in colour greene, or grassie, in part coloured and bespotted with Purple speckes and bloud coloured vaines. This is a marvellous Jugler, for it wil cause things object to be presented to our eies as it listeth. It being put into a Basan of water chaungeath to a mans eiesight the Sunne his beames, and giveth them a contrarie colour. Being also mooved and beaten in the ayre, maketh to appeare a bloudie Sunne, and darkneth the ayre in maner of an Eclipse: and therefore it is called *Elutropia* as you would say, the Sunne his enimie. There is of this name also a certaine Hearbe which Enchaunters and Witches have oftentimes used, and doe use, as also that above said, whereby they have mocked and deluded many, which by meanes and working of enchauntment, have so dazeled the beholders eies, that they have gone by them invisibly.

John Maplet

TAISHITARAUGHK

They generally term this second-sight in Irish Taishita-raughk, and such as have it Taishatrin, from Taish, which is properly a shadowy substance, or such naughty, and imperceptible thing, as can only, or rather scarcely be discerned by the eye; but not caught by the hands: for which they assigned it to Bugles or Ghosts, so that Taishtar, is as much as one that converses with ghosts or spirits, or as they commonly call them, the Fairies or Fairy-Folks. Others call these men

Phissicin, from Phis, which is properly fore-sight, or fore-knowledge. . . ."

JOHN AUBREY

. . . My eyes are a burthen,
Now unwillingly closed, now open and aching with darkness.
O! what a life is the eye! what a strange and inscrutable
　　essence!
Him that is utterly blind, nor glimpses the fire that warms him;
Him that never beheld the swelling breast of his mother;
Him that smiled in his gladness as a babe that smiles in its
　　slumber;
Even for him it exists, it moves and stirs in its prison;
Lives with a separate life, and " Is it a Spirit? " he murmurs:
" Sure it has thoughts of its own, and to see is only a lan-
　　guage." . . .

SAMUEL TAYLOR COLERIDGE

I will not refrain from setting among these precepts a new
device for consideration which, although it may appear trivial
and almost ludicrous, is nevertheless of great utility in arous-
ing the mind to various inventions. And this is that if you look
at any walls spotted with various stains or with a mixture of
different kinds of stones, if you are about to invent some scene
you will be able to see in it a resemblance to various different
landscapes adorned with mountains, rivers, rocks, trees,
plains, wide valleys, and various groups of hills. You will also
be able to see divers combats and figures in quick movement,
and strange expressions of faces, and outlandish costumes,
and an infinite number of things which you can then reduce
into separate and well conceived forms. With such walls and
blends of different stones it comes about as it does with the
sound of bells, in whose clanging you may discover every
name and word that you can imagine.

LEONARDO DA VINCI

. . . In day-dreaming we are conscious of a sensation
which tells that certain of our faculties have fallen into rest —

Will, for instance; while at the same time others are advanced into far greater freedom and activity. But perhaps the word should be not "others" but "one other" — Imagination: Imagination with its tributaries, such as hope, fear, memory, retrospection, and that which is the contrary of retrospection and is rather difficult to name: let us say forecast. And since this is our experience in day-dreaming (whether it be specially provoked, or whether it be the idle desultory mind-rambling in which so much of our time is passed), it may fairly be inferred that it is also our experience in sleep-dreaming. That certain of our faculties are in abeyance at such times becomes much less hypothetical at any rate; though it would be rash to infer that they are *always* in abeyance, and not unreasonable to ask whether Imagination itself is not sometimes a substitute for them or for some of them. . . .

FREDERICK GREENWOOD

. . . I pity the man who can see the connection of his own ideas. Still more do I pity him, the connection of whose ideas any other person can see. Sir, the great evil is, that there is too much common-place light in our moral and political literature; and light is a great enemy to mystery, and mystery is a great friend to enthusiasm. Now the enthusiasm for abstract truth is an exceedingly fine thing, as long as the truth, which is the object of the enthusiasm, is so completely abstract as to be altogether out of the reach of the human faculties; and, in that sense, I have myself an enthusiasm for truth, but in no other, for the pleasure of metaphysical investigation lies in the means, not in the end; and if the end could be found, the pleasure of the means would cease. The mind, to be kept in health, must be kept in exercise. The proper exercise of the mind is elaborate reasoning. Analytical reasoning is a base and mechanical process, which takes to pieces and examines, bit by bit, the rude material of knowledge, and extracts therefrom a few hard and obstinate things called facts, every thing in the shape of which I cordially hate. But synthetical reasoning, setting up as its goal some unattainable abstraction, like an imaginary quantity in algebra, and commencing its course with taking for granted some two assertions which cannot be proved, from the union of these two assumed truths produces a third assumption, and so on in infinite series, to the unspeakable benefit of the human intellect. The beauty of this process is, that at every step it strikes out into two branches, in a compound ratio of ramification; so that you are perfectly sure of losing your way, and keeping your mind in perfect health, by the perpetual exercise of an interminable quest. . . .

THOMAS LOVE PEACOCK

At my alighting, I was surrounded by a crowd of people, but those who stood nearest seemed to be of better quality. They beheld me with all the marks and circumstances of wonder, neither indeed was I much in their debt, having never till then seen a race of mortals so singular in their shapes, habits, and countenances. Their heads were all reclined, either to the right or the left; one of their eyes turned inward, the other directly up to the zenith. Their outward garments were adorned with the figures of suns, moons, and stars, interwoven with those of fiddles, flutes, harps, trumpets, guitars, harpsichords, and many more instruments of music, unknown to us in Europe. I observed here and there many in the habit of servants, with a blown bladder, fastened like a flail to the end of a short stick, which they carried in their hands. In each bladder was a small quantity of dried pease, or little pebbles, as I was afterwards informed. With these bladders they now and then flapped the mouths and ears of those who stood near them, of which practice I could not then conceive the meaning: it seems the minds of these people are so taken up with intense speculations, that they neither can speak, nor attend to the discourses of others, without being roused by some external taction upon the organs of speech and hearing: for which reason, those persons who are able

[578]

to afford it always keep a flapper (the original is *climenole*) in their family, as one of their domestics; nor ever walk abroad, or make visits, without him. And the business of this officer is, when two or three more persons are in company, gently to strike with his bladder the mouth of him who is to speak, and the right ear of him or them to whom the speaker addresses himself. This flapper is likewise employed diligently to attend his master in his walks, and upon occasion to give him a soft flap on his eyes; because he is always so wrapped up in cogitation, that he is in manifest danger of falling down every precipice, and bouncing his head against every post, and in the streets, of justling others, or being justled himself into the kennel. . . .

JONATHAN SWIFT, from *Gulliver's Travels: Laputa*

. . . The argument is that in ordinary reflective thought, and more especially still in scientific investigation, we uncritically and unconsciously assume that in seeking explanations of fact we are getting into closer contact with fact and thereby knowing fact more perfectly. The direct opposite is true. In pursuing explanations we are of necessity moving away from fact; and the more we succeed in explaining, the more the fact itself is left behind, and the more unlike fact becomes the factors of the explanation; so that we find at last not only that the immediacy and integrity of fact is gone, but that the supposed elemental constituent parts are pitiful distortions of the reality. If, then, explaining fact is not a way of knowing fact, what is the value of explanation, and what is the way of knowing fact? Briefly, the answer to the first part of the question is that action and not knowledge is the guiding motive in explanation, and that the intellect in its mode of working is purely practical. And the answer to the second part of the question is that the only way to get closer to fact, to know reality as it is in itself, is to turn by an intellectual effort from the attention to life which keeps us forward-looking, intent on the future and the preparing action in order to intuit fact not as the already made, but as becoming. . . .

WILDON CARR

One of the dangers that scientific people run is that they become so interested in the resemblances between things, and the words that stand for them, that they lose sight of the things themselves. . . . They talk as though weight, density, pressure, temperature were things that existed of themselves. This is because they are seeking scientific knowledge for its own sake; their interest in building up a pattern of scientific ideas makes them forget the things which they are really talking about. As a result, their picture of the world contains nothing but " things " which seem very shadowy and unreal to anyone else.

To discover resemblances on which to build laws the scientist has usually to take the things he is studying to pieces; the result of this is that something is inevitably left out. If you parse a poem and break it up into its separate parts of speech, you may find out a good deal about its construction, and how this resembles the construction of other poems. But so long as you fix your attention only on the grammar you must miss all that is really important about the poem. The same is true of all analysis. If you were to be handed over to the chemist for him to work on, he would analyse your body into its chemical constituents and could find out exactly what substances it was made of. He might even present your executors with a row of little bottles, all neatly labelled, containing the separate substances of which you were made. But still there would remain a good deal about you of which he could say nothing, for all his analysis. A physiologist would analyse you in a different way. He would dissect your body, and show how each part of your body resembled the parts of other people's bodies, and the bodies of other mammals, but still he could say nothing about all that made you yourself. The same applies to the psychologist. He would study what you said and what you did, and would show how this corresponded with what other people said and did. But he too would have to leave out all that made you different from other people.

What it comes to is that no scientist can ever say anything about you as an individual person differing from everyone else. All he can say is that in some respects you resemble one group of other persons and in other respects another group; but these are the respects in which you are not different from other persons. The people who are interested in you *as yourself* are the people who love you; perhaps too the people who hate you. If they wanted to tell other people about you, they would have to write a book about you. They would not set out to show that you were made up of this and that constituent, but would show you acting in a variety of circumstances so chosen that you would be most typically yourself. In this they could only really succeed if they were artists.

JOHN PILLEY

For those who are inspired by the scientific method, to whom God has granted the rare talent of thinking scientifically, there is, in my opinoin, but one way out — the philosophy of creative art. It is possible to gather together all the best that has been created by artists throughout the ages, and, employing the scientific method, to grasp that common element which makes them like one another and conditions their value. That common element will be the law. Works which are called immortal have a great deal in common; if that common element were excluded from each of them the work would lose its value and its charm. It follows then that that universal element is essential and forms the *conditio sine qua non* of every work that aspires to immortality.

ANTON TCHEKHOV
to A. S. Souvorin

. . . I was mounted upon a very easie-going nag, but not very sure. At my returning home againe, a sudden occasion being offered me to make use of this nag in a peece of service whereto he was neither trained nor accustomed, one of my men (a strong sturdy fellow), mounted upon a young strong-headed horse, and that a desperate hard mouth, fresh, lusty and in breath, to shew his courage, and to out-goe his fellowes, fortuned with might and maine to set spurres unto him, and giving him the bridle, to come right into the path where I was, and as a Colossus with his weight riding over me and my nag, that were both very little, he overthrew us both, and made us fall with our heels upward: so that the nag lay along astonied in one place, and I in a trance groveling on the ground ten or twelfe paces wide of him; my face all torne and brused, my sword which I had in my hand a good way from me, my girdle broken, with no more motion or sense in me than a stocke. It is the only swowning that ever I felt yet. Those that were with me, after they had assayed all possible meanes to bring me to my self againe, supposing me dead, tooke me in their armes, and with much adoe were carrying me home to my house, which was about halfe a French league thence: upon the way, and after I had for two houres space by all beene supposed dead and past all recoverie, I began to stir and breathe: for so great aboundance of bloud was falne into my stomake, that to discharge it nature was forced to rowse up her spirits. I was immediately set upon my feet, and bending foward, I presently cast up in quantitie as much clottie pure bloud as a bucket will hold, and by the way was constrained to doe the like divers times before I could get home, whereby I began to recover a little life, but it was by little and little, and so long adoing, that my chiefe senses were much more enclining to death than to life.

> *Perche dubbiosa ancor del suo ritorno*
> *Non s'assicura attonita la mente.*

> For yet the minde doubtfull of its returne
> Is not assurèd, but astonishèd.

The remembrance whereof (which yet I beare deepely imprinted in my minde) representing me her visage and Idea so lively and so naturally, doth in some sort reconcile me unto her. And when I began to see, it was with so dim, so weake and so troubled a sight, that I could not discerne anything of the light,

> . . . *come quel ch'or apre, or chiude*
> *Gli occhi, mezzo tra 'l sonno e l'esser desto.*

> As he that sometimes opens, sometimes shuts
> His eyes, between sleepe and awake.

Touching the functions of the soule, they started up and came in the same progresse as those of the bodie. I perceived my selfe all bloudy; for my doublet was all sullied with the bloud I had cast. The first conceit I apprehended was that I had received some shot in my head; and in truth, at the same instant, there were divers that shot round about us. Me thought my selfe had no other hold of me but of my lips-ends. I closed mine eyes to help (as me seemed) to send it forth, and tooke a kind of pleasure to linger and languishingly to let my selfe goe from my selfe. It was an imagination swimming superficially in my minde, as weake and as tender as all the rest: but in truth, not only exempted from displeasure, but rather commixt with that pleasant sweetnesse which they feel that suffer themselves to fall into a soft-slumbring and sense-entrancing sleepe. I believe it is the same state they find themselves in, whom in the agony of death we see to droop and faint thorow weaknesse: and am of opinion we plaine and moane them without cause, esteeming that either they are agitated with grievous pangs, or that their soule is pressed with painful cogitations. It was ever my conceit, against the opinion of many, yea and against that of Estienne de la Boëtie, that those whom we see so overwhelmed and faintly-drooping at the approaches of their end, or utterly cast downe with the lingring tediousnesse of their deseases, or by accident of some apoplexie or falling-evill, . . . or hurt in the head, whom we heare throb and rattle, and send forth grones and gaspes, although we gather some tokens from them, whereby it seemeth they have yet some knowledge left and certaine motions we see them make with their body: I say, I have ever thought they had their soule and body buried and asleepe. . . .

Montaigne, translated by John Florio

The famous philologist Gherardini, after a terrible domestic tragedy, had his nervous system so shaken that he became seriously ill. Professor A. Verga, who published the history of this illness, writes —

"Sensation, internal and external, was abolished. Doctor Gherardini perceived neither hunger nor thirst, neither heat nor cold, neither taste nor smell. Stuporose, sleepless, without energy, he seemed likely to die of inanition. But one morning, after having slept at last, he felt the desire for a pinch of snuff. He roused himself, seated himself at the table, seized a pen, and wrote his work, *Voci e maniere di dire additate ai futuri vocabolaristi.* But if the intelligence appeared to emerge from that illness strengthened, the physical powers retained a bitter souvenir."

After seven years he had a relapse, with the same profound stupor. Artificial nourishment was necessary. He no longer swallowed, and the saliva flowed from his mouth. After presenting this melancholy spectacle for a year and a half, he recovered his intelligence all at once, and began to write another treatise, the *Lessigrafia e il Supplemento ai Vocabolari.* After other seven years he had a third attack, but Dr. Gherardini was now seventy-seven years of age, and strength was wanting for a third resurrection. . . .

A. Mosso, translated by M. and W. B. Drummond

. . . Our inner life is like a stream, moving quickly on the surface, moving very slowly along its bed below. It is sometimes rushing at the surface, surging like a river in flood; or again it is rippling gently, singing as it goes. But it is always hurrying on. Perceptions jostle one another and combine in imaginings; they link themselves in concepts and purposes;

and there is often a struggle among the concepts. The unity of our mind establishes control and harmony. Recent memories are also stirred and join in the stream, or send contributions which join in the stream. Below this is the undercurrent of appetites and urges — sometimes breaking violently to the surface. And here, also, are habitual desires often brought to the focus of consciousness.

Deep down on the floor of the stream is the primary unconscious. It consists of inborn general tendencies, the framework of our inner life, the fundamental conative elements such as the will to live. It also normally includes, we think, the sex-urge during early years, but in adolescence this rises to be part of the undercurrent nearer the surface, raised . . . by the activity of hormone-producing glands. The primary unconscious also includes very deep racial memories, some of them, perhaps, pre-human, as is illustrated by the almost universal shrinking from the snake. The primary unconscious also includes the influences of nurture (environmental and habitudinal) that soaked in without our knowing of them, especially in youth. " As is the world on the banks," Arnold wrote, " so is the mind of man." Or, as Whitman said, " There was a child who went forth every day, and what that child saw became part of him for a day, or for a year, or for stretching cycles of years." Such is the general nature of the primary unconscious, which ought to remain as the slowly-moving deep current of our being. It may send eddies to the surface stream; it is always doing so, just as the water in a pond rises to the surface as it approaches the freezing-point; but it is not meant to be seen. The controlled vividly conscious life is the crown of evolution and supreme; the under-current is fundamental. We should not pull up our flowering plant to see how the roots are looking. That is for the botanist.

Nearer the surface, yet below the under-current of appetencies and desires, there is the secondary or Freudian unconscious, consisting of memory-traces and the like which once were in the light of consciousness (or fore-consciousness), but have been sunk down or repressed, because painful to, or out of harmony with, the normal mind. They are repressed by barriers, which are relaxed a little during sleep — and then the prisoners steal out like ghosts. . . .

J. Arthur Thomson

Jung [like Freud] also postulates something he calls Libido, but his Libido is quite different from that of Freud. According to Jung the Libido is an undifferentiated primal life-force from which all the instincts derive. In the infant it assumes the form of the instinct of nutrition. It is only much later that it assumes the sexual form. Then he denies that the unconscious is a region inhabited by desires which have been repressed after conflict. The unconscious, according to Jung, arises as a consequence of the individual's one-sided mental growth. . . . Naturally, with this outlook, Jung gives an entirely different interpretation of dreams. He believes that dreams record the attitude of the unconscious towards the tasks of life.

Adler's interpretation is again different, but is equally plausible. Adler sees the driving force of life as the urge to acquire power and superiority over one's fellows. This outlook enables Adler to give analyses which are quite as convincing and penetrating as those that follow from entirely different theories. . . . Besides rejecting Freud's Libido, Adler also ignores the unconscious and makes no use of the notion of repression. . . . In fact, psycho-analysis bids fair to rival Christianity in the number of its sects.

J. W. N. Sullivan

The immense popularity of psycho-analysis has not been on account of the cures it has found for neuroses, but on account of its method; and the study of psycho-analysis has in our time become perhaps only another way of becoming neurotic, of going down into one's unconscious, and finally of " going down." . . .

Now the perversity, strained curiosity, and bad conscience

in this attitude toward sex is generally resumed under the summary term " neurotic " — a word which we need nowadays, but which we love more than we need. What does one mean by neurotic? It is precisely the descent into oneself instead of development outward: it is, first, desire for darkness and concealment; then fear of them; and finally the intense, silent struggle in the deepening toils. The problem is whether man attains his fulfilment by throwing himself out into existence, and there achieving his real form, or by knowing himself, by exploring his own chaos; and it is the great modern problem, the extreme results of which we are working out in our own time and in ourselves. . . .

Man is a sea in which all riches are hidden; but if he pries into it the most beautiful things turn into slime, and the freest, happiest creatures into frightened monsters who, with the furtive courage of things which are watched, turn at last and attack him. One can not discover what one is, because one's very self makes distorting grimaces, out of some mysterious instinct. Perhaps it would be a violation of ourselves if we could know ourselves. . . .

The soul is unfathomable, beyond all computation, beyond all conception, of depth and height; and the chasms which St. Augustine and Pascal found in it were only, could be only, the gigantic shadows of tremendous fears, gulfs of darkness concealing the smiling infinity. The soul is unfathomable; it can only be expressed. Dostoyevsky has been written of as the last word in the book of introspection. This is psychologically a mistake which Dostoyevsky himself would never have committed. He did not gain his terrible clairvoyance in psychology by turning his eye inward; it was with him a piece of sheer imagination, second sight, whereby what was unconscious in men became to him conscious. . . . The psychological novel is, in spite of appearances, one of the least introspective forms of art: it is concerned not only with other people's actions but with the hidden movements behind them, and it requires in its adepts a capacity to be uniquely and vigilantly conscious. This is how the soul has been enriched and diversified; not by a withdrawal into itself, but by an expression outward which breaks one bond after another, and in which the hidden riches of one's soul rise up and are revealed. Then every paradox is a delight, a spangled, laughing cross of life, the eternal cross, the cross which has not to be borne. . . .

EDWIN MUIR

It is true that in very profound slumber the law that regulates the reappearance of memories may be very different. We know almost nothing of this profound slumber. The dreams which fill it are, as a general rule, the dreams which we forget. Sometimes, nevertheless, we recover something of them. And then it is a very peculiar feeling, strange, indescribable, that we experience. It seems to us that we have returned from afar in space and afar in time. These are doubtless very old scenes, scenes of youth or infancy that we live over then in all their details, with a mood which colours them with that fresh sensation of infancy and youth that we seek vainly to revive when awake.

It is upon this profound slumber that psychology ought to direct its efforts, not only to study the mechanism of unconscious memory, but to examine the more mysterious phenomena which are raised by " psychical research." . . . If telepathy influences our dreams, it is quite likely that in this profound slumber it would have the greatest chance to manifest itself. . . . To explore the most secret depths of the unconscious, to labour in what I have just called the subsoil of consciousness, that will be the principal task of psychology in the century which is opening. . . .

HENRI BERGSON, translated by Edwin E. Slosson

There is nothing astonishing in the fact that the language of savages abounds in concrete terms whose variety and precision overwhelm us. This is true of all rural tongues. It has been observed in Lithuanian, where one tale can be related in a series of onomatopes. The same may be observed in any country patois. Compare some story in a genuine rural patois with the discourse of any French political writer of the eighteenth century brought up in the school of logic. The first abounds in concrete ideas; it is disjointed, abrupt, illogical, but nevertheless very expressive; the other progresses by a succession of abstract and general formulæ, linked together in order like the terms of a syllogism. They are two different types of language representing two different types of thought. Let us not flatter ourselves that even our highly elaborated languages are completely void of mysticism. They are only so in appearance. The mystical element lies not in the language, but in the thought. Or rather, when it is found in language, it is because it was already present in the thought. It is not necessary to probe very deep beneath the surface of the language of illiterate folk anywhere in order to see the mystical appear, as in its proper element. The power of the name, the creation of onomastic legends, the use of formulæ and spells, the verbal taboos in our country folk-lore; are these anything but the natural fruit of an uncivilized mentality cropping up in the language of a civilized people?

Still, if we can imagine a political or social cataclysm overthrowing the present barriers which divide human groups, flinging into one whirlpool the representatives of different classes, nationalities, and races, destroying even our time-honoured civilization in order to clear the way for a new civilization, to be established upon another foundation, would not language be the first thing to suffer? Would not this mystical and concrete mentality, which has been almost eliminated from the great common languages, become sufficiently powerful again to recreate them in its own image and impose its own habits of thought upon them? What would French or English become in that case? Nothing more nor less than an uncivilized tongue. They would travel over again, in the reverse direction, the road by which they came to their present state. They would pass from the expression of the abstract to that of the concrete; and would be full of mystical and subjective categories. Would this be progress or decadence?

Neither — at least if we treat the matter from the linguistic point of view. We need not consider the purely relative advantages or inconveniences of a change of civilization or even of a return to the state known as barbarism. We have no right to consider a rational and abstract language, because it happens to be our own, as in any way superior to a mystical and concrete one. It is entirely a question of two different types of mentality, each of which may have its merits. There is nothing to prove that, in the eyes of an inhabitant of Sirius, the civilized person's mentality does not represent degeneration. . . .

J. VENDRYES, translated by Paul Radin

. . . We are not only dominated by the suggestion of our visions, but we are unable adequately to appreciate and criticise the situations which are presented to us. We instinctively continue to reason, and to reason clearly and logically with the material at our disposal, but our reasoning is hopelessly absurd. We perceive in dreams, but we do not apperceive; we cannot, that is to say, test and sift the new experience, and co-ordinate it adequately with the whole body of our acquired mental possessions. The phenomena of dreaming furnish a delightful illustration of the fact that reasoning, in its rough form, is only the crudest and most elementary form of intellectual operation, and that the finer forms of thinking involve much more than logic. "All the thinking in the world," as Goethe puts it, "will not lead us to thought."

HAVELOCK ELLIS

Locke, writing with a knowledge of Newtonian dynamics, places mass among the primary qualities of bodies. In short, he elaborates a theory of primary and secondary qualities in accordance with the state of physical science at the close of the seventeenth century. The primary qualities are the essential qualities of substances whose spatio-temporal relationships constitute nature. The orderliness of these relationships constitutes the order of nature. The occurrences of nature are in some way apprehended by minds, which are associated with living bodies. Primarily, the mental apprehension is aroused by the occurrences in certain parts of the correlated body, the occurrences in the brain for instance. But the mind in apprehending also experiences sensations which, properly speaking, are qualities of the mind alone. These sensations are projected by the mind so as to clothe appropriate bodies in external nature. Thus the bodies are perceived as with qualities which in reality do not belong to them, qualities which in fact are purely the offspring of the mind. Thus nature gets credit which should in truth be reserved for ourselves: the rose for its scent: the nightingale for his song: and the sun for his radiance. The poets are entirely mistaken. They should address their lyrics to themselves, and should turn them into odes of self-congratulation on the excellency of the human mind. Nature is a dull affair, soundless, scentless, colourless; merely the hurrying of material, endlessly, meaninglessly.

However you disguise it, this is the practical outcome of the characteristic scientific philosophy which closed the seventeenth century.

In the first place, we must note its astounding efficiency as a system of concepts for the organisation of scientific research. In this respect, it is fully worthy of the genius of the century which produced it. It has held its own as the guiding principle of scientific studies ever since. It is still reigning. Every university in the world organises itself in accordance with it. No alternative system of organising the pursuit of scientific truth has been suggested. It is not only reigning, but it is without a rival.

And yet — it is quite unbelievable. This conception of the universe is surely framed in terms of high abstractions, and the paradox only arises because we have mistaken our abstractions for concrete realities.

ALFRED NORTH WHITEHEAD

[591]

Perhaps we shall find that neither philosophy, science, nor religion in themselves are directly in contact with what is real, but only through those moments of insight, of mystical experience, closely allied to the appreciation of the beautiful which all three of them give us. When, like Mozart, we see in an instant of time, all the sonata of the universe circling round the point from which we started — a profound theory in science, a meditation in religion — then we may say that we are, though in the midst of time, in our eternal home. . . .

Bacon thought the scientific mind was in a sense legal, but actually it has proved to be far more truly artistic; after all, his opportunities of studying the real thing at work were meagre.

But so it has turned out, and surely the scientific view of the world, with its three hall-marks, mathematics, mechanics and materialism, gains somewhat in significance when it is realised that there is an element of intuition in it as well as of reason, and when indeed it is not at all sure that the former element is not more powerful than the latter. For the conviction is forced upon one that the scientific view of the world, and the method of abstraction by which it is arrived at, is an autonomous and authentic manner of dealing with what is real in the world in which we live; that it is not an instrument of merely practical utility, nor on the other hand a philosophy, much less the only true philosophy. It is not an art, it is not a religion, it is not history, it is not a philosophy; it is something different from all of these, it is a special department and activity of the human spirit. . . .

JOSEPH NEEDHAM

. . . Shall men for whom our age
Unbaffled powers of vision hath prepared,
To explore the world without and world within,
Be joyless as the blind? Ambitious spirits —
Whom earth, at this late season, hath produced
To regulate the moving spheres, and weigh

The planets in the hollow of their hand;
And they who rather dive than soar, whose pains
Have solved the elements, or analysed
The thinking principle — shall they in fact
Prove a degraded Race? and what avails
Renown, if their presumption make them such?
Oh! there is laughter at their work in heaven!
Enquire of ancient Wisdom; go, demand
Of mighty Nature, if 'twas ever meant
That we should pry far off yet be unraised;
That we should pore, and dwindle as we pore,
Viewing all objects unremittingly
In disconnection dead and spiritless;
And still dividing, and dividing still,
Break down all grandeur, still unsatisfied
With the perverse attempt, while littleness
May yet become more little; waging thus
An impious warfare with the very life
Of our own souls! . . .

WILLIAM WORDSWORTH,
from *The Excursion, Book IV*

. . . Intellectualists like Aristotle, the Schoolmen, Descartes, or most modern Scientists look for this illumination [i.e. "the contact of our mind with what we call realities"] in formal logic. . . .

There is another, quite contrary, method, which has always charmed people of a religious or poetic turn, viz., immediate contact with spiritual realities. A lyrical poet does not refer to encyclopædias when he feels the coming of inspiration. We, humdrum church-goers, are glad of a good sermon or a serviceable book to help us with our plodding meditation, but great mystics have no need of any such adjuvants: their minds are soon ravished, they do not know where, and they stay there rapt in contemplation. That their minds are not the victims of a fascination, no matter how noble, but, on the contrary, follow the rules of some logic, is made evident from the fact that, as appears from their writings, contemplation reveals substantially the same things to them all. . . . From Plotinus to Swedenborg all illuminists have descanted on the floods of light produced by the contemplative process in which they delighted. But is there a single man or woman who has not experienced something of the kind?

Modern Intuitionists, like Newman or Bergson, are closely related to Mystics. Men of such culture and such vast reading cannot but know the value of accurate information, but they believe in a superior logic making use of it. Pasteur was constantly visited by intuitions which he was afterwards at great pains to check off by the ordinary canons of science. Such intuitions are not revelations, they are only the result of flash-like comparisons or oppositions of sets of images stored up in the mind and incredibly more elastic than the formulas in our intellect which Newman calls the " notional " as opposed to the " real." . . . A process of lovingly bending over one's consciousness is preferred to an exterior one, but the possession of the rich pregnant notions is the end in view just as well. . . .

ERNEST DIMNET

. . . One impulse from a vernal wood
　　May teach you more of man,
　　Of moral evil and of good,
　　Than all the sages can.

Sweet is the lore which Nature brings;
Our meddling intellect
Mis-shapes the beauteous forms of things: —
We murder to dissect.

Enough of Science and of Art;
Close up those barren leaves;
Come forth, and bring with you a heart
That watches and receives.

WILLIAM WORDSWORTH,
from " The Tables Turned "

SONG BY THE UNCONSCIOUS SELF

[in a Dream]

I know not what my secret is,
    I only know 'tis mine;
I know to dwell with it were bliss,
    To die for it divine.
I cannot yield it in a kiss,
    Nor breathe it in a sigh,
I know that I have lived for this;
    For this, my love, I die.

ANDREW LANG

. . . For Freud, as for Adler, imagination is simply the veil called "symbolic," under which the tendencies and primitive wishes which these two investigators suppose dissimulate themselves. But one may object to this opinion — not on a theoretical principle but for essentially practical reasons — that if it is possible to explain and to depreciate imagination in its causation, *the former is nevertheless the creative source of everything that has ever meant for humanity a progress in life*. Imagination has its own irreducible value as a psychic function, with roots plunging at the same time into the contents of consciousness and into those of unconsciousness. This statement agrees better with our findings. . . .

Others before me have pointed out that day-dreaming offers an escape from a censorship that is too stringent in its repression, and consequently constitutes a safety-valve for the abreaction of strong affects. This is the cathartic aspect of mind-wandering. Maeder in this respect speaks of the appeasing function of day- and night-dreaming. . . .

J. VARENDONCK

Imagination, . . . the power by which one image or feeling is made to modify many others, and by a sort of fusion to force many into one; — that which afterwards showed itself in such might and energy in *Lear,* where the deep anguish of a father spreads the feeling of ingratitude and cruelty over the very elements of heaven; — and which, combining many circumstances into one moment of consciousness, tends to produce that ultimate end of all human thought and human feeling, unity, and thereby the reduction of the spirit to its principle and fountain, who is alone truly one. Various are the workings of this the greatest faculty of the human mind, both passionate and tranquil. . . .

SAMUEL TAYLOR COLERIDGE

. . . The imagination is conscious of an indestructible dominion; — the Soul may fall away from it, not being able to sustain its grandeur; but, if once felt and acknowledged, by no act of any other faculty of the mind can it be relaxed, impaired, or diminished. . . .

WILLIAM WORDSWORTH

Men are ruled by imagination: imagination makes them into men, capable of madness and of immense labours. We work dreaming. Consider what dreams must have dominated the builders of the Pyramids — dreams geometrical, dreams funereal, dreams of resurrection, dreams of outdoing the pyramid of some other Pharaoh! What dreams occupy that fat man in the street, toddling by under his shabby hat and bedraggled rain-coat? Perhaps he is in love; perhaps he is a Catholic, and imagines that early this morning he has partaken of the body and blood of Christ; perhaps he is a revolutionist, with the millennium in his heart and a bomb in his pocket. The spirit bloweth where it listeth; the wind of inspiration carries our dreams before it and constantly refashions them like clouds. Nothing could be madder, more irresponsible, more dangerous than this guidance of men by

[596]

dreams. What saves us is the fact that our imaginations, groundless and chimerical as they may seem, are secretly suggested and controlled by shrewd old instincts of our animal nature, and by continual contact with things. The shock of sense, breaking in upon us with a fresh irresistible image, checks wayward imagination and sends it rebounding in a new direction, perhaps more relevant to what is happening in the world outside.

When I speak of being governed by imagination, of course I am indulging in a figure of speech, in an ellipsis; in reality we are governed by that perpetual latent process within us by which imagination itself is created. Actual imaginings — the cloud-like thoughts drifting by — are not masters over themselves nor over anything else. They are like the sound of chimes in the night; they know nothing of whence they came, how they will fall out, or how long they will ring. There is a mechanism in the church tower; there was a theme in the composer's head; there is a beadle who has been winding the thing up. The sound wafted to us, muffled by distance and a thousand obstacles, is but the last lost emanation of this magical bell-ringing. Yet in our dream it is all in all; it is what first entertains and absorbs the mind. Imagination, when it chimes within us, apparently of itself, is no less elaborately grounded; it is a last symptom, a rolling echo, by which we detect and name the obscure operation that occasions it; and not this echo in its aesthetic impotence, but the whole operation whose last witness it is, receives in science the name of imagination, and may be truly said to rule the human world. . . .

Whilst dreams entertain us, the balance of our character is shifting beneath: we are growing while we sleep. The young think in one way, the drunken in another, and the dead not at all; and I imagine — for I have imagination myself — that they do not die because they stop thinking, but they stop thinking because they die. How much veering and luffing before they make that port! The brain of man, William James used to say, has a hair-trigger organization. His life is terribly experimental. He is perilously dependent on the oscillations of a living needle, imagination, that never points to the true north. . . .

Imagination changes the scale of everything, and makes a thousand patterns of the woof of nature, without disturbing a single thread. Or rather — since it is nature itself that imagines — it turns to music what was only strain; as if the universal vibration, suddenly ashamed of having been so long silent and useless, had burst into tears and laughter at its own folly, and in so doing had become wise.

GEORGE SANTAYANA

The further limits of our being plunge, it seems to me, into an altogether other dimension of existence from the sensible and merely " understandable " world. Name it mystical region, or the supernatural region, whatever you choose. So far as our ideal impulses originate in this region (and most of them do so originate in it, for we find them possessing us in a way for which we cannot articulately account) we belong to it in a more intimate sense than that in which we belong to the visible world, for we belong in the most intimate sense wherever our ideals belong. Yet the unseen region in question is not merely ideal, for it produces effects in this world. When we commune with it, work is actually done upon our finite personality, for we are turned into new men.

This overcoming of all the usual barriers between the individual and the Absolute is the great mystic achievement. In mystic states we both become one with the Absolute and we become aware of oneness. This is the everlasting and triumphant mystical tradition, hardly altered by differences of clime or creed. In Hinduism, in Neoplatonism, in Sufism, in Christian mysticism, in Whitmanism, we find the same recurring note, so that there is about mystical utterances an eternal unanimity which ought to make a critic stop and think, and which brings it about that the mystical classics have, as has been said, neither birthday nor native land. Perpetually telling of the unity of man with God, their speech antedates languages, and they do not grow old.

WILLIAM JAMES

It is not so much the imagination that acts, as the spirit, that being only the organ of the spirit. Thus it is true that *it is the spirit that quickeneth, the flesh* and the image of the flesh, merely considered as such, *profiteth nothing.* A look of love [revealing itself on any human face] from the sanctuary of the soul, has, certainly, greater forming power than hours of deliberate contemplation of the most beautiful images. This forming look, if so I may call it, can as little be premeditatedly given as any other naturally beautiful form can be imparted by a studious contemplation in the looking glass. All that creates, and is profoundly active, in the inner man, must be internal, and be communicated from above; as I believe it suffered itself not to be occasioned, at least, not by forethought, circumspection, or wisdom in the agent, to produce such effects. . . . Moments unforeseen, rapid as the lightning, in my opinion, form and deform. Creation, of whatever kind, is momentaneous: the development, nutriment, change, improving, injuring, is the work of time, art, industry, and education. Creative power suffers itself not to be studied. Creation cannot be meditated. . . .

JOHN CASPAR LAVATER,
translated by Thomas Holcroft

. . . Inspiration, as we conceive it, does not come to us from without. It is not a gift of the stars or the Muses, but an impulse from sources that are inside ourselves. The Pierian Spring, the Fountain of Castalia, are still flowing, but their streams murmur deep within us; and although our conscious intelligence has no direct control over these springs of power, yet by labour and study it can clarify and enrich them; and can form standards and ideals which, long brooded over, may then sink down from the conscious into the unconscious strata

of our mental existence, and mould and elaborate the unknown stores of energy which exist there, amorphous and
concealed. . . .

LOGAN PEARSALL SMITH

. . . A man's body is a sort of husk of which his Psyche
(itself material) is the kernel; and it is out of the predisposi-
tions of this living seed, played upon by circumstances, that
his character and his mind are formed. . . .

At first, when she was only a vegetative Psyche, she waited
in a comparatively peaceful mystical torpor for the rain or
the sunshine to foster her, or for the cruel winter or barbarous
scythe to cut her down. . . . Later, she found a new means
of safety and profit in locomotion; and it was then that she
began to perceive distinct objects, to think, and to plan her
actions — accomplishments by no means native to her. Like
the Chinese, she is just as busy by night as by day. Long before the sunrise she is at work in her subterranean kitchen
over her pots of stewing herbs, her looms, and her spindles;
and with the first dawn, when the first ray of intuition falls
through some aperture into those dusky spaces, what does it
light up? The secret springs of her life? The aims she is
so faithfully but blindly pursuing? Far from it. Intuition,
floods of intuition, have been playing for ages upon human
life: poets, painters, men of prayer, scrupulous naturalists
innumerable, have been intent on their several visions; yet
of the origin and of the end of life we know as little as ever.
And the reason is this: that intuition is not a material organ of
the Psyche, like a hand or an antenna; it is a miraculous child,
far more alive than herself, whose only instinct is play, laughter, and brooding meditation. This strange child — who
could have been his father? — is a poet; absolutely useless
and incomprehensible to his poor mother, and only a new
burden on her shoulders, because she can't help feeding and
loving him. He *sees;* which to her is a mystery, because although she has always acted as if, in some measure, she felt
things at a distance, she has never seen and never can see

anything. Nor are his senses, for all their vivacity, of any use to her. For what do they reveal to him? Always something irrelevant: a shaft of dusty light across the rafters, a blue flame dancing on the coals, a hum, a babbling of waters, a breath of heat or of coolness, a mortal weariness or a groundless joy — all dream-images, visions of a play world, essences painted on air, such as any poet might invent in idleness. . . .

GEORGE SANTAYANA

. . . All things are subject to the mind, which . . . is the commander of them all. No resistance is against it; it breaks through the orbs and immense circles of the Heavens, and penetrates even to the centre of the Earth; it opens the fountains of antiquity, and runs down the stream of time, below the period of all seasons; it dives into the dark counsels of Eternity, and the abstruse secrets of nature it unlocks; all places, all occasions are alike obvious to this: this does observe those subtle passages in the air, and the unknown paths and traces in the deeps. There is that great power of operation in the mind, that quickness and celerity of motion, that in an instant it does pass from extremity to extremity, from the lowest to the highest, from the extremest point o' the west, to the horoscope and ascendant in the east, it measures in one thought the whole circumference of Heaven, and by the same line it takes the geography of the earth, the seas, the air, the fire, all things of either, are within the comprehension of the mind, it has an influence on them all, whence it takes all that may be useful, all that may be helpful in its government. No limitation is prescribed it, no restriction is upon it, but in a free scope it has liberty upon all. And in this liberty is the excellence of the mind, in this power and composition of the mind is the perfection of a man. . . . The mind for this has that transcendence given it, that man, though otherwise the weakest, might be the strongest and most excellent of all creatures; in that only is the excellence we have. . . .

SIR JOHN ELIOT

[601]

It is too little to call man a little world: except God, man is a diminutive to nothing. Man consists of more pieces, more parts, than the world; than the world doth, nay, than the world is. And if those pieces were extended and stretched out in man, as they are in the world, man would be the giant, and the world the dwarf, the world but the map, and the man the world. If all the veins in our bodies were extended to rivers, and all the sinews to veins of mines, and all the muscles, that lie upon one another, to hills, and all the bones to quarries of stones, and all the other pieces to the proportion of those which correspond to them in the world, the air would be too little for this orb of man to move in, the firmament would be but enough for this star; for, as the whole world has nothing, to which something in man doth not answer, so hath man many pieces, of which the whole world hath no representation. Enlarge this meditation upon this great world, man, so far, as to consider the immensity of the creatures this world produces: our creatures are our thoughts, creatures that are born giants; that reach from east to west, from earth to heaven, that do not only bestride all the sea and land, but span the sun and firmament at once; my thoughts reach all, comprehend all. Inexplicable mystery. . . .

JOHN DONNE

. . . There is no Matereal thing, that can hurt or afflict the *Soul,* but only its own *Imaginations* or *Turba;* and what it forms unto it self in the principal of *Evil,* and which it self is comprehended being the Root and Fountain whence all *sorrow* and *fear* takes its Birth. . . .

T. TRYON

If in every world we are liable to find nothing but ourselves, the unspeakable folly of setting our hearts upon *external* goods comes into clearest light. What we *have,* however delighting and desirable, is truly a matter of small importance compared to what we *are,* and if we could but see it, the habits of our mind, our thoughts, wishes, and aspiration are really bills of exchange upon our future lot, be it on this or the other side of bodily dissolution. . . . We were lost if the Love which is the life of the world of light were not as eager to combine with the faintest beginnings of spiritual rebirth. . . . Hence the inexpressible importance of fixing imagination on Divine love. . . .

" Hold fast to love in your imaginations," says Gichtel . . . " Nothing can take it from you but your own imagination: as soon as our imagination goes out of the love, darkness enters the imagination. All things are generated out of imagination, so also the soul shall receive its property in the imagination: and *every imagination reapeth its own work which it hath wrought.*

" That which breaketh the divine image [in man] is the *essential* fierce wrathfulness, and it is done through the imagination; or false or wicked love and imaging; therefore, it lieth wholly in the imagination; whatsoever a man letteth into his desire, in that standeth the image. . . . There is nothing in this world that can touch or kill the soul, no fire nor sword, but only the *imagination;* that is its poison; for it originally proceeded out of the imagination, and continueth eternally therein. All things are existed through *divine imagination.* . . ."

A. J. PENNY

. . . Fun I love, but too much Fun is of all things the most loathsom. Mirth is better than Fun, & Happiness is better than Mirth. I feel that a Man may be happy in This World. And I know that This World Is a World of Imagination & Vision. I see Every thing I paint In This World, but Every body does not see alike. To the Eyes of a Miser a Guinea is far more beautiful than the Sun, & a bag worn with the use of Money has more beautiful proportions than a Vine filled with Grapes. The Tree which moves some to tears of joy is in the Eyes of others only a Green thing which stands in the way. Some see Nature all Ridicule and Deformity, . . . and some scarce see Nature at all. But to the Eyes of the Man of Imagination, Nature is Imagination itself. As a man is, so he sees. As the

Eye is formed, such are its Powers. You certainly Mistake, when you say that the Visions of Fancy are not to be found in This World. To Me This World is all One continued Vision of Fancy or Imagination, & I feel Flattered when I am told so. What is it sets Homer, Virgil & Milton in so high a rank of Art? Why is the Bible more Entertaining & Instructive than any other book? Is it not because they are addressed to the Imagination, which is Spiritual Sensation, & but mediately to the Understanding or Reason? . . .

I am happy to find a Great Majority of Fellow Mortals who can Elucidate My Visions, & Particularly they have been Elucidated by Children, who have taken a greater delight in contemplating my Pictures than I even hoped. Neither Youth nor Childhood is Folly or Incapacity. Some Children are Fools & so are some Old Men. But There is a vast Majority on the side of Imagination or Spiritual Sensation. . . .

Wᴵᴸᴸᴵᴬᴹ Bᴸᴬᴷᴱ, from a letter to the Rev. Dr. Trusler

I have been very near the gates of death, and have returned very weak and an old man, feeble and tottering, but not in spirit and life, not in the real man, the imagination, which liveth for ever. In that I am stronger and stronger, as this foolish body decays. . . .

Wᴵᴸᴸᴵᴬᴹ Bᴸᴬᴷᴱ, from a letter to George Cumberland, April 12, 1827

WILLIAM BLAKE

If ever I saw angel, I told none;
If, before grass was dry, I plucked therefrom
Fairies, and bore them, fading, to my room;
If, darkling, censed by scattered rays of sun,
I took Truth to my heart, and lost her, won;
I have still held those memories in a tomb
Of solitude, imagination's womb,
And unresurgent ere my span was run.

[604]

There came a Vision with two books aloft,
Innocence this, and that *Experience;*
They told of matters deathly or unknown:
Yet, as I read, the pathway and the croft,
By child's feet traced, were thus revealed to sense,
And I no longer knew myself alone.

E. H. W. Meyerstein

 . . . The forces which mould the thought of men change,
or men's resistance to them slackens; with the change of men's
thought comes a change of literature, alike in its inmost essence and in its outward form: after the world has starved its
soul long enough in the contemplation ar.d the re-arrange-
ment of material things, comes the turn of the soul; and with
it comes the literature . . . in which the visible world is no
longer a reality, and the unseen world no longer a dream. . . .

Arthur Symons

The Artist

. . . But like an artist in his mood
  Who reckons all as nought,
So he may quickly paint his nude
  Unutterable thought. . . .

The life so short, the craft so long to learn . . .

The Artist

Of his one meeting with Coleridge, Keats tells us that, " I walked with him at his alderman-after-dinner pace, for near two miles, I suppose. In those two miles he broached a thousand things. Let me see if I can give you a list — nightingales — poetry — on poetical sensation — metaphysics — different genera and species of dreams — nightmare — a dream accompanied with a sense of touch — single and double touch — a dream related — first and second consciousness — the difference explained between will and volition — so say metaphysicians from a want of smoking — the second consciousness — monsters — the Kraken — mermaids — Southey believes in them — Southey's belief too much diluted — a ghost story — Good morning — I heard his voice as he came towards me — I heard it as he moved away — I had heard it all the interval — if it may be called so. . . ."

. . . My night-fancies have long ceased to be afflictive. I confess an occasional night-mare: but I do not, as in early youth, keep a stud of them. Fiendish faces, with the extinguished taper, will come and look at me; but I know them for mockeries, even while I cannot elude their presence, and I fight and grapple with them. For the credit of my imagination, I am almost ashamed to say how tame and prosaic my dreams are grown. They are never romantic, seldom even rural. They are of architecture and of buildings — cities abroad, which I have never seen, and hardly have hope to see. I have traversed, for the seeming length of a natural day, Rome, Amsterdam, Paris, Lisbon — their churches, palaces, squares, market-places, shops, suburbs, ruins, with an inexpressible sense of delight — a map-like distinctness of trace — and a day-light vividness of vision, that was all but being awake. . . . The poverty of my dreams mortifies me. There is Coleridge, at his will can conjure up icy domes, and pleasure-houses for Kubla Khan, and Abyssinian maids, and songs of Abara, and caverns,

> Where Alph, the sacred river, runs,

to solace his night solitudes — when I cannot muster a fiddle. Barry Cornwall has his tritons and his nereids gamboling before him in nocturnal visions, and proclaiming sons born to Neptune — when my stretch of imaginative activity can hardly, in the night season, raise up the ghost of a fish-wife. To set my failures in somewhat a mortifying light — it was after reading the noble Dream of this poet, that my fancy ran strong upon these marine spectra; and the poor plastic power, such as it is, within me set to work, to humour my folly in a sort of dream that very night. Methought I was upon the ocean billows at some sea nuptials, riding and mounted high, with the customary train sounding their conchs before me, (I myself, you may be sure, the *leading god*), and jollily we went careering over the main, till just where Ino Leucothea should have greeted me (I think it was Ino) with a white embrace, the billows gradually subsiding, fell from a sea-roughness to a sea-calm, and thence to a river-motion, and that river (as happens in the familiarization of dreams) was no other than the gentle Thames, which landed me, in the wafture of a placid wave or two, alone, safe and inglorious, somewhere at the foot of Lambeth palace.

The degree of the soul's creativeness in sleep might furnish no whimsical criterion of the quantum of poetical faculty resident in the same soul waking. An old gentleman, a friend of mine, and a humorist, used to carry this notion so far, that when he saw any stripling of his acquaintance ambitious of becoming a poet, his first question would be, — " Young man, what sort of dreams have you? " . . .

CHARLES LAMB

. . . Do there not sometimes, as you fall asleep, come swimming before your eyes in vivid portraiture, shapes and scenes and faces, grotesque or beautiful, but of such speaking realness that they make you move? Or do you ever wake at midnight to find your soul naked to the touch of the world? Little things that you care for, yesterday's, or to-morrow's, or a lifetime's — they are too real. Sometimes the trees stand out this way before a storm. Each being is as though it had non-being for a background. In these hours none too sober, I think we are not far from the well-springs of poetry. Activity has ceased and the senses sleep, but there is energy of perception under the eyelids, and the world re-creates itself with fervour there.

Neither dreams nor the complete illusions of hypnosis, but just on the moonlight verge of them — the wakeful lethargy in which a creak of the floor seems an earthquake, and things with the special values of unreality acquire all the vividness of the real — this is the condition in which imaginative realization can vie in its intensity with the sensuous experience of a Bacchanalian. This is the condition into which the poet must bring us. He must lull us into our exaltation. And for this purpose, like a mother to her child in the night, he brings music. He cradles us in rhythm and soothes us with a perpetual and half-monotonous melody. . . .

MAX EASTMAN

HOST. What say you to young Master Fenton? he capers, he dances, he has eyes of youth, he writes verses, he speaks holiday, he smells April and May: he will carry't, he will carry't; 'tis in his buttons; he will carry't.

WILLIAM SHAKESPEARE,
from *The Merry Wives of Windsor, Act III, Scene II*

We have an idea that thought — as diamonds are wrongly supposed to do — can exist in a pure state, is elaborated without images. We feel sure that we are not infrequently conscious of conclusions, practical or speculative, arrived at without the help of images. What are those?

Ah! what are they? But, first of all, are there any? How can we be sure that there are any? Every time we really succeed in watching our mental process we discover the presence of images. You say " thoughts," " pure thought," and you are persuaded that you say this without any accompanying image, but are you right or wrong? While you say " thought," is it, or is it not, possible that you see a man's head, or his brow, or the inside of his head visualised, not as the horrible brain jelly, but perhaps as a more or less complicated wire frame destined to classify and keep in place the results arrived at, or like infinitely delicate clockwork?

The names of mental operations which are now abstract were not so originally. To *see* and to *know* are the same word in Greek; to ponder, which sounds so intellectual, obviously means to weigh, to *think* is the ghostlike descendant of a much rougher word meaning to seem; *logic* and *speech* are the same word; so, in fine — as if to protest against too much intellectual pride — are *idea* and *image!*

Images can be subconscious and harder to detect than people who have not tried suppose. We can be conscious of one reel unrolling itself — with many crazy interruptions — in our inward cinema, and not be quite conscious of another fixed image, visible, but not easily visible, through the film. Nothing is more frequent than this superposition of two sets of images progressing with variable speeds. They account for the unexpected conclusions at which we arrive while apparently attentive to entirely different matters. . . .

ERNEST DIMNET

Artists have been defined as adults partly in the infantile stage. What has been called their infantilism would be more appropriately designated their primitiveness. For an artist without a delicate emotivity is unthinkable, and visualization plays an important role in all the expressions of art. It is not only in the plastic art that the practitioner has a special eye for colour or line, or both at the same time. Hebbel's statement that " the poet creates from contemplation " is true of novelists and orators as well; and composers, too, know how to utilize their auditory hallucinations. As to scientists, I have promised to myself to prove in a later essay that a certain amount of visualization and affect is not absent from their labours either. Bergson's assertion that " speech only marks out the several halting-places of thought " is true in more than one sense, and it has required all the foregoing pages of this book [*Psychology of Daydreams*] summarily to describe the different psychic mechanisms of which the human word does not give the slightest account. . . .

J. VARENDONCK

The state of ecstasy, of rapture, of absent-mindedness, in a poet, an artist, or a philosopher composing under the influence of inspiration, is, at bottom, identical with the secondary state of the medium. Let it not be said that the medium speaks, acts, and writes quite automatically, whilst the artist, even when his conscious will does not intervene, nevertheless knows what he is producing. This distinction does not always obtain. Many mediums know quite well what is about to be given through them; just as the artist knows bit by bit what he will produce under an inspiration of which he is neither the master nor the guide.

Rousseau covering pages of writing without reflection or effort, in a state of rapture which drew tears, Musset listening to the mysterious " genius " who dictated his verses, Socrates listening to his dæmon, Schopenhauer refusing to believe that his unexpected and unsought postulates were his own work, all behaved exactly like mediums. . . .

GUSTAVE GELEY,
translated by Stanley de Brath

. . . The atmosphere into which genius leads us, and indeed all art, is the atmosphere of the world of dreams. The

[613]

man of genius, it is often said, has the child within him; he is, according to the ancient dictum, which is still accepted, not without an admixture of insanity, and he is unquestionably related to the primitive myth-maker. All these characteristics, as we see, bring him near to the sphere of dreaming, and we may say that the man of genius is in closer touch with the laws of the dream world than is the ordinary civilised man. " It would be no great paradox," remarks Maudsley, " to say that the creative work of genius was excellent dreaming, and dramatic dreaming distracted genius." This has often been recognised by some of the most typical men of genius. Charles Lamb, in speaking of Spenser, referred to the analogy between dreaming and imagination. Coleridge, one of the most essential of imaginative men, argued that the laws of drama and of dreaming are the same. Nietzsche, more recently, has developed the affinity of dreaming to art, and in his *Birth of Tragedy* argued that the Apollonian or dream-like element is one of the two constituents of tragedy. Mallarmé further believed that symbolism, which we have seen to be fundamental in dreaming, is of the essence of art. " To name an object," he said, " is to suppress three-quarters of the enjoyment in a poem which is made up of the happiness of gradually divining; to suggest — that is our dream. The perfect usage of this mystery constitutes symbolism: to evoke an object, little by little, in order to exhibit a state of the soul, or, inversely, to choose an object, and to disengage from it a state of the soul by a series of decipherments." It may be added that imaginative and artistic men have always been prone to day-dreaming and reverie, allowing their fancies to wander uncontrolled, and in so doing they have found profit to their work. From Socrates onwards, too, men of genius have sometimes been liable to fall into states of trance, or waking dream, in which their mission or their vision has become more clearly manifested; the hallucinatory voices which have determined the vocation of many great teachers belong to psychic states allied to these trances. . . .

HAVELOCK ELLIS

[614]

It has been decided by the scientific that dreams are entirely profitless. My suggestion is that that is an undiscriminating mistake; and that imagination, which is a teaching faculty, reveals in dreams an originality and force far beyond all that it displays when we are awake. . . .

Though imagination may mislead, as electricity may destroy, it is by nature the revealing quality of the human mind. Revelation, the unveiling of hidden things, is its daily business. With all our thought for them, the commonest affairs of life would go in darkness and confusion but for the flashing of its light; and if we look above common affairs, we see that what imagination has done for Science (usually under the name of "inspiration") goes so far beyond all that Science could do for itself that Reason is quite unable to explain its ways and means. . . .

It is the common experience of men of genius that their noblest "thoughts," their keenest intuitions, seem to flash into the mind from without rather than to spring up from within. They seem to proceed from some independent agency external to mind and yet at home in it; which is just what might be said of dreams. And madness being mentioned, another remark occurs. Insanity is robbed of half its terrors by the extremely probable supposition that the state of madness is a state of constant dreaming; and wherever insanity appears it certainly seems that the mental faculties have fallen apart from each other, and that imagination takes full possession in unbridled strength. . . .

FREDERICK GREENWOOD

"The taste of arsenic was so really in my mouth when I described how Emma Bovary was poisoned, that it cost me two indigestions one upon the other — quite real ones, for I vomited my dinner."

GUSTAVE FLAUBERT

I by no means rank poetry or poets high in the scale of intellect. This may look like affectation, but it is my real opinion. It is the lava of the imagination whose eruption prevents an earthquake. They say poets never or rarely go *mad*. Cowper and Collins are instances to the contrary (but Cowper was no poet). It is, however, to be remarked that they rarely do, but are generally so near it that I cannot help thinking rhyme is so far useful in anticipating and preventing the disorder. I prefer the talents of action — of war, of the senate, or even of science, — to all the speculations of those mere dreamers of another existence (I don't mean religiously but fancifully) and spectators of this apathy. Disgust and perhaps incapacity have rendered me now a mere spectator; but I have occasionally mixed in the active and tumultuous departments of existence, and on these alone my recollection rests with any satisfaction, though not the best parts of it. . . .

BYRON, to Anne Isabella Milbanke [1813]

THESEUS. . . . Lovers and madmen have such seething
     brains,
    Such shaping fantasies, that apprehend
    More than cool reason ever comprehends.
    The lunatic, the lover, and the poet,
    Are of imagination all compact:
    One sees more devils than vast hell can hold,
    That is, the madman; the lover, all as frantic,
    Sees Helen's beauty in a brow of Egypt:
    The poet's eye, in a fine frenzy rolling,
    Doth glance from heaven to earth, from earth to heaven;
    And, as imagination bodies forth
    The forms of things unknown, the poet's pen
    Turns them to shapes, and gives to airy nothing
    A local habitation and a name. . . .

WILLIAM SHAKESPEARE
from *A Midsummer-Night's Dream, Act V, Scene I*

So far from the position holding true, that great wit (or genius, in our modern way of speaking) has a necessary alliance with insanity, the greatest wits, on the contrary, will ever be found to be the sanest writers. It is impossible for the mind to conceive a mad Shakespeare. . . . The ground of the mistake is, that men, finding in the raptures of the higher poetry a condition of exaltation, to which they have no parallel in their own experience, besides the spurious resemblance of it in dreams and fevers, impute a state of dreaminess and fever to the poet. But the true poet dreams being awake. He is not possessed by his subject, but has dominion over it. . . . Herein the great and the little wits are differenced; that if the latter wander ever so little from nature or actual existence, they lose themselves, and their readers. Their phantoms are lawless, their visions nightmares. They do not create, which implies shaping and consistency. Their imaginations are not active . . . but passive, as men in sick dreams.

CHARLES LAMB

" Do not class the artist's inward vision with those of the hallucinated. During what is properly called hallucination, terror is always present; you feel your personality escaping, you think yourself about to die. With the poetic vision, on the contrary, joy comes, something enters into you. Yet none the less truly you know not where you are. . . . Such a vision often forms slowly, piece by piece as the parts of a scene slide on to the stage; but often also it is sudden and fugitive like the hallucinations of sleep. Something passes before your eyes; then you must throw yourself eagerly upon it."

GUSTAVE FLAUBERT

No one can thoroughly realize Mangan's life without some knowledge of Dublin: not knowledge of Ireland at large, for Mangan had practically none, save by reading; but knowledge of that Dublin " dear and dirty," splendid and squalid, fascinating and repulsive, which was Mangan's from the cradle to the grave. There is there an unique piteousness of poverty and decay, a stricken and helpless look, which seem appropriate to the scene of the doomed poet's life. It was a life of dreams and misery and madness, yet of a self-pity which does not disgust us, and of a weakness which is innocent; it seems the haunted, enchanted life of one drifting through his days in a dream of other days and other worlds, golden and immortal. He wanders about the rotting alleys and foul streets, a wasted ghost, with the " Dark Rosaleen " on his lips, and a strange light in those mystical blue eyes, which burn for us yet in the reminiscences of all who ever saw him and wrote of the unforgettable sight. And, with all his remoteness, all his wretchedness, there was a certain grimly pathetic and humourous common-sense about him, which saved him from being too angelic a drunkard, too ethereal a vagabond, too saintly a wastrel. Hard as it is to believe at all times, he was an intelligible, an explicable human being, and not some " twy-natured " thing, some city faun. . . .

LIONEL JOHNSON

. . . I saw Mallarmé alone on several occasions. " Poe," he remarked, on one of these visits, " I regard as an Irish genius transplanted to America."

" Hugo," I said, at another time, " advises writers never to dream."

" He is wrong," answered Mallarmé; " dreams have as much influence as actions."

And truth to say, this dreamer of dreams exercised a power seldom attained by any Frenchman before or during his day. Everything comes to him who seeks for nothing. The dreamer contents himself in a world of meditation and contemplation; his ideas are many, but his words are few. He dislikes action, yet he attracts the active. He seeks no réclames, yet he is acclaimed. . . .

FRANCIS GRIERSON

MY DEAR CLARE — you see Jane is where you left her, and minus the fat Hogg and the scraggy Prue her daughter, is as she was — her life a routine of what she calls duties. Prue's husband is an old gouty port wine Beak (i.e. Magistrate) of the old school. Your letters are exceedingly interesting — the present and future is nothing — so I look back — and the Shelleyan episode in my life is the most interesting — by the by why did he not project a sect on the Mormon plan? I would gladly have joined him and founded a settlement. . . . Hogg says the Poet could never distinguish truth from falsehood — I found the Poet always truthful — his vivid imagination might occasionally delude him as it does others — for instance his account of the parson assaulting him at the post office — I doubted; but it may have been — in all the ordinary occurrences of life he was truthful. You say he was womanly in some things — so he was, and we men should all be much better if we had a touch of their feeling, sentiment, earnestness, and constancy; but in all the best qualities of man he excelled — the best qualities of the sexes he had — not exactly all — he was inconstant in Love as men of vehement temperament are apt to be — his spirit hunting after new fancies: nothing real can equal the ideal. Poets and men of ardent imagination should not marry — marriage is only suitable to stupid people. . . .

E. J. TRELAWNY, from a letter to Claire Clairmont

Within our happy Castle there dwelt One
Whom without blame I may not overlook;
For never sun on living creature shone
Who more devout enjoyment with us took:
Here on his hours he hung as on a book,
On his own time here would he float away,
As doth a fly upon a summer brook;
But go to-morrow, or belike to-day,
Seek for him, — he is fled; and whither none can say. . . .

Ah! piteous sight it was to see this Man
When he came back to us, a withered flower, —
Or like a sinful creature, pale and wan.
Down would he sit; and without strength or power
Look at the common grass from hour to hour:
And oftentimes, how long I fear to say,
Where apple-trees in blossom made a bower,
Retired in that sunshiny shade he lay;
And, like a naked Indian, slept himself away.

Great wonder to our gentle tribe it was
Whenever from our Valley he withdrew;
For happier soul no living creature has
Than he had, being here the long day through.
Some thought he was a lover, and did woo:
Some thought far worse of him, and judged him wrong;
But verse was what he had been wedded to;
And his own mind did like a tempest strong
Come to him thus, and drove the weary Wight along. . . .

WILLIAM WORDSWORTH

ANIMAL TRANQUILLITY AND DECAY

The little hedgerow birds,
That peck along the road, regard him not.
He travels on, and in his face, his step,
His gait, is one expression; every limb,
His look and bending figure, all bespeak
A man who does not move with pain, but moves
With thought. — He is insensibly subdued
To settled quiet: he is one by whom
All effort seems forgotten; one to whom
Long patience hath such mild composure given,

That patience now doth seem a thing of which
He hath no need. He is by nature led
To peace so perfect that the young behold
With envy, what the Old Man hardly feels.

WILLIAM WORDSWORTH

KARMA

Who paints a picture, writes a play or book
Which others read while he's asleep in bed
O' the other side of the world — when they o'erlook
His page the sleeper might as well be dead;
What knows he of his distant unfelt life?
What knows he of the thoughts his thoughts are raising,
The life his life is giving, or the strife
Concerning him — some cavilling, some praising?
Yet which is most alive, he who's asleep
Or his quick spirit in some other place,
Or score of other places, that doth keep
Attention fixed and sleep from others chase?
    Which is the " he " — the " he " that sleeps, or " he "
That his own " he " can neither feel nor see?

SAMUEL BUTLER

. . . [William Blake's] work is full of . . . visions: his pictures swarm with them. And the personages represented can
only be recognised after a careful reading of the Prophetic
Books. Thus his supernatural visitors became more and more
numerous; but they had their birth always in the invisible
world of his thoughts, his reading, his mental conceptions.
This parallel development can only be regarded as proving
the subjective nature of these heavenly visitations. They
were simply the ideas of a thinker, clothed with a symbolical
and visible form, and perceived, as having an objective existence, by an abnormally sensitive brain.

There were even some cases in which this last feature was lacking, and the visions were nothing but vivid poetical creations. On one occasion, when he had been describing a certain vision in minute detail, someone asked him where he had seen it; and he touched his forehead and replied " Here! " Such an answer shows us how a great many of Blake's assertions as to what he had " seen " are to be interpreted. He often saw only in the same sense as other great poets. But while the others could always dismiss their visions, as it were, into nothingness, and recognise their unreality as soon as the moment of inspiration had gone, Blake remained always conscious of the real existence of his visions. To him, they were the only reality, while our real world was but a shadow and an illusion. . . .

P. BERGER, translated by Daniel H. Conner

. . . Mrs. Blake had but one fault to find with him, that his visions occupied so much of his time. They were her only rivals. In them he found the source of his internal strength and of his confidence in himself. To them he looked for his chief happiness. From them sprang the great light which shone in his eyes, and threw its dazzling brilliance over his sombre and monotonous life.

No poet has ever surpassed Blake in visionary power. Even those whose imagination was strongest have very rarely seen visions like his. Their dreams have had no existence save in the imagination; and they have felt that their visions belonged to some invisible, impalpable sphere, outside of our world. They recognised them as creations of their own, which they could alter or destroy at will. They never saw them with their bodily eyes; and they scarcely ever felt an actual presence confronting them. Dante knew well that his *Inferno,* though he described and measured it with such vivid exactness, was but a fiction of his brain. Bunyan, in spite of his hallucinations, made no mistake as to the nature of the allegorical dream which he embodied in the *Pilgrim's Progress.*

Shelley, who saw and felt so acutely the life around him, and whose nervous system was so morbidly excitable, did not see more than two or three real visions, nor did he take these as subjects for his poems. Even the most fantastic nightmares of Poe and the weirdest evocations of De Quincey are only artificial dreams, set before us as if they were real and palpable. And if at times the intensity of the poet's imaginative power has brought his artistic fancies visibly before his eyes, if Poe did really see the beak of his ill-omened raven or the long, waving hair of his Ligeia, he must have felt immediately that these things were only a part of his own thought projected outside of him, and not separate beings with a life of their own. No poet, however exactly he may have described his creations, has seen them entirely outside of himself, or felt absolutely sure that they came to him from another world, and that he was only the spectator or the enforced listener. To all of them, as to Prospero, these things have been only " such stuff as dreams are made on." . . .

P. BERGER

. . . In [William Blake's] verse there is, if it is to be found in any verse, the " lyrical cry "; and yet, what voice is it that cries in this disembodied ecstasy? The voice of desire is not in it, nor the voice of passion, nor the cry of the heart, nor the cry of the sinner to God, nor of the lover of nature to nature. It neither seeks nor aspires nor laments nor questions. It is like the voice of wisdom in a child, who has not yet forgotten the world out of which the soul came. It is as spontaneous as the note of a bird; it is an affirmation of life; in its song, which seems mere music, it is the mind which sings; it is lyric thought. What is it that transfixes one in any couplet such as this: —

> " If the sun and moon should doubt
> They'd immediately go out "?

It is no more than a nursery statement, there is not even an image in it, and yet it sings to the brain, it cuts into the very flesh of the mind, as if there was a great weight behind it. Is it that it is an arrow, and that it comes from so far, and with an impetus gathered from its speed out of the sky? . . .

Where other poets use reality as a spring-board into space, [William Blake] uses it as a foothold on his return from flight. Even Wordsworth seemed to him a kind of atheist, who mistook the changing signs of " vegetable nature " for the unchanging realities of the imagination. . . .

" There are three powers in man of conversing with Paradise," said Blake, and he defined them as the three sons of Noah who survived the flood, and who are Poetry, Painting, and Music. Through all three powers, and to the last moments of his life on earth, Blake conversed with Paradise. We are told that he used to sing his own songs to his own music, and that, when he was dying, " he composed and uttered songs to his Maker," and " burst out into singing of the things he saw in heaven." And with almost the last strength of his hands he had made a sketch of his wife, before he " made the rafters ring," as a bystander records, with the improvisation of his last breath.

Throughout life, his desire had been, as he said, "To converse with my friends in eternity, see visions, dream dreams, and prophesy and speak parables unobserved." He says again: —

"I rest not from my great task
To open the eternal worlds, to open the immortal eyes
Of Man inwards into the worlds of thought, into eternity,
Ever expanding in the bosom of God, the human imagination."

ARTHUR SYMONS

A Spirit and a Vision are not, as the modern philosophy supposes, a cloudy vapour, or a nothing: they are organized and minutely articulated beyond all that the mortal and perishing nature can produce. He who does not imagine in stronger and better lineaments, and in stronger and better

[624]

light than his perishing and mortal eye can see, does not imagine at all. The painter of this work asserts that all his imaginations appear to him infinitely more perfect and more minutely organized than any thing seen by his mortal eye. . . .

WILLIAM BLAKE

In the life and art of Coleridge, the hours of sleep seem to have been almost more important than the waking hours. " My dreams became the substance of my life," he writes, just after the composition of that terrible poem on " The Pains of Sleep," which is at once an outcry of agony, and a yet more disturbing vision of the sufferer with his fingers on his own pulse, his eyes fixed on his own hardly awakened eyes in the mirror. In an earlier letter, written at a time when he is trying to solve the problem of the five senses, he notes: " The sleep which I have is made up of ideas so connected, and so little different from the operations of reason, that it does not afford me the due refreshment."

To Coleridge . . . there was no conscious division between day and night, between not only dreams and intuitions, but dreams and pure reason. And we find him, in almost all his great poems, frankly taking not only his substance, but his manner from dreams, as he dramatises them after a logic and a passion of their own. His technique is the transposition into his waking hours of the unconscious technique of dreams. It is a kind of verified inspiration, something which came and went, and was as little to be relied upon as the inspiration itself. On one side it was an exact science, but on the other a heavenly visitation. Count and balance syllables, work out an addition of the feet in the verse by the foot-rule, and you will seem to have traced every miracle back to its root in a natural product. Only, something, that is, everything, will have escaped you. As well dissect a corpse to find out the principles of life. That elusive something, that spirit, will be what distinguishes Coleridge's finest verse from the verse of, well, perhaps of every conscious artist in our language. For it is not, as in Blake, literally unconscious, and wavering on every breath of that unseen wind on which it floats to us; it is faultless; it is itself the wind which directs it, it steers its way on the wind, like a seagull poised between sky and sea, and turning on its wings as upon shifted sails.

This inspiration comes upon Coleridge suddenly, without warning, in the first uncertain sketch of " Lewti," written at twenty-two: and then it leaves him, without warning, until the great year 1797, three years later, when " Christabel " and the " Ancient Mariner " are begun. Before and after, Coleridge is seen trying to write, like Bowles, like Wordsworth, like Southey. . . . But here, in " Lewti," he has his style, his lucid and liquid melody, his imagery of moving light and the faintly veiled transparency of air, his vague, wildly romantic subject-matter, coming from no one knows where, meaning one hardly knows what; but already a magic, an incantation.

" Lewti " is a sort of preliminary study for " Kubla Khan "; it too, has all the imagery of a dream, with a breathlessness and awed hush, as of one not yet accustomed to be at home in dreams. " Kubla Khan " . . . has just enough meaning to give it bodily existence; otherwise it would be disembodied music. It seems to hover in the air, like one of the island enchantments of Prospero. It is music not made with hands, and the words seem, as they literally were, remembered. " All the images," said Coleridge, " rose up before me as *things,* with a parallel production of the correspondent expressions." Lamb, who tells us how Coleridge repeated it " so enchantingly that it irradiates and brings heaven and elysian bowers into my parlour when he says or sings it to me," doubted whether it would " bear daylight." It seemed to him that such witchcraft could hardly outlast the night. It has outlasted the century, and may still be used as a touchstone; it will determine the poetic value of any lyric poem which you place beside it. Take as many poems as you please, and let them have all the merits you please, their ultimate merit as poetry will lie in the degree of their approach to the exact, unconscious, inevitable balance of qualities in the poetic art of " Kubla Khan." . . .

ARTHUR SYMONS

To be with Lawrence was a kind of adventure, a voyage of discovery into newness and otherness. For, being himself of a different order, he inhabited a different universe from that of common men — a brighter and intenser world, of which, while he spoke, he would make you free. He looked at things with the eyes, so it seemed, of a man who had been at the brink of death and to whom, as he emerges from the darkness, the world reveals itself as unfathomably beautiful and mysterious. For Lawrence, existence was one continuous convalescence; it was as though he were newly re-born from a mortal illness every day of his life. What these convalescent eyes saw his most casual speech would reveal. A walk with him in the country was a walk through that marvellously rich and significant landscape which is at once the background and the principal personage of all his novels. He seemed to know, by personal experience, what it was like to be a tree or a daisy or a breaking wave or even the mysterious moon itself. He could get inside the skin of an animal and tell you in the most convincing detail how it felt and how, dimly, inhumanly, it thought. Of Black-Eyed Susan, for example, the cow at his New Mexican ranch, he was never tired of speaking, nor was I ever tired of listening to his account of her character and her bovine philosophy.

" He sees," Vernon Lee once said to me, " more than a human being ought to see. Perhaps," she added, " that's why he hates humanity so much." Why also he loved it so much. And not only humanity: nature too, and even the supernatural. For wherever he looked, he saw more than a human being ought to see; saw more and therefore loved and hated more. To be with him was to find oneself transported to one of the frontiers of human consciousness. For an inhabitant of the safe metropolis of thought and feeling it was a most exciting experience. . . .

He regarded no task as too humble for him to undertake,
nor so trivial that it was not worth his while to do it well.
He could cook, he could sew, he could darn a stocking and
milk a cow, he was an efficient wood-cutter and a good hand
at embroidery, fires always burned when he had laid them
and a floor, after Lawrence had scrubbed it, was thoroughly
clean. Moreover, he possessed what is, for a highly strung
and intelligent man, an even more remarkable accomplishment: he knew how to do nothing. He could just sit and be
perfectly content. . . .

ALDOUS HUXLEY

. . . So it is that while in a sense he [Henry James] was the
most personal of writers — for he could not put three words
together without marking them as his own and giving them
the very ring of his voice — yet, compared with other such
deliberate craftsmen as Stevenson or Gustave Flaubert, he
baffles and evades curiosity about the private affairs of his
work. If curiosity were merely futile it would be fitting to
suppress the chance relic I shall offer in a moment — for it
so happens that a single glimpse of unique clarity is open
to us, revealing him as no one saw him in his life. But the
attempt to picture the mind of an artist is only an intrusion
if it is carried into trivial and inessential things; it can never
be pushed too far, as Henry James would have been the first
to maintain, into a real sharing of his aesthetic life.

The relic in question consists of certain pencilled pages,
found among his papers, in which he speaks with only himself for listener. . . . It is as though for once, at an hour of
midnight silence and solitude, he opened the innermost
chamber of his mind and stood face to face with his genius.
There is no moment of all his days in which it is now possible
to approach him more closely. Such a moment represented
to himself the pith of life — the first tremor of inspiration, in
which he might be almost afraid to stir or breathe, for fear
of breaking the spell, if it were not that he goes to meet it
with a peculiar confidence.

"I take this up again after an interruption — I in fact throw myself upon it under the *secousse* of its being brought home to me even more than I expected that my urgent material reasons for getting settled at productive work again are of the very most imperative. Je m'entends — I have had a discomfiture (through a stupid misapprehension of my own indeed;) and I must now take up projected tasks — this long time *entrevus* and brooded over, with the firmest possible hand. I needn't expatiate on this — on the sharp consciousness of this hour of the dimly-dawning New Year, I mean; I simply make an appeal to all the powers and forces and divinities to whom I've ever been loyal and who haven't failed me yet — after all: never, never yet! Infinitely interesting — and yet somehow with a beautiful sharp poignancy in it that makes it strange and rather exquisitely formidable, as with an unspeakable deep agitation, the whole artistic question that comes up for me in the train of this idea . . . of the *donnée* for a situation that I began here the other day to fumble out. . . . Causons, causons, mon bon — oh celestial, soothing, sanctifying process, with all the high sane forces of the sacred time fighting, through it, on my side! Let me fumble it gently and patiently out — with fever and fidget laid to rest — as in all the old enchanted months! It only looms, it only shines and shimmers, *too* beautiful and too interesting; it only hangs there too rich and too full and with too much to give and to pay; it only presents itself too admirably and too vividly, too straight and square and vivid, as a little organic and effective Action. . . .

"Thus just these first little wavings of the oh so tremulously passionate little old wand (now!) make for me, I feel, a sort of promise of richness and beauty and variety; a sort of portent of the happy presence of the elements. The good days of last August and even my broken September and my better October come back to me with their gage of divine possibilities, and I welcome these to my arms, I press them with unutterable tenderness. I seem to emerge from these recent bad days — the fruit of blind accident — and the prospect

clears and flushes, and my poor blest old Genius pats me so
admirably and lovingly on the back that I turn, I screw
round, and bend my lips to passionately, in my gratitude,
kiss its hands."

PERCY LUBBOCK

TO HIS OWN MIND

O weaver, will you not forget
To spin your airy web and slight?
Too nimble Dancer, dancing yet
On the thin meshes of the night!
Beneath my feet your ropes are set,
You hang the stars within my brain; —
I too could weave a wiry net
And dance upon a thoughtful chain,

But that, in pauses, I have heard
Dim sounds that mock the polished mind,
Have seen the lovely and absurd
Things of the country of the blind;
A country where a flaming word
Found by an idiot in his sleep
Is yet the peering poised white bird
That scans the pavement of the deep.

GEOFFREY SCOTT

THE IMAGE–MAKER

Hard is the stone, but harder still
The delicate preforming will
That guided by a dream alone,
Subdues and moulds the hardest stone,
Making the stubborn jade release
The emblem of eternal peace.

[630]

★   *The Artist*   ★

If but the will be firmly bent,
No stuff resists the mind's intent;
The adamant abets his skill
And sternly aids the artist's will,
To clothe in perdurable pride
Beauty his transient eyes descried.

OLIVER ST. JOHN GOGARTY

"Animus and Anima"

*The smallest thing may speak to a
man of the whole round world.*

"Animus and Anima"

In the most remarkable cases of subconscious collaboration, it seems that the work consciously begun is elaborated little by little in the subconsciousness, with a definite plan, with all its divisions and details, till it reaches completion. But these divisions and details come only by degrees and not in a regular order and sequence. It is only when the work is far advanced that the plan and the arrangement of its parts appear. The action resembles putting together a kind of subconscious puzzle, and the artist or the writer (and it is more especially to writers that we refer) has to make an effort to allocate correctly the pages or the phrases which have been subconsciously inspired.

When the work is finished it is found to be quite different from the plan sketched out; but it may give an impression of beauty and order above the writer's own powers; it seems to be partly strange to him and he may even admire it as if it were not his own. . . .

Inspiration, however, except in very rare cases, does not dispense from effort. It simply fertilises effort and reduces it to a minimum. Effort, however, cannot dispense with inspiration, and it is in the collaboration of both that the highest and best work is produced. Without rationalised effort and conscious control, even the inspiration of genius is liable to stray. Disordered and uncontrolled inspiration may result in fine work disfigured by want of proportion, by want of order, by redundance, errors, and mistakes. . . .

GUSTAVE GELEY,
translated by Stanley de Brath

[635]

. . . Many lines of evidence are converging to show that all great accomplishment in human endeavour depends on processes which go on outside those regions of the mind of the activity of which we are clearly conscious. There is reason to believe that the processes which underlie all great work in art, literature, or science, take place unconsciously, or at least unwittingly. It is an interesting question to ask whence comes the energy of which this work is the expression. There are two chief possibilities; one, that it is derived from the instinctive tendencies which, through the action of controlling forces, fail to find their normal outlet; the other, that the energy so arising is increased in amount through the conflict between controlled and controlling forces. Many pathological facts, and especially the general diminution of bodily energy accompanying so many forms of psycho-neurosis, point to the truth of the second alternative. Whatever be the source of the energy, however, we can be confident that by the process of sublimation the lines upon which it is expended take a special course, and in such case it is not easy to place any limit to its activity. We do not know how high the goal that it may reach.

We have, I think, reason to believe that the person who has attained perfection of balance in the control of his instinctive tendencies, in whom the processes of suppression and sublimation have become wholly effective, may thereby become completely adapted to his environment and attain a highly peaceful and stable existence. Such existence is not, however, the condition of exceptional accomplishment, for which there would seem to be necessary a certain degree of instability of the unconscious and subconscious strata of the mind which form the scene of the conflict between instinctive tendencies and the forces by which they are controlled. . . .

W. H. R. RIVERS

. . . It is not enough to say that the whole episode [of the Cave of Mammon in Spenser's *Faerie Queene*] is a copy of the mind's conceptions in sleep; it is, in some sort — but what a copy! Let the most romantic of us, that has been entertained all night with the spectacle of some wild and magnificent vision, recombine it in the morning, and try it by his waking judgment. That which appeared so shifting, and yet so coherent, while that faculty was passive, when it comes under cool examination, shall appear so reasonless and so unlinked, that we are ashamed to have been so deluded; and to have taken, though but in sleep, a monster for a god. But the transitions in this episode are every whit as violent as in the most extravagant dream, and yet the waking judgment ratifies them.

CHARLES LAMB

. . . True Poetry . . . is *not*, as some suppose, a kind of verbal confectionery, with cramp fantastic laws that impose great labour to little purpose.

If one has anything to express in words, why go thus roundabout? asks our sternly prosaic friend. The relations of the human mind with the world are not so simple as he takes for granted. Men are not only intellectual and moral, but emotional and imaginative. Sorrow and joy are very real, yet often very illogical; and so also, and oftener, are those faint rapid shadows and gleams that pass continually over the mind, composing the multiplex hue of life. The moods of the sagest, are they never submissive to the wind in a keyhole, the crackling of the flame, a vernal odour, or the casual brightness or gloom upon a landscape? At the least touch of any sense gates to Infinity are ready to fly open. . . .

WILLIAM ALLINGHAM

. . . It is difficult indeed to become a critic and remain a man. Fitly, therefore, to examine even the shortest genuine Poem is the rarest success of literary judgment. Perhaps it is not venturing too far to say that a true Poem is always conceived by a sort of happy chance — descending, as it were,

[637]

out of the sky; but, as a finished whole, is the fruit of a most actively attentive condition (yet with ease — not strained) of the rarest natural endowment. . . .

WILLIAM ALLINGHAM

. . . In order that a new world may step in, this world must for a time disappear. The murderers, and the murder [of King Duncan, in *Macbeth*], must be insulated, — cut off by an immeasurable gulf from the ordinary tide and succession of human affairs — locked up and sequestrated in some deep recess; we must be made sensible that the world of ordinary life is suddenly arrested — laid asleep, — tranced, — racked into a dread armistice; time must be annihilated; relation to things without abolished; and all must pass self-withdrawn into a deep syncope and suspension of earthly passion. Hence it is, that when the deed is done, when the work of darkness is perfect, then the world of darkness passes away like a pageantry in the clouds; the knocking of the gate is heard; and it makes known audibly that the reaction has commenced; the human has made its reflex upon the fiendish; the pulses of life are beginning to beat again; and the re-establishment of the goings-on of the world in which we live, first makes us profoundly sensible of the awful parenthesis that had suspended them.

O mighty poet! Thy works are not as those of other men, simply and merely great works of art; but are also like the phenomena of nature, like the sun and the sea, the stars and the flowers — like frost and snow, rain and dew, hail-storm and thunder, which are to be studied with entire submission of our own faculties, and in the perfect faith that in them there can be no too-much or too-little, nothing useless or inert, — but that, the further we press in our discoveries, the the more we shall see proofs of design and self-supporting arrangement where the careless eye had seen nothing but accident!

THOMAS DE QUINCEY

[638]

It was my custom to study my characters at night, when all the domestic cares and business of the day were over. On the night preceding that in which I was to appear in this part for the first time, I shut myself up, as usual, when all the family were retired, and commenced my study of Lady Macbeth. As the character is very short, I thought I should soon accomplish it. Being then only twenty years of age, I believed, as many others do believe, that little more was necessary than to get the words into my head; for the necessity of discrimination, and the development of character, at that time of my life, had scarcely entered into my imagination. But, to proceed. I went on with tolerable composure, in the silence of the night (a night I can never forget), till I came to the assassination scene, when the horrors of the scene rose to a degree that made it impossible for me to get farther. I snatched up my candle, and hurried out of the room, in a paroxysm of terror. My dress was of silk, and the rustling of it, as I ascended the stairs to go to bed, seemed to my panic-struck fancy like the movement of a spectre pursuing me. At last I reached my chamber, where I found my husband fast asleep. I clapt my candlestick down upon the table, without the power of putting the candle out, and threw myself on my bed, without daring to stay even to take off my clothes. . . .

SARAH SIDDONS

. . . So far as any single function of spiritual life can be said to have an intrinsic value, poetry, it seems to me, possesses it just as other functions do, and it is in each case irreplaceable. And further, it seems to me, poetry attains its own aim, and in doing so makes its contribution to the whole, most surely and fully when it seeks its own end without attempting to reach those of co-ordinate functions, such as the attainment of philosophic truth or the furtherance of moral progress. But then I believe this because I also believe that the unity of human nature in its diverse activities is so intimate and pervasive that no influence can effect any one of them alone, and that no one of them can operate or change without transmitting its influence to the rest. If I may use the language of paradox I would say that the pursuit of poetry for its own sake is the pursuit both of truth and of goodness. Devotion to it is devotion to " the good cause of the world "; and wherever the imagination is satisfied, there, if we had a knowledge we have not, we should discover no idle fancy but the image of a truth.

A. C. Bradley

Infinite mountains of the interior mind
    cast their long shadow over field and town;
whence, from the melting glaciers far behind,
    comes the tumultuous torrent, rushing down
the deep-hewn watercourse of speech, and roars
    its meaning in its passage: our poor thought
feels how that sound old fruitfulness restores;
    flush with its banks philosophy is brought,
and metaphysic thunders once again
    over the pebbled channels of our time,
o'er rocky meditations to our plain
    of common hearing dashed, in rhythm and rhyme —
there, by the force of its creative will,
flows into poetry, surges, and is still.

Charles Williams

. . . [Poesy] is (as hath been said) one of the principal portions of learning, and is nothing else but Feigned History, which may be styled as well in prose as in verse.

The use of this Feigned History hath been to give some shadow of satisfaction to the mind of man in those points wherein the nature of things doth deny it; the world being in proportion inferior to the soul; by reason whereof there is agreeable to the spirit of man a more ample greatness, a more exact goodness, and a more absolute variety, than can be found in the nature of things. Therefore, because the acts or events of true history have not that magnitude which satisfieth the mind of man, poesy feigneth acts and events greater and more heroical; because true history propoundeth the successes and issues of actions not so agreeable to the merits of virtue and vice, therefore poesy feigns them more just in retribution, and more according to revealed providence; because true history representeth actions and events more ordinary and less interchanged, therefore poesy endueth them with more rareness, and more unexpected and alternative variations. So as it appeareth that poesy serveth and conferreth to magnanimity, morality, and to delectation. And therefore it was ever thought to have some participation of divineness, because it doth raise and erect the mind, by submitting the shows of things to the desires of the mind; whereas reason doth buckle and bow the mind into the nature of things. . . .

Neither is the Imagination simply and only a messenger; but is invested with or at leastwise usurpeth no small authority in itself, besides the duty of the message. For it was well said by Aristotle, "That the mind hath over the body that commandment, which the lord hath over a bondman; but that reason hath over the imagination that commandment which a magistrate hath over a free citizen"; who may come also to rule in his turn. For we see that in matters of Faith and Religion we raise our Imagination above our Reason; which is the cause why Religion sought ever access to the mind by similitudes, types, parables, visions, dreams. And again in all persuasions that are wrought by eloquence and other impression of like nature, which do paint and disguise the true appearance of things, the chief recommendation unto Reason is from the Imagination. . . .

Francis Bacon

. . . The poet [declares Shelley] creates, but this creation is no mere fancy of his; it represents " those forms which are common to universal nature and existence," and " a poem is the very image of life expressed in its eternal truth." We notice, further, that the more voluntary and conscious work of invention and execution is regarded as quite subordinate in the creative process. In that process the mind, obedient to an influence which it does not understand and cannot control, is driven to produce images of perfection which rather form themselves in it than are formed by it. The greatest stress is laid on this influence or inspiration; and in the end we learn that the origin of the whole process lies in certain exceptional moments when visitations of thought and feeling, elevating and delightful beyond all expression, but always arising unforeseen and departing unbidden, reach the soul; that these are, as it were, the interpretation of a diviner nature through our own; and that the province of the poet is to arrest these apparitions, to veil them in language, to colour every other form he touches with their evanescent hues, and so to " redeem from decay the visitations of the divinity in man. " . . .

The enemy [Shelley] has to meet [in his " Defence of Poetry " " something very much wider than poetry in the usual sense "], is the contention that poetry and its influence steadily decline as civilisation advances, and that they are giving place, and ought to give place, to reasoning and the pursuit of utility. His answer is that, on the contrary, imagination has been, is, and always will be, the prime source of everything that has intrinsic value in life. Reasoning, he declares, cannot create, it can only operate upon the products of imagination. Further, he holds that the predominance of mere reasoning and mere utility has become in great part an evil; for while it has accumulated masses of material goods and moral truths, we distribute the goods iniquitously and fail to apply the truths, because, for want of imagination, we have not sympathy in our hearts and do not feel what we know. The " Poetry " which he defends, therefore, is the whole creative imagination with all its products. . . .

The imagination — that is to say, the soul imagining — has before it, or feels within it, something which, answering perfectly to its nature, fills it with delight and with a desire to realise what delights it. This something, for the sake of brevity, we may call an idea, so long as we remember that it need not be distinctly imagined and that it is always accompanied by emotion. The reason why such ideas delight the imagining soul is that they are, in fact, images of forebodings of its own perfection — of itself become perfect — in one aspect or another. These aspects are as various as the elements and forms of its own inner life and outward existence; and so the idea may be that of the perfect harmony of will and feeling (a virtue), or of the perfect union of soul with soul (love), or of the perfect order of certain social relations or forces (a law or institution), or of the perfect adjustment of intellectual elements (a truth). . . .

A. C. BRADLEY

Poetry is not like reasoning, a power to be exerted according to the determination of the will. A man cannot say, " I will compose Poetry." The greatest poet even cannot say it; for the mind in creation is as a fading coal, which some invisible influence, like an inconstant wind, awakens to transitory brightness; this power arises from within, like the colour of a flower which fades and changes as it is developed, and the conscious portions of our natures are unprophetic either of its approach or its departure.

PERCY BYSSHE SHELLEY

As to the poetical Character itself (I mean that sort of which, if I am anything, I am a Member; that sort distinguished from the Wordsworthian or egotistical sublime; which is a thing per se and stands alone) it is not itself — it has no self — it is every thing and nothing. It has no character — it enjoys light and shade; it lives in gusto, be it foul or fair, high or low, rich or poor, mean or elevated. It has as much delight in conceiving an Iago as an Imogen. What shocks the virtuous philosopher, delights the chamelion Poet. It does no harm from its relish of the dark side of things any more than from its taste for the bright one; because they both end in speculation. A poet is the most unpoetical of anything in existence; because he has no Identity — he is continually in for [?] and ing some other Body. The Sun, the Moon, the Sea, and Men and Women who are creatures of impulse are poetical and have about them an unchangeable attribute — the poet has none; no identity — he is certainly the most unpoetical of all God's Creatures. If then he has no self, and if I am a Poet, where is the Wonder that I should say I would write no more? Might I not at that very instant have been cogitating on the Characters of Saturn and Ops? It is a wretched thing to confess; but it is a very fact that not one word I ever utter can be taken for granted as an opinion growing out of my identical nature — how can it when I have no nature? When I am in a room with People if I ever am free from speculating on creations of my own brain, then not myself goes home to myself: but the identity of every one in the room begins [so] to press upon me that I am in a very little time annihilated — not only among Men; it would be the same in a Nursery of children. . . .

I am ambitious of doing the world some good: if I should be spared, that may be the work of future years — in the interval I will assay to reach to as high a summit in poetry as the nerve bestowed upon me will suffer. The faint conceptions I have of poems to come bring the blood frequently into my forehead. All I hope is, that I may not lose all interest in human affairs — that the solitary indifference I feel for applause, even from the finest spirits, will not blunt any acuteness of vision I may have. I do not think it will. I feel assured I should write from the mere yearning and fondness I have for the beautiful, even if my night's labours should be burnt every morning, and no eye ever shine upon them. But even now I am perhaps not speaking from myself, but from some character in whose soul I now live. . . .

JOHN KEATS to Charles Woodhouse

. . . The poet himself would fain believe that the vision uplifting him will bring its own song with it, that the beauty and splendour of the one will be the infallible beauty and splendour of the other. He will agree that the song may rush straight upon his lips from the thing seen, or that the certainty of a poem may come in some rare uplifting of the mind though that poem will lie buried for months, its shape and fashion all unknown, to flow forth finally with a deeper earthly wisdom, though not with so clear a light: he will agree that the vision itself, for all that it is, will not be clear to him till its poem come, and that he will make the vision his by the making of the poem, rising upon it by being now finished with it: but it will seem to him that these things should argue a poem to match equally with the exaltation given to him, and that if the poem be faulty there was something amiss with the exaltation. So, indeed, at heart it mostly is; but not always. All men are more than they can express of themselves. No man can give another all of his own enlightenment. . . .

DARRELL FIGGIS

. . . As we are superfluous in the midst of nature, so is the best part of ourselves superfluous in us. Poetry, music and pictures, inspired and shaded by human emotion, are surely better worth having than the inarticulate experience they spring from. Even in our apprehension of the material world, the best part is the adaptation of it to our position and faculties, since this is what introduces boundaries, perspectives, comparison and beauty. It is only what exists materially that exists without excuse, whereas what the mind creates has some vital justification, and may serve to justify the rest. . . .

GEORGE SANTAYANA

The argument of this book [*Art and Understanding*], is based upon the following five beliefs. (i) That reality is in mind, not in matter: (ii) That we have to deal with a world of reality and a world of appearance: (iii) That the world of reality, or spiritual world, is true and good and permanent and is outside time and space, while the world of appearance, or material world, which appears to combine good and evil, truth and error, is, in reality, a temporal world, without permanent value: (iv) That the world known as the world of art presents a parallel to the temporal world. Although necessarily a world of appearance (for works of art are material structures) it has its higher and lower aspects. True art is a symbol of reality. Counterfeit art stands for unreality, or ignorance of good. We have therefore not good art and bad art (for bad art would be as unreasonable a thing to believe in as bad virtue) but true art and counterfeit: (v) That a true aesthetic is to be found in the living experience, the true understanding of true art by the race. . . .

The belief that art is connected with reality is generally, although vaguely, accepted. The view that the visible world of appearance made known to us through the physical senses is not the real world, but is only a symbol for the invisible or permanent world outside time and space and the flux of mortal experience has been held, not only by simple people but by many of the profoundest minds of all ages. . . . It is based on personal experience, but if it contains truth it is no personal hypothesis but an individual experience of truth. It takes as its point of departure the belief that a true work of art is a witness to beauty in its profoundest aspect. The awareness of this beauty is the awareness of the real world, of the underlying spiritual reality of things, hidden behind the clouds of appearance or material sense. . . . To explain these things further, we must envisage a creative Mind, wholly good, and a spiritual creation also wholly good, reflecting the conceptions of this Mind. These conceptions range from the smallest to the greatest, from the simple to the complex, and of all of them *man* is the greatest. He alone is capable of understanding his true nature and that of the universe. Each individual man is unique and reflects a different variation of Mind's ideal. Reality, therefore, consists of Mind and its ideas or conceptions, entirely separate from material conceptions or forms since immortality and mortality can never become one but are only associated in appearance. It is spiritual man who is aware, not of appearance, but of reality. His thoughts and ideas are impartations of truth; they are good and beautiful. . . .

The case having been thus stated we must now postulate, for practical purposes, a material universe and a man compounded of mind, body and spirit. This man appears to have a double experience. Sometimes he is aware of his true identity and of the truth about the universe. Sometimes he is only conscious of his material selfhood and of the material world. This is the experience of everyday life in accordance with our present state of thinking and feeling. In this life good must be made manifest and in terms of this life it must be understood and enjoyed. We are conscious of matter and think in terms of matter, although science dissolves it under our eyes. We believe the evidence of the senses although it is now generally accepted that their witness is largely if not entirely false and that extra sensory perception exists. How this material and illusory experience arose, how it communicates itself, or in what its nature consists we cannot say, since nothing true or consistent can be said of what is untrue except that it can only exist as a negation, as "a lie and the father of lies." . . .

The artist, whatever he may think, is the man who is aware of the unseen world. His experience can be shared, in different ways, by all who seek disinterestedly for goodness and truth. It is reflected through the medium of words in the form of poetry, of sounds in the form of music, and of visible form in the visual arts. The form is implicit in the idea which determines the work. . . . The sense of visual beauty or harmony is a natural thing, potential in us all, continually entertained. It comes to us in the form of an idea, impression or mind-picture. But the artist responds to it more profoundly and in special fashion. . . .

MARGARET H. BULLEY

. . . There is no question of likening the poet's dim nightlight to the sun of the contemplative; a profane, and, after all, a fairly common experience, to an experience that is wholly supernatural, and one not granted to all Christians, even to those who are very devout? It is solely a question of seeking in the most wonderful introspective literature that exists, some lights on the mechanism of poetic experience. Poetic experience is, in my opinion, a gift of God — indeed, a grace, an activity essentially directed towards prayer, as Mr. Middleton Murry has said; but even if it were less supernatural than as a fact it is, were it completely profane, worldly, frivolous even, it would none the less be a sort of knowledge distinct from notional knowledge, a " simple gaze of the spirit, without formation of species," a direct, immediate, global perception or an obscure seizing of the real, a feeling of presence, a contact, a profound touch, a " unitive knowledge," the outline of a possession, a realisation, a "real knowledge." . . .

HENRI BREMOND, translated by Algar Thorold

. . . Blake was probably right in believing that the greatest artists had worked from vision; " students of nature " clumsily supply their physical defect by handicapped labour. Michael Angelo and Rembrandt watched the world in order to enrich their visions, not each item piecemeal for each several work; hence, as in fine literature, their observation is thoroughly assimilated. On a lower plane, Wordsworth's " bliss of solitude," and " eye upon the object," suppose a visionary habit perhaps less vivid but possibly better trained than Blake's: but in Flaubert's case we have indisputable evidence that one as exceptional can be treated seriously.[1] . . .

Imagination cultivated to the point of vision, if of great service to an artist, needs a constant supply of trustworthy material, and correction by a free critical reference to logic and aesthetic judgment; for, like any other human faculty, it must be disciplined and not worshipped blindly. Flaubert was at vast pains to acquire a stock of precise information about objects, persons, places, and periods with which his

[1] See pp. 617 and 615.

work was concerned, though we are to understand that he often wrote his actual descriptions from visions for which his mind had been thus prepared. Blake would have dreaded the influence of any preparation other than prayer or good deeds, since, in his belief, it could only have imposed on the real spiritual world shadows, stains, and contortions, characteristic of the outward spectacle, which was inherently false. . . .

T. Sturge Moore

. . . Now, is it wonderful that that pen of his [Shakespeare's] should some times be at fault for a while, — that it should pause, write, erase, rewrite, amend, complete, before he satisfies himself that his language has done justice to the conceptions which his mind's eye contemplated?

In this point of view, doubtless, many or most writers are elaborate; and those certainly not the least whose style is furthest removed from ornament, being simple and natural, or vehement, or severely business-like and practical. Who so energetic and manly as Demosthenes? Yet he is said to have transcribed Thucydides many times over in the formation of his style. Who so gracefully natural as Herodotus? yet his very dialect is not his own, but chosen for the sake of the perfection of his narrative. Who exhibits such happy negligence as our own Addison? yet artistic fastidiousness was so notorious in his instance that the report has got abroad, truly or not, that he was too late in his issue of an important state-paper, from his habit of revision and re-composition. Such great authors were working by a model which was before the eyes of their intellect, and they were labouring to say what they had to say, in such a way as would most exactly and suitably express it. It is not wonderful that other authors, whose style is not simple, should be instances of a similar literary diligence. Virgil wished his Æneid to be burned, elaborate as is its composition, because he felt it needed more labour still, in order to make it perfect. . . .

Now in all these instances, I wish you to observe, that what

I have admitted about literary workmanship differs from the doctrine which I am opposing in this, — that the mere dealer in words cares little or nothing for the subject which he is embellishing, but can paint and gild anything whatever to order; whereas the artist, whom I am acknowledging, has his great or rich visions before him, and his only aim is to bring out what he thinks or what he feels in a way adequate to the thing spoken of, and appropriate to the speaker.

CARDINAL NEWMAN

. . . In all the biographical studies I had read, Goethe always appeared to me as a man whom labour did not fatigue. . . .

Later, however, I had to change my mind, when in the last volume of Goethe's work on the *Theory of Colour* I read this confession: "From the first appearance of my poetic attempts, my contemporaries showed themselves sufficiently benevolent towards me, recognising at least that I had poetic talent and inclination. Yet I myself had towards the poetic art a quite peculiar relation which was only practical when I for a long time cherished in my mind a subject which possessed me, a model which inspired, a predecessor who attracted me, until at length, after I had moulded it in silence for years, something resulted which might be regarded as a creation of my own; and finally all at once, and almost instinctively, as if it had become ripe, I set it down upon paper."

Flaubert worked fourteen hours a day, and every one knows that in him the endeavour after perfection of style had become a disease. Of this many anecdotes are told; among others that he rose during the night to correct a word; that he remained motionless for some hours, his hands in his hair, bent down over an adjective. Style was a tyrant to him; it became his passion to wear himself out in the insatiable search for the mysterious law of a beautiful phrase, and this ceaseless striving ended by becoming an insuperable obstacle to work. . . .

A. MOSSO

. . . And, while the many use language as they find it, the man of genius uses it indeed, but subjects it withal to his own purposes, and moulds it according to his own peculiarities. The throng and succession of ideas, thoughts, feelings, imaginations, aspirations, which pass within him, the abstractions, the juxtapositions, the comparisons, the discriminations, the conceptions, which are so original in him, his views of external things, his judgments upon life, manners, and history, the exercises of his wit, of his humour, of his depth, of his sagacity, all these innumerable and incessant creations, the very pulsation and throbbing of his intellect, does he image forth, to all does he give utterance, in a corresponding language, which is as multiform as this inward mental action itself and analogous to it, the faithful expression of his intense personality, attending on his own inward world of thought as its very shadow: so that we might as well say that one man's shadow is another's as that the style of a really gifted mind can belong to any but himself. It follows him about *as* a shadow. His thought and feeling are personal, and so his language is personal. . . .

Cardinal Newman

. . . Who has not a thousand times seen snow fall on water? Who has not watched it with a new feeling from the time that he has read Burns' comparison of sensual pleasure to —

> " Snow that falls upon a river,
> A moment white — then gone for ever! "

In poems, as in philosophic disquisitions, genius produces the strongest impressions of novelty, while it rescues the most admitted truths from the impotence caused by the very circumstance of their universal admission. Truths of all others the most awful and mysterious, yet being at the same time of universal interest, are too often considered as *so* true, that they lose all the life and efficiency of truth, and lie bedridden

[651]

in the dormitory of the soul, side by side with the most despised and exploded errors.

SAMUEL TAYLOR COLERIDGE

What, for the most part, mean we by Genius, but the Power of accomplishing great things without the means generally reputed necessary to that end? A *Genius* differs from a *good Understanding,* as a Magician from a good Architect; *That* raises his structure by means invisible; *This* by the skillful use of common tools. Hence Genius has ever been supposed to partake of something Divine. . . .

So boundless are the bold excursions of the human mind, that in the vast void beyond real existence, it can call forth shadowy beings, and unknown worlds, as numerous, as bright, and, perhaps, as lasting, as the stars; such quite-original beauties we may call Paradisaical, *Natos sine semine flores.* . . .

EDWARD YOUNG

REYNOLDS AND BLAKE

. . . Our minds should be habituated to the contemplation of excellence . . . we should to the last moment of our lives continue a settled intercourse with all the true examples of grandeur. Their inventions are not only the food of our infancy, but the substance which supplies the fullest maturity of our vigour.

Reynolds Thinks that Man Learns all that he knows. I say on the Contrary that Man Brings All that he has or can have Into the World with him. Man is born Like a Garden ready Planted and Sown. This World is too poor to produce one Seed.

The mind is but a barren soil; a soil which is soon exhausted, and will produce no crop. . . .

The mind that could have produced this Sentence must have been a Pitiful, a Pitiable Imbecillity. I always thought that the Human Mind was the most Prolific of All Things &

Inexhaustible. I certainly do Thank God that I am not like
Reynolds.

WILLIAM BLAKE

> . . . Visionary power
> Attends the motions of the viewless winds,
> Embodied in the mystery of words:
> There, darkness makes abode, and all the host
> Of shadowy things work endless changes, — there,
> As in a mansion like their proper home,
> Even forms and substances are circumfused
> By that transparent veil with light divine,
> And, through the turnings intricate of verse,
> Present themselves as objects recognised,
> In flashes, and with glory not their own.

WILLIAM WORDSWORTH,
from *The Prelude, Book V*

The purpose of rhythm, it has always seemed to me, is to
prolong the moment of contemplation, the moment when we
are both asleep and awake, which is the one moment of creation, by hushing us with an alluring monotony, while it holds
us waking by variety, to keep us in that state of perhaps real
trance, in which the mind liberated from the pressure of the
will is unfolded in symbols. If certain sensitive persons listen
persistently to the ticking of a watch, or gaze persistently on
the monotonous flashing of a light, they fall into the hypnotic
trance; and rhythm is but the ticking of a watch made softer,
that one must needs listen, and various, that one may not be
swept beyond memory or grow weary of listening; while the
patterns of the artist are but the monotonous flash woven to
take the eyes in a subtler enchantment. I have heard in meditation voices that were forgotten the moment they had
spoken; and I have been swept, when in more profound meditation, beyond all memory but of those things that came from
beyond the threshold of waking life. I was writing once at a

very symbolical and abstract poem, when my pen fell on the ground; and as I stooped to pick it up, I remembered some phantastic adventure that yet did not seem phantastic, and then another like adventure, and when I asked myself when these things had happened, I found that I was remembering my dreams for many nights. I tried to remember what I had done the day before, and then what I had done that morning; but all my waking life had perished from me, and it was only after a struggle that I came to remember it again, and as I did so that more powerful and startling life perished in its turn. Had my pen not fallen on the ground and so made me turn from the images that I was weaving into verse, I would never have known that meditation had become trance, for I would have been like one who does not know that he is passing through a wood because his eyes are on the pathway. So I think that in the making and in the understanding of a work of art, and the more easily if it is full of patterns and symbols and music, we are lured to the threshold of sleep, and it may be far beyond it, without knowing that we have ever set our feet upon the steps of horn or of ivory.

W. B. YEATS

. . . I know very well that many who pretend to be wise by the forms of being grave, are apt to despise both poetry and music as toys and trifles too light for the use or entertainment of serious men. But whoever find themselves wholly insensible to these charms, would I think do well to keep their own counsel, for fear of reproaching their own temper and bringing the goodness of their natures, if not of their understandings, into question. It may be thought at least an ill sign, if not an ill constitution, since some of the fathers went so far as to esteem the love of music a sign of predestination, as a thing divine and reserved for the felicities of Heaven itself. While this world lasts, I doubt not but the pleasure and requests of these two entertainments will do so too: and happy those that content themselves with these or any other so easy and so innocent, and do not trouble the world or other men, because they cannot be quiet themselves, though nobody hurts them!

When all is done, human life is, at the greatest and the best, but like a froward child, that must be played with and humoured a little to keep it quiet till it falls asleep, and then the care is over.

Sir William Temple

. . . All children, under nine or ten years of age, are poets and philosophers. They pretend to live with the rest of us, and the rest of us imagine that we influence them so that their life is only a reflection of our own. But, as a matter of fact, they are as self-contained as cats and as continuously attentive to the magical charm of what they see inwardly. Their mental wealth is extraordinary; only the greatest artists or poets, whose resemblance to children is a banal certainty, can give us some idea of it. A golden-haired little fellow playing with his blocks in the garden may be conscious all the time of the sunset while pretending not to look at it. "Come along!" the nurse said to Felicité de la Mennais, eight years old, "you have looked long enough at those waves and everybody is going away." The answer: "*ils regardent ce que je regarde, mais ils ne voient pas ce que je vois*," was no brag, but merely a plea to stay on. Who can tell what the four Brontë tots saw or did not see in the moors through which, day after day, they rambled holding hands? Cannot you remember looking for long spells at a mere patch of red on a sheet of paper or in your little paint-box? Most intelligent children, as was the case with Newman, have the philosopher's doubts about the existence of the world. You see them looking curiously at a stone; you think "children are so funny" and all the time they are wondering if the stone may not be eternal, and what it is to be eternal. Have I not heard a little girl of nine interrupt a conversation of dons who talked about nothing with the astounding question: "Father, what is beauty? What makes it?" . . .

Ernest Dimnet

At the very instant when the already projected work is definitely conceived in germ like every other living being, inspiration takes hold of it, inflames it, transfigures it, and makes it shine before the poet's eyes with a bright, mysterious light. He sees in a twinkling of an eye his work, not yet made, but somehow exciting, move and live. . . . In these rare but sublime moments time and space disappear; the work thus created has no limits, or, if it has, the poet does not see them. His thought embraces and penetrates him at so great a depth, that for a moment he is set free from the conditions of the human lot. . . . This is the first (and for the writer of this book the last) note of inspiration. It does not last long, but nothing can take its place when it is over. It gives to a work of poetry that primitive swing, that unlimited movement which is necessary to it; for it must have begun by being too vast in the soul of the poet, in order, afterwards, to be great enough in the eyes of other men. . . .

EDMOND ARNOULD, quoted by Henri Bremond

. . . The possession of an *Anima*, and the consequent capacity for this concrete, real, unitive knowledge which I have tried to describe, is not the exclusive privilege of the poet and the mystic. The most prosaic of men, the least religious, and the most intellectually conceited has his *Anima*, as much as St. John of the Cross and Virgil, and it is impossible to imagine any kind of rational knowledge in which the activity of *Anima* does not intervene or insinuate itself. It is the intensity of these activities of the deeper soul in poet and mystic that distinguish them from the run of men. From the point of view of psychological mechanism, at which we still remain, it is merely a question of more or less. At the highest stage come the mystical states, properly so called; then the higher poetical states; then the lower poetical states, meaning by them the experience of the thousands of poets who do not arrive at expression, and of the thousands of readers who are not content only to " understand " the poets; then the " real " knowledge, at the level of everybody, in which the apprehension of the real is so weak and evanescent that nothing betrays the passage of the current. It is in this more or less vivid apprehension of the real that these diverse states resemble each other. . . .

HENRI BREMOND, translated by Algar Thorold

Animus and *Anima:* reason and poetry. Words considered in their natural being — *i.e.*, as signs of ideas — belong to the sole master of ideas, *Animus.* He has made them in his own image, rationalising them through and through. When *Anima* wants to talk, she can only borrow the dictionary of *Animus.* But, without robbing them of what makes their substance — the property, that is, of representing ideas — she possesses the secret of associating them just as they are with her own activity, transmitting to them her own vibrations, breathing into them her own life. A transmutation impossible to define, but a fact of experience. *Animus* hears her song and laughs in his coarse way. " Ah! " says he, " she has stolen all my words, and has not added the shadow of a new meaning to the ideas which they represent. Why, then, all this trouble? " That is . . . precisely the very just reasoning of the rationalist aesthetic; reason only being acceptable to didacticism, all poetry is closed to it. Yes or no, do you teach reason anything new? If yes, you are only doing what prose can do as well, and better. So be silent. . . .

> Et pourtant elle est immortelle
> Et ceux qui se sont passés d'elle
> Ici-bas ont tout ignoré. . . .

HENRI BREMOND

All is not going well in the home of Animus and Anima. It is a long time since their short honeymoon, during which Anima had the right of speaking at her ease, while Animus listened to her ravished with delight. After all, did not the household live on the fortune brought by Anima? But not for long did Animus allow himself to be reduced to this inferior position; very soon did he show his true nature — vain, pedantic, and tyrannical. Anima is a ignoramus and a fool, she has never been to school; whereas Animus knows a heap of things, he has read a heap of things in books . . . all his friends say it is impossible to be a better talker. . . . Anima has no longer the right to say a word . . . he knows better than she what she wants to say. Animus is not faithful, but that does not prevent him being jealous, for *au fond* he knows well (no, he has finished by forgetting it) that all the fortune belongs to Anima, and that he is a beggar, and lives on what she gives him. So he is endlessly exploiting and tormenting her to get money out of her. . . . She stays silently at home to do the cooking and clean the house as best she can. . . . *Au fond* Animus is a bourgeois; he has regular habits, and likes to eat the same dinner every day. But something strange has happened. . . . One day Animus came in unexpectedly . . . he heard Anima singing to herself behind closed doors a curious song, something that he did not know; there was no way of discovering the notes, or the words, or the key — a strange and wonderful song. Since then he has slyly tried to make her repeat it, but Anima pretends not to understand. She is silent as soon as he looks at her. The soul is silent when the mind looks at it. Then Animus thinks he will play a trick on her; he takes steps to make her think he is not present . . . little by little Anima reassures herself, she looks here and there, she listens, she sighs, she thinks herself alone, and noiselessly she goes and opens the door to her divine lover.

PAUL CLAUDEL, quoted by Henri Bremond

The lover knocks at the door of the Beloved, and a voice replies from within: "Who is there?" "It is I," he said; and the voice replied: "There is no room for thee and me in this house." And the door remained shut. Then the lover retired to the desert, and fasted and prayed in solitude. After a year he came back, and knocked once more at the door. Once more the voice asked: "Who is there?" He replied: "It is thyself." And the door opened to him.

From the Persian, translated by Edward Fitzgerald

People dislike and despise symbols so much nowadays, and yet how necessary they are. They are most inadequate, but that doesn't matter. Once when I was very ill, I dwelt all the time on a picture of the Sacred Heart. It was everything to me, I looked at it and prayed to it all the time, it was the only thing that seemed to make my illness bearable. After some years I saw this picture again: it was odious, vulgar, such a trashy picture! I was ashamed to think what it had been to me — yet it had been everything! You see how the sensible always conveys the spiritual: the invisible in the visible. Christ everywhere makes use of the sensible to convey the spiritual, never the spirit alone. . . .

BARON FRIEDRICH VON HÜGEL, in a letter to a Niece

THE CREDITOR

The quietude of a soft wind
Will not rescind
My debts to God, but gentle-skinned
His finger probes. I lull myself
In quiet in diet in riot in dreams,
In dopes in drams in drums in dreams
Till God retire and the door shut.
But
Now I am left in the fire-blaze
The peacefulness of the fire-blaze
Will not erase
My debt to God for His mind strays
Over and under and all ways
All days and always.

LOUIS MACNEICE

[659]

With fainting soul athirst for Grace,
I wandered in a desert place,
And at the crossing of the ways
I saw the sixfold Seraph blaze:
He touched mine eyes with fingers light
As sleep that cometh in the night:
And like a frightened eagle's eyes,
They opened wide with prophecies.
He touched mine ears, and they were drowned
With tumult and a roaring sound:
I heard convulsion in the sky,
And flights of angels' hosts on high,
And beasts that move beneath the sea,
And the sap creeping in the tree.
And bending to my mouth he wrung
From out of it my sinful tongue,
And all its lies and idle rust,
And 'twixt my lips a-perishing
A subtle serpent's forkèd sting
With right hand wet with blood he thrust
And with his sword my breast he cleft,
My quaking heart thereout he reft,
And in the yawning of my breast
A coal of living fire he pressed.
Then in the desert I lay dead,
And God called unto me and said:
"Arise, and let My voice be heard,
Charged with My Will go forth and span
The land and sea, and let My Word
Lay waste with fire the heart of man."

ALEXANDER PUSHKIN,
translated by Maurice Baring

CONTINUITY

No sign is made while empires pass.
The flowers and stars are still His care,
The constellations hid in grass,
The golden miracles in air.

Lift in an instant will be rent
Where death is glittering blind and wild —
The Heavenly Brooding is intent
To that last instant on Its child.

It breathes the glow in brain and heart,
Life is made magical. Until
Body and spirit are apart
The Everlasting works Its will.

In that wild orchid that your feet
In their next falling shall destroy,
Minute and passionate and sweet
The Mighty Master holds His joy.

Though the crushed jewels droop and fade
The Artist's labours will not cease,
And of the ruins shall be made
Some yet more lovely masterpiece.

G. W. RUSSELL (A.E.)

SOUL AND BODY

Body. Art thou for breaking faith, after these years,
These many married years
Wherein we have ourselves so well delighted?
Why art thou sick? Art thou beginning fears
That our dear joys have been unholy things?
Trust me, since we have been so long plighted, —

Whate'er be this white worship thou dost mean
To reach on these unlucky wings, —
Thou wilt miss the wonder I have made for thee
Of this dear world with my fashioning senses,
The blue, the fragrance, the singing, and the green.
And thou wilt find, not having me,
Crippled thy high powers, gone to doubt
Thy indignation and thy love, without
Help of my lust, and the anger of my blood,
And my tears.
Try me again; dost thou remember how we stood
And lookt upon the world exultingly?
What is for rapture better than these? —
Great places of grassy land, and all the air
One quiet, the sun taking golden ease
Upon an afternoon;
Tall hills that stand in weather-blinded trances
As if they heard, drawn upward and held there,
Some god's eternal tune;
I made them so, I with my fashioning senses
Made the devoted hills: have their great patiences
Not lent thee any health of ecstasy?
Or when the north came shouting to the beach,
Wind that would gag in his throat a lion's speech,
And spindrift with a whining hiss went by
Like swords, — wert thou not glad with me?
O who will lodge these better than I have done
In exultation? — I who alone
Can wash thee in the sacring of moonlight,
Or send thee soaring even that above
Into the wise and unimaginable night,
The chambers of the holy fear,
Or bring thee to the breasts of love.

Soul.　Dear Body, my loved friend, poor thanks have I
　　For all this service. As if fires had made me clean,
　　I come out of thy experience,

Thy blue, thy fragrance, thy singing, and thy green,
Passions of love, and most, that holy fear:
Well hast thou done to me with every sense.
But there's for me a fiercer kind
Of joy, that feels not, knows not, deaf and blind:
And these but led to it, that we did try
When we were person, thou and I;
Woe for me if I should dare
Partake in person now I see
The lights of unware ecstasy.
I must not in amazement stay,
Henceforth I am for a way
Beyond thy senses, beauty and fear,
Beyond wonder even.
I want neither earth nor heaven,
I will not have ken or desire,
But only joy higher and higher
Burning knowledge in its white fire,
Till I am no more aware
And no more saying "I am I,"
But all is perfect ecstasy.

LASCELLES ABERCROMBIE

SUDDEN HEAVEN

All was as it had ever been —
The worn familiar book,
The oak beyond the hawthorn seen,
The misty woodland's look:

The starling perched upon the tree
With his long tress of straw —
When suddenly heaven blazed on me,
And suddenly I saw:

Saw all as it would ever be,
In bliss too great to tell;
For ever safe, for ever free,
All bright with miracle:

Saw as in heaven the thorn arrayed,
The tree beside the door;
And I must die — but O my shade
Shall dwell there evermore.

RUTH PITTER

ROTATION

Even the owls are lyrical
  When the moon's right,
And we have no patience with the stars
  On a dusty night.

Love is dull with the mood wrong,
  And age may outsing youth,
For there is no measuring a song,
  Nor counting upon truth.

All's well, and then a flood of loss
  Surges upon delight,
While the rose buds upon the cross,
  And the blind have sight.

Morning wisdom vanishes,
  And dusk brings dread
That stalwart sleep banishes
  Ere primes are said.

He who is sure, has all to learn;
  Who fears, but fears in vain?
For never a day does the year turn,
  But it shall turn again.

JOHN DRINKWATER

EVENING

The burden of these beauties is too much.
They strain my passion for mortality.
They ring my world with falsity of touch
As fingers can the far dim rims of sea.
They overcrowd with their reality
The small and casual places of the brain,
Till what is edged most passionately with me
Is lost too easily for errant pain.

Empty the sack of this too varied sky
Of sails and lights and children. Let there lie
A vacant vastness of expectancy
As in the mind before the last dreams free.
Let doom be everywhere the sign of grace,
And each thing stand for death in its true place.

L. AARONSON

"THE MOON HATH NOT"

The moon hath not got any light;
All that beauty, all that power,
Is a cheat upon the sight,
Is come and gone within the hour!
What is pure,
Or what is lovely?
Nothing is that will endure!

An apple-blossom in the spring,
When spring awakens everything,
Is pure or lovely as it please,
Or not as it knows not of these!
What is pure,
Or what is lovely?
Nothing is that will endure!

[665]

Pure is cherished in a dream,
Loveliness in little thought;
Out of nowhere do they gleam,
Out of nothing are they wrought!
What is pure,
Or what is lovely?
Nothing is that will endure!

Courage, goodness, tenderness:
Beauty, wisdom, ecstasy:
Wonder, love, and loveliness:
Hope, and immortality:
What is pure,
Or what is lovely?
Nothing is that will endure!

Pure and lovely sleep and wait,
Where not good nor ill is done,
In the keep, within the gate,
At the heart of everyone:
What is pure,
Or what is lovely?
All is, and doth all endure.

JAMES STEPHENS

THE UNICORN

Hate me or love, I care not, as I pass
To those hid citadels
Where in the depth of my enchanted glass
The changeless image dwells;
To where for ever blooms the nameless tree;
For ever, alone and fair,
The lovely Unicorn beside the sea
Is laid, and slumbers there.

Give or withhold, all's nothing, as I go
On to those glimmering grounds
Where falling secretly and quiet as snow
The silent music sounds;
Where earth is withered away before the eyes,
And heaven hangs in the air,
For in the oak the bird of paradise
Alights, and triumphs there.

Slay me or spare, it matter not: I fly
Ever, for ever rest
Alone and with a host: in the void sky
There do I build my nest:
I lay my beams from star to star, and make
My house where all is bare;
Hate, slay, withhold, I rear it for thy sake
And thou art with me there.

RUTH PITTER

Conclusion

As he was walking one day in the fields, says Jakob Boehme, the mystery of creation was suddenly opened to him. " In one quarter of an hour I saw and knew more than if I had been many years together at an university; at which I did exceedingly admire, and I knew not how it happened to me; and thereupon I turned my heart to praise God for it . . ."

Man knoweth but as in a dream of his own desire
The thing that is good for man, and he dreameth well . . .

Conclusion

Progress?' writes our author [Benjamin Paul Blood]. 'And to what? Time turns a weary and a wistful face; has he not traversed an eternity? and shall another give the secret up? We have dreamed of a climax and a consummation, a final triumph where a world shall burn *en barbecue;* but there is not, cannot be, a purpose of eternity; it shall pay mainly as it goes, or not at all. The show is on; and what a show, if we will but give our attention! Barbecues, bonfires, and banners? Not twenty worlds a minute would keep up our bonfire of the sun; and what banners of our fancy could eclipse the meteor pennants of the pole, or the opaline splendours of the everlasting ice? . . . Doubtless we *are* ostensibly progressing, but there have been prosperity and high jinks before. Nineveh and Tyre, Rome, Spain, and Venice also had their day. We are going, but it is a question of our standing the pace. It would seem that the news must become less interesting or tremendously more so — "a breath can make us, as a breath has made." ' . . ."

WILLIAM JAMES

THE LITTLE GIRL LOST

In futurity
I prophetic see
That the earth from sleep
(Grave the sentence deep)

[671]

Shall arise and seek
For her Maker meek;
And the desart wild
Become a garden mild. . . .

WILLIAM BLAKE

If, in the silent mind of One all-pure,
    At first imagined lay
The sacred world; and by procession sure
From those still deeps, in form and colour drest,
Seasons alternating, and night and day,
The long-mused thought to north south east and west
    Took then its all-seen way:

O waking on a world which thus-wise springs!
    Whether it needs thee count
Betwixt thy waking and the birth of things
Ages or hours: O waking on Life's stream!
By lonely pureness to the all-pure Fount
. (Only by this thou canst) the coloured dream
    Of Life remount.

Thin, thin the pleasant human noises grow;
    And faint the city gleams;
Rare the lone pastoral huts: marvel not thou!
The solemn peaks but to the stars are known,
But to the stars, and the cold lunar beams:
Alone the sun arises, and alone
    Spring the great streams. . . .

MATTHEW ARNOLD, from *In Utrumque Paratus*

DREAMS

We suffer the Arguments of Religion to have so little impression upon our spirits, that they operate but like the discourses of childhood, or the Problems of uncertain Philosophy: A man talks of Religion but as of a dream, and from

thence he awakens into the Businesses of the world, and acts
them deliberately, with perfect Action and full Resolution,
and contrives, and considers, and lives in them: But when he
falls asleep again, or is taken from the Scene of his own employment and choice; then he dreams again, and Religion
makes such Impressions as is the conversation of a Dreamer,
and he acts accordingly. . . . He was prettily and fantastically troubled, who having used to put his trust in Dreams,
one night dreamed, that all dreams were vain; For he considered, If so, then This was vain, and then dreams might be
true for all this: But if they might be true, then this dream
might be so upon equall reason; And then dreams were vain,
because This dream, which told him so, was true, and so
round again. In the same Circle runs the Heart of man; All
his cogitations are vain, and yet he makes especiall use of this,
that, that Thought which thinks so, That is vain; and if That
be vain, then his other Thoughts, which are vainly declared
so, may be Reall, and Relied upon; And so we do. Those religious thoughts, which are sent into us, to condemne and
disrepute the thoughts of sin and vanity, are esteemed the
onely dreams; And so all those Instruments, which the grace
of God hath invented for the destruction of Impiety, are ren-
dred ineffectuall, either by our direct opposing them, or
(which happens most commonly) by our want of considering
them. . . .

JEREMY TAYLOR

ATTENDANT. Come lift your head from that sad pillow, lady,
　　　Let comfort kiss thee dry. Nay, weep no more:
　　　Oh! sure thy brain has emptied all its tears,
　　　Thy breast outsighed its passion, leaving room
　　　For sleep to pour her sweetness into them,
　　　And the cored sleep of sleep, tranquillity,
　　　That opens but one window of the soul,
　　　And with her hand on sorrow's face, does keep her
　　　Dark in her bed and dayless. Quiet now —
　　　Will you take peace?

ERMINIA.   Good-night; you must go in:
  The door of life is shut upon me now;
  I'm sepulchred alone. Look in the west;
  Mark you the dusty traveller,
  That stumbles down the clouds?
ATTEND.   I see the sun
  Silently dying.
ERMIN.   Weep till your sight is found.
  I have been one that thought there was a sun,
  A joyful heat-maker; and like a child
  By a brook's side spooning the sparkles out,
  I caught at his reflection in my soul,
  And found 'twas water painted with a lie. . . .

THOMAS LOVELL BEDDOES,
from *Erminia Abbandonata*

. . . Sleep is nothing else but death painted in a night-
piece; it is a prelibation of that deep slumber, out of which
we shall not be awaked until the Heavens be no more: We go
to bed under a Scene of Stars and darkness, but when we
awake, we find Heaven changed, and one great luminary
giving light to all: We die in the state of corruption, errors,
and mistiness: But we shall be raised in glory, and perfection, when these clouds of blackness that are carried about
with diverse winds, and every Enemy of truth shall vanish
for ever, and God alone shall be all in all. We affect sleep
naturally, it is the reparation of man, & a laying by of cares.
The Copy cannot match the pattern: if we love sleep then,
why should we hate the Idea of it; why should we fear death,
whose shadow refresheth us, which nature never made, nor
meant to fright us with? It was her intention to strengthen
our hope of dying, by giving us the fruition of this resemblance of death; lest we should grow impatient with delay,
she favoured us with the shadow and Image of it, as Ladies
comfort themselves with the pictures of their absent lovers.
There is no part of life without some portion of death, as

dreams cannot happen without sleep, so life cannot be without death. As sleep is said to be the shadow of death; So I think dreams to be the shadows of life, for nothing deceives us more frequent than it: When we shall be raised from death, we shall not grieve so much because the joys of life were not real, as because there were none at all. It was said by one, that he had rather dream of being tormented in Hell, then glorified in *Paradise:* for being awaked, he should rejoice to find himself in a soft featherbed, and not in a lake of unquenchable fire: But having dreamt of Heaven, it would grieve him that it was not real. *Paracelsus* writes, that the watching of the body is the sleep of the Soul, and that the day was made for Corporeal Actions, but the night is the working-time of Spirits. Contrary natures run contrary courses: Bodies having no inherent light of their own, make use of this outward light, but Spirits need it not. Sunbeams cannot stumble, nor go out of their way. Death frees them from this dark Lantern of flesh. *Heraclitus* used to say, that men were both dead and alive, both when they died, and when they lived: when they lived their Souls were dead, and when they died, their Souls revived. Life then is the death of the Soul, and the life of the body: But death is the life of the Soul, and the death of the body. . . .

Henry Vaughan

The sun is a glorious creature, and its beams extend to the utmost stars; by shining on them it clothes them with light, and by its rays exciteth all their influences. It enlightens the eyes of all the creatures: it shineth on forty kingdoms at the same time, on seas and continents in a general manner; yet so particularly regardeth all, that every mote in the air, every grain of dust, every spire of grass is wholly illuminated thereby as if it did entirely shine upon that alone. Nor does it only illuminate all these objects in an idle manner; its beams are operative, enter in, fill the pores of things with spirits, and impregnate them with powers, cause all their emanations, odors, virtues, and operations; springs, rivers, minerals and vegetables are all perfected by the sun; all the motion, life and sense of birds, beasts and fishes dependeth on the same. Yet the sun is but a little spark among all the creatures that are made for the Soul; the Soul, being the most high and noble of all, is capable of far higher perfections, far more full of life and vigour in its uses. The sphere of its activity is illimited, its energy is endless upon all its objects. It can exceed the heavens in its operations, and run out into infinite spaces. Such is the extent of knowledge that it seemeth to be the Light of all Eternity. All objects are equally near to the splendour of its beams: As innumerable millions may be conceived in its Light, with a ready capacity for millions more; so can it penetrate all abysses, reach to the centre of all Nature, converse with all beings, visible and invisible, corporeal and spiritual, temporal and eternal, created and increated, finite and infinite, substantial and accidental, actual and possible, imaginary and real; all the mysteries of bliss and misery, all the secrets of heaven and hell are objects of the Soul's capacity, and shall be actually seen and known here.

THOMAS TRAHERNE

Are we not Spirits, that are shaped into a body, into an Appearance; and that fade-away again into air and Invisibility? This is no metaphor, it is a simple scientific *fact;* we start out of Nothingness, take figure, and are Apparitions; round us, as round the veriest spectre, is Eternity; and to Eternity minutes are as years and aeons. Come there not tones of Love and Faith, as from celestial harp-strings, like the Song of beatified Souls? And again, do not we squeak and jibber (in our discordant, screech-owlish debatings and recriminatings); and glide bodeful, and feeble, and fearful; or uproar (*poltern*), and revel in our mad Dance of the Dead, — till the scent of the morning air summons us to our still Home; and dreamy Night becomes awake and Day? Where now is Alexander of Macedon: does the steel Host, that yelled in fierce battle-shouts at Issus and Arbela, remain behind him; or have they all vanished utterly, even as perturbed Goblins must? Napoleon too, and his Moscow Retreats and Austerlitz Campaigns! Was it all other than the veriest Spectre-hunt; which has now, with its howling tumult that made Night hideous, flitted away? — Ghosts! There are nigh a thousand-million walking the Earth openly at noontide; some half-hundred have vanished from it, some half-hundred have arisen in it, ere thy watch ticks once. . . .

O Heaven, it is mysterious, it is awful to consider that we not only carry each a future Ghost within him; but are, in very deed, Ghosts! These Limbs, whence had we them; this stormy Force; this life-blood with its burning Passion? They are dust and shadow; a Shadow-system gathered round our ME; wherein, through some moments or years, the Divine Essence is to be revealed in the Flesh. . . .

THOMAS CARLYLE

O Joys! Infinite sweetness! with what flowers,
And shoots of glory, my soul breaks, and buds!
     All the long hours
     Of night, and Rest
     Through the still shrouds
     Of sleep, and Clouds,
   This Dew fell on my Breast. . . .
     O let me climb
When I lie down! The Pious soul by night
Is like a clouded star, whose beams though said
     To shed their light
     Under some Cloud
     Yet are above,
     And shine, and move
   Beyond that misty shroud.
     So in my Bed
That Curtained grave, though sleep, like ashes, hide
My lamp, and life, both shall in thee abide.

HENRY VAUGHAN, from " The Morning Watch "

. . . PANTHEA. Look, sister, where a troop of spirits gather,
  Like flocks of clouds in spring's delightful weather,
  Thronging in the blue air!
IONE.   And see! more come,
   Like fountain-vapours when the winds are dumb,
   That climb up the ravine in scattered lines.
   And, hark! is it the music of the pines?
   Is it the lake? Is it the waterfall?
PANTHEA. 'Tis something sadder, sweeter far than all.
CHORUS OF SPIRITS.
   From unremembered ages we
   Gentle guides and guardians be
   Of heaven-oppressed mortality;
   And we breathe, and sicken not,
   The atmosphere of human thought:
   Be it dim, and dank, and grey,
   Like a storm-extinguished day,
   Travelled o'er by dying gleams;
    Be it bright as all between
   Cloudless skies and windless streams,
    Silent, liquid, and serene;
   As the birds within the wind,
    As the fish within the wave,
   As the thoughts of man's own mind
    Float thro' all above the grave;
   We make there our liquid lair,
   Voyaging cloudlike and unpent
   Through the boundless element. . . .

       PERCY BYSSHE SHELLEY,
       from " Prometheus Unbound "

THE CAGED SKYLARK

As a dare-gale skylark scanted in a dull cage
 Man's mounting spirit in his bone-house, mean house,
  dwells —
That bird beyond the remembering his free fells;
This in drudgery, day-labouring-out life's age.

[678]

Though aloft on turf or perch or poor low stage,
  Both sing sometimes the sweetest, sweetest spells,
  Yet both droop deadly sómetimes in their cells
Or wring their barriers in bursts of fear or rage.

Not that the sweet-fowl, song-fowl, needs no rest —
Why, hear him, hear him babble and drop down to his nest,
  But his own nest, wild nest, no prison.

Man's spirit will be flesh-bound when found at best,
But uncumbered: meadow-down is not distressed
  For a rainbow footing it nor he for his bónes risen.

G. M. Hopkins

THE VISIONARY

Silent is the house: all are laid asleep:
One alone looks out o'er the snow-wreaths deep,
Watching every cloud, dreading every breeze
That whirls the 'wildering drift, and bends the groaning trees.

Cheerful is the hearth, soft the matted floor;
Not one shivering gust creeps through pane or door;
The little lamp burns straight, its rays shoot strong and far:
I trim it well, to be the wanderer's guiding star.

Frown, my haughty sire! chide, my angry dame;
Set your slaves to spy; threaten me with shame!
But neither sire nor dame, nor prying serf shall know
What angel nightly tracks that waste of frozen snow.

What I love shall come like visitant of air,
Safe in secret power from lurking human snare;
What loves me, no word of mine shall e'er betray,
Though for faith unstained my life must forfeit pay.

Burn, then, little lamp; glimmer straight and clear —
Hush! a rustling wing stirs, methinks, the air:
He for whom I wait, thus ever comes to me;
Strange Power! I trust thy might; trust thou my constancy!

EMILY BRONTË

THE OBSCURE NIGHT OF THE SOUL

Upon an obscure night,
Fevered with love in love's anxiety,
(O hapless-happy plight!)
I went, none seeing me,
Forth from my house where all things quiet be.

By night, secure from sight,
And by the secret stair, disguisedly,
(O hapless-happy plight!)
By night, and privily,
Forth from my house where all things quiet be.

Blest night of wandering,
In secret, where by none might I be spied,
Nor I see anything;
Without a light or guide,
Save that which in my heart burnt in my side.

That light did lead me on,
More surely than the shining of noontide,
Where well I knew that one
Did for my coming bide;
Where he abode might none but he abide.

O night that didst lead thus,
O night more lovely than the dawn of light,
O night that broughtest us,
Lover to lover's sight,
Lover with loved in marriage of delight!

Upon my flowery breast,
Wholly for him, and save himself for none,
There did I give sweet rest
To my beloved one;
The fanning of the cedars breathed thereon.

When the first moving air
Blew from the tower, and waved his locks aside,
His hand, with gentle care,
Did wound me in the side,
And in my body all my senses died.

All things I then forgot,
My cheek on him who for my coming came;
All ceased and I was not,
Leaving my cares and shame
Among the lilies, and forgetting them.

ARTHUR SYMONS, from " San Juan de la Cruz "

That there are distinct orders of *Angels,* assuredly I be-
leeve; but what they are, I cannot tell; *Dicant qui possunt; si
tamen probare possunt quod dicunt,* saies that Father, Let
them tell you that can, so they be able to prove, that they tell
you true. They are Creatures, that have not so much of a
Body as *flesh* is, as *froth* is, as a *vapor* is, as a *sigh* is, and yet
with a touch they shall molder a rock into lesse Atomes, then
the sand that it stands upon; and a milstone into smaller
flower, then it grinds. They are Creatures *made,* and yet not
a minute elder now, then when they were first made, if they
were made before all measure of time began; nor, if they were
made in the beginning of Time, and be now six thousand
yeares old, have they one wrinckle of Age in their face, or one
sobbe of wearinesse in their lungs. They are *primogeniti Dei,*
Gods eldest sonnes; They are super-elementary meteors, they
hang between the nature of God, and the nature of man, and
are of middle Condition; And, (if we may offencelessly ex-

[681]

presse it so) they are *ænigmata Divina,* The Riddles of
Heaven, and the perplexities of speculation.

JOHN DONNE

The Door of Death is made of Gold,
That Mortal Eyes cannot behold;
But when the Mortal Eyes are closed,
And cold and pale the Limbs reposed,
The Soul awakes; and, wondering, sees
In her mild Hand the golden Keys:
The Grave is Heaven's golden Gate,
And rich and poor around it wait;
O Shepherdess of England's Fold,
Behold this Gate of Pearl and Gold! . . .

I give you the end of a golden string;
    Only wind it into a ball,
It will lead you in at Heaven's gate,
    Built in Jerusalem's wall.

WILLIAM BLAKE

By this time the Pilgrims had a desire to go forward, and
the Shepherds a desire they should; so they walked together
towards the end of the mountains. Then said the Shepherds
one to another, Let us here shew to the Pilgrims the gates of
the Celestial City, if they have skill to look through our per-
spective glass. The Pilgrims then lovingly accepted the motion; so they had them to the top of a high hill, called Clear,
and gave them their glass to look.

Then they essayed to look, but the remembrance of that
last thing that the Shepherds had shewed them, made their
hands shake; by means of which impediment, they could not
look steadily through the glass; yet they thought they saw
something like the gate, and also some of the glory of the
place. . . .

JOHN BUNYAN

"ENGLAND! AWAKE!"

England! awake! awake! awake!
　Jerusalem thy Sister calls!
Why wilt thou sleep the sleep of death
　And close her from thy ancient walls?

Thy hills and valleys felt her feet
　Gently upon their bosoms move:
Thy gates beheld sweet Zion's ways:
　Then was a time of joy and love.

And now the time returns again:
　Our souls exult, and London's towers
Receive the Lamb of God to dwell
　In England's green and pleasant bowers.

WILLIAM BLAKE

To the Accuser who is
The God of This World

Truly, My Satan, thou art but a Dunce,
And dost not know the Garment from the Man.
Every Harlot was a Virgin once,
Nor can'st thou ever change Kate into Nan.

Tho' thou art Worshipped by the Names Divine
Of Jesus and Jehovah, thou art still
The Son of Man in weary Night's decline
The lost Traveller's Dream under the Hill.

WILLIAM BLAKE

　　Seek no more abroad, say I,
　　House and Home, but turn thine eye
　　Inward, and observe thy breast;
　　There alone dwells solid Rest. . . .

[683]

Say not that this House is small,
Girt up in a narrow wall:
In a cleanly sober mind
Heaven itself full room doth find. . . .
Contented here make thine abode
With thy self and with thy God.
Here in this sweet privacy
May'st thou with thyself agree,
And keep House in peace, tho' all
The universe's fabric fall.

JOSEPH BEAUMONT,
from "House and Home"

VENATOR. Well, master . . . here I must part with you, here in this now sad place where I was so happy as first to meet you: but I shall long for the ninth of May; for then I hope again to enjoy your beloved company at the appointed time and place. And now I wish for some somniferous potion, that might force me to sleep away the intermitted time, which will pass away with me as tediously, as it does with men in sorrow; nevertheless, I will make it as short as I can by my hopes and wishes. And, my good master, I will not forget the doctrine which you told me Socrates taught his scholars, that they should not think to be honoured so much for being philosophers, as to honour philosophy by their virtuous lives. You advised me to the like concerning angling, and I will endeavour to do so; and to live like those many worthy men of which you made mention in the former part of your discourse. This is my firm resolution; and as a pious man advised his friend, that to beget mortification he should frequent churches, and view monuments, and charnel-houses, and then and there consider how many dead bones time had piled up at the gates of death: so when I would beget content, and increase confidence in the power, and wisdom, and providence of Almighty God,

I will walk the meadows by some gliding stream, and there contemplate the lilies that take no care, and those very many other various little living creatures, that are not only created but fed (man knows not how) by the goodness of the God of nature, and therefore trust in him. This is my purpose; and so, let everything that hath breath praise the Lord: and let the blessing of St. Peter's master be with mine.

PISCATOR. And upon all that are lovers of virtue, and dare trust in his providence, and be quiet, and go a-angling.

IZAAC WALTON

THE SWANS

How lovely are these swans,
That float like high proud galleons
Cool in the summer heat,
And waving leaf-like feet
Divide with narrow breasts of snow
In a smooth surge
This water that is mostly sky;
So lovely that I know
Death cannot kill such birds,
It could but wound them, mortally.

ANDREW YOUNG

The maidens came
When I was in my mother's bower;
I had all that I would.
    The bailey beareth the bell away;
    The lily, the rose, the rose I lay.
The silver is white, red is the gold;
The robes they lay in fold.
    The bailey beareth the bell away;
    The lily, the rose, the rose I lay.

And through the glass windows shines the sun.
How should I love, and I so young?
   The bailey beareth the bell away;
   The lily, the lily, the rose I lay.

January 12, 1822.

. . . After this cat's departure Agnes took to heart a kitten, who was very fond of her. This kitten, the first night she slept in her room, on wakening in the morning looked up from the hearth at Agnes, who was lying awake, but with her eyes half-shut, and marked all pussy's motions; after looking some instants, puss jumped up on the bed, crept softly forward and put her paw, with its glove on, upon one of Miss Baillie's eyelids and pushed it gently up. Miss Baillie looked at her fixedly, and Puss, as if satisfied that her eyes were *there* and safe, went back to her station on the hearth and never troubled herself more about the matter. . . .

Maria Edgeworth, to Lucy Edgeworth

Acknowledgments

M y grateful thanks for their kind permission to include certain poems and passages in prose in this volume are due to the following authors (or their executors, trustees or representatives) and publishers: Mr. L. Aaronson (and Victor Gollancz Ltd.); Mr. Lascelles Abercrombie (and Messrs. Secker & Warburg Ltd.); Mr. J. Redwood Anderson (and the Oxford University Press); Mr. W. H. Auden (the Hogarth Press and Lawrence & Wishart); the Hon. Maurice Baring (and Peter Davies Ltd.) for his translation of a poem by Alexander Pushkin; Mr. Laurence Binyon (and Macmillan & Co. Ltd.); Mr. Edmund Blunden (and R. Cobden-Sanderson Ltd.); Miss Elizabeth Bridges [Mrs. Elizabeth Daryush] (and Bowes & Bowes); Mr. Gerald Bullett (and J. M. Dent & Sons Ltd.); Mr. Roy Campbell (and Faber & Faber Ltd.); Mr. Padraic Colum (Macmillan & Co. Ltd., and the Macmillan Company); Mrs. Francis Cornford; Mr. R. P. T. Coffin (and Harlan Logan, Inc.); Mr. Edward Davison; Mr. T. S. Eliot (Faber & Faber Ltd., and Harcourt, Brace and Company, Inc.); Mr. Robert Frost (Jonathan Cape Ltd., Longmans, Green & Co. Ltd., and Henry Holt & Co., Inc.); Mr. Barrington Gates (and the Hogarth Press); Mr. Monk Gibbon (and Victor Gollancz Ltd.); Mr. Wilfred Gibson (Macmillan & Co. Ltd., the Oxford University Press, and the Macmillan Company); Mr. St. John Gogarty; Mr. James Guthrie; Mr. G. Rostrevor Hamilton (and William Heinemann Ltd.); Mr. Richard Hughes (and Chatto & Windus); Mr. Eugene Lee Hamilton; Mr. Cecil Day Lewis (and the Hogarth Press); Mr. Vivian Locke Ellis; Miss Sylvia Lynd (and Victor Gollancz Ltd.); Mr. Hugh M'Diarmid (and Victor Gollancz

Ltd.); Mr. Louis MacNeice (and Faber & Faber Ltd.); Mr. Charles Madge; Mr. John Masefield (William Heinemann Ltd., and the Macmillan Company) for a poem from his *Collected Poems;* Mr. E. H. W. Meyerstein (and Macmillan & Co. Ltd.) for two poems from his *Selected Poems;* Mr. Edwin Muir (J. M. Dent & Sons Ltd., and B. W. Huebsch, Inc.); Mr. Alfred Noyes (and William Blackwood & Sons Ltd.); Miss Ruth Pitter (the Cresset Press, and the Macmillan Company); Mr. Herbert Read (and Faber & Faber Ltd.); Mr. Siegfried Sassoon (and William Heinemann Ltd.); Miss Marjorie Seiffert [Mrs. Otto Seiffert]; Miss Edith Sitwell (and Duckworth & Co. Ltd.); Mr. William Soutar (and the Moray Press); Sir John Squire; Mr. James Stephens; Miss Muriel Stuart (and William Heinemann Ltd.); Mr. Arthur Symons; Miss Pamela Travers; Mr. Walter J. Turner (and Sidgwick & Jackson Ltd.); Miss Helen Waddell (and Constable & Co. Ltd.); Lady Gerald Wellesley (and Macmillan & Co. Ltd.); Mr. Charles Williams (and the Oxford University Press); the Hon. Mrs. Wingfield; and to Mr. Andrew Young (and Jonathan Cape Ltd.). My thanks are also due to Mr. Norman Ault for very kindly permitting me to include certain poems taken from his *Elizabethan Lyrics, Seventeenth Century Lyrics,* and *Treasury of Unfamiliar Lyrics;* to the author's trustees for " Soul and Body " by Lascelles Abercrombie; to the author's executors (and John Lane The Bodley Head Ltd.) for a poem by A. C. Benson; the author's executors (Macmillan & Co. Ltd., and the Macmillan Company) for a poem from *The Poetical Works of Wilfrid Scawen Blunt;* Mrs. Bridges (and the Clarendon Press) for two poems from the *Shorter Poems of Robert Bridges* (1931); the author's representatives (Sidgwick & Jackson Ltd., and Dodd, Mead & Company, Inc.) for a poem by Rupert Brooke; Jonathan Cape Ltd. for a poem by Samuel Butler; the trustees of Sir Henry Newbolt (and Elkin Mathews & Marrot Ltd.) for three poems by Mary Coleridge; Mrs. Herbert Paul (and the Oxford University Press) for a poem by Digby Dolben; the author's representatives (and Sidgwick & Jackson Ltd.) for a poem by John

Drinkwater; Mrs. Flecker (and Secker & Warburg Ltd.) for a poem by James Elroy Flecker; the author's representatives (Macmillan & Co. Ltd., and the Macmillan Company) for three poems from the *Collected Poems of Thomas Hardy* and extracts from Parts I and III of *The Dynasts;* the author's family (and the Oxford University Press) for three poems by G. M. Hopkins; the author's trustees (the Richards Press and Henry Holt and Company, Inc.) for a poem by A. E. Housman; Longmans, Green & Co. Ltd. for two poems from the *Collected Poems of Andrew Lang;* the author's trustees (Constable & Co. Ltd., and Charles Scribner's Sons) for an extract from *Modern Love* by George Meredith; Mr. Wilfrid Meynell (and Burns Oates & Washbourne Ltd.) for a poem by Alice Meynell; Mrs. Monro (and the Poetry Bookshop) for three poems by Harold Monro, and for two poems by Charlotte Mew; Mrs. Myers (Macmillan & Co. Ltd., and the Macmillan Company) for a poem from the *Collected Poems* of Frederick Myers; the author's trustees (and Thomas Nelson & Sons Ltd.) for a poem from *New Paths on Helicon* by Sir Henry Newbolt; Mrs. Owen (Chatto & Windus and the Viking Press) for two poems by Wilfred Owen; the author's executors (and George Bell & Sons Ltd.) for six poems by Coventry Patmore; the author's representatives (Macmillan & Co. Ltd., and the Macmillan Company) for a poem from the *Collected Poems* of G. W. Russell — AE; the Society for Promoting Christian Knowledge for a poem by Christina Rossetti; the author's executors (and the Oxford University Press) for two poems by Geoffrey Scott; William Heinemann Ltd. for extracts from four poems by Algernon Charles Swinburne; Mrs. Helen Thomas (and Faber & Faber Ltd.) for two poems from the *Collected Poems* of Edward Thomas; Mr. Wilfrid Meynell (and Burns Oates & Washbourne Ltd.) for two poems by Francis Thompson; Frederick Warne & Co. Ltd., and Houghton Mifflin Company for extracts from two poems by John Greenleaf Whittier; Mr. Vyvyan B. Holland for two stanzas from " The Ballad of Reading Gaol " by Oscar Wilde; and to Mrs. Yeats (Macmillan & Co. Ltd., and the Macmillan Company) for a poem from the *Collected Poems* of W. B. Yeats.

Also (for passages in prose) to Mr. Owen Barfield (and Methuen & Co. Ltd.) for extracts from *History in English Words;* Mr. William Beebe (and Henry Holt and Co., Inc.) for an extract from *Jungle Peace;* Chapman & Hall Ltd. for extracts from Dr. P. Berger's *William Blake;* the Editor of the *British Medical Journal* for an extract from an article by Dr. Weir Mitchell; Miss Margaret Bulley (and B. T. Batsford Ltd.) for extracts from *Art and Understanding;* Miss Anna Robeson Burr for an extract from *Religious Confessions and Confessants;* Dr. E. Classen and the Swedish Chamber of Commerce for an extract from *The Psychology of Murder* by A. Bjerre; Professor G. G. Coulton (and Methuen & Co. Ltd.) for extracts from *Chaucer and His England;* Jonathan Cape Ltd., and Simon and Schuster, Inc. for extracts from the Abbé Ernest Dimnet's *The Art of Thinking;* Mr. J. W. Dunne (Faber & Faber Ltd., and the Macmillan Company) for an extract from *An Experiment with Time;* Mr. Max Eastman (and Charles Scribner's Sons) for an extract from *Enjoyment of Poetry;* Mr. Havelock Ellis (Constable & Co. Ltd., and Houghton Mifflin Company) for extracts from *The World of Dreams;* Mr. J. W. Flavell for an extract from the *Saturday Westminster Gazette;* Sir James Frazer (Macmillan & Co. Ltd., and the Macmillan Company) for extracts from *Folk-Lore in the Old Testament* and *The Golden Bough;* Mr. J. A. Gotch (and the Oxford University Press) for an extract from F. P. Barnard's *Companion to English History;* Mr. Aldous Huxley (Mrs. Frieda Lawrence, William Heinemann Ltd., and the Viking Press) for an extract from the Introduction to *The Letters of D. H. Lawrence;* Mr. S. S. Koteliansky (and Cassell & Co. Ltd.) for extracts from his translation of the *Life and Letters of Anton Tchekhov;* Mr. Percy Lubbock (Mr. Henry James Jnr., and Macmillan & Co. Ltd.) for an extract from the Introduction to *The Letters of Henry James;* George Allen & Unwin Ltd. for an extract from Mr. Maurice Maeterlinck's *Life and Flowers,* translated by

A. Teixeira de Mattos; Sir Edward Marsh (and William Heinemann Ltd.) for an extract from *The Fables of Jean de la Fontaine;* Mr. Bernard Miall (and Ernest Benn Ltd.) for an extract from his translation of J. H. Fabre's *Social Life in the Insect World;* Mr. Neil Montgomery (and Faber & Faber Ltd.) for an extract from his Introduction to Professor Denis Saurat's *The End of Fear;* Mr. T. Sturge Moore (and Methuen & Co. Ltd.) for an extract from *Art and Life;* George Allen & Unwin Ltd. for extracts from Professor A. Mosso's *Fatigue,* translated by M. & W. B. Drummond; Mr. Edwin Muir (Andrew Melrose Ltd., and B. W. Huebsch, Inc.) for extracts from *Latitudes;* Mr. Joseph Needham (and Chatto & Windus) for an extract from *The Sceptical Biologist;* Mr. Logan Pearsall Smith (Constable & Co. Ltd., and Houghton Mifflin Company) for an extract from *Words and Idioms;* Mr. John Pilley (and Victor Gollancz Ltd.) for an extract from his essay "What Science Can Do" in *An Outline for Boys and Girls and their Parents;* the Duke of Portland (and Faber & Faber Ltd.) for an extract from his *Men, Women and Things;* Mr. Forrest Reid for an extract from *Apostate;* Professor George Santayana (Constable & Co. Ltd., and Charles Scribner's Sons) for extracts from *Soliloquies in England;* Professor Denis Saurat (and Faber & Faber Ltd.) for extracts from *The End of Fear;* Mr. Bernard Shaw for an extract from his Introduction to *The Life of Frank Harris;* Mr. Arthur Symons (and Constable & Co. Ltd.) for extracts from *The Romantic Movement in English Poetry* and *The Symbolist Movement in Literature;* Mr. H. M. Tomlinson (William Heinemann Ltd., and Harper & Brothers) for extracts from *The Sea and the Jungle;* Kegan Paul, Trench, Trubner & Co. Ltd. for an extract from M. J. Vendryes's *Language: A Linguistic Introduction to History,* translated by Mr. Paul Radin; and to Dr. Alfred North Whitehead (the Cambridge University Press and the Macmillan Company) for extracts from *Science and the Modern World.* Also to Ernest Benn Ltd. for extracts from Henri Bergson's *Dreams,* translated by Edwin E. Slosson, and from Dr. John Bigelow's *The Mystery of Sleep;* the author's representatives (Macmillan & Co. Ltd., and the Macmillan Company) for extracts from A. C. Bradley's *Oxford Lectures on Poetry;* Mrs. Thorold (and Burns Oates & Washbourne Ltd.) for extracts from Algar Thorold's translation of the Abbé Henri Bremond's *Prayer and Poetry;* the author's trustees (and Chapman & Hall Ltd.) for an extract from Dr. Allen Brockington's *Mysticism and Poetry;* Baillière, Tindall & Cox for an extract from Dr. P. Brouardel's *Death and Sudden Death,* translated by F. Lucas Benham; Jonathan Cape Ltd., and E. P. Dutton & Co., Inc. for an extract from *The Note Books of Samuel Butler;* George Allen & Unwin Ltd. for an extract from Edward Carpenter's *Pagan and Christian Creeds;* C. Arthur Pearson Ltd. for extracts from Mr. Joseph Elgie's *The Stars, Night by Night;* the Talbot Press Ltd. for an extract from Darrell Figgis's *AE — A Study of a Man and a Nation;* William Collins, Sons & Co. Ltd. and Harper & Brothers for extracts from Dr. Gustave Geley's *From the Unconscious to the Conscious,* translated by Stanley de Brath; John Lane The Bodley Head Ltd. for extracts from Frederick Greenwood's *Imagination in Dreams,* and for an extract from Francis Grierson's *Parisian Portraits;* the author's representatives (Macmillan & Co. Ltd., and Harper & Brothers) for extracts from Thomas Hardy's *The Return of the Native;* the author's family (and the Oxford University Press) for an extract from G. M. Hopkins's *Letters;* J. M. Dent & Sons Ltd., and E. P. Dutton & Co., Inc. for an extract from Baron Friedrich von Hügel's *Letters to a Niece,* and from W. H. Hudson's *Far Away and Long Ago;* Williams & Norgate Ltd. for an extract from Dr. Montagu James's *Eton and Kings;* Mr. Henry James Jnr. (and Longmans, Green & Co. Ltd.) for extracts from William James's *Varieties of Religious Experience* and *Memories and Studies;* Elkin Mathews & Mariot Ltd. for an extract from Lionel Johnson's *Post Liminium;* the author's trustees (and the Clarendon Press) for extracts from Benjamin Jowett's translation of *The Republic of Plato* and the *Phaedo;* William Blackwood & Sons Ltd. for an extract from A. W. Kinglake's

Eothen; Longmans, Green & Co. Ltd. for extracts from Andrew Lang's *Dreams and Ghosts;* Burns Oates & Washbourne Ltd. for an extract from Alice, Lady Lovat's *Life of St. Teresa;* the Clarendon Press for an extract from Percy Macquoid's essay on " The Home " in *Shakespeare's England;* Methuen & Co. Ltd., and Dodd, Mead & Company for an extract from Eugene Marais's *The Soul of the White Ant,* translated by Miss Winifred de Kok; Mr. Wilfrid Meynell (and Burns Oates & Washbourne Ltd.) for an extract from Alice Meynell's *Essays;* Longmans, Green & Co. Ltd. for an extract from William Morris's *A Dream of John Ball,* and for an extract from Cardinal Newman's *Idea of a University;* the author's executors (and the Oxford University Press) for extracts from Coventry Patmore's *Courage in Politics and other Essays;* the Cambridge University Press for extracts from W. H. Rivers's *Instinct and the Unconscious;* Mrs. White (and the Oxford University Press) for an extract from Mark Rutherford's *An Epoch — More Pages from a Journal;* Chatto & Windus and Charles Scribner's Sons for an extract from R. L. Stevenson's *Travels with a Donkey;* James B. Pinker & Son and Chatto & Windus for an extract from J. W. N. Sullivan's *Limitations of Science;* Lady Thomson (Methuen & Co. Ltd., G. P. Putnam's Sons, J. M. Dent & Sons Ltd., and E. P. Dutton & Co., Inc.) for extracts from Sir Arthur Thomson's *What is Man?* and *Biology for Everyman;* the Manager of *The Times* for an extract from Wildon Carr's review of *The Misuse of Mind* by Karin Stephen; Mr. Percy J. Dobell for extracts from Thomas Traherne's *Centuries of Meditations;* and to George Allen & Unwin Ltd. for extracts from Dr. J. Varendonck's *The Psychology of Day Dreams;* and to Mrs. Yeats (Macmillan & Co. Ltd., and the Macmillan Company) for an extract from *Ideas of Good and Evil* by W. B. Yeats. For valuable suggestions, help or counsel in the preparation of this book I am much indebted to many friends: Mr. J. Redwood Anderson; Miss Agnes Drew; Mr. Ronald Fuller; Mr. Monk Gibbon; Mr. R. N. Green-Armytage; Miss Olive Jones; Mr. James Mac-Lehose; Mrs. M. R. Nicholas; Mr. Frank Sidgwick; Dr. J. C.

★ *Acknowledgments* ★

Smith; Mr. W. McC. Stewart of St. Andrews University; Dr. Maxwell Summers; Mr. Charles Williams; Dr. G. Scott Williamson; my son Colin; my son-in-law Mr. Rupert Thompson; and my secretary, Miss Brenda Sayers.

It has not in every case been possible to trace the authors of copyright material contained in this volume. If, on this account, or by inadvertence, anything in copyright has been included without permission, or if I have failed to return thanks to anyone to whom thanks are due, I hope my apologies will be accepted. Finally, brief and scattered extracts, either in verse or prose, of which there are many in the preceding pages, may give only a partial and inadequate impression of their context, and occasionally perhaps even a misleading one. This, I hope, will be forgiven if, as they may, they attract any reader unfamiliar with them to the sources from which they came.

Index of Authors

Index of First Lines of Poems

*of extracts from plays, and of the titles of poems of which
the opening lines have been omitted*

Index of Plays and Works in Prose

A NOTE ON THE TYPE

This book is set in Caledonia, a new Linotype face designed by W. A. Dwiggins. Caledonia belongs to the family of printing types called " modern face " by printers — a term used to mark the change in style of type-letters that occurred about 1800. Caledonia is in the general neighborhood of Scotch Modern in design, but is more freely drawn than that letter.

The book was composed, printed, and bound by The Plimpton Press, Norwood, Massachusetts. The paper was made by S. D. Warren Company, Boston. The binding design is by W. A. Dwiggins.